Comparative Philosophy and Method

Also available from Bloomsbury

Chinese and Buddhist Philosophy in Early Twentieth-Century German Thought, by Eric S. Nelson

Comparative Studies in Asian and Latin American Philosophies, edited by Stephanie Rivera Berruz and Leah Kalmanson

Comparative Philosophy without Borders, edited by Arindam Chakrabarti and Ralph Weber

Doing Philosophy Comparatively, by Tim Connolly

The Public Sphere from outside the West, edited by Divya Dwivedi and Sanil V

Comparative Philosophy and Method

Contemporary Practices and Future Possibilities

Edited by
Steven Burik, Robert Smid, and
Ralph Weber

BLOOMSBURY ACADEMIC
LONDON • NEW YORK • OXFORD • NEW DELHI • SYDNEY

BLOOMSBURY ACADEMIC
Bloomsbury Publishing Plc
50 Bedford Square, London, WC1B 3DP, UK
1385 Broadway, New York, NY 10018, USA
29 Earlsfort Terrace, Dublin 2, Ireland

BLOOMSBURY, BLOOMSBURY ACADEMIC and the Diana logo are trademarks of Bloomsbury Publishing Plc

First published in Great Britain 2022
This paperback edition published 2023

Copyright © Steven Burik, Robert Smid, Ralph Weber and Contributors, 2022

Steven Burik, Robert Smid, and Ralph Weber have asserted their right under the Copyright, Designs and Patents Act, 1988, to be identified as Editors of this work.

Cover image © Frances Alleblas

All rights reserved. No part of this publication may be reproduced or transmitted in any form or by any means, electronic or mechanical, including photocopying, recording, or any information storage or retrieval system, without prior permission in writing from the publishers.

Bloomsbury Publishing Plc does not have any control over, or responsibility for, any third-party websites referred to or in this book. All internet addresses given in this book were correct at the time of going to press. The author and publisher regret any inconvenience caused if addresses have changed or sites have ceased to exist, but can accept no responsibility for any such changes.

A catalogue record for this book is available from the British Library.

A catalog record for this book is available from the Library of Congress.

ISBN: HB: 978-1-3501-5502-2
PB: 978-1-3502-9704-3
ePDF: 978-1-3501-5503-9
eBook: 978-1-3501-5504-6

Typeset by Newgen KnowledgeWorks Pvt. Ltd., Chennai, India

To find out more about our authors and books visit www.bloomsbury.com and sign up for our newsletters.

Contents

Introduction ... 1
Steven Burik, Robert Smid, and Ralph Weber

Constellation I Necessary Conditions

1   Reflections on Methods of Comparative Philosophy ... 17
    Robert Cummings Neville
2   Necessary Preconditions of the Practice of Comparative Philosophy ... 31
    Jaap van Brakel and Lin Ma

Constellation II Generalization and Essentialization

3   Unloading the Essentialism Charge: Some Methodological Reflections in Doing Philosophy of Culture ... 55
    Roger T. Ames
4   From the Écart to the Unfamiliar: Thinking Paths—Reference Points ... 71
    François Jullien (trans. Steven Burik)

Constellation III Translation

5   Translation as Method ... 89
    Souleymane Bachir Diagne (trans. Philippe Major)
6   Thinking Along with Texts from Afar: Why One Doesn't Understand Texts without Philosophical Reflection and Can't Do Philosophy without Inspiration ... 97
    Elisa Freschi

Constellation IV Postcolonialism and Globalization

7   Reflections for Comparative Method from a Latin American Philosophical Perspective ... 119
    Gabriel Soldatenko

Contents

8 Why Philosophy Needs Sanskrit, Now More than Ever 139
   Jonardon Ganeri
9 Global Post-Comparative Philosophy as Just Philosophy 159
   Arindam Chakrabarti and Ralph Weber

Constellation V Plurality, Neutrality, and Method

10 On the Taming of Comparison: Methodological Myopathy, Plurality, and Creativity 181
    Robert Smid
11 Comparative Philosophy without Method: A Plea for Minimal Constraints 203
    Steven Burik
12 Two Problems of Comparative Philosophy: Why Conversational Thinking Is a Veritable Methodological Option 223
    Jonathan O. Chimakonam and Amara E. Chimakonam

Epilogue 241
Steven Burik, Robert Smid, and Ralph Weber

Notes on Contributors 257
Index 261

Introduction

Steven Burik, Robert Smid, and Ralph Weber

This volume was brought to fruition out of a recognition that, while comparative philosophy is thriving, and while a number of texts within that field of study have been written in a manner that is explicit about its methodological commitments, very little work has been done to bring these many considerations on method and methodology in comparative philosophy together. This might have to do with the nature of comparative philosophy itself. While it is true that in recent times comparative philosophy has increasingly become institutionalized in journals, monograph series, and study programs, it remains a "specialization" that is "neither encouraged nor rewarded" (Kirloskar-Steinbach, Ramana, and Msffie 2014: 44). Textbooks like the one by Tim Connolly (2015) or the elaborate volume by Lin Ma and Jaap van Brakel (2016) that discuss comparative philosophy generally are still rare. As a "specialization," comparative philosophy seems to straddle a myriad of philosophical styles, from analytic to continental and beyond, overlapping with religious traditions, spotlighting texts both ancient and modern if not also postmodern, and more often than not requiring very specialized philological expertise. No single scholar could possibly master it all. Comparative philosophy in this sense is certainly a collective enterprise. It is therefore wrong to think of the specialist in comparative philosophy only in terms of their particular area of expertise; both the impetus for specialized research and its application are directly related to broader developments in the field. That the field might be considered unduly large of course has to do with the many languages and cultures possibly involved with it. But this is not in itself an unusual setting. Most disciplines today have a global reach and therefore cover a large spectrum with no one able to stay on top of it all. Still, if the many languages and cultures make comparative philosophy seem a daunting task, this only provides more reason why method and methodology should be the privileged meeting point, particularly since many of the central issues appear to be pertinent across languages and cultures.

Against this background, it is quite natural that those few who do attempt higher order reflection on comparative philosophy still tend to be limited to a specific subset of traditions. For example, Robert Smid's (2009) book offers mostly the pragmatist and process tradition while also discussing methodology in general, while Steven Burik's (2009) book draws on the continental tradition in comparison with classical Daoism. The *Bloomsbury Research Handbook of Chinese Philosophy Methodologies* edited by

Sor-hoon Tan (2016) presents an up-to-date discussion of methods that would be relevant to comparative philosophy in general but is focused on Chinese philosophy only, as are Bo Mou's (2010) writings on constructive engagement. As a result, while comparative philosophy abounds, with its various siloes of methodological tradition, there is still too little communication across these traditions. One consequence of this situation is that there is little agreement about what comparative philosophy entails, who is qualified to undertake it, and under what conditions its claims are to be considered legitimate. But this, again, is a condition that also marks several disciplines today, and it is an open question whether or not such diversity is actually preferable to a more mainstreamed situation.

In fact, in recent times, we have seen a lively discussion of alternative labels for comparative philosophy, adding to the somewhat older strand of work labeled intercultural philosophy. Among them, we find transcultural philosophy, cosmopolitan philosophy, fusion philosophy, post-comparative philosophy, global philosophy, world philosophy/philosophies, and so on. These labels stand for different proposals for the direction in which comparative philosophy should be heading and are helpful for understanding what different scholars find important in the comparative endeavor. But in an important sense they still represent partisan attempts to reduce the plurality in the field and seldom include reflections at the level of meta-philosophical discussion.

More than a merely theoretical problem, the relative lack of overarching second-order methodological discussion has led to a very practical inefficiency in comparative philosophy. While there are some notable opportunities for cross-methodological engagement—such as during the East-West Philosophers Conferences and in periodicals such as *Philosophy East and West* or *Dao: A Journal of Comparative Philosophy*—the larger part of comparative philosophy takes place in the context of smaller conferences and more focused publications, which tend to privilege certain aspects of philosophy (e.g., intellectual history, philology, ethics), traditions (e.g., Continental, analytic, pragmatist), or regions (e.g., Chinese, Indian, Latin American). As a result, such work is often not readily available to comparativists with different interests, even when it addresses broader challenges of methodology. This problem is compounded by the prevalence of particular methodological options in each of these siloes, which can make it appear that there is more methodological consensus than there actually is. Indeed, for those not attuned to the broader array of options, it can appear that there are only a small number of methods available—or at least worthwhile. This manifests itself in presentations and publications that are able to take for granted the methodological approach that they employ, thus eliding the methodological challenges that they would otherwise need to address. In such cases, it is difficult to distinguish between disinterest in, indifference toward, and obliviousness of those challenges, but the end result is the same: not only are methodological issues not addressed, but the assumptions regarding their presumed resolution are only further reinforced.

Incidentally, this problem is not limited to comparativists. Those who argue against the possibility of comparative philosophy often point to the lack of methodological consensus to claim that there is no distinctive characteristic of comparative philosophy—that it is simply one or another variety of philosophy more generally.

Such critiques fail to acknowledge the cross-methodological deliberation that, while limited, nonetheless indicates a set of overlapping concerns that define the landscape of comparative philosophy, particularly its truly global reach and the indispensable reflection on what difference in place, language, and culture implies philosophically. At the same time, others argue against the possibility of comparative philosophy precisely because of the perceived failures of one or more of those methods. What they fail to register, however, are the methods that successfully evade those critiques, such that they can proceed only because of the lack of broader awareness of methodological diversity.

It is difficult to definitively identify the causes for this problem. Those whose methodological options predominate in any context have usually done their part to draw their readers' attention to methodological alternatives, although this has almost always been for the purpose of demonstrating the superiority of their own option. This is understandable, given their aims, but it can have only a limited effect on encouraging any further engagement. It is also understandable why those whose comparative interests are not primarily methodological would spend so little time on questions of method, as it could be seen to sidetrack or detract from their primary concern. Indeed, one gets the sense that questioning a presentation or publication on method would be inappropriate if it were not presented as an explicitly stated concern. Furthermore, those whose interests are primarily methodological have attempted to highlight the diversity of methods, but—as noted above—those efforts have been understandably limited by the expertise of their authors and their influence limited to the traditions they have been able to address. And, finally, those who argue against the very possibility of comparative philosophy can hardly be blamed for failing to see coherent methodological deliberation over the diverse and disparate array of what is taken to be comparative philosophy.

This is, of course, not sufficient as an explanation, as it lets everyone off the hook and still the problem remains. Whose responsibility is it to address questions of comparative method? In one sense, the responsibility belongs to anyone and everyone who engages in philosophical comparison. This seems to have been the understanding of the early pioneers of modern comparative philosophy. While the endeavor of a comparative history of philosophy harks back to texts such as Joseph Marie Degérando's *Histoire Comparée des systèmes de philosophie* from 1804, an important new and more global outlook emerged from the colonial position. Some of the first uses of the expression "comparative philosophy" can be traced to the nineteenth-century Indian scholars Virchand Raghavji Gandhi and Brajendra Nath Seal (Halbfass 1997: 298–9). The latter advocated "the systematic study of comparative philosophy and comparative disciplines, with the goal of furnishing 'new and comprehensive material for more correct generalizations'" (Halbfass 1990: 423).

Seal sought to strip Hegelianism of its Eurocentrism and its subordination of "non-Western tradition to European thought" (Halbfass 1997: 299), but remained committed to a view of history in terms of linear teleology, revolving around the eventual realization of universal humanity where each "national personality" would have found its place (quoted in Gupta, 2014: 761). He was also deeply positivist, seeing in comparative philosophy a tool to discover "the general laws of the social organism."

His was perhaps more the comparison of philosophy than philosophical comparison, although Chatterjee (2015) gives a compelling account of him as a precursor to fusion philosophy. Be that as it may, there is a strong affinity with the positivist program of Paul Masson-Oursel (Halbfass suggests a historical connection between the two scholars). Masson-Oursel studied with the likes of Henri Bergson, Emile Durkheim, and Marcel Mauss and had learned Sanskrit, Tibetan, Chinese, and Arabic. He was a prominent figure of his time and proved instrumental in raising the question of method in comparative philosophy, which he dealt with as early as in his essay "Objet et méthode de la philosophie comparée" (Masson-Oursel 1911).

The translation of Masson-Oursel's *Philosophie comparée* (1923) into English in 1926 might have contributed to an interest that was developing in the United States. Charles A. Moore stands at the forefront of this development and he watched over a series of initiatives that came to shape the contours of comparative philosophy for decades. Moore took up a position in Hawaii in 1936 and founded both the East-West Philosophers Conference and the journal *Philosophy East and West*. Of particular note in the earliest conferences and the ensuing journal articles associated with them is a strong interest in issues of comparative method: this was a prevalent theme over the course of the first three conferences (1939, 1949, and 1959), and perhaps best captured by the series on philosophical synthesis run by the journal over its first three years. Bringing together such early pioneers as Dewey, Radhakrishnan, Santayana, Hocking, Dasgupta, Mukerji, and Suzuki, along with Masson-Oursel and Moore, these opportunities not only energized and focused discussions of method but also demonstrated—both among the many contributions and as enumerated in many of them—the prevailing pluralism of possible methods (see, e.g., Kwee Swan Liat's *Methods of Comparative Philosophy* (1953), which is built on his 1951 article in *Philosophy East and West*).

The concern with method and second-order reflection, however, loses its prominence shortly after the 1950s, showing up only sporadically. As demonstrated by the persistent plurality of comparative methods, this is not because of any ensuing consensus on the matter. Rather, it appears to be due to the increasing emphasis on specialization within comparative philosophy. One demonstrates one's credentials in comparative philosophy by demonstrating expertise in at least one of the traditions compared, and such expertise is more easily demonstrable the more focused and specific it is. One should, of course, adopt an academically credible method but—by the logic of specialization—if method is not one's expertise then one is not responsible for any further interrogation of that method.

There are, in turn, those who take methodological issues as a primary area of expertise, and for them it would be inexcusable to elide such further interrogation. Yet those who do so are relatively few and face a countervailing set of obstacles. On the one hand, their deliberations about method may be taken to be only the deliberations internal to a specific area of expertise. If one's comparative credentials are determined by one's primary area of expertise, then immersing oneself in methodological deliberations can only be a secondary concern. On the other hand, comparative methodology is a strange thing to take as one's area of expertise, as it is difficult to assess the success of methods without also having expertise in what they compare. Thus, methodologists are usually under pressure to demonstrate expertise in specific traditions as well. What these countervailing obstacles suggest is that methodology cannot be the concern of only specialists in methodology or specialists in specific philosophical traditions; it must be assessed in conjunction with both groups. Effectively, it requires a revalorization of the generalists' perspective, whether by and for methodologists as such or in part by all comparativists.

Whatever the cause may be, and indeed whatever its solution turns out to be, the current problem is itself readily apparent. There is a diversity of live methodological options in comparative philosophy, and yet the actual practice of comparative philosophy operates as if this were not the case. There is a certain irony to this, as one of the hallmarks of the comparative endeavor has been to recognize diversity where it is otherwise suppressed and to engage it on its own terms. Thus, comparative philosophy that cannot recognize and engage the diversity of its own methodological options is ultimately at odds with itself.

Comparative philosophy has knowingly or unknowingly always stood in close connection with and even depended on the larger political realities within which it was pursued. Positionality is crucial. Seal, coming to think about comparative philosophy from within the colonial context, is a good example. Like in many comparative scholarly endeavors, colonialism forms a most important background, the consequences of which we are still occupied with. There is a strong sense in which comparative philosophy seeks a level playing field in the global arena against charges of Eurocentrism and epistemic injustices of all sorts. The *Journal of World Philosophies* (initially named *Confluence: Journal of World Philosophies*), for example, has tackled this dimension more consistently than other publications in the field. There are other contexts, too. In the early texts of *Philosophy East and West*, a lot of discussion revolved around world philosophical synthesis (Behuniak 2017) and the desire for world peace is palpable, given that the Second World War had just ended. One would have to assume that our own positionalities and political environments have similar impacts not only on the aims and purposes we attach to our work in comparative philosophy but also to discussions of method within it.

This book seeks to join ongoing efforts to remedy this situation by presenting, in a concise and accessible format, a diverse set of methodological considerations for comparative philosophy. While it would not be possible to include all of the available alternatives within one volume, presenting a substantially diverse array of such alternatives is enough to challenge myopic understandings of comparative method and encourage a more informed consideration of method. Accordingly, this book includes essays by scholars from East Asia, South Asia, the Middle East, Africa, Europe, and America, with representatives from a wide variety of philosophical traditions. Each essay is meant to be cutting edge insofar as it reflects the authors' latest work in methodology, so that every chapter can serve as an up-to-date methodological resource and viable methodological alternative for any would-be philosophical comparativist.

The intended audience for this book is intentionally broad. On the one hand, it is meant to serve as a primer for anyone looking to undertake the task of comparative philosophy. Because there are currently no clear and accessible resources laying out the variety of methodological considerations that are available, younger scholars should find this a valuable resource for weighing these considerations, making an informed choice among them, or perhaps even developing their own approach. On the other hand, it is also intended to broaden the awareness of even seasoned veterans, who would benefit from a more concise, explicit, and recent account of these methods for use in their own work. Ultimately, then, this should be an important resource for anyone writing on comparative philosophy, since upon publication of this text there should be no excuse for any lack of methodological awareness in such works.

Chapter Summaries

The primary purpose of this volume has been to present a variety of diverse perspectives on comparative method in philosophy, and thus from an editorial perspective our effort has been to allow each of these perspectives to speak for themselves through their respective chapters. At the same time, however, some order must be given to the volume, at least with respect to which chapter follows upon which. Our solution to this challenge is to encourage readers to consider the connections among the chapters from two perspectives. The first perspective is holistic, seeing each chapter as a distinctive response to the question of method in comparative philosophy. In soliciting contributions to the volume, we asked each author to focus on the question of method, and so in that sense each of the chapters should be read as staking a distinctive claim about method. Taken as a whole, then, the chapters are meant to provide a rough cross section of the methodological options available at this moment in the history of comparative philosophy.

The second perspective, in turn, acknowledges the presence of noteworthy themes running across several of the chapters. In some chapters these themes were central, in others more peripheral, and in some perhaps not notably present at all. In an effort to highlight these shared themes, and to underscore the mutual relevance of these chapters for readers particularly interested in those themes, we have arranged the chapters in clusters according to the shared themes most pronounced in each case. We refer to these as "constellations" both to indicate the provisional character of the groupings and also to remind the reader that they inevitably overlap. Readers will find that chapters placed in one constellation often make strong claims related to other constellations, such that the constellations could have been arranged in other, perhaps equally compelling ways.

In addition to these perspectives, we have attempted to capture some of these additional connections through the necessarily linear structure of modern print publication: aware that chapters must nonetheless follow one another in sequence, we have utilized some of these extra-constellational connections as transitions, so that some of the issues raised at the end of one constellation are picked up to some degree by the first chapter of the next constellation. The linear structure of this volume, then, should not be taken to convey either priority or culmination, but rather the ongoing conversation of a variety of distinct perspectives.

As editors, our common interests in methodological pluralism lead us to extend the following invitation to our readers: instead of looking for the approach they find most plausible, we ask our readers to contemplate the inevitable pros and cons of *all* the diverse approaches encountered in this volume, and by doing so share in our methodological meta-level thinking about comparative philosophy, and thus to see this volume as a contribution to what will surely be an ongoing and continuously evolving discussion on comparative philosophy in the years to come.

Constellation I: Necessary Conditions

Robert C. Neville

Robert Neville asserts that "the critical problem for comparative philosophy is Western bias" (18). While bias is a problem more generally for comparison, Western bias is a particular problem because of the current predominance of Western philosophical traditions across the globe—including in many historically non-Western regions. Neville reviews and assesses several approaches to addressing bias, ultimately arguing in favor of what he calls "two-faced comparison," which attends to the development and ongoing correction of both comparisons and the categories that inform them. Comparative philosophy, he argues, has generally neglected the latter process, refusing to indicate explicitly the respects in which a comparison is made and rendering itself unable to assess whether the respect of comparison is appropriate to what is compared. As a result, it remains vulnerable to charges of excessive bias. However, if it attends adequately to the development and correction of those categories as well as how everything that is interpreted in terms of that category relates to each other, then it can move toward what he calls "objective comparison," the truth-value of which can be assessed by the broader academic community.

Jaap van Brakel and Lin Ma

In their contribution, van Brakel and Ma propose what they call an XYZ model of interhuman interpretation, and discuss six necessary conditions and principles of the practice of comparative philosophy. Building on their previous books and articles in this area, they argue that the interpreter (comparativist, investigator) *must* presuppose a number of things for comparative philosophy to be possible. Based on concepts of Wittgenstein, Heidegger, Davidson, classical Chinese thinkers, and others, they extend and apply such concepts to the practice of comparative philosophy, (re-)introducing such ideas found throughout their work as "mutually recognizable human practices," "family-resemblance-concepts," "quasi-universals," and a threefold principle of mutual attunement that consists of the (extended and reworked) principles of reasonableness, of charity, and of humanity. Their paper lastly discusses the idea of epistemic virtues that are to be present in good comparative efforts, while also touching on the ideas of ideal language paradigms, translation, and embeddedness in *some* forms of life (hermeneutic relativity). For those yet unfamiliar with van Brakel and Ma's work, this contribution forms a valuable overview of the concepts and methodology they propose for comparative philosophy.

Constellation II: Generalization and Essentialization

Roger T. Ames

In his essay, Roger Ames addresses the charge leveled against some comparativists—including himself—of cultural essentialism: the belief that traditions are monolithic wholes that share a distinctive (though evolving) set of guiding (though perhaps unstated) principles. At issue is whether it is accurate and/or responsible for comparativists to assess traditions in general terms (including ascriptions of difference among them), or whether comparativists must necessarily restrict their interpretations solely to the immediate context of what is interpreted. Yet the flight to particularity offers no safer haven, he argues, as even the most particular interpretations will inevitably be shaped by the cultural assumptions of its interpreter(s). Indeed, abjuring self-conscious generalization risks unselfconsciously essentializing one's own cultural assumptions and projecting them onto what is interpreted. The more responsible approach is one that is self-consciously historicist, striving diligently to engage what is interpreted in its own particularity but also taking responsibility for the ways that engagement requires translation across a range of contingent historical contexts— including and especially one's own.

François Jullien

Presented in the form of an interview, Jullien sketches his journey to Chinese philosophy and comparative philosophy. It is a journey those familiar with his work will recognize: seeking access to Western thought through a detour into Chinese thinking, with the aim of questioning the grand theorems of Western philosophy from the outside through a different conceptuality. While wishing to be seen as neither a Sinologist nor a comparativist, Jullien offers his own way through his explanations of the relevance of his notions of blandness, the allusive, availability, and "silent transformation." Aside from this, Jullien takes us through the critiques from Sinologists and others on his work, explains his focus on language and conceptual schemes as important drivers for the differences in philosophies, and explores his quest to lay open the "unthought" background of understanding operable in different ways of thinking, exactly through setting up the confrontation or encounter of such different ways of thinking and placing himself in the "between" or the "écart" opened by such encounters.

Constellation III: Translation

Souleymane Bachir Diagne

In his essay, Diagne explores the relation between language and philosophy and its implications for comparative methodology. Following Merleau-Ponty, he maintains that, while there can be no "vertical universality" (i.e., no overarching universal) in a pluralistic world, this need not lead to relativism; there can also be a "lateral universality" that is uncovered and built up through the encounter and confrontation with other persons, experiences, ideas, and so on. Focusing on the embeddedness of philosophy within language, Diagne argues that translation is one way to achieve such lateral universality, but that it can only be achieved when no single language is given priority and learning other languages is taken to be necessary for the task of philosophy. In this respect, translation is not merely a precursor or attendant to philosophy; it is a method in itself. He demonstrates the possibilities and challenges of this approach in the context of tenth-century debates among Islamic intellectuals and shows how it continues to inform debates among contemporary African philosophers. Diagne's argument has postcolonial implications not only for intellectual traditions marginalized by the predominance of Western languages but also for those embedded within those languages alone.

Elisa Freschi

Pointing out that comparison is always present and is a necessary part of any philosophical enterprise, Freschi argues that intercultural or comparative philosophy should be seen in terms of a philosophical confrontation or combat between different positions, with the aim of changing those positions or at least accepting the risks involved to one's own position. Such risks arise because the time and effort invested in the encounter forces one out of one's comfort zone philosophically, and this makes the encounter productive, as it entails a development not gotten without the comparative encounter. This development leads to a (re-)gaining of identity through the encounter. Freschi then argues that translation is a litmus test for one's philosophical engagement with a text, as it forces the interpreter/translator into thinking through entireties of thought systems as represented in a text, rather than just thinking via snippets or sections.

Constellation IV: Postcolonialism and Globalization

Gabriel Soldatenko

Soldatenko's essay is an exploration of the possibility and function of Latin American philosophy as a contribution to comparative philosophy. Soldatenko discusses first the unique position of Latin American thought, in that it is neither "completely" other to Western philosophy, as Chinese philosophy would be, and this is because Latin American philosophy consists of a reaction to the dominance of Western philosophy within the Latin American sphere, to the exclusion of native thought systems. Nor should Latin American philosophy be thought of as a return to these native thought systems. So Latin American philosophy finds itself in an awkward position, which brings about an interesting discussion of the role of colonization and decolonization for the practice of comparative philosophy. Introducing two major Latin American thinkers with the aim of extracting methodological considerations, Soldatenko then moves to deliberate how Latin American thought may offer a different angle to ideas about methodology in comparative philosophy, since Latin American thought has developed in this rather unique circumstance of being both or neither Western and non-Western.

Jonardon Ganeri

Starting from the claim that the marked lack of diversity in philosophy is largely due to the Western legacy of colonial patterns of thought and organization, Ganeri argues against the claim of exceptionalism of the Greek "miracle," and aims to show that other traditions (most notably the Indian tradition) were equally exceptional. He identifies the problems of Western thinking in its focus on abstract and syllogistic approaches, and contrasts that with the blueprint+adaptation style of thought found in Classical India. Philosophy should not focus too much on abstract and mechanical rationality, but following India's example, consist more of an "aesthetic sympathy" approach, or in other words, philosophy should be a form of life based on phenomenological immersion, rather than analytic detachment. What is needed to bring philosophy back to life (assuming its Western focus has killed its living component) is something found in the philosophizing of the Sanskrit tradition and which Ganeri terms "stance pluralism," and which consists of an epistemic pluralism that does not succumb to relativism.

Arindam Chakrabarti and Ralph Weber

Chakrabarti and Weber revisit some recent controversies around the apparent difficulty of integrating comparative and "non-European philosophy" into philosophy departments dominated by analytic philosophy. Although constituting intricately related concerns, they choose to distinguish between political and philosophical concerns, focusing on the latter. They claim that the framing and labelling of philosophical concerns is important for the political discussion and crucial for achieving a more just philosophy and argue for a global post-comparative approach. Philosophically, their project amounts to a variant of "fusion philosophy," which is interested in producing arguments from working across different philosophical traditions that come to stand for nothing more or less than just philosophy. The chapter offers two methodological arguments, one pertaining to the significance of a weak historicism and the other to the philosophical value of a polyglotism that needs to be unflaunted if the future of comparative philosophy is to lead to doing just philosophy.

Constellation V: Plurality, Neutrality, and Method

Robert Smid

In his essay, Smid explores the intersection between carefully regulated method and philosophic creativity. He argues that, while the former has been the primary focus of comparative methodology for the past several decades, it runs the risk of stifling the latter—not because ill-conceived and distorted comparisons should be protected under the banner of creativity (they shouldn't), but because even the most carefully crafted methods occlude one another by their exclusivist focus. There is an irony in any comparativist's dogmatic adherence to a single method within a context of contested methods, and it comes at a cost to the comparative endeavor itself. Smid argues that, while individual methods each have a creative potential of their own, a greater creativity can be achieved through the embrace of methodological pluralism. He provides three recommendations for increasing cross-methodological engagement that are designed to prevent comparativists from finding, again and again, only what their preferred method allows them to discover and encourage the further cultivation of novel and unanticipated connections.

Steven Burik

In his essay, Burik argues that comparative philosophy cannot have one method or even one methodology. His contribution centers around two claims: firstly, that comparative philosophy cannot by its very nature have one method or methodology, because with ever finer comparisons and ever less or finer generalizations, comparative philosophy is increasingly becoming more site-specific so that it will become impossible to assign any single meaningful identity to it. Burik argues that assigning any single identity is something comparative philosophy should be adamant to avoid. Secondly, he claims that we neither need nor should we want a specific methodology for comparative philosophy. Any philosophy is in a way comparative philosophy, so comparative philosophy does not really have any special methodology, instead it relies on ever varying bits and pieces of both Western and non-Western sources. Based on these two claims, Burik then argues that methodology understood as "studying the various methods employed" in comparative philosophy is of course still useful, and can provide us with some provisional minimum requirements, which he proceeds to provide. He concludes that these requirements should, however, stay as minimal as possible, and that this is the only way comparative philosophy can stay true to its intended openness to diverse ways of thought.

Jonathan O. Chimakonam and Amara E. Chimakonam

Chimakonam and Chimakonam turn their attention to a long-standing problem in comparative philosophy—the persistence of bias in method—and propose conversational thinking as a promising solution. Comparative philosophy, they argue, requires a degree of neutrality, an ability to think across significant cultural (and other) borders, and this distinguishes it from philosophy more generally. To substantiate this claim, they outline six tasks for comparative philosophy, composed of three dimensions (philosophical, methodological, and logical) manifesting themselves across two spheres (the discursive and meta-sphere), and argue that it is the third dimension—the logical/meta-logical—that is most crucial to the development of a more neutral method. Dissatisfied with comparative methods rooted in the bivalent logic of Western traditions, they introduce conversational thinking as a more comprehensive method. The advantage of this method, they argue, is its grounding in the trivalent system of Ezumezu logic, which can account for but is not limited to bivalent logic. This, they conclude, gives it significantly more expressive power across traditions, allowing for greater complementarity and contextual considerations and thus staking a more credible claim for methodological neutrality.

Conclusion

Our goal in putting this volume together was to provide a handbook on methodological issues in comparative philosophy, both as it is currently practiced and with an eye toward its ongoing development. As a handbook, it is meant to be reasonably representative but not exhaustive, which has meant that we could not include all relevant perspectives on the issues addressed. Our guiding principle was to prioritize the diversity of methodological perspectives, including and especially the diversity of philosophical traditions from which they emerge. This is necessarily an imperfect process, as some forms of diversity must be sacrificed in favor of others, but we believe that these choices allow for a certain coherence that provides both a reasonable introduction to the methodological concerns prevalent at this moment in time and also a basis for considerations on how to address those concerns moving forward.

References

Behuniak, Jim (2017), "John Dewey and East-West Philosophy," *Philosophy East and West*, 67 (3): 908–16.
Burik, Steven (2009), *The End of Comparative Philosophy and the Task of Comparative Thinking: Heidegger, Derrida, and Daoism*, Albany, NY: SUNY Press.
Chatterjee, Amita (2015), "Brajendra Nath Seal: A Disenchanted Hegelian," in Sharad Deshpande (ed.), *Philosophy in Colonial India*, Sophia Studies in Cross-cultural Philosophy of Traditions and Cultures, 13, 81–101, New Delhi: Springer.
Connolly, Tim (2015), *Doing Philosophy Comparatively*, London: Bloomsbury Academic.
Gupta, Sujata, Prabir K. Gupta, and Supratim Gupta (2014), "Brajendra Nath Seal—a Sesquicentenary Birth Anniversary Tribute," *Current Science*, 106 (5): 760–62.
Halbfass, Wilhelm (1990), *India and Europe: An Essay in Philosophical Understanding*, New Delhi: Motilal Banarsidass.
Halbfass, Wilhelm (1997), "Research and Reflection: Responses to my Respondents. III. Issues of Comparative Philosophy," in Eli Franco and Karin Preisendanz (eds.), *Beyond Orientalism: The Work of Wilhelm Halbfass and Its Impact on Indian and Cross-Cultural Studies*, 297–315, Amsterdam: Rodopi.
Kirloskar-Steinbach, Monika, Geeta Ramana, and James Maffie (2014), "Introducing Confluence: A Thematic Essay," *Confluence: Journal of World Philosophies*, 1: 7–63.
Kwee, Swan Liat (1951), "Methods of Comparative Philosophy," *Philosophy East and West*, 1 (1): 10–15.
Kwee, Swan Liat (1953), "Methods of Comparative Philosophy," PhD dissertation, Leiden University.
Ma, Lin, and Jaap van Brakel (2016), *Fundamentals of Comparative and Intercultural Philosophy*, Albany: SUNY Press.

Masson-Oursel, Paul (1911), "Objet et Méthode de la Philosophie Comparée," *Revue de Métaphysique et de la Morale*, 19 (4): 541–8.

Masson-Oursel, Paul (1923), *La Philosophie Comparée*, Paris: Imprimerie des Presses Universitaires de France. Translated into English in 1926 as *Comparative Philosophy*, New York: Harcourt, Brace.

Mou, Bo (2010), "On Constructive-Engagement Strategy of Comparative Philosophy: A Journal Theme Introduction," *Comparative Philosophy*, 1 (1): 1–32.

Smid, Robert W. (2009), *Methodologies of Comparative Philosophy: The Pragmatist and Process Traditions*, Albany, NY: SUNY Press.

Tan, Sor-hoon (ed.) (2016), *The Bloomsbury Research Handbook of Chinese Philosophy Methodologies*, London: Bloomsbury Academic.

Constellation I

Necessary Conditions

1

Reflections on Methods of Comparative Philosophy

Robert Cummings Neville

The Situation for Comparative Philosophy

Philosophy has been comparative since its beginnings. As philosophy arose during the Axial Age, it formulated general conceptions about the universe and noted that alternative conceptions existed or were being formulated also. The definiteness of one conception depended on its distinction from other conceptions. In East Asia, pre-Qin philosophers debated between philosophies of Confucian, Daoist, Legalist, and Moist leanings; Buddhist philosophy entered the picture during the Han dynasty. In South Asia, the early Vedic philosophies rearticulated themselves over against the emerging Buddhist philosophies to form the Six Orthodox Schools, as well as the unorthodox ones; by the sixth century of the common era, Bhaviveka could write a detailed comparative analysis of the Buddhist and Hindu schools of his day, setting them out as alternatives to one another.[1] In the West, Plato wrote almost only dialogues, which are comparative arguments to begin with, though mostly within classical Greek culture and a bit of Egyptian philosophy; Aristotle began his *Physics* with comparative philosophy establishing the "four causes" theory.

Comparative philosophy (and theology) came to mean comparing philosophies from different cultures, although the distinctions among cultures were themselves fluid and contentious. East Asians had moments of great comparison in the period of neo-Confucianism in which Buddhist, Daoist, and early Confucian texts were distinguished and compared. Beginning in the sixth and then again in the nineteenth centuries, Chinese philosophers of all schools encountered and interpreted Western philosophies, Christian and then Marxist. Buddhist, Hindu (in various senses), and Moghul Muslim philosophies interpreted each other in South Asia. In West Asia, the philosophies looking to the East slowly separated from those looking toward Western Europe and so the medieval Christians looked upon medieval Muslims and Jews as coming from different cultures, however common many of their roots.

The contemporary situation for comparative philosophy began in the nineteenth century with the great translation projects that brought texts from East Asia and South Asia into European languages. Translation inevitably involves comparison across the texts translated and the philosophical vocabulary of the European and American traditions. James Legge and Max Mueller are the great names associated with the translation of "Eastern" texts into English, although many others worked in this field and still do.[2] Although sometimes criticized as colonialist, these great translation efforts initiated extraordinary projects of comparative philosophy and theology, often more associated with religion than philosophy. We are in great debt to these European-cultured scholars who brought massive amounts of philosophy into European languages that already had a leg up in making explicit comparisons. In contrast to contemporary comparativists who tend to be on the margins of the academy, Legge and Mueller were giants at Oxford in the nineteenth century, subject to criticism mainly from those who were jealous of their power. The juggernaut translation projects as the venue for comparative philosophy pretty much came to an end with the twentieth-century work of William Theodore de Bary and his many generations of students at Columbia University.

The critical problem with this European and American scholarship, of course, is that the categories used initially to understand the non-Western texts were those of the Western texts, a problem addressed by de Bary's project. These were categories not only for translating non-Western philosophical terms but also those for deciding what counts as philosophy or theology and for determining what is important. So from the beginning of the nineteenth-century project until today there has been sensitivity to Western reductionism, the translation of non-Western texts into what they might mean as variants on Western philosophies. The translated non-Western texts usually appear to be poor substitutions for Western ideas, often missing the Western point. Also, those texts that cannot quickly be compared to Western terms have been late in translation.

Since early times, we have recognized a significant difference between translating things into what Westerners already understand and translating Western and other texts into non-Western languages. Comparison requires all sides to understand the comparisons. As comparative philosophy has become more and more embedded in the academy, however, and the global academy has come more and more to be the Western academy no matter where the schools are located, the critical problem of comparative philosophy has focused on dealing with Western bias. To be sure, many non-Western academies remain, especially in lands dominated by Islam. By and large, however, the critical problem for comparative philosophy is Western bias.

Let me make four contingent qualifications to this statement of the situation of comparative philosophy. First, most Western analytic philosophy departments are not interested in comparative philosophy. Bryan Van Norden (2017) has written a blistering indictment of them for being so monocultural. The situation is improving some under pressure from students and interests outside of philosophy departments. But most non-Western philosophies are not considered to be serious philosophy by most analytic philosophers, except within the field of ethics in some instances. So, for better or worse, there is no critical problem for comparative philosophy within analytic philosophy departments.

Second, most, though not all, Continental philosophy departments have been moved toward some version of postmodernism with its Marxist roots. This gives them a strong interest in liberation, or critical theory, which usually means liberation from some kind of social oppression such as economic inequality, racism, or human-caused climate change. Nevertheless postmodernism usually takes the form of criticizing the past of its own dialectic, usually a European one. Non-European cultures enter consideration mainly insofar as they show up as victims of Western colonialism. Even there they are not heard on their own terms but rather only in how they delegitimate some aspect of the Western philosophical dialectic, usually only the Continental dialectic.

The anticolonialist bent in postmodern Continental philosophy has two main arguments against comparative philosophy. One is that Continental philosophy needs to be humble and limit its comments only to its own tradition. Ironically, this serves only to marginalize further the non-European philosophies, not to involve them in a global conversation. A second reason to neglect comparative philosophy is postmodernism's alleged bias against large-scale theories, logocentrism. The postmodern identification of its own dynamic is of course a logocentric story; but that aside. Genuine comparative philosophy needs to work at many levels of comparison, including very general ones such as whether everything is substances or processes. At any rate, comparative philosophy is not an important topic in most areas of contemporary Continental philosophy, which thinks its categories receive determinateness because of its own historical dialectic and not by comparison with whole other philosophic approaches.

Third, the American philosophic tradition beginning with Ralph Waldo Emerson in the first half of the nineteenth century and working through the pragmatists, process philosophers, and contemporary Americanists have long been interested in major figures in non-Western philosophies. So, American philosophers identifying with the classic trajectory are very much involved in comparison and its contemporary problems.

Fourth, comparative philosophy is practiced often, although not always, around theological topics. Sometimes comparative theology, of the sort studied and practiced primarily by Francis X. Clooney, SJ, and by the American Academy of Religion group he founded is the main kind of serious comparative philosophy. Comparative theology is comparative philosophy about theological topics.

Fighting Bias

Let me return to the major problem facing contemporary comparative philosophy, namely bias. The first way to fight bias is simply to accept it.[3] This happens most often in comparative theology where the intent is to have the outcome of the comparative inquiry to be fully theological, making first-order theological claims. In principle, this strategy could be employed in any area of comparative philosophy, for instance metaphysics, epistemology, ethics, and logic, where the comparativist is convinced of the truth of his or her home tradition. Whereas Clooney speaks frankly of comparative theology as "faith seeking understanding," other forms of philosophy are not likely to use that religious language. But we all know of philosophers whose commitment to Aristotelian metaphysics, or liberal democracy, or symbolic logic, is a nearly unquestionable faith. Comparison consists in reading the texts of some other tradition alongside one's own. In the happiest of circumstances, the new tradition simply adds something new to what is known in the home tradition and perhaps sheds new light on understanding the traditions together. In one of the saddest circumstances, the new tradition is simply dismissed where it differs from the old. In another of the saddest circumstances, the new tradition is overwhelmingly attractive and the old tradition is simply abandoned. In between are the many circumstances in which new questions are asked about the old and new traditions; one understands the original tradition better by seeing it from the outside and perhaps one adds new understanding to the new tradition by seeing it in the light of the old.

Good scholars in this approach, such as Clooney and Catherine Cornille, are scrupulous in their interpretations of all the traditions. They are also quick to learn from the new traditions for the sake of expanding, perhaps even correcting, their old home traditions. Scholars who do not share their commitment of their home traditions often learn much from them, as I have. This approach to comparison is most common among Roman Catholic theologians who need to maintain loyalty to their capacious yet limited tradition as they make assertions of theological truth. In light of this, Catherine Cornille (2014: 12) writes:

> The goal of comparative theology, however, is not in the end the understanding of the other on its own terms but the meaning of the other tradition (or some elements within it) for one's own religious self-understanding. As such it may be presumed that the ultimate interpretation of the other tradition will be colored by one's own tradition.

To be sure, one's own historical location might be impossible to prevent from biasing comparison, even in the long run.

Nevertheless, I say that the goal of comparison is *first* to understand all the traditions on their own terms and in terms of how they relate to one another, and that the determination of one's own religious self-understanding needs to come *after* doing one's best to be fair to all sides.[4]

A second approach to bias aims to be fair to all the traditions or positions involved by following the natural suggestions for comparison, where increasing knowledge of diverse positions suggests comparisons to be made. This approach is what I had in mind generally when claiming that philosophy has been comparative from its earliest beginnings, as Aristotle compared his view to Plato's, and Wang Bi his view to the Daodejing's. We do not think of this as comparative these days, however, unless the positions had been nurtured by different traditions that had little to do with one another earlier.

Even a little knowledge of "other" traditions prompts all sorts of comparative suggestions. After two millennia of Aristotelian substance philosophy in the West, the discovery that the Chinese suppose that things are made of yin-yang changes that are somewhat in balance but that themselves are always changes prompts an interesting comparison regarding the stuff of the cosmos: "substance" versus "changes." Then again, reflection on the diversity in the Chinese "change" position where changes are measured by the structures of coherences or Heaven or Principle might suggest that we regard Plato as being, not a proto Aristotelian, but rather on the side of the Chinese. Or consider the history of the idea of God in the great Western translation projects begun in the nineteenth century. Monotheism was supposed to be the mature view, with pantheons such as the Greeks' and the Romans' being immature; the Indians were pluralistic but ordered their gods in hierarchies that marked out one as supreme, the "henotheist" positions. When it was noticed that the Chinese had altogether too many gods and regarded none of them as ultimate, Chinese philosophies were dismissed as not religious. But the Chinese did have conceptions of ultimacy, just not those based on theistic models of intentional agency, at least after the pre-Qin philosophers. So it has become popular now to compare personal theisms with naturalistic conceptions of spontaneous emergence and pattern formation, all under the category of "ultimacy."

These stories are told in many different ways that do not need rehearsal here. But they all have the logic of noting apparent similarities, checking that out, finding differences, and noting how far the differences go. In complex comparison the terms of the original comparison are changed and become detailed in many ways. The dialectic of comparison involves noting similarities and differences and following them out. It does not lead to the development of a comparative scheme versus content distinction. Comparativists such as David Decosimo sometimes explicitly call upon Donald Davidson's (1973/4) attack on the scheme–content distinction in order to agree with it. The aim is to reject any appeal to a scheme of comparative categories or "bridge concepts," as Aaron Stalnaker (2010) calls them. The argument is that we would not be able to understand and use the categories from such a scheme if we did not already have the language to articulate what the scheme compares.

The heart of this approach is in the accidents of comparative work, achieving new connections as they arise and being chastened in making hasty comparisons. Jonathan Z. Smith was surely right that "in comparison a magic dwells." Furthermore, comparison is never-ending, with each comparative explanation vulnerable to being corrected by the next thing discovered. This approach to comparison is best understood to be undertaken by a community of investigators, or rather, by a noncommunity of investigators who come at similar topics from different angles. To be sure, many levels of comparison exist, with comparisons being supposed on some levels while others are under investigation. Distant comparison might suddenly be brought into mutual contestation by new discoveries in material or in point of view. This approach accurately sees the actual jumble of comparisons being made by academic communities over time.

Nevertheless, I believe this approach does not take bias seriously enough. Of course, no one completely transcends historical location, and it is foolish to hope to be completely bias free. But a step can be taken, and insisted upon all through comparison, to ask about the respect in which things are compared. Some "respect of comparison" is always functioning in any suggestion of a comparison. Things are similar in some respects and different in some respects. But the possibility of bias is always especially present when the respect of comparison is not examined on its own. Sometimes this is as gross as equivocation on the middle term: warm beer is better than nothing, nothing is better than God, therefore warm beer is better than God. Other times the respect of comparison can be subtly ambiguous and hence distorting. The distortion *derives* from lack of clarity about the respects in which the things are being compared. The distortion *consists* in some meaning of the respect of comparison that comes from one's own preferences or assumptions being taken to evaluate the items compared. The result is a diminishment of the importance of the other things being compared, and a distortion of them in comparison with one's own. Therefore, I would insist that comparison make explicit the respects in which things are compared, and I call these respects "comparative categories."

Two-Faced Comparison

Aaron Stalnaker's "bridge concepts" are a move in the right direction. They acknowledge that different traditions have such different languages that some fresh language needs to connect them, like building a bridge over a chasm. But I believe they represent a very sophisticated version of comparative categories, not the actual beginning work of constructing comparative categories themselves. Comparison consists as much in constructing the comparative categories as it does in making comparisons according to them. Therefore, I say that comparison is two-faced: developing and correcting actual comparisons and developing and correcting the categories that constitute the respects in which things are being compared.

This supposes that there is no such thing as the "beginning" of comparison. We are always in the middle. Always there are some comparative categories at work, and always there are some comparisons assumed and used to orient new comparisons. So we should think of comparison as a process with many comparativists. Although we publish papers and books that report comparisons, these should not be thought of as finished products. They rather should be regarded as reports on stages in the processes. Moreover, the comparative processes are not well structured. Rather, they are lumpy and connected only from time to time. These days, the comparative processes that are active are those for which there exist scholars or groups of scholars with a particular interest in comparing certain things at hand. Most academic comparison also requires money, and money is available for some projects and not others. Moreover, comparative processes are much affected by accidental discoveries of new texts, new ways of reading symbols, new materials for putting philosophies in social contexts, and the like. Although we usually think of philosophic comparisons these days as academic processes, those processes are punctuated by many accidental findings that turn comparisons in new directions.

Therefore, we find ourselves working in loosely connected pockets of comparison, often defined by friendships and sometimes enmities. When I say, then, that comparison is two-faced, I am not suggesting that comparative work be organized in two steady streams of comparison: one developing the comparative categories and the other making comparisons in respect of those categories. Rather, I say that there are at least two elements in comparison that need to be attended to, one of which is usually neglected. Whenever we make a comparison, we are assuming and employing a comparative category, comparing two or more things in some alleged respect or other. We commonly think of comparison as identifying and analyzing what the things compared say about the respect in which they are compared. We commonly neglect to identify explicitly what that respect is and to inquire as to whether the way we think about that respect is fair to the things compared. This sets up comparison for the postmodern criticism that comparison is always biased and that it is therefore better not to compare at all.

My point is that examination of the comparative categories is itself a process. On the surface, it might seem as if that process *merely* aims to correct the bias of assuming that the categories basic to one's own philosophic culture identify the important things to notice in comparison. Of course, this kind of correction is always desirable. Earlier I noted the process of comparison regarding what philosophies take to be ultimate moves from assuming that the ultimate is really some kind of personal theism to making room for nontheistic kinds of ultimate reality. I noted also that Aristotelian substance thinkers, when doing comparison, need to allow for process- or change-oriented philosophies. But something more is going on in these kinds of processes of reflecting about comparative categories. In each instance, the comparative category was changed to something deeper. In the case of ontological ultimate reality, the category itself allows of exemplification by notions of personal gods, transpersonal supreme infinite beings, combinations of gods plus the world, forces of existence beyond the karma that controls the gods, emptiness of many kinds, the Dao conceived in many ways, Heaven and Earth, Principle and Qi, to name only a few of the commonly recognized ways of specifying ultimacy. Without suggesting that each of these is as good as the others or that each of them has something important to contribute to the understanding of ultimate reality, we can see that each is its own line of development in articulating the respect in which we compare them. Similarly with regard to cosmological conceptions of what the world consists in: there are many conceptions of substances and many conceptions of change. To compare them requires us to ask what really is at stake in identifying the things of the world. I shall return to the problem of discerning the "true" philosophy in comparison shortly.

So far I have spoken as if a comparative process were to compare two or more philosophical ideas in some respect, and we all know that this is far too abstract. In any significant comparison, many things are being held steady and other things are being compared at once. For instance, the metaphorical systems of West Asian and South Asian religious philosophies can be compared in respect of how they symbolize ultimacy. Both begin with ideas of the human person and transform those notions to transcendent, indeterminate ultimacy. But what the Western philosophies find interesting in the human is agency, intentionality, emotion, will, and creative action. To be sure, Western philosophies of God, for instance neo-Platonism or Aristotelian Thomism, acknowledge that God is infinitely full with no unfulfilled agency or intention. But those philosophies carry traces of personal action and so can relate to mythic and biblical images of God or the gods acting with a sense of justice. The South Asian philosophies in Hinduisms and Buddhisms, quite to the contrary, believe that the traits of agency, intention, and action are what is problematic in the human person and seek in various ways to limit them. Rather, what is important in the human is pure consciousness. Even ordinary people can meditate so as to remove or at least trivialize the arising and ceasing of dharmas in consciousness, and ultimate reality is imagined to be pure consciousness with no content, such as Brahman. Buddhists in different ways say that pure consciousness is empty. So, the comparison of Western and South Asian conceptions of ultimate personhood also involves many kinds of comparisons of differences in their conceptions of selfhood at all other levels. To be sure, each of those traditions has many different conceptions of selfhood. One of the large-scale differences is that South Asians generally assume that persons as agents are subject to the laws of karma. Karma is more ultimate than persons, and hence the South Asians are not much interested in developing agential theories of personhood as metaphors for ultimacy. They do, however, have elaborate theories of agency and karma, with competing theories of how people should live as finite agents. When the South Asian philosophers think about gods and ultimacy, they transform their conceptions so that agency is left out, and what remains as a metaphoric reference to ultimate reality is only pure consciousness, somehow conceived. Comparing how any thinkers from West and South Asia might compare regarding ultimate reality also involves comparing how they compare regarding the nature of selfhood, whether there is karma, and how to distinguish the ultimate from finite lives.

Real comparison of those traditions thus involves comparing vast numbers of related items brought together in some respect. I would be tempted to say that the comparisons are those of systems of comparative categories. But that temptation should be resisted because in those traditions, each of the notions has a history of changes with regard to the others. The ideas in any one person's philosophy have a history, and that person ranks them differently at different stages of life. To compare the South and West Asian philosophies of ultimacy is a vast generalizing project. It is legitimate because it provides a context for making more particular comparisons. But most active comparative projects these days are likely to be far less general than this. I shall return to philosophy of history in comparison shortly.

Comparison and Truth in Comparative Philosophy

So far I have focused on the two-faced character of comparative philosophy: the development of comparative categories and the making of comparisons of different positions under those categories. But there exists a third element in comparison, namely, the statement of just how the things compared compare. This requires two steps, assuming that the comparative category is settled. The first step is to say what each of the philosophers or traditions has to say about the comparative category, say ultimacy. Plato, Aristotle, Abhinavagupta, Nagarjuna, Wang Bi, and Zhou Dunyi have different theories of ultimacy, and the first step in comparison is to state just how each one specifies the category of ultimate reality. This requires the development of the language of the comparative category with different languages of specification, in this instance the Platonic, Aristotelian, Shaivite, Buddhist, Daoist, and neo-Confucian. Given the complex interrelations of this comparative category with so many others, this means the complex description of all the different approaches.

The second step, however, is to say explicitly how each of the philosophies compares with the others, where they agree and disagree, what they emphasize and what they diminish, and why, and all the other ways in which the positions might compare. It is one thing to note how the different philosophies say what they do about the comparative topic. It is another to draw out explicitly how these relate to one another. Only when a comparativist draws out explicit comparisons can the comparison be called "objective."

"Objective comparisons" are explicit claims about how two or more philosophies compare in some respect. Any comparative philosopher ought to be able, in principle, to check out those claims. The original comparative argument should be checkable. Of course, given the complexity of any comparison, this is highly fallible. A second comparativist invariably will have different interests from the first and will be more acquainted with different material. But an explicit objective comparison is a claim that is laid before the community of comparativists to be tested, modified, and judged. Hopefully, it will also be helpful to the other comparativists. The claim is intended to be objectively true in stating how the positions compare.

I have argued in this paper that the attainment of truth in this objective sense is a primary goal of comparative philosophy. "Such and such" is how the philosophies compare in this respect with as little bias as possible. This is an essential goal for comparison. As I have said, comparative philosophy is multidisciplinary in many ways. Some comparativists might identify themselves primarily as historians. In this regard, they would not aim for more normative study than is involved in the objective comparisons. They could say, for instance, that the Thomists and neo-Confucians compare in such and such a way regarding ultimacy and in this and that ways regarding whether the units of the cosmos are substances or changes. They would avoid making much more serious comparative claims as to which of the sides compared is more true. In comparative *theology*, this is a serious temptation for those who have an authoritative commitment to some home theological tradition, which must trump any more mind-altering views about theological truth.

Nevertheless, there is a more normative sense of truth at work here, namely, that the comparative categories involved are the important ones for comparing the philosophies. The comparative categories are developed by detecting and correcting bias. They reveal more connections with other categories, the subtler they are. Although the comparative categories are more and more complexly related to other comparative categories, and the layout of their connections is increasingly dense, the categories increasingly layout the important joints of reality about which different philosophies might be compared. There are huge lacunae in the categoreal connections, always, but there are increasingly dense connections in processes of comparison.

So I would insist that the two-faced character of philosophical comparison finds a way, in developing its comparative categories, to discern something about what is really real and philosophically noteworthy. Although philosophies can be compared with regard to whether they are more "realistic" or "historicistic," in the long run they are realistic. They pick up on what is interesting, however differently they frame that. If something is a problem for only one philosophy, chances are it is not a real problem. But the categories that emerge through complex and dense comparison are likely to be on to something.

Immediately I need to qualify this further normativity. First, no clear line exists between the objective claims that a comparison explains how things compare fairly and the more normative claims that the respects of comparison are the real lines of the universe according to which philosophical positions ought to be compared. If there were no serious grounds to believe in the importance of the comparative categories, no one would even bother to make the objective comparisons. The question is how far the comparativist goes in stating the importance of the comparisons.

Second, no clear rule determines when a serious comparison ought to be checked out with regard to other specifications of the vulnerable comparative category, which would be a logical follow-up. Academic comparativists today are trained in silos, even when they are connected dual or triple silos. Christian–Confucian expert comparativists might move around in different time periods and in sub-traditions of their comparative subjects, but are not likely to move to compare these with South Asian or Islamic traditions, except by moving up some levels of generality.

Third, to be sure, most academic comparativists might publish learned articles comparing just a few authors from detailed angles, but would also teach advanced courses in whole traditions and introductory courses in comparative world philosophies. The texture of comparative thinking operates at many different levels with different approaches at each. Comparative learning is not only with regard to detailed specifics but also with regard to generalizations at many levels.

Fourth, after a while, the pursuit of solid, well-grounded judgment on the importance of comparative categories shifts its balance from *comparative* philosophy to comparative *philosophy*. The concern becomes less to inquire into new comparisons and rather becomes to assume a wide range of comparisons, at many levels of generality and specificity. From the standpoint of this kind of assumption, the philosopher can begin to ask what the best philosophy is. The broad background of comparative knowledge of world philosophies can be assumed as important for doing philosophy, not just the knowledge of a narrow "home tradition." This is "comparatively informed" philosophy. I believe myself that all philosophy today should be comparatively informed, even when it is not much interested in further research in specifically comparative inquiries.

Fifth, at this point, comparative informed philosophy begins to take on a systematic character. The "system" is not merely a system of the comparative categories, although they should register somehow or other in the system. Many forms of system exist, from Plato's lifetime of dialogues without himself as a character to Aristotle's prose lying out of categories based on some serious comparative work, from Zhuangzi's ironic speech to Mencius's essays, and from the Samkhya Sutras to the Buddhist systems of Asanga and Vasubandu. Kierkegaard and Nietzsche had systems attacking systematic thinking. All I mean by "system" here is a more or less inclusive vision that comments on just about all philosophic topics, at least the central ones. Kierkegaard and Nietzsche had visions of this sort, as did Nishitani who thought everything is empty. Formal logic has an ambiguous relation to philosophical systems because many philosophers ignore it. Nevertheless, approaches to epistemology and formal logic exist in all major philosophic traditions.

Sixth, though hard to imagine concretely, some comparatively informed philosophers might believe that the objectively valid comparative categories and specific comparisons are so seriously mistaken as to require rejection. Probably no contemporary philosopher would accept any given philosophical position or comparatively informed system except their own. On the other hand, it would be inconceivable to be totally new in philosophy. How would we identify that work as philosophy? Nevertheless, nearly all the great philosophers now included in any tradition for comparison contributed something novel in their own time, sometimes things that seemed outlandish then or now.

Seventh, any philosophy has an obligation to be true to the world, which means it is obligated to take responsibility for what it says. This is so whether it is primarily *comparative* philosophy focusing on a few texts, comparative *philosophy* focusing on the truth to be found in various comparative schemes and expressed in compared ways, comparatively *informed* philosophy dealing with its own philosophic agenda, or comparatively *uninformed* philosophy. That philosophy has an obligation to take responsibility for what it says about the world means that it is a normative as well a descriptive way of thought. The ten thousand things of the world can be "merely described" in an indefinitely rich number of alternative ways. Philosophy needs to describe the important ways, and to justify why it thinks these are important and how they fit together. Few philosophers face up to the depth of this kind of intellectual responsibility, even though we all have it.

Philosophy of the History of Philosophy

Although histories of philosophy, or at least small bits of history of philosophy, go back to the ancient world, grand philosophies of the history of philosophy are products of the modern era in Europe and then the rest of the world. Hegel was the first really grand philosopher who had a detailed, multivolume philosophy of how the world philosophies as he knew them fit together both historically and conceptually regarding the truth. What he knew about the world's major philosophic and theological traditions was astonishing for his day.

Karl Jaspers's *Origin and Goal of History* ([1953] 2010) was a twentieth-century masterpiece. He developed a capacious view of world philosophies and invented the brilliant new historical category of the "Axial Age" to make sense of them together. The "Axial Age" is not exactly an historian's historical category; it does not deal closely enough with detailed empirical data and depends too much on generalizations. For a long time, it was out of favor for that and other reasons. Among the other reasons was the seriously biased philosophy of history of Martin Heidegger who for a long time dominated Jaspers in the Western Continental world. But something obviously true shines through Jaspers's work. In the same way, something obviously true shines through the philosophies of history of Charles Taylor (1989, 2007). Robert Bellah (2011), a philosophical sociologist, has shown how true the notion of the Axial Age is for orienting historical and philosophical thought in many fields for understanding the world.

My final reflection on philosophy of the history of philosophy is that we need much more of it these days as a kind of culminating stage of comparative philosophy. Jaspers's is not the only way our origins and resources might be understood. We need East and South as well as West Asian, African, Islamic, and American approaches to the philosophy of the history of philosophy. Disputes among alternatives will take generations. But that is the historical context necessary for us to do global philosophy today.

Much more comparative philosophy of the objective sort needs to be done, and many comparative philosophers will content themselves with that. The attractiveness of understanding the importance of the categories according to which we understand the connections of philosophy will continue to stimulate normative comparisons. Regional and global normative comparisons will become more common, will fill in much that we now only guess at, and will provide an assumable background within which to think. Soon we will have contributions toward genuine global philosophies and will come to understand more and more about what is important and how to live in the world and our skies. Comparative philosophy is only a stage in the development of global philosophy. But without it we cannot move on.

Notes

1. See Malcolm David Eckel's *Bhaviveka and His Buddhist Opponents* (2008) for a translation into English and a detailed analysis of part of this comparative philosophy.
2. See Norman J. Girardot's *The Victorian Translation of China: James Legge's Oriental Pilgrimage* (2002), a massive and brilliant study of Legge's major orientalist work in China and at Oxford with Max Mueller. This is a major study of the strengths and limits of the colonialist approach to comparative philosophy in a missionary context.
3. The most sophisticated version I know of defending this approach is that of Francis X. Clooney, SJ (2010: 10), who defines comparative theology as follows: "*Comparative theology—comparative* and *theological* beginning to end—marks acts of faith seeking understanding which are rooted in a particular faith tradition but which, from that foundation, venture into learning from one or more other faith traditions. This learning is sought for the sake of fresh theological insights that are indebted to the newly encountered tradition/s as well as the home tradition."
4. I have discussed this approach to comparison in relation to my own at much greater length in "On Comparative Theology: A Confucian Case" (forthcoming).

References

Bellah, Robert N. (2011), *Religion in Human Evolution: From the Paleolithic to the Axial Age*, Cambridge, MA: Harvard University Press.

Clooney, Francis X., SJ (2010), *Comparative theology: Deep Learning Across Religious Borders*, Chicester, UK: John Wiley & Sons.

Cornille, Catherine (2014), "The confessional Nature of Comparative Theology," *Studies in Interreligious Dialogue*, 24 (1): 9–17.

Davidson, Donald (1973-4), "On the Very Idea of a Conceptual Scheme," *Proceedings and Addresses of the American Philosophical Association*, 47: 5–20.

Eckel, David (2008), *Bhaviveka and His Buddhist Opponents*, Cambridge, MA: Harvard University Press.

Girardot, Norman J. (2002), *The Victorian Translation of China: James Legge's Oriental Pilgrimage*, Berkeley: University of California Press.
Jaspers, Karl ([1953] 2010), *The Origin and Goal of History*, trans. Michael Bullock, Routledge Revivals edition, London: Routledge.
Neville, Robert Cummings (forthcoming), "On Comparative Theology: A Confucian Case," in Wilhelmus Valkenberg (ed.), *Brill's Companion to Comparative Theology*.
Norden, Bryan W. Van (2017), *Taking Back Philosophy: A Multicultural Manifesto*, with a Foreword by Jay L. Garfield, New York: Columbia University Press.
Stalnaker, Aaron (2010), *Overcoming our Evil*, Washington, DC: Georgetown University Press.
Taylor, Charles (1989), *Sources of the Self: The Making of Modern Identity*, Cambridge, UK: Cambridge University Press.
Taylor, Charles (2007), *A Secular Age*, Cambridge, MA: Harvard University Press.

2

Necessary Preconditions of the Practice of Comparative Philosophy

Jaap van Brakel and Lin Ma

In this contribution, we embrace a rather broad notion of comparative philosophy.[1] We consider that it involves such a wide range of activities as translation, interpretation, exposition of the conceptual schemes of an "alien" philosophical tradition in terms of the conceptual schemes of the interpreter's "own" tradition, as well as comparison of these conceptual schemes in a learnable meta-language constructed by the interpreter.[2] Our use of the word "interpretation" includes translations and any other form of interpretation of human actions, experiences, and utterances/inscriptions (including comparative philosophy). We ask: What are the necessary conditions and/or unavoidable constraints of interpretation practice, in particular comparative interpretation of philosophical traditions?[3] In clarifying more abstract considerations, we shall draw our examples from comparison of classical Chinese texts and their interpretations in modern languages (including modern Chinese).

We consider that an interpretation or comparison of interpretations is always already a *theory*, with defining features similar to other theories in the sciences and humanities. The methodology of comparative philosophy bears resemblances to the methodology of any interpretative practice. Interpretation is a feature of all human activities.

We will present an outline of the process of interpretation starting from the earliest stages when little or nothing is known concerning (the language of) the other. Today, any investigation concerning some features of classical Chinese philosophy presupposes various assumptions that formed the basis of "received wisdom" about the classical Chinese language as well as the reflections of classical Chinese literati. Any part of this interpretative tradition can be reassessed again. Therefore, the assumptions underlying earlier translations and interpretations remain part of any more recent investigations.

We shall employ the terms of concept and conceptual scheme, but we emphasize that there are no essences or fixed meanings to them. A conceptual scheme consists in a cluster of concepts, while a concept is already a conceptual scheme, because of the holism of concepts. We do not ascribe only one conceptual scheme to a tradition or to an individual. When one is thinking and acting, s/he always is deploying a plurality of (dynamic and possibly incommensurable) conceptual schemes at the same time. In our terminology, the word "language" covers any kind of language games, including the language games that hint at so-called nonconceptual thought.

Our proposals have drawn resources from such philosophers such as Wittgenstein, Zhuangzi (莊子 369?–286?BCE), Davidson, Gadamer, Nelson Goodman, and Heidegger. After some terminological introduction, including a so-called XYZ model of interhuman interpretation, we address the following features of comparative philosophy as we see it.

The interpreter (henceforth: Y) *must* acknowledge the existence of mutually recognizable human practices (alternatively speaking the family resemblances of human forms of life). This is the basis relative to which similarities and differences are observed.

Y *must* assume that *all* general concepts in *all* languages are family-resemblance-concepts (henceforth: FR-concepts). This is a *necessary* condition for interpretation and translation; FR-concepts are not merely a tool.

Y *must* construct a meta-language, the lexicon of which contains many quasi-universals that connect FR-concepts from a limited number of traditions by extension of FR-concepts from both sides.

Y *must* assume a principle of mutual attunement, which consists of principles of reasonableness (already required in the prelinguistic stage of interpretation), of charity (X is, *for most of the time*, sincere, consistent, and right, according to Y's criteria), and of humanity (similar to the principle of charity but now according to the standards of X's community).

Interpreters *must* assume a standard of evaluation for their work and that of their colleagues. We call these standards "epistemic virtues." Y *must* be committed to a number of epistemic virtues, which curtail underdetermination.

Interpretation is constrained by the background of Y (hermeneutic relativity). This includes Y's commitments to and specifications of items one to five above and XYZ in the next section.

These are the necessary conditions and/or constraints of interpretation. No more are needed; in particular the *not-so-necessary* conditions, as mentioned in the family resemblance principle section, are not needed. Only after the necessary conditions are fulfilled can Y focus on differences, realizing that the latter is only possible relative to a background of similarities.

XYZ Model for Interhuman Interpretation

In this section we present a model of Y interpreting X (or Z comparing X and Y).[4] We use Y and Z to refer to interpreters, and we use X (or X and Y) to refer to what is being interpreted: either the author or his/her text or corpus (or that of a school or tradition). For the moment, we assume that Y's and Z's native language is English; X's language is classical Chinese.

When Y interprets X, Y is engaged in comparing the practices of two traditions; that is, comparing two forms of life. Y uses observations regarding X to provide interpretations of X's sayings, inscriptions, and other actions. The observations (based on self-descriptions and descriptions by X's contemporaries) include the following:

1. identifying the relevant (uninterpreted) texts of X;
2. observing circumstances (the *Umwelt*) in which X is situated (both socio-historical context and physical environment);
3. noticing similarities in forms of life; recognizing unfamiliar human practices as being (somewhat) similar to practices which Y is already familiar with; and
4. describing X's actions and attitudes (in Y's language).

These observations are not neutral but depend on Y's background knowledge, which consists of:

1. Y's beliefs, expectations, values; Y's concepts employed in forming her/his beliefs, interests, and so on; Y's values that guide her/his interests and related practices; and
2. Y's awareness of what has been said about X and about X's language community.

This background knowledge is the result of interpretation of other texts. Observations and background knowledge together allow Y to generate hypotheses concerning:

1. the meaning of X's utterances (or, translations in terms of Y's language);
2. the beliefs, desires, motivations, illocutions, and other attitudes that are to be ascribed to X;
3. X's background (meanings, attitudes, and so on, just mentioned; language games, practices); and in particular,
4. hypotheses concerning (clusters of) conceptual schemes that are to be ascribed to X.[5]

The general features of the model are supposed to hold no matter how close or how far the "distance" between X and Y is. The particular subdivision of observations, background, and interpretation is not rigid. Finer discriminations and more parameters can be added, but the model is sufficiently complicated to pin down most of what is important in interpretation. First of all, there is not just one thing that is being interpreted, but numerous things are involved in the process of interpretation, thus forming a holistic whole. For example, the beliefs of X and the meanings of X's words (and other things) are interpreted at the same time.

Results of interpretation can be added to or replace part of the background of Y or X. However, the original background of an interpreter cannot be eliminated or transcended completely. This may be called hermeneutic relativity (see also the section on hermeneutic relativity). Y's background will determine what things Y will find salient, relevant, important, and so on.

Usually a large number of Ys are involved in the project of interpreting X. Some may focus more on philological reconstruction of the text; others only on its translation or interpretation of specific concepts and conceptual schemes. Perhaps some may claim to have access to the "original meaning" of X and claim to speak on behalf of (the author of) X. Others may aim for an interpretation that is relevant to and directed at a particular audience. X's "words" may already have been in transmission for a long time, to which all kind of commentaries have been added. The text may have been translated into foreign languages and received various interpretations in other traditions. X may have contributed to all kinds of contemporary philosophical discussions via the "original" text and via later interpretations, commentaries, and translations. Therefore, we propose that interpreting X can be conceived as a dialogue among all interpreters, translators, and commentators who are involved. Deceased commentators can be represented by later interpreters.

The model we propose for comparative philosophy is slightly more complicated. Consider the comparison of texts, philosophers, or traditions represented by the letters X and Y. A group of philosophers, $Z_j(X)$, are involved in interpreting X, being in dialogue among one another concerning their interpretations; and another group, $Z_k(Y)$ are similarly interpreting Y. A comparison of X and Y can be given in the form of an imaginary dialogue between X and Y, being constructed by a group of contemporary philosophers Z_i.[6] That is to say, interpreters Z_i set up an imaginary dialogue between some X and some Y. Both X and Y are represented by a group of interpreters, $Z_j(X)$ and $Z_k(Y)$ respectively, each of these groups being in dialogue among one another. The group of interpreters setting up such an imaginary dialogue, Z_i, are in dialogue with the groups $Z_j(X)$ and $Z_k(Y)$, as well as in dialogue among one another.

Underdetermination

Underdetermination is an intrinsic feature of interpretation. Interpreting a text, a philosopher, or a tradition is always underdetermined by the evidence (the data). Meanings, beliefs, and such like are all interpreted *at the same time*. No specific entity can be interpreted independently of numerous other interpretations. Every interpretation is relative to a context or background that cannot be described completely. Underdetermination already starts at the theoretically unavoidable indeterminacy of the reference of terms, the indeterminacy of translation, and the principled underdetermination of a theory or interpretation by the data.[7]

Underdetermination entails that there is no such thing as *the* correct interpretation. There is an indefinite manifold of more or less plausible interpretations. Each particular facet of interpretation is connected to other facets of interpretation by hermeneutic circles (or holistic relations). Changing the interpretation of the one requires changing the interpretation of the other, and vice versa. For example, if Y notices an inconsistency in the beliefs of X, the conclusion of inconsistency (according to Y's criteria) may be well supported, but it may also be possible to disclaim the inconsistency by suggesting that the meanings of some of X's utterances are different.

Beliefs can be attributed only holistically through their location in a structural pattern. This leads to the more general holism of language (or meanings) and thinking (beliefs about the *Umwelt*) and the holism of text and embedding forms of life. The analytic philosophers' holism can be considered as a counterpart of continental philosophers' hermeneutic circle. Hermeneutic efforts are directed at finding an interpretation that can both make sense of the individual parts of a text and integrate them into a consistent whole. Here the "consistent whole" may refer to the whole text (work), the whole corpus of a philosopher or a school, or an even larger semantic horizon at a particular time. But this account is still too simplistic. There are *numerous* other hermeneutic circles. Whatever detail of the XYZ model one zooms onto, one would encounter more varieties of holisms or hermeneutic circles; for example, meanings of words are interpreted synchronically, not consecutively. There are no basic concepts that can be exempted from holism.

The possibility of interpretation may seem to be undermined by two extreme and mutually opposed positions. One is that no interpretation/translation is possible, which is the source of the so-called threat of incommensurability. Our alternative to this stance is to adhere to family resemblance across the board (which we develop in the next three sections). The other position is that too many interpretations are possible, which is derived from the so-called freedom of underdetermination. Our alternative to this is to uphold the principle of mutual attunement and the requirement to be committed to particular epistemic virtues (which we develop in later sections).

Mutually Recognizable Human Practices

For interpretation to be possible, it is necessary to assume that (the author of) X is a human being and engages in practices many of which are immediately recognizable as *human* practices. This attitude-toward-a-soul principle underlies the necessity of family resemblances of human forms of life.[8] No attempt is made to find "universally" recognizable human practices. Family resemblance between the practices of a small number of traditions suffices to construct quasi-universals that connect FR-concepts in these traditions. Very different practices can be recognized as human practices because they show some similarity with practices Y is familiar with.

Y *must* assume that there are MRHP,[9] including, as seen from a modern perspective, such things as using language (communicating, translating, interpreting, discussing/arguing, and enjoying), experiencing, making distinctions, evaluating, forming a community, birth, death, and living.[10]

Down-to-earth actions, crafts, and behaviors often have a close resemblance across traditions and are presupposed in more sophisticated interpretations of ancient texts. For example, to compare the "emptiness" of Heidegger's jug and Laozi's vessel (*qi* 器) requires that we first recognize, among other things, the everyday practice of molding a jug or vessel.[11] Similarly, in the *Zhuangzi*, many human and animal practices are involved. Consider the following two references to a huge "useless" tree in the *Zhuangzi*:[12]

> Its trunk is too gnarled and bumpy to apply a measuring line to, its branches too bent and twisty to match up to a compass or square.
> Make boats out of it and they'd sink; make coffins and they'd rot in no time; make vessels and they'd break at once. Use it for doors and it would sweat sap like pine; use it for posts and the worms would eat them up.

These descriptions already presuppose a number of everyday practices and familiarity with boats, coffins, doors, and so on. Hui Shi 惠施 (370–310 BCE) suggests that Zhuangzi's "big words" are as useless as the "huge tree" is. Zhuangzi in response makes several suggestions to the effect that people do not see the usefulness of the useless. The importance of this theme is repeated in, for example, the rhymed essay *Rongmufu* 榕木賦 ("Rhapsody on the Banyan Tree") by Li Gang 李綱 (1083–1140), and by Heidegger in the twentieth century.[13]

Consider the following passages in chapter four of the *Zhuangzi* (transl. Watson 1968):

Carpenter Shi (referring to an oak tree, which serves as a village shrine): "It's a worthless tree!" "It's not a timber tree–there's nothing it can be used for. That's how it got to be that old!"

Oak tree (appearing in a dream to the carpenter): "As for me, I've been trying a long time to be of no use, and though I almost died, I've finally got it. This is of great use to me. If I had been of some use, would I ever have grown this large?"

Zhuangzi (at the end of the chapter): "The cinnamon can be eaten, and so it gets cut down; the lacquer tree can be used, and so it gets hacked apart. All men know the use of the useful, but nobody knows the use of the useless!"

The (sacred) oak tree is useless from the point of view of the carpenter (the quality of the wood is not good). The villagers pay homage to the sacred tree (as a village shrine); hence, for them, the tree is useful. The tree is useful to itself, because it is sacred and thus has survived.

Sophisticated interpretations of the idea of the usefulness of the useless in Zhuangzi or Heidegger would not be possible if most people (whether in ancient China or the modern world) did not agree that one cannot make large planks from a crooked tree. There is no beginning for an interpretation of what Zhuangzi's stories and parables might possibly convey, if there is no familiar consensus on simple examples of (mutually recognizable) human practices.

Observing similarities and differences is part of ordinary practices. However, "similar" does not mean "identical," though usually (often, but not always), there are family resemblances as seen from the perspective of the meta-language that Y is developing.

Even if denotations (extensions) of words are rather similar, connotations (and contexts of use) may differ substantially. For example, there are similarities between contemporary FIFA-type football and the football engaged in by soldiers in the Han dynasty or by ladies in the Tang dynasty.[14] However, understanding and contextual embedment of these games differ greatly. In order to say something about their differences, one must presuppose some similarities. For example, by saying that {*cujü* 蹴鞠 ⇔ football} is a quasi-universal.[15]

That Y recognizes strange practices as similar to practices Y is familiar with is both a necessary (transcendental) condition of interpretation and a well-confirmed empirical fact. There are always family resemblances between (human) forms of life, although what the resemblances are in a particular case is relative to the languages and conceptual schemes involved (and hence may be judged differently by different parties).

Absence of practices taken to be quasi-universals is possible, but this can only be observed given a background of many cases of family resemblance of practices and language games. It is the recognition of practices of humans that lie at the basis of similarities of (human) forms of life.

Family Resemblance Principle

The necessary condition that makes most impact on the practice of interpretation is family resemblance across the board, which we call the family-resemblance-principle. It consists of three interrelated parts:

1. Y *must* assume that *all* concepts in *whatever* tradition are FR-concepts. Concepts can be *stipulated* to be exact and precise, but the stipulation itself involves FR-concepts.
2. Y *must* assume mutually recognizable human practices. Similarities and differences are grounded in family resemblances of forms of life. Considering a limited number of traditions at a time will always show some mutually recognizable human practices. This is both a transcendental condition and an empirically well-supported fact concerning interactions of human traditions. See further in the next section.
3. Extension of FR-concepts across traditions and the construction of quasi-universals form the basis of quasi-universals (QUs). The latter are working hypotheses that connect conceptual schemes from a limited number of traditions. Assuming the availability across traditions of quasi-universals is a *necessary* condition for the practice of interpretation. See further in the next section.[16]

The phrase "family resemblance" and the reference to Wittgenstein are omnipresent throughout the humanities and also in comparative philosophy (Angle 2010). However, most of the time, how to understand the phrase is left unexplained. Our account differs from others with respect to the following important features:[17]

1. We have given a detailed exposition of Wittgenstein's notion of "family resemblance," which is closely related to Wittgenstein's notions of language game, forms(s) of life, and rule following. Contrary to most uses of the phrase "FR-concepts," we assume that a FR-concept not only has vague borders, but also has no fixed core.[18]
2. We argue that *all* concepts involved in comparative philosophy are FR-concepts. This holds for concepts at all levels: everyday concepts such as green and *qing* 青, philosophical concepts such as emotion(s) and *qing* 情, philosophical categories such as form(s) of life and *dao* 道, and meta-concepts such as thing(s) and *wu* 物.

3. We considerably extend Wittgenstein's notion of family resemblance by assigning it a *necessary* role for any discourse that interprets, explains, or compares concepts of one tradition in terms of the concepts of another tradition. The notion of "family resemblance" is not merely a helpful tool, as is commonly assumed in comparative philosophy; it is a *necessary* condition.

Because FR-concepts have no essences ("cores") and no strict borders, they can be extended across traditions, which makes it possible to construct quasi-universals. For example, *youxi* 游戏 and games are FR-concepts that can be extended across traditions. There are many differences between *youxi* and games, but FR(games) can be extended to include many (features of) *youxi* and FR(*youxi*) can be extended to include many (features of) games.[19] Similarities and differences "crop up and disappear" (Wittgenstein 2009a: §66). In order to compare *youxi* and games, Y has to construct a meta-language (which usually is an extension of Y's language).

We suggest that the family-resemblance-principle is a feasible alternative to what we call the "not-so-necessary" conditions for interpretation across traditions: (1) the ideal language assumption, (2) the assumed necessity of a shared, or common, or in-between language, and (3) the assumption of a number of (linguistic, cognitive, cultural, philosophical) universals.[20] In particular, we suggest that we replace the idea of an ideal language with fixed and exact meanings by the notion of FR-concepts, which are dynamic and extendable across traditions.

The family-resemblance-principle dissolves the false antinomy of universalism versus relativism, as well as worries about incommensurability and about the Sapir–Whorf hypothesis. This is because both universalism and relativism take for granted a language with rigidly defined concepts (which are either universal or only belonging to a particular tradition). Moreover, in almost all examples discussed in the literature, the relativist is actually a universalist at one remove. For example, when s/he argues that different traditions segment the color spectrum in different ways, s/he is in fact assuming the category of color is a universal. The family-resemblance-principle allows us to be more universalistic than a universalist by making the most tradition-specific notions accessible by extension of Y's FR-concepts; and it also allows to be more relativistic than the relativist by not only allowing, for example, color classifications to be different across traditions, but by revealing that the notion of color itself is not a universal.

Considering family resemblance across the board includes the principle of "no need to speak the same language." Natural language is full of ambiguities, malapropisms, and hybridities, but this does not obstruct communication or interpretation in a principled way. Speaking the same language is not a necessary condition for communicative interaction and conventions of use are not strict rules. A language is not governed by just one theory of meaning. Instead, there are dynamic "momentary" passing theories of interpretation, which varies for individual speakers.[21] No need to speak the same language leads to our suggestion that, ideally, the results of investigations in comparative philosophy should be reported in at least two unrelated languages.

A common objection to our approach, that is rooted in the notions of FR-concepts and MRHP, is that it leaves the application of a concept too unrestricted, not telling one which FR-concepts are the "objectively" relevant ones. By presenting MRHP as the final ground of interpretation, we propose to resolve the alleged "problem of relevance."[22] The first step toward an answer to this problem is to acknowledge that there is no such answer. There is no solution; only a natural history of successive forms of life or MRHP. Both the secondary literature on Wittgenstein and the work by logicians such as Quine and Nelson Goodman have convincingly shown this. As Goodman (1972: 440) puts it: "In the case of ordinary actions, the principle of classification varies with our purposes and interests."[23]

In the Wittgensteinian tradition, critics had argued from the outset that family resemblance does not suffice to limit the extension of concepts. One can always find *some* resemblance between instances of two concepts.[24] Around 1970 this critique was formulated most strongly by Nelson Goodman (1972) and Quine (1969) in the context of the ideal language tradition. Goodman famously argued, "Anything is in some way like anything else" (1972: 444). However, this is not part of *our* notion of "mutually recognizable human practices." The relevant respects are always already given by the conceptual schemes of the interpreter or forms of life the interpreter is familiar with. As a logician, Goodman concluded that no theoretical (logical) explication of the relation of similarity is possible. However, he added: "If statements of similarity ... cannot be trusted in the philosopher's study, they are still serviceable in the streets." Neither Wittgensteinians nor logicians can avoid dependence on background. Recourse to similarity is unavoidable, though it cannot be formalized. We should (dis)solve the problem of relevance, and so on by dropping the ideal language assumption, replacing it with a Wittgensteinian inspired ordinary language approach. There is no way denying that similarities are relative to contextual theories or forms of life.

Inevitably, the investigator starts with *some* MRHP, which is the basis for constructing a meta-language and QUs to be constructed. Potentially this meta-language can absorb any *natural* language and leave out *unnatural* ones, such as a language containing "grue" (= being blue before 2050 and green after 2050). A concept such as "grue" is outside the limits of natural forms of life (but it is part of an artificial ideal language game). Any critique of our approach must use a natural language that is grounded in a prevailing understanding of MRHP. The limits of human life-form(s) are given by the possible family resemblances that crop up and disappear in the different practices or life-forms of human beings and their encounters with one another.

The practices of human beings always show similarities (because they are *human* practices). Were this not so, communicative interaction or interpretation across traditions would be impossible. It is a necessary requirement for communication (or translation) that these similarities appear to be there. There are always enough (perceived) similarities for an interpreter to make a start at interpreting difference. That there will always be relevant similarities between human forms of life is both an empirical fact and a transcendental condition of possibility. However, spelling out what the specific similarities are is dependent on the forms of life involved and the conceptual resources available to those who make the comparison.

Constructing Quasi-Universals

The construction of quasi-universals is the most central task in the practice of interpretation and comparative philosophy.[25] Our notion of quasi-universal is different from all other uses of the phrase in that:

1. Quasi-universals belong to the meta-language Y is developing.
2. Quasi-universals are newly constructed FR-concepts, grounded in the mutual recognition of human practices.
3. A quasi-universal connects conceptual schemes from a limited number of traditions.
4. Quasi-universals are working hypotheses; in other words, they are revisable as a consequence of the continuing process of interpretation.
5. Quasi-universals fulfill a necessary role in interpretative practice. Without assuming a sufficient number of quasi-universals, interpretation across traditions would not be possible.
6. Data and background underdetermine the choice of quasi-universals in any particular case.

A quasi-universal, for example, {*zhi* 知 ⇔ know(ing)}, has two sides, in (classical) Chinese and English, respectively.[26] The concept *zhi* can be extended to include features of know(ing) and similarly for extending know(ing) to cover features of *zhi*. That is to say: a Chinese concept shows similarities to a European concept as judged from European conceptual schemes; and a European concept shows similarities to a Chinese concept as judged from Chinese conceptual schemes. The similarities as seen from the Chinese and European side respectively are not the same, although there are family resemblances. Therefore, it is misleading to speak of an English word and a Chinese word or character having the same meaning or being synonymous.

We propose distinguishing between ordinary (everyday) language and sophisticated (theoretical) language. Y starts with identifying possible quasi-universals in everyday language (on both sides). Differences in everyday classifications are to be noted. But most of them can be easily explained. For example, the sentences "the cat sat on the mat" and *mao zai xizi shang* 猫在席子上 (a translation of the former sentence) are incommensurable. Why? One may assume that *mao* is the correct translation of cat. But, contrary to "the cat sat on the mat," *mao zai xizi shang* is "true even if the cat has never before now sit on the mat, false if it sat on a cloth mat" (Graham 1992: 65). But it is easy to see that bilingual speakers would agree on the truth or falsity of both the English and Chinese sentence in any concrete situation.

Not all FR-concepts in a language/tradition can easily participate in quasi-universals, and they must be left untranslated or given a stipulated translation (after embedding it in "its own terms" or construct hybrid concepts). Different languages usually allow the construction of different quasi-universals.[27]

Already in ordinary language the idea of a simple quasi-universal can break down. Perhaps *youxi*/games and cat/*mao* are simple quasi-universals (with appropriate extension of FR-concepts on both sides). However, a simple looking pair such as *zhi* 知/know(ing), already breaks down; *zhi* also means "understanding." For such more complex cases, one must distinguish hybrid concepts from what we call quasi-homonyms (see further van Brakel and Ma Lin 2015).

Dictionaries and many other sources favor listing a variety of *different* meanings for a Chinese word/character. For example (Harbsmeier 2004):

> FR(*qing* 情) ⇔ {real/basic facts} or {basic instinctive feelings} or {state of perfect genuineness} or {emotional response to situations} or …

This example illustrates that *qing* 情 is a quasi-homonym. From the English side it seems that *qing* is a proper homonym (but perhaps not from the Chinese side). The option of constructing *new* hybrid concepts may be more appropriate. Hybrid concepts are *new* concepts in Y's language, but they already exist in the language to be interpreted. Such hybrid concepts can be explained in terms of English as illustrated in the following example, using as an example again *qing* 情:[28]

> {*qing* 情} ⇔ {real/basic facts, principles/essentials, passions, virtues, sentiments (basic instinctive feelings), desires, sensibilities, state of perfect genuineness, ultimate motives, deep convictions, authenticity, emotional response to situations, distinguishing right from wrong}

To the left of the sign ⇔, there is a Chinese FR-concept; to the right, a hybrid FR-concept in English. The latter is constructed by blending or merging the notions mentioned on the right side. A neologism could be chosen in English as a shorthand for the right-hand side; for example, by simply introducing "qing" as a new English word in Y's meta-language and by claiming that {*qing* 情 ⇔ qing}. "*Qing*" and "qing" are *different* words/concepts! These merged or blended or mingled concepts are constructed in order to get access to a concept in the alien tradition for which there is no suitable word or FR-concept to construct a simple quasi-universal. Merging concepts amounts to making *new* FR-concepts in Y's language that can serve as to connect with alien (perhaps polysemous) concepts.[29]

Yet another possibility is to embed *qing* 情 among a cluster of FR-concepts in classical Chinese. For example:

> {*qing* 情} ⇔ {*xin* 心, *xing* 性, *yü* 欲; *qi* 氣, *li* 理, *li* 禮; *shi* 事, *shi* 實, *shi* 是, *cheng* 誠, *gan* 感, *huai* 懷, *duan* 端}

This way of presenting the matter suggests that the meaning of *qing* 情 can be explained in Chinese in terms of *xin*, *xing*, and so on. This approach seems to avoid having to construct quasi-universals or identifying quasi-homonyms. *Qing* is left untranslated and explained "on its own terms,"[30] but note that the meaning of the characters listed on the right-hand side must already be grasped in English. In fact, all of them require (indirect) participation in quasi-universals that connect the Chinese character with English concepts, either in terms of hybrid concepts (in English) or quasi-homonyms (ascribed, in English, to Chinese).

As interpretation of a particular tradition becomes more sophisticated, it may transpire that most of everyday language is "tainted" with the holism within ordinary language and the holism between ordinary and sophisticated language. For example, the assumed simple quasi-universal *le* 樂/happiness will break down if the background of interpretations of *qing* 情 and of binomes containing *le* are considered.[31]

The more sophisticated or idiosyncratic the proposed interpretation of a text is, the more often simple quasi-universals will disappear. Does it suffice to assume, as regards the *Zhuangzi*, {FR(*wuyong* 无用) ⇔ FR(useless)}? With respect to ordinary language *yong*/use and *wuyong*/useless are simple quasi-universals. But when Zhuangzi appears to make a plea for the usefulness of the useless, perhaps one should consider a wider cluster in a modern language to be linked to *wuyong*; for example by constructing a hybrid of FR(unnecessary—unneeded—unprofitable).

Mutual Attunement

In addition to the family-resemblance-principle (developed in the previous sections), Y *must* assume a degree of mutual attunement between Y and X.[32] The principle of mutual attunement is a fundamental constraint on the underdetermination of interpretation. It consists of three parts: the principles of reasonableness, of charity, and of humanity. These three principles are not horizontal either-or options, but principles that start to work in consecutive stages of interpretation. However, the earlier emerging ones remain in force during more advanced stages such that Y has to balance the relative weight of the three principles.

Although in hermeneutics one may speak of Y aiming for mutual attunement with a text, we think this puts too much potentially disturbing weight on the hermeneutic relativity of Y. Mutual attunement is operative within the community of all interpreters and commentators of the relevant texts. It is a dynamic process in which interlocutors interact with one another. There happens attunement among interpreters and commentators, but one does not primarily aim at reaching consensus. There is no singing together in a concert but instead: solely fine-tuning of hermeneutic circles across traditions relative to an indefinite variety of background conceptual schemes of interpreters and commentators. In a certain face-to-face situation (such as cross-traditional philosophical dialogue), interaction goes in both directions. If the original "author" of a text is deceased, as is the case with most textual interpretation, the dynamism of attunement is operative in the dialogue among traditional as well as contemporary interpreters and commentators.

The "principle of reasonableness" refers to the principle of mutual attunement already required in the prelinguistic stage of interpretation, including interpretation of the use of human-made artifacts in mutually recognizable practices. Y *must* presuppose that, *in most cases*, X (the maker of artifacts) has reasonable beliefs (according to the criteria of reasonableness of Y) given X's *Umwelt* (as perceived by Y). A somewhat more concrete description is to say that Y should ascribe to X those attitudes that Y would have, were Y in X's place (allowing for some as yet unexplained exceptions).

Already "before" interpretation and the principle of reasonableness become "active," there is mutual attunement of humans with their local *Umwelt* (which includes other humans). Invariants constrain the course of events in the system of humans *cum* environment taken together as a whole.[33] If there were no such invariants or affordances, there would not be a biological basis for mutual attunement. A human being (or a group of human beings) creates and reshapes his or her or their *Umwelt* when interacting with the world (which includes humans).

In the primordial "radical" stage of linguistic interpretation,[34] Y *must* presuppose that X is, *for most of the time*, sincere, consistent, and right. This necessary presupposition resembles Davidson's principle of charity. Only by assuming that X is sincere, consistent, and right in general is it possible to ascribe error to X (by the standards of Y). However, our principle of charity differs on a number of points from that of Davidson. We formulate our revised principle of charity as follows: Y *must* presuppose that X usually is sincere, is by and large consistent, and is on the whole right—all of this according to Y's criteria and formulated in Y's language. Being right includes having true beliefs concerning both "facts" and "values." A degree of emotional and moral attunement is as necessary for successful communicative interaction and interpretation as pragmatic agreement on the happenings in the *Umwelt*. There must also be some agreement on meta-epistemic virtues such as coherence ("fitting"). Finally, the principle of charity includes cases of agreeing that two incommensurable statements (in two different languages) may both be true.[35]

In comparative philosophy awareness of the mutual recognition of human practices cannot be based on direct observations but depends on descriptions in language. Usually, such descriptions are dependent on interpreting the language of X and X's community. Hence, the principle of reasonableness and the principle of charity are operative together. In some sense the principle of charity is the most fundamental: it is only possible to establish differences or have disagreements, *given* a background of agreements (in terms of the mutual recognition of human practices, the principle of reasonableness and quasi-universals).

The principle of humanity is similar to the principle of charity but now according to the standards of X's community. Often the principles of charity and humanity are discussed in terms of favoring either the one or the other.[36] This is not helpful. In advanced stages of interpretation, both principles apply, but the principle of humanity can only be known *given* that the principle of charity governs earlier states of linguistic interpretation. That is to say, the principle of charity is presupposed in order to find out what the standards are in X's community.

As interpretation moves on, or as a result of discussions among scholars, one may reach a stage where a reformulation of (part of) the principle of mutual attunement may be advised. For example, the concepts used in the most common formulations of the principle of charity may not easily allow for extension across traditions, in particular not when definitions of the principle of charity are formulated with reference to the truth predicate (already avoided in our definition above). A possibly needed reformulation of the principle of charity is not to use "true/truth" in its "definition," but a generic quasi-universal notion of correctness instead. The latter has a wide scope, covering (or fusing) right, permissible, true, cohere, sincere, appropriate, fitting, as well as *yi* 宜, *ran* 然, *shi* 是, *zhen* 真, *cheng* 誠, *dang* 當, and other kinds of being correct.³⁷

Epistemic Virtues

Epistemic virtues are the properties a good interpretation should have; for example, overall coherence on the one hand and faithfulness to the text and tradition on the other. In the context of comparative philosophy, epistemic virtues are effective in comparing competing interpretations; in assessing the balancing of the subsidiaries of the principle of mutual attunement; in the choice of quasi-universals; and in combating any other form of underdetermination. Concrete examples of debates involving epistemic virtues include Mozi's three tests/standards (*biao* 表) understood as criteria for evaluating teachings, policies, or claims in general; Roetz's proposals for validity criteria in pre-Han times (Roetz 1993); standards of evidence as used by ancient Chinese ministers when presenting their views to the ruler (Olberding 2012), and so on.

We suggest that epistemic virtues (as discussed in modern philosophy of science) can be ordered in six groups:³⁸

1. *empirical adequacy*: faithfulness to the text(s), verification, falsification;
2. *coherence*: logical consistency, consonance with other knowledge/*zhi*, hermeneutic circles between levels of abstraction;
3. *scope*: comprehensibility, exhaustiveness;
4. *pragmatic aspects*: simplicity, clarity, being informative, being illuminating;
5. *social criteria*: respect for alternative hypotheses, impartiality, appropriateness; and
6. *metaphysical concerns*: simplicity, aesthetic qualities, accounting for the ontological heterogeneity or homogeneity of the subject of study.

Anybody reflecting on this list would soon conclude that there is no simple rule for deciding whether a particular interpretation meets the requirements of particular epistemic criteria.³⁹

Specification of epistemic virtues varies among interpreters and across traditions. There is no single set of epistemic virtues that characterizes a "good" interpretation. Different epistemic virtues have been proposed by different scholars. There is no consensus on the classification of epistemic virtues. No single virtue is straightforwardly determinable. No matter how one draws the dividing line between epistemic and pragmatic virtues (to claim truth, empirical adequacy, an economic rendering of sensory input, or whatever as the goal of inquiry) that goal is a value, not a fact (Putnam 2002). For some concepts used in the list of epistemic virtues, one may not easily find a suitable quasi-universal. For example, "facts," or "true to the facts," notwithstanding its current popularity, is not a universal, and it is difficult to construct a fruitful quasi-universal related to it.⁴⁰

Even if agreement could be reached on what "the" epistemic virtues are, they will almost always come into conflict when concrete choices have to be made, as a neutral weighing of different virtues governed by "rational decisions" is impossible. In particular, neutral weighing of background knowledge is impossible. There are neither universal nor domain-specific rules for "weighing" different virtues when they conflict.

There are discussions (and dissensus) about every conceivable virtue; for example, about the ineffability of the notion of simplicity.[41] Simplicity (with respect to a theory, interpretation, explanation) may refer to, for example: harmony, elegance, parsimony, economy, efficiency, clearness and distinctness, idealization, coherence, appropriateness, and smoothness. Hence, saying (a theory of) interpretation should preferably be simple is a rather empty statement if not further specified.

In modern discourse the notion of epistemic virtues is related to the notion of knowledge. Interpreters seem to agree that the quasi-universal "knowing-how" works rather similarly in all traditions (perhaps because it is closely related to survival), but "knowing that," in particular when understood as knowing the truth of propositions or sentences, is more specifically tied to European traditions. There are passages in classical Chinese for which a translation in terms of "knowledge that" is not obviously wrong. However, they are not central, but marginal (Harbsmeier 1993). What is central is what one might call "knowledge of," that is, correctly discriminating the referent of a word or name (*ming* 名) that denotes the object of knowledge (Fraser 2011). Drawing distinctions replaces determining facts or truths. This is an important difference between FR(*zhi* 知) and FR(know). On the other hand, it is not difficult to see similarities between, for example, modern epistemic virtues and Mozi's well-known three tests/standards. Mozi's criteria may be compared with the following three groups of epistemic virtues: coherence with background knowledge, empirical adequacy, and economy (practical use) respectively.[42] Whatever the details of alternative ways of translating and interpreting this passage from Mozi, we suggest that Mozi's three tests (at least the first two) may exemplify what might be considered to be quasi-universal epistemic meta-virtues, formulated in nonphilosophical language as follows:[43] taking FR(know) and FR(experience) very broadly, knowing has to fit experience and earlier knowledge. And similarly, FR(*zhi*) has to fit experience and earlier *zhi*.

Even if we stipulate that fitting experience is a quasi-universal, there are no general let alone strict criteria for how this "fitting experience" and "earlier knowledge/*zhi*" is to be worked out in concrete cases or how they should be balanced, or whether a third criterion concerning the utility of knowledge must be distinguished from the other two.[44] Whether such vague criteria are met or not in concrete cases is ultimately a matter of consideration and contestation among groups of people in light of prevailing (and yet revisable) everyday maxims. In the end, epistemic virtues are grounded in the manifest life-forms and are concerned with survival.

Hermeneutic Relativity

As already noted in the section on the XYZ model, interpretation is constrained by the background of Y, which is called hermeneutic relativity.[45] More generally speaking, hermeneutic relativity refers to various choices, constraints, and stances of Y (for example, Y's stance concerning the best way of doing philosophy).[46] Whether Y likes it or not, he/she *must* make a large number of often implicit choices, which derive from the guidance or constraint originating from his/her background and situatedness. Some degree of transcendental pretense is unavoidable.[47] Hopefully this unavoidable constraint can be "softened" by the interaction of the various Y involved in interpreting X; by including the commentarial tradition in Y's background; by interpreting/translating X in different (modern) languages; and by comparisons of different translations of the relevant texts. Hermeneutic relativity includes, for example:[48]

1. The choice of the goal of investigation, including choice of texts to be studied, and the context of these texts.
2. The choice of interpretative context, for example, the choice to assume a particular fundamental difference between (modern) European and (classical) Chinese thought.
3. The commitment to a particular philosophical method or approach; that is, choice of (background of) favored theory of interpretation.
4. Commitments with respect to the notion of language; for example, the stance taken with respect to the Sapir–Whorf hypothesis.

We will refer to such constraints or presuppositions (or Gadamerian prejudices) as "choices" or "commitments" because *in principle* Y can "choose" to be guided by other constraints.

Some features of hermeneutic relativity have already been discussed as necessary presuppositions, for example, the choice of criteria for the evaluation of competing interpretations (epistemic virtues). The favored specification of mutual attunement and the choices made in the construction of quasi-universals can also be considered part of hermeneutic relativity.

In a somewhat different ordering of the aspects of hermeneutic relativity, assumptions concerning what is shared across traditions may be considered a separate item (shared concepts? shared experiences? shared problems?). Views as to what is shared among traditions usually derive from "deep" commitments concerning philosophy and language.

One virtually unavoidable constraint not yet mentioned is the regimentation of the languages of the world relative to the dominant language(s) of the center in the current epoch of globalization (following the aftermath of colonization and global exploration). This contingent fact drastically constrains alternative interpretations of texts from ancient traditions—a bias which is difficult to overcome.[49]

Conclusion

Reflection on language shows undeniably that in a natural language, there are no words with rigid meanings. One can construct ideal languages consisting in rigidly defined concepts, but the evaluation of their relevance requires that one uses a natural language.

The family-resemblance-principle removes the threat of relativism and/or incommensurability, which only makes sense from the perspective of an ideal language. It is certainly possible to judge one interpretation to be "better" than another, but convergence to a single "ultimately true" interpretation will not be achieved, because of "deep" disagreements hidden in hermeneutic relativity.

Any (kind of) interpretation presupposes a range of quasi-universals that help connect different traditions. Divergences and differences are only possible against a background of similarities displayed in the construction of quasi-universals (including hybrid concepts).

Interpreting X using the standards that prevail amongst X's contemporaries (i.e., applying the principle of humanity) is only possible after these standards have been "found," relying on the principle of charity (applying Y's standards) and principle of reasonableness (governing the prelinguistic stage).

The mutual recognition of human practices, the principles of mutual attunement, and the epistemic virtues work together to constrain possible versions of interpretations. This is conducive to a kind of pragmatism or what can be called "soft" universalism.

Notes

1. We have published a range of texts on parts of this theme to which we refer to for more detailed arguments, embedment in relevant literature, and illustrative examples taken from Chinese philosophy.
2. For our understanding of the notion of tradition see Ma and van Brakel (2016a: 20–2); for forms of life see ibid. (165–72). We avoid using the word "culture" and use "tradition" or "forms of life" instead.
3. For our understanding of the notion of philosophy, see Ma and van Brakel (2016a: 14–20).
4. This section is an updated explication of the XYZ model first presented in Ma and van Brakel (2013: 305–7).
5. Y has to learn how X's concepts are embedded in clusters of X's conceptual schemes and language games. One can learn the use and sense of an unknown concept by learning its use in many different contexts.
6. For example, Stambaugh (1991) constructs an imaginary dialogue between Heidegger and a Buddhist. In presenting this imaginary dialogue, Stambaugh is (potentially) in dialogue with the interpreters of Heidegger, with the interpreters of Buddhism, and with scholars who compare the stances of Heidegger and Buddhism.
7. For details on indeterminacy and underdetermination, see Ma and van Brakel (2016a: 255–7).
8. The name of this principle derives from Wittgenstein's remark: "My attitude [*Einstellung*] toward him is an attitude toward a soul [*zur Seele*]. I am not of the opinion [*Meinung*] that he has a soul" (Wittgenstein 2009b: §22). For more discussion of this principle, see Ma Lin and van Brakel (2016a: 136–9).
9. Cf. Ma and van Brakel (2016b: 579–81).
10. The examples listed may not be true for all languages.

11. See *Daodejing*, ch. 11 (埏埴而為器—"Molding clay to make a vessel") and Lin Ma (2008: ch. 6).
12. Citations from the *Zhuangzi*, chs. 1 and 4 respectively; transl. Watson (1968).
13. See the *Zhuangzi* (ch. 26): "A person must first have recognised the unnecessary [*wuyong* 无用] before one can talk with him about the necessary [*yong* 用]." Heidegger: "Only one who has learned to know the necessity of the unnecessary can appreciate anything at all of the pain that arises when the human is barred from thinking" (Heidegger 2010: 155). *Rongmufu*: The huge tree "can avoid premature death by hewing and striking of hatchet and axe" (Li Gang 2004: line 51; cited from Schafer 1953). For discussion see van Brakel (2014).
14. FIFA = *Fédération Internationale de Football Association*.
15. The symbol ⇔ means "similar as judged from a given perspective."
16. For a detailed discussion of the variety of options for extension of FR-concepts see van Brakel and Ma (2015: 483–94). Concepts of the other tradition can also be learnt in various ways from scratch, but this is only possible against the background of a host of extended FR-concepts.
17. See Ma and van Brakel (2016a: ch. 4; 2016c). We use the phrase "family resemblance" as a technical term ("defined" by us). It does not have the colloquial meaning of the resemblance of members of the same family. There is some similarity of our notion of family resemblance with "productive vagueness" (instead of precise meanings) as advocated by Hall and Ames (1995: 165–9). Lloyd's advocacy of the relevance of semantic stretch points in the same direction (Lloyd 2002: ch. 5).
18. Cf. the *Zhuangzi*, ch. 2: 言者有言，其所言者特未定也 — "When we speak, we speak of something, but what it is, is never determined [*weiding* 未定]." For details see Ma and van Brakel (2019: ch. 9).
19. "FR(…)" is short for "FR-concept of …"
20. See Ma and van Brakel (2016a: ch. 2).
21. The phrase "passing theory of meaning" stems from Davidson. For discussion of the principle of no need to speak the same language, see Ma and van Brakel (2016a: ch. 5).
22. In the Wittgensteinian commentarial tradition, numerous unsuccessful attempts have been made to resolve the problem of relevance, also referred to as the underdetermination of extension or the problem of wide-open texture. There cannot be a list of *relevant* resemblance characteristics. One cannot even find a paradigm case. Proposals in terms of basic predicates, simple properties, normal conditions, or bidirectional determination of concepts, none of these can provide successful (re)-solution. See for discussion Ma and van Brakel (2021).
23. Similarly, Murphy and Medin (1985) in the cognitive science tradition and Bellaimey (1990: 41) in the Wittgensteinian tradition.
24. Beardsmore (1992: 142), Bellaimey (1990: 31), Beardsmore (1992: 142), Andersen (2000: 313).
25. This section is a somewhat shortened and updated version of Ma and van Brakel (2015). By the way, there is some similarity between our notion of quasi-universals and what Merleau-Ponty (1964: 120) calls lateral universals.
26. The expression "know(ing)" includes known, know-how, know-of, and knowledge, etc.
27. Consider English "games," German *Spiele*, and Chinese *youxi* 游戲. Games/*youxi*, *Spiele*/*youxi*, and games/*Spiele* are three different quasi-universals in Y's meta-meta-language.
28. We do not claim that this "definition" of *qing* is particularly good. It serves as an example to give an idea of how a hybrid concept might be constructed. Similar

proposals can be traced back at least as far as to Richards (1932). See Ma and van Brakel (2020) concerning the possible meaning "distinguishing right from wrong" (*shifei* 是非) for *qing* 情.
29. Hybrid concepts may also be considered to be intermediaries. This suggestion can be seen as an extension of "the importance of finding *connecting links*" (Wittgenstein 1993: 133; emphasis original).
30. Probably more characters are listed than any interpreter wants to use in explaining the embedment of *qing*. Different interpreters may select a different subset or add other characters, in particular if they focus on different texts.
31. Background of *le* 樂 includes: binomes consisting of two "emotions" (examples of *qing*) such as *aile* 哀樂, *haole* 好樂, *beile* 悲樂, *youle* 憂樂, *xile* 喜樂; *le*'s relation to music (*yue* 樂); *le*'s distinction from *xi* 喜 and other characters that are located in the (English) semantic field of "joy"; parallel constructions of "emotions" and the four seasons; *le*'s relation to *wuwei* 無為 (or *wuqing* 無情) and serenity (*tian* 恬); and the distinction of *renle* 人樂, *tianle* 天樂, and *zhile* 至樂. See for details Despeux (2004) and Middendorf (2006).
32. This section is an updated explication of the notion of mutual attunement in Ma and van Brakel (2016b: 581–6).
33. See Gibson (1979). Invariants are lawlike relations among different modes or dimensions of activity (involving social, cultural, as well as physical and biological factors). One's grasp of affordances is the attunement to such invariants.
34. The adjective "radical" indicates the earliest stages of Y interpreting X's language. Any sophisticated interpretation remains relative to its underlying radical interpretation of everyday language on which the sophisticated language supervenes.
35. Cf. Graham's example of "the cat sat/*zai* on the mat/*xizi*."
36. Cf. the debate between Wong and Hansen, as discussed in Ma and van Brakel (2016b: 584–6).
37. See Ma and van Brakel (2019).
38. This section is an updated version of Ma and van Brakel (2018: 467–70).
39. Our favorite list of epistemic virtues (applicable to both the sciences and the humanities) is derived from Goodman's proposal: fitting in with the rest of knowledge (tradition, inertia, structural coherence), being attractive (initial credibility, providing understanding, future value, usefulness, relevance, simplicity), increasing our understanding of all interpretations, theories, and stories (Goodman 1978: 19).
40. Today, "facts" is a leftover concept from late-nineteenth century (European) positivism. According to the reports of Sima Guang 司馬光 (1019–86), debates at Chinese courts did not invoke any clear notion of "facts" (Olberding 2012: chs. 7–8). Therefore, such characters as *shi* 實 should not be translated as "facts" or "truth."
41. Note that we have listed "simplicity" under pragmatic as well as metaphysical virtues. There is little consensus on its preferable meaning and relevance.
42. The alternate versions (chs. 36 and 37) are slightly different. Chapter 36 defines verifiability in terms of "books of the early kings."
43. Here we use the notion of "fitting" in the sense of Goodman (1978), but still regard it as an everyday notion. For more details on this notion of fitting see Ma and van Brakel (2019: ch. 6).
44. One might argue that Mozi's third criterion and the epistemic virtue of practical usefulness are already contained in the first two criteria.
45. Cf. Gadamer's notion of prejudgment (*Vor-urteil*) and Heidegger's notion of preconception.

46. This section is a shortened version of Ma and van Brakel (2018).
47. Transcendental pretence shows itself in that particular concepts are taken to be universals having one defining characteristic (the "essence"). It assumes that, by proceeding with such (home grown) universals, truth in other traditions can be revealed. It is apparent in the common practice of assuming and applying a fixed system of philosophical branches and a determinate set of basic philosophical terminology to classical Chinese texts and philosophers, such that Laozi is viewed as a metaphysician and Zhuangzi a relativist. See further Ma and van Brakel (2016a: 215–18).
48. See for detailed discussion of hermeneutic relativity Ma and van Brakel (2018).
49. See Ma and van Brakel (2016a: ch. 8).

References

Andersen, Hanne (2000), "Kuhn's Account of Family Resemblance: A Solution to the Problem of Wide-Open Texture," *Erkenntnis*, 52: 313–37.
Angle, Stephen C. (2010), "The Minimal Definition and Methodology of Comparative Philosophy: A Report from a Conference," *Comparative Philosophy*, 1 (1): 106–10.
Beardsmore, R. W. (1992), "The Theory of Family Resemblances," *Philosophical Investigations*, 15 (2): 131–45.
Bellaimey, James E. (1990), "Family Resemblances and the Problem of the Under-Determination of Extension," *Philosophical Investigations*, 13 (1): 31–43.
Despeux, Catherine (2004), "Feeling in *Zhuangzi*: From Joy to Serenity," in Paolo Santangelo (ed.), *Expressions of States of Mind in Asia*, 73–94, Napoli: Università degli Studie di Napoli 'L'Orientale'.
Fraser, Chris (2011), "Knowledge and Error in Early Chinese Thought," *Dao: A Journal of Comparative Philosophy*, 10: 127–48.
Gibson, James (1979), *The Ecological Approach to Visual Perception*, Boston: Houghton Mifflin.
Goodman, Nelson (1972), *Problems and Projects*, Indianapolis: Bobbs-Merrill.
Goodman, Nelson (1978), *Ways of Worldmaking*, Indianapolis: Hackett.
Graham, Angus C. (1992), "Conceptual Schemes and Linguistic Relativism in Relation to Chinese," in Angus C. Graham (ed.), *Unreason within Reason: Essays of the Outskirts of Rationality*, 59–83, La Salle, IL: Open Court.
Hall, David L., and Roger T. Ames (1995), *Anticipating China: Thinking Through the Narratives of Chinese and Western Culture*, Albany, NY: SUNY Press.
Harbsmeier, Christoph (1993), "Conceptions of Knowledge in Ancient China," in Hans Lenk and Gregor Paul (eds.), *Epistemological Issues in Classical Chinese Philosophy*, 11–30, New York: SUNY Press.
Harbsmeier, Christoph (2004), "The Semantics of *Qing* 情 in Pre-buddhist Chinese," in Halvor Eifring (ed.), *Love and Emotions in Traditional Chinese Literature*, 69–148, Leiden: Brill.
Heidegger, Martin (2010), *Country Path Conversations*, Bloomington and Indianapolis: Indiana University Press.
Li, Gang 李綱 (2004), "Rongmufu 榕木賦," in *Quanji* 《全集》, 19–20, Changsha, China: Yuelu shushe.
Lloyd, Geoffrey Ernest Richard (2002), *The Ambitions of Curiosity: Understanding the World in Ancient Greece and China*, Cambridge, MA: Cambridge University Press.

Ma, Lin (2008), *Heidegger on East-West Dialogue: Anticipating the Event*, New York: Routledge.
Ma, Lin, and Jaap van Brakel (2013), "On the Conditions of Possibility for Comparative and Intercultural Philosophy," *Dao: A Journal of Comparative Philosophy*, 12: 297–312.
Ma, Lin, and Jaap van Brakel (2016a), *Fundamentals of Comparative and Intercultural Philosophy*, Albany, NY: SUNY Press.
Ma, Lin, and Jaap van Brakel (2016b), "A Theory of Interpretation for Comparative and Chinese Philosophy," *Dao: A Journal of Comparative Philosophy*, 15: 575–89.
Ma, Lin, and Jaap van Brakel (2016c), "Revisiting Wittgenstein on Family Resemblance and Colour(S)," *Philosophical Investigations*, 39 (3): 254–80.
Ma, Lin, and Jaap van Brakel (2018), "On the Interpreter's Choices: Making Hermeneutic Relativity Explicit," *Dao: A Journal of Comparative Philosophy*, 17: 453–78.
Ma, Lin, and Jaap van Brakel (2019), *Beyond the Troubled Water of Shifei: From Disputation to Walking-Two-Roads in the Zhuangzi*, Albany, NY: SUNY Press.
Ma, Lin, and Jaap van Brakel (2020), "Re-Visiting the Exchange between Zhuangzi and Huizi on Qing 情," *Dao: A Journal of Comparative Philosophy*, 20: 133–48.
Ma, Lin, and Jaap van Brakel (2021), "The Impossibility of Translation," in preparation.
Merleau-Ponty, Maurice (1964), *Signs*, Evanston, IL: Northwestern University Press.
Middendorf, Ulrike (2006), "Basic Emotion Terms in Warring States Texts: Sequences and Patterns," in Paolo Santangelo and Donatella Guida (eds.), *Love, Hatred, and Other Passions: Questions and Themes on Emotions in Chinese Civilization*, 126–48, Leiden: Brill.
Murphy, G. L., and D. L. Medin (1985), "The Role of Theories in Conceptual Coherence," *Psychological Review*, 92: 289–316.
Olberding, Garret P. S. (2012), *Dubious Facts*, Albany, NY: SUNY Press.
Putnam, Hilary (2002), *The Collapse of the Fact/Value Dichotomy*, Cambridge, MA: Harvard University Press.
Quine, Willard V. O. (1969), "Natural Kinds," in Willard V. O. Quine (ed.), *Ontological Relativity and Other Essays*, 114–38, New York: Columbia University Press.
Richards, Ivor Armstrong (1997), *Mencius on the Mind: Experiments in Multiple Definition*, London: Curzon. (Original edition in 1932.)
Roetz, Heiner (1993), "Validity in Chou Thought: On Chad Hansen and the Pragmatic Turn in Sinology," in Hans Lenk and Gregor Paul (eds.), *Epistemological Issues in Classical Chinese Philosophy*, 69–113, New York: SUNY Press.
Schafer, Edward H. (1953), "Li Kang: A Rhapsody on the Banyan Tree," *Oriens*, 6 (2): 344–53.
Stambaugh, Joan (1991), "Imaginary Dialogue between Heidegger and a Buddhist with Apologies for Possible Implausibilities of Personalities," *Eastern Buddhist*, 24 (1): 123–34.
van Brakel, Jaap (2014), "Heidegger on Zhuangzi and Uselessness," *Journal of Chinese Philosophy*, 41 (3–4): 387–406.
van Brakel, Jaap, and Lin Ma (2015), "Extension of Family Resemblance Concepts as a Necessary Condition of Interpretation across Traditions," *Dao: A Journal of Comparative Philosophy*, (4): 475–97.
Watson, Burton (1968), *The Complete Works of Chuang Tzu*, New York: Columbia University Press.
Wittgenstein, Ludwig (1993), "Remarks on Frazer's Golden Bough," in James C. Klagge and Alfred Nordmann (eds.), *Philosophical Occasions 1912-1951*, 118–55, Indianapolis: Hackett.

Wittgenstein, Ludwig (2009a), *Philosophical Investigations*, 4th ed., trans. G. E. M. Anscombe, P. M. S. Hacker, and J. Schulte, Oxford: Wiley-Blackwell.
Wittgenstein, Ludwig (2009b), *Philosophy of Psychology—a Fragment*, trans. G. E. M. Anscombe, P. M. S. Hacker, and J. Schulte, 4th ed., Oxford: Wiley-Blackwell. Formerly part II of PI.

Constellation II

Generalization and Essentialization

3

Unloading the Essentialism Charge: Some Methodological Reflections in Doing Philosophy of Culture

Roger T. Ames

A familiar criticism leveled against those of us who attempt to excavate cultural differences in service to responsible cultural comparisons is that, in doing so, we are guilty of essentializing these same cultures. A recent example of this charge is Ted Slingerland in his monograph, *Mind and Body in Early China: Beyond Orientalism and the Myth of Holism* (2019), wherein he describes me (and many other contemporary students of Chinese philosophy) as purveyors of "the myth of holism" with respect to early Chinese cosmology and epistemology. Slingerland (2013: 9) would have it that I with my "strong" holist position hold "that, for the early Chinese (or 'the Chinese' or even the 'East' more generally), there exists no qualitative distinction at all between anything we could call *mind* and the physical body or other organs of the body."[1] As putative "postmodern neo-Orientalists" we all believe that "holistic" Chinese philosophers were incapable of making any such distinctions, and further we would claim on the basis of this same strong holism, that our different cultural traditions are monolithic and incommensurable (Slingerland 2019).[2]

Slingerland is not alone in offering such characterizations. Indeed, he has been encouraged by some other interpreters of Chinese philosophy who, to avoid such essentializing themselves, would go so far as to recommend that in discussing Chinese culture, we would all do well to abjure generalizations entirely. Paul Goldin and Michael Puett have indicted me and my collaborators as offering what Goldin again calls "an updated Orientalism." For Puett, not only David Hall and I, but Marcel Granet, Fritz Mote, Joseph Needham, Angus Graham, and K. C. Chang are all "cultural essentialists" in our best attempts to articulate an interpretive context for understanding Chinese culture. Goldin (2008: 3) likewise charges us and these fellow travelers with presenting "China as a reified foil to a reified West, an antipodal domain exemplifying antithetic mores and modes of thought."

What we and this group of alleged "cultural essentialists" share in common is the belief that there is a distinctive yet always evolving way of thinking that needs to be taken into account in understanding an unbounded and holistic Chinese cosmology. Further, we assert that this dynamic Chinese cosmology posits a world that is naturalistic, autogenerative, and self-construing without appeal to some external metaphysical principle as its unilateral source of order. To appreciate what is philosophically at issue in this debate, we need to maintain a clear distinction between the ahistorical implications of rational or logical thinking that is analytical and that seeks closure in patterns of fixed regularity, and the historical entailments of correlative thinking that is synthetic and that seeks open-ended, aesthetic disclosure in ad hoc unities constituted by unique details. This distinction is captured in the difference A. N. Whitehead (1938: 60–3) asserts in defining a logical and an aesthetic order, where the former as an act of closure is universalistic, while the latter as an act of disclosure is radically historicist. Logic requires a notion of strict ontological identity as the ground for its formal essentialism; art only allows for analogical relations among unique and always particular details. And we and the other interpreters who share this approach are self-consciously historicist in tracing the evolution of this worldview through the corpus of canonical texts and again historicist in our understanding of its application to and elaboration in different dimensions of the Chinese experience, including the cosmology as it is made explicit in the Han dynasty.

Puett goes on to rehearse this same distinction between the rational and aesthetic sensibilities that Hall and Ames refer to as the difference between first and second problematic thinking and the difference between analogical and causal thinking. Puett (2002: 17) would allow that through such distinctions, Hall and Ames like Granet before them, "attempt to illumine the contrasting assumptions shaping classical Chinese and Western culture." True enough. And that like Graham, they "see each of these ways of thinking as existing to some degree in both Chinese and Western cultures, and ... are thus able to argue that Chinese thought is something that can be fully assimilated into contemporary Western thinking" (18). Again confirmed.

If essentialism is to be understood as a generalization stating that certain properties possessed by a given population are universal within that culture and at the same time exclusive to them, that these properties are thus not dependent on contingencies of context, and that again these same properties bring with them a relativism and incommensurability among cultures, how can Puett describe us or any of these scholars as proffering a "cultural-essentialist model" of interpretation? The account given by these interpreters sounds instead like an open-ended and inclusive pluralism. And given that their characterization of Chinese culture anticipates a productive dialogue among importantly different cultural narratives, I would in fact describe it as "evolutionary" in the best sense of that term.

Returning to Goldin (2008: 21), as his alternative to our alleged Orientalism, he would argue categorically that:

> if there is one valid generalization about China, it is that China defies generalization. Chinese civilization is simply too huge, too diverse, and too old for neat maxims.

And again for Puett (2002: 25), "all of these interpretive strategies—reading in terms of schools, essentialized definitions of culture, evolutionary frameworks—have the consequence of erasing the unique power that particular claims had at the time." Explicitly rejecting our self-consciously interpretive strategies, Puett (2002: 24–5) argues:

We should instead work towards a more nuanced approach in which we make no *a priori* assumptions regarding single statements made in single texts and the significance of any individual claims.

I think that Goldin and Puett, while both presumably aspiring to some ostensive interpretive objectivity, are advocating for nothing short of a naïve realism that fails to acknowledge the profoundly subjective coloration of all interpretative experience. Hillary Putnam (1990: 28) challenges this kind of realism by rejecting any such mind-independent understanding of reality, arguing :

> Elements of what we call "language" or "mind" penetrate so deeply into what we call "reality" that the very project of representing ourselves as being "mapper's" of something "language-independent" is fatally compromised from the start. Like Relativism, but in a different way, Realism is an impossible attempt to view the world from Nowhere.

Putnam (1990: 178) continues by insisting that this kind of human penetration and transformation of our contextualizing environments extends to our attention and valorization of the world in which we live, requiring us to accept our own reflexivity as "beings who cannot have a view of the world that does not reflect our interests and values." Putnam (1987: 83) argues it is this always collaborative experience that is the one and only reality:

> The heart of pragmatism, it seems to me—of James' and Dewey's pragmatism if not of Peirce's—was the supremacy of the agent point of view. If we find that we must take a certain point of view, use a certain "conceptual system," when engaged in a practical activity, in the widest sense of practical activity, then we must not simultaneously advance the claim that it is not really "the way things are in themselves."

In our earlier forays into translating the Chinese canons, I and my several collaborators, rather than beginning from some uncritical assumptions about being literal or objective, have produced what we have upfront called self-consciously interpretive translations. In describing our translations as "self-consciously interpretive," however, we are not allowing in any way that we are recklessly speculative or given to license in our renderings. Nor are we willing to accept the reproach that we are less "literal" and thus more "creative" than other translators. On the contrary, I would insist that any pretense to a "literal" translation is not only naïve, but is itself an "objectivist" prejudice of the first order. Just as each generation selects and carries over earlier thinkers to reshape them in their own image, each generation reconfigures the classical canons of world philosophy to its own needs.

At the most general level, I would suggest that modern English as the target language carries with it such an overlay of cultural assumptions that, in the absence of such "self-consciousness," the philosophical import of the classical Chinese text can be seriously compromised. Our conventional translation of the classical term *tian* 天

being "Heaven" with a reverentially capital "H," for example, is to insinuate theological assumptions into what is a fundamentally an atheistic cosmology. Again, a failure of naïve translators to be self-conscious and to take fair account of their own Gadamerian "prejudices" with the excuse that they are relying on an existing "objective" dictionary that gives us this equation between *tian* and "Heaven" is to fail to acknowledge that in the case of China at least this lexical resource, given its missionary origins, is itself so heavily colored with cultural biases that Chinese philosophy is for the most part taught in religion or Asian studies departments in our universities, and shelved in the religion or literature sections of our libraries.[3] To fail to be self-conscious as translators is to betray our readers not once, but twice. That is, not only do we fail to provide the "objective" reading of the text we have promised, but we also neglect to warn our unsuspecting readers of the cultural assumptions we willy-nilly insinuate into our translations.

Encountering the unsummed richness of the original texts, we as interpreters are ourselves always collaborators from a specific time and place. Such an interface between fundamentally different interpretive contexts is in itself a formula for an inescapable cultural reductionism. Certainly our too hastily constructed interpretive strategies and overarching theories—"philosophical" or otherwise—when applied in the practice of cultural and textual translation, cannot help but put the concrete detail of another tradition at some considerable risk. When Robert Frost remarks that "what is lost in translation is the poetry," I think that he as an artist is quite properly concerned that the project of translation is a literary transaction, and thus in its outcomes at the very least makes the text different, and in many (but not all) cases, makes it much less.

Indeed, in order to maximize our efforts in translation, we first and foremost need a commitment to a Heideggerian *Destruktion* that itself was initially controversial and provocative in Heidegger's recovery of classical Greek terms. That is, we must struggle to retrieve the situated, primordial meanings by "polishing" the key terminology. This process is "conservative" in the archaeological sense of working backward through each stratum of the distortions layered over the terminologies across the ages in order to return to their origins. It is recovering as much of the contextualizing detail as possible and is "radical" as we seek to root out the meanings within the soil of Chinese culture itself. In spite of our inescapable interpretive limitations, to the extent that we can, we must struggle with imagination to allow a text that belongs to another cultural narrative to reveal its poetry—the unmediated, non-referential bottomlessness of its own particularity.

But in this best effort, the image of Jorge Luis Borges's "Funes the Memorious" comes to mind, raising the question of whether we can actually "think" particularity.[4] We have to ask to what extent and in what degree is it ever possible to escape our own facticity and read these texts with naiveté and innocence, free from our own cultural assumptions. Clearly, instead of pretending to an impossible objectivity, we need a self-conscious hermeneutical openness in the project of cultural interpretation. That is, beyond the necessary commitment to respect the particularity of the text, we are in need of hermeneutical sensibilities that begin from an awareness of our own prejudgments and that allows for both textual detail and interpretive generalizations in the ongoing and inevitable fusion of horizons.

In fact, when we ask the question: Why do we pursue comparative studies in the first place? my answer would be that understanding different traditions of philosophy provides us with resources for further philosophizing. If *philosophia* is the pursuit of wisdom, it can be argued that "wisdom" itself emerges analogically through establishing and aggregating a pattern of truly productive correlations between what we already know and what we would know. Such correlations are "productive" in that they increase meaning and provide us with the possibility of actually achieving intelligent practices to the extent that we are able to optimize these meaningful correlations effectively in our practical life situations.

Of course, not all such analogies and correlations are equally apposite. As we know from the history of having translated and thus "carried over" Chinese philosophy into the Western academy, poorly chosen comparisons can be a persisting source of distortion and of cultural condescension. A heavy-handed and impositional "Christian," "Heideggarian," and yes, even "Pragmatic" or "Whiteheadian" reading of Chinese philosophy betrays the reader by distorting both the Chinese tradition and the Western analog in the comparison. Even so, we have no choice but to identify productive analogies that, with effort and imagination, can in the fullness of time be qualified and refined in such a way as to introduce culturally novel ideas into our own world to enrich our own ways of thinking and living. As inescapably correlative thinkers, we need to be analogically retail and piecemeal rather than working in whole cloth.

To take one example, when turning to *Focusing the Familiar* (*Zhongyong*) that numbers as one of the Confucian Four Books in which the sagacious human being is celebrated as cocreator with the heavens and the earth, we might find analogy with Whitehead in his concern to reinstate "creativity" as an important human value. For Whitehead, the aseity or self-sufficiency and perfection of God in traditional theology, precludes any interesting or coherent sense of human creativity. Following his sustained challenge to conventional ways of thinking about creativity, the word "creativity" itself becomes an individual entry in a 1971 supplement to the *Oxford English Dictionary* with two of the three references being made to Whitehead's *Religion in the Making*. At the same time, however, we might be keenly aware that when the same Whitehead invokes the primordial nature of God and the Eternal Objects that are sustained in His thinking, the long shadow of Aristotelian metaphysics sets a real limit on the relevance of this dimension of Whitehead's philosophy for classical Chinese process cosmology.

Again, analogies can be productive of both associations and contrasts, and we can learn much from both. Aristotle's teleology, his substance ontology, and his reliance upon logic as the demonstrable method that will secure us truth might serve as a point of contrast with a Chinese process cosmology that abjures fixed beginnings and ends, that precludes any strict formal identity, and that will not yield up the principle of noncontradiction which enables erstwhile apodictic knowledge. On the other hand, Aristotle's resistance to Platonic abstraction in promoting an aggregating practical wisdom correlates rather productively with one of the central issues in classical Confucian moral philosophy. That is, Aristotelian *phronesis* with its commitment to the cultivation of excellent habits (*hexis*) in the practical affairs of everyday living has some immediate resonance with the ubiquitous Confucian assumption that knowing and doing are inseparable and mutually entailing (*zhixingheyi* 知行合一). In our project of cultural translation, we must certainly be deliberate in the picking and choosing of our analogies—but at the end of the day, pick and choose we must.

This self-consciousness in translation then, is not to disrespect the integrity of the Chinese philosophical narrative. On the contrary, it is to endorse one of the hermeneutical premises of this commentarial tradition captured in one of the basic cosmological postulates of the *Book of Changes*, "continuity in change" (*biantong* 變通):

> According to the *Book of Changes*, with everything running its course, there is flux (*bian*), and where there is such flux, there is continuity (*tong*), and where there is such continuity, the process is enduring.⁵

What this postulate means when applied to the interpretation of the philosophical canons is that textual meaning emerges at the intersection between change and persistence, and that we as translators of the culture, far from being passive or secondary or epiphenomenal in our interpretive work, are integral to the growth of any living tradition. Indeed, risking here a thick generalization that emerges from a contrast between early Greek substance ontology and this *Book of Changes* process cosmology, I would suggest that these early Confucian philosophers were less inclined to ask *what* makes something real or *why* things exist, and more interested in *how* the complex relationships that obtain among the changing phenomena in their cosmic surroundings can be correlated and negotiated for optimum productivity and value. These thinkers were not given to positing any predetermined necessity in teleologically-derived assumptions about origins, or to offering causal speculations about some grand, rationalizing design. Rather, a fundamental guiding value for these early Chinese philosophers was the pursuit of superlative quality in an achieved personal, social, and ultimately cosmic harmony, and the opportunity to participate in the production of cosmic meaning through the aestheticization of the human experience captured in the contemporary Chinese expression, *wenhua* 文化.

But again, this term *wenhua* that emerged in the nineteenth century throughout East Asia as an equivalency to translate and appropriate the complex word "culture" differs markedly in its metaphorical implications from those assumed by Western modernity.⁶ The strongly teleological agricultural and husbanding associations of the European term "culture" are bypassed as points of metaphorical departure in favor of *wenhua* 文化, a compound expression that combines the characters for the "transforming" (*hua* 化) of the human experience effected by "the inscribing and embellishing processes undertaken by literary, civil, and artistic traditions" (*wen* 文). This modern expression *wenhua* 文化 created to synchronize Chinese with modernity's word "culture" is an allusion to the *Book of Changes*, where it states: "through observing carefully the heavenly patterns we can gain insight into the changing seasons; through observing carefully the embellishments made by human beings, we can transform the world."⁷ In a word, *wenhua* is the attempt to aestheticize and civilize the human experience in all of its parts.

Metaphorically rooting "culture" in the agricultural practices of plant and animal domestication invites us to see cultural norms as having a transcendent disciplinary force with respect to that which is being "cultured," thereby enabling us to regulate its spontaneous growth. *Wen* by contrast is understood (with significant political implications) as the disclosing processes of civilization: that is, of *collaborating* with nature's beauty, *elaborating* upon it, *elevating* it, and through a critical self-awareness *achieving* a decidedly aesthetic if not spiritual product. In this contrast between culture driven by teleology and culture as *wenhua*, we have an important distinction between rationalized closure and aesthetic disclosure, between retrospective necessity when what is an intrinsic potential is then actualized, and prospective possibility when what is imagined is then realized.

As a self-confessed philosopher of culture, I find myself tasked to excavate, identify, and articulate generalizations that distinguish different cultural narratives, as is exemplified here in the contrast between the metaphorical ground of the English word "culture," and its erstwhile Chinese equivalent, *wenhua*. It is only in being cognizant of these uncommon cultural assumptions that, in some degree at least, we are able to respect their most fundamental differences by locating the philosophical discussion somewhere between their alternative worldviews. Just as with the watershed of the Western cultural narrative we would identify with Plato and Aristotle and Hellenistic culture, certain enduring commitments were made explicit in the formative period of Chinese philosophy that are more persistent than others and that allow us to make useful generalizations about the evolution of this continuing tradition. In fact, one of the premises that allows for such generalizations is the importance of trying to recover and understand the earliest conditions available to us as the history of an emergent cultural process unfolds. As Nathan Sivin (1974: xi) observes: "man's prodigious creativity seems to be based on the permutations and recastings of a rather small stock of ideas." I would argue that the fundamental distinctions between a Greek substance ontology grounded in the self-sufficiency of "being" (*ousia*) and a classical Chinese cosmology that begins from the procreativity inherent in an always contextualized process of "becoming" (*shengsheng* 生生) must number among this stock.

In my attempt to unload the essentialism charge, I want to appeal to two historical examples of distinguished philosophers of culture—one from Europe and one from China—who were themselves willing to risk thick generalizations. In the preface to his *Novissima Sinica* written over the period of 1697–9, an astute and penetrating Leibniz offers a synoptic comparison between the contributions of European and Chinese culture. Leibniz argues that in the specifically theoretical disciplines such as mathematics, logic, metaphysics, and in particular theology, there is a clear European superiority. Indeed, for Leibniz (1994: 46–7), we Europeans "excel by far in the understanding of concepts which are abstracted by the mind from the material." We own the theoretical sciences and surpass the Chinese in those rational tools of the intellect that promise us demonstrable truth, while the Chinese would struggle with a kind of empirical geometry owned by most artisans.

On Leibniz's reading, contrasting with this European advantage in the highly abstract and theoretical, the Chinese excel in the pursuit of civil philosophy. Indeed,

Chinese "civilization" has set a standard in ethics and politics far superior to that found in Europe. In Leibniz's own words:

> But who would have believed that there is on earth a people who, though we are in our view so very advanced in every branch of behavior, still surpass us in comprehending the precepts of civil life? Yet now we find this to be so among the Chinese, as we learn to know them better. And so if we are their equals in the industrial arts, and ahead of them in contemplative sciences, certainly they surpass us (though it is almost shameful to confess this) in practical philosophy, that is, in the precepts of ethics and politics adapted to the present life and use of mortals. Indeed, it is difficult to describe how beautifully all the laws of the Chinese, in contrast to those of other peoples, are directed to the achievement of public tranquility and the establishment of social order, so that men shall be disrupted in their relations as little as possible. ... Certainly the Chinese above all others have attained a higher standard. In a vast multitude of men they have virtually accomplished more than the founders of religious orders among us have achieved within their own narrow ranks. (1994, 46–7)

Considering the dearth of information on China available to Leibniz in his own time, this philosopher resists his own formalist and universalistic philosophical proclivities that should have inclined him steeply in the opposite direction. Indeed, in advancing his own generalizations about European and Chinese cultures, he is a surprisingly keen and honest observer of the cultural continuities and differences. In these writings we can actually discern Leibniz's grasp of the seminal and peculiar cluster of terms that are defining of Confucian ethical and political philosophy: that is, *xiao* 孝 as the intergenerational embodiment and transmission of the cultural tradition through patterns of deference in lived and always familial relations, and following from this prime moral imperative *li* 禮 as aspiring to an achieved propriety in our family-centered roles and relations, *yi* 義 as seeking after an optimizing appropriateness and decorum in our roles and relations, *he* 和 as the unrelenting pursuit of an optimizing symbiosis within the diversity of our familial, communal, political, and cosmic roles and relations, and so on. Leibniz saw and registered a clear contrast between the value invested in those abstract, theoretical disciplines in the European academy that are in search of axiomatic-deductive demonstration, and the more aesthetic and pragmatic applications of the Chinese tradition—a distinction that broadly distinguishes European confidence in the dividends of the rational sciences from those alternative rewards that can be derived from virtuosity in the art of living in family and community. In fact, it was more than a fundamental sympathy and respect for Chinese culture that led Leibniz to defend Matteo Ricci's advocacy of an accommodationist Christianity in the long simmering Rites Controversy that came to a boil in Rome toward the end of Leibniz's own life. Leibniz's commitment to accommodationism was clearly based on his conviction that the precepts of any universal civil philosophy that would seek to construct a framework for optimizing the social, political, and indeed religious life of human beings in community would do well to take into account the substantial accomplishments that Chinese culture has achieved in this same effort.

As a second example of a distinguished philosopher of culture, the twentieth-century "New Confucian" (*xinruxuejia* 新儒學家), Qian Mu 錢穆, in his attempt to provide a corrective to the key Confucian philosophical terms that have been compromised by their Christian conversion, is adamant that this same vocabulary expressing the unique and complex Confucian vision of a moral life simply has no counterpart in other languages. (Dennerline 1988: 9) Qian Mu's point in making this claim is not to argue for cultural purism and incommensurability. On the contrary, he would allow that with sufficient exposition made through thick generalizations (the ambitious objective of philosophers of culture), the Confucian world can, in important degree, be expanded upon and further "appreciated" by those from without. Qian Mu's claim is on behalf of the uniqueness and the value of a tradition that has defined its terms of art through the lived experience of its people over millennia and anticipates the real difficulty we must face in attempting to capture its complex and organically related vocabulary in other languages without substantial qualification and explanation.

In service to Qian Mu's project, I want to contest the resistance among some contemporary scholars to accept the kind of thick cultural generalizations being made by both Leibniz and Qian Mu that I believe are necessary if we are to respect the rich differences that are obtained among traditions and if we are to avoid as best we can an impoverishing cultural reductionism. I would posit that the canopy of an always emerging cultural vocabulary is itself rooted in and grows out of a deep and relatively stable soil of unannounced assumptions sedimented over succeeding generations into the language, the customs, and the life-forms of a living tradition. And further, I would argue that to fail to acknowledge the fundamental character of cultural difference as an erstwhile safeguard against the sins of "essentialism" is not itself innocent. Indeed, ironically, this antagonism to cultural generalizations leads to the uncritical essentializing of one's own contingent cultural assumptions and to the insinuating of these same presuppositions into one's interpretations of the ways of thinking and living of other traditions.

One might go further and argue that the bugbear of "essentializing" itself, like any such corollary of "universalism," is largely a culturally specific deformation. After all, we can only "essentialize" if we are predisposed to believe there are such things as "essences" and the dualisms that follow from such assumptions, a way of thinking about the world that did not recommend itself to the formative, analogizing thinkers of classical China. Essentialism itself arises from classical Greek ontology as "the science of being *per se*"—the self-sufficiency of being—and from the application of strict identity as the principle of individuation. It is this notion of "essences" (*eidos*) that grounds Platonic idealism and his search for formal definitions as the source of knowledge. Essentialism is the basis of Aristotelian logic with its "A or not-A" principle of noncontradiction, and his doctrine of species (*eidos*) as immutable natural kinds.

But essences aside, there are still important cultural continuities that allow for responsible generalizations. A point that was drilled into me by my teachers was that different cultures think differently and that we elide important distinctions among them at our peril. Angus Graham, for example, ascribes unique and evolving categories and conceptual structures to different cultural traditions and, in so doing, is challenging the Saussurian structuralist distinction between *langue* (universal and systematic linguistic structures and rules governing all languages) and *parole* (diverse and open-ended speech acts in any of our natural languages).⁸ Like many (but not all) of us, Graham is persuaded that different populations within always changing cultural milieus appeal to different concepts and ways of thinking and living. And Graham spent his illustrious career doing his very best to bring some clarity to these differences.

Contra Graham, however, Zhang Longxi 張隆溪 (1999), in his equally sincere commitment to pursuing intercultural understanding, is quite critical of those of us (singling out Jacques Gernet [1985] as one primary example) who would describe the tension between Christianity and Chinese as not only one "of different intellectual traditions" but also "of different mental categories and modes of thought."⁹ Zhang becomes impatient when "the cultural difference between the Chinese and the Western is formulated as fundamentally distinct ways of thinking and speaking, as the ability, or lack of it, to express abstract ideas." Above we saw that Leibniz quite proudly took the equation between abstraction and a higher reality to be a distinctively European assumption. In Zhang's (1999: 44) assuming uncritically that abstraction is indeed the source of spiritual and theoretical assent, he does not recognize that in thus giving abstract and theoretical ideas pride of place, he is advocating for decidedly Western philosophical assumptions that are not only absent in the classical Chinese tradition but in fact have for more than a century now been under assault within the narrative of Western philosophy and its own ongoing, internal critique. It must be noted that, beginning in the late nineteenth century and captured succinctly in Nietzsche's proclamation that "God is dead," this now old, foundationalist way of thinking has been sternly rejected as a shared target in the post-Darwinian internal reassessment of the Western philosophical narrative.

Why would our colleagues describe putatively essentializing philosophers of culture as "post-modern, neo-Orientalists?" How did "oriental" as the opposite of "occidental" become a bad word? In service to the idea that many voices should be heard, Edward Said in his influential book *Orientalism* (1978) made the claim that largely for political reasons "Oriental Studies" in the Western academy has constructed a distorted and condescending description of Islamic cultures in service to its own self-image and understanding. In the decades since the cautions of Said were made regarding the projection of "orientalist" prejudices in the study and teaching of other cultures, the tendency in academic circles has been to steer clear of what has become understood as "essentialist" constructions of culture. This cautionary corrective has resulted in valuable efforts to peel back layers of exotic and universalizing veneer that previous generations of scholarship had effectively laid over cultural realities, and to bring to light the often complex and convoluted striations of living, changing cultures. In rejecting cultural essentializing, a genuine endeavor has been made in the scholarship to try with imagination to take other cultures on their own terms. However, this important attempt to rethink and get past the naïve constructions of cultural others now runs the risk of obscuring the crucial and still vital role played by assaying differences in ways of thinking and living, and by acknowledging persistent cultural ideals in engendering and sustaining cultural change.

Returning to Graham's (1990: 360) advocacy of different ways of thinking, he allows that getting at such conceptual differences is not an easy task:

That people of another culture are somehow thinking in other categories is a familiar idea, almost a commonplace, but one very difficult to pin down as a topic for fruitful discussion.

We might recall Nietzsche's philosophy of grammar as having anticipated Graham in this respect. Nietzsche asserts that a particular worldview has over time been sedimented into the family of Indo-European languages to both shape and to constrain the semiotic structures of these disparate yet in some ways continuous cultures. As a consequence of this shared history, our culturally specific Indo-European languages in their various modes of expression encourage certain philosophical possibilities while discouraging others:

> The strange family resemblance of all Indian, Greek, and German philosophizing is explained easily enough. Where there is an affinity of languages, it cannot fail, owing to the common philosophy of grammar—I mean owing to the unconscious domination and guidance by similar grammatical functions—that everything is prepared at the outset for a similar development and sequence of philosophical systems; just as the way seems barred against certain other possibilities of world-interpretation. (Nietzsche 1966: 20)

Graham, like Nietzsche before him, looks to what languages reveal grammatically and by extension, conceptually, to get at the slippery issue of other cultures "thinking in other categories." Graham has consistently warned us that serious equivocations emerge when we elide the distinction between classical Greek ontological commitments and those assumptions grounding a classical Chinese processive, procreative cosmology. Ontology privileges "being *per se*" and a substance language with its reality and appearance, essence and attribute dualisms—that is, substances as necessary property bearers and the contingent properties that are borne, respectively. Process cosmology, on the other hand, gives privilege to "becoming" and the vital, interdependent, and correlative categories needed to "speak" process and its eventful content. Graham (1991: 287) is quite explicit about the nature of these philosophical differences and their linguistic entailments:

> In the Chinese cosmos all things are interdependent, without transcendent principles by which to explain them or a transcendent origin from which they derive. ... A novelty in this position which greatly impresses me is that it exposes a preconception of Western interpreters that such concepts as *Tian* "Heaven" and *Dao* "Way" must have the transcendence of our own ultimate principles; it is hard for us to grasp that even the Way is interdependent with man.

Thus, my defense against the familiar charge made by some scholars that philosophy of culture "essentializes" the Other is first to insist that cultural narratives are contingent. We are referencing holistic, protean, and always reflexively inflected and thus overlapping historical *narratives* of populations—not reified and discrete *other minds*. In Graham's (1990: 360–411) comparison of Chinese and Greek categories, and specifically in reference to the classical Chinese language with its alternative philosophy of grammar, he concludes that in reporting on the eventful flow of *qi* cosmology, "the sentence structure of Classical Chinese places us in a world of process about which we ask ... 'Whence?' and also, since it is moving, 'At what time?'" I have followed him in consistently advocating for a holistic, narrative understanding of experience as being more revealing of underlying cultural assumptions than any detemporalizing and essentializing analytical approach.

As I have argued, the entertainment of other cultural narratives is always a reflexive exercise. If we acknowledge that the experiencing of other cultures is a matter of mutually shaping stories, then in failing to articulate apposite generalizations, we are at real risk of imposing on them cultural importances not their own. After all, without struggling with imagination to identify, refine, and ultimately defend such characterizations, the default position is an uncritical cultural assimilation. Such cultural reductionism follows from the seemingly respectful and inclusive assumption that we are all the same, a claim that, far from being innocuous, is in fact asserting that "they" are the same as "us." And in the cautionary language of Richard Rorty, such forced redescription is not only condescending but, indeed, is cruel and humiliating.

My teachers thought that to claim peoples and cultures are either too complex to make the necessary generalizations that allow them their differences or, by default, are somehow "equal" in their ability to think, might at first blush seem to be inclusive and liberating and respectful. And while such assurances might be so for some interpreters, I would argue that such an assertion is anything but innocent. Why would we assume that in allowing other traditions have their own culturally contingent modalities of thinking is to claim that such traditions do not know how to think unless we ourselves believe that in fact there is only one way of thinking and that this way of thinking— that is, *our* way of thinking—is the only way? Indeed, the uncritical assumption that other cultures must think the same way as we do is for me, the very definition of an ethnocentric essentialism. I would argue that it is precisely the hard work needed to excavate, to recognize, and to appreciate the degree of difference obtaining among cultures in living and thinking that properly motivates cultural translation in the first place, and that ultimately rewards the effort. Surely arguing that there are culturally contingent modalities of thinking can be pluralistic rather than relativistic, can be accommodating rather than condescending, and can be a source of shared cultural growth rather than diminution. At the very least, if comparative studies is to provide us with the mutual enrichment it promises, we must strive to take other cultures on their own terms and to appreciate fully the differences that obtain among them.

This same point can be made another way. I would argue that the only thing more dangerous than striving to make responsible cultural generalizations is failing to make them. Generalizations do not have to preclude appreciating the richness and complexity of always evolving cultural traditions; in fact, it is generalizations that locate and inform specific cultural details and provide otherwise sketchy historical developments with the thickness of their content. There is no alternative in making cultural comparisons to an open, hermeneutical approach that is ready to modify always provisional generalizations with the new information that additional detail yields as it is interpreted within the grid of generalizations.

But the argument for unloading the essentialism charge against philosophers of culture is even more complex. As a consequence of the challenge of new directions in historiographical thinking, the assumption that cultural families develop their distinctive patterns of values, norms, and practices in relative isolation from one another has become markedly less trenchant over the past several decades. Both historians and philosophers have come to recognize significant distortions that attend any unreflective tendencies to compartmentalize the ancient and premodern worlds according to currently prevailing spatial and conceptual divisions and their underlying (often highly political) rationales. In particular, critical assessment is now well underway regarding the degree to which persistent prejudices about metageography—especially the "myth of continents"—have shaped and continue to shape representations of history and cultural origins. The classic assertion of "independently originating" European and Asian cultures on either side of the Ural Mountains, for example, is being abandoned in favor of highlighting "Eurasian" characteristics in the complex cultural genealogies of both "West" and "East." Indeed, given that cultures arise interculturally, or better yet, *intra*-culturally, in wide-ranging, intimate commerce with one another over time as a borderless ecology of cultures having an inside without an outside, it would seem that no culture *can* be fully understood in isolation from others. It was thus that, years ago, we asked the question: Is there more than one culture? If we follow Wittgenstein with his "family resemblances" and "language games," then given the contingency of culture, the context that contains mutually incoherent games without attempting reduction or sublation may be called "culture." Perhaps the best way to understand the vagueness of culture is to declare that there is *at most* only one language and *at most* only one culture. The engagement between two cultures, then, is the articulation of alternative importances within a single (incoherent) complex. This understanding of culture resonates rather closely with the "focus and field" understanding of *dao* 道 as the unbounded and unsummed totality of orders as they are construed from insistently particular perspectives (*de* 德). In this manner, one needs to make no final distinction among different cultures and their languages (Hall and Ames 1995: 175–9).

The development and growth of particular cultures do not take place, however, only by way of historical interactions among them, resulting either in accommodation of differences as conditions for mutual contribution or in competition for acknowledged superiority. Cultures change not only in adaptive response to others and to political, economic, or environmental exigencies but are also animated by an internal impulse as an expression of their own particular aspirations. Quite often, this change involves and requires envisioning ways of life distinctively other than those that are near and familiar, revealing with greater or lesser clarity what present cultural realities are not, and do not promise. Cultural change *does* occur in response to differing circumstantial realities, but it also takes place as a function of pursuing new or not-yet-actualized ideals. Said differently, ideals as "ends-in-view"—what Charles Taylor calls "hypergoods"—are also realities that live in history, and that at least in degree have the force of directing the patterns of change.[10]

This recognition of the indigenous impulse has as its own corollary the insight that the histories through which cultures narrate their own origins and development are not primarily aimed at accurately depicting a closed past, but rather at disclosing arcs of change projected into open and yet more or less distinctly anticipated futures. The cliché that history is written by the winners is perhaps better couched in terms of history being written to affirm that what has occurred *amounts to* a victory. Cultural change is inseparable from the process, at some level, of both valorizing and actualizing new (or at least alternative) interpretations of the changes that have occurred. Thus, in trying to glean resources from our past cultural narratives, we must be self-conscious of the fact that our redescriptions of these cultures while certainly being informed by their past, are also being reformulated to serve our own contemporary needs and interests.

Notes

1. Slingerland's 2013 essay was preliminary to the later monograph cited below.
2. I am entirely sympathetic with Jim Behuniak's critical review of this book in *Dao: A Journal of Comparative Philosophy* (2019a) in which Behuniak defends me and a legion of other contemporaries against Slingerland's rather wanton and gratuitous caricatures where he ascribes to us positions that we simply do not hold. See also the further exchange between Slingerland (2019) and Behuniak (2019b) in the same journal.
3. Hans-Georg Gadamer uses "prejudices" not in the sense of blind prejudice, but on the contrary, in the sense that our prejudgments can facilitate rather than obstruct our understanding. Our assumptions can positively condition our experience. For Gadamer, we must always entertain these assumptions critically, being aware that the hermeneutical circle in which understanding is always situated requires that we continually strive to be conscious of what we are bringing to our experience. In thus being self-conscious in our interpretation of experience, we must pursue increasingly felicitous prejudgments that can inform our behaviors in better and more productive ways.
4. In this story, Borges introduces a character who, with perfect memory of every detail of his day, requires a full twenty-four hours to remember twenty-four hours. Such interpretive completeness turns Greek abstraction on its head, precluding any possibility of rising above the detail to reflect upon and think through one's experience.
5. *Book of Changes* B2:《易》，窮則變，變則通，通則久。.
6. Raymond Williams (1976) has famously described "culture" as one of the two or three most complicated terms in the English language. He attributes this complexity in part to the relative recency with which the meaning of "culture" has been metaphorically extended from its original sense of the physical processes of nurturing and cultivation—i.e., perhaps the mundane yet vital practices of agriculture that includes both horticulture and husbandry—to point toward a characteristic mode of human material, intellectual, spiritual, and aesthetic development.
7. 《周易・賁・彖》：「觀乎天文，以察時變；觀乎人文，以化成天下」.
8. Saussure uses the analogy of a chess game, where *langue* are the fixed rules that govern the game while *parole* are the actual, varied moves made by different people that come to constitute any particular game.
9. See Zhang's "Translating Cultures: China and the West" (1999). He cites Jacques Gernet, *China and the Christian Impact: A Conflict of Cultures* (1985).

10. "Hypergoods" is a useful neologism introduced by Charles Taylor in his *Sources of the Self: The Making of the Modern Identity* (1989: 62–3):

> Most of us not only live with many goods but find that we have to rank them, and in some cases, this ranking makes one of them of supreme importance relative to the others. ... Let me call higher-order goods of this kind "hypergoods," i.e. goods which not only are incomparably more important than others but provide the standpoint from which these must be weighed, judged, decided about.

References

Behuniak, Jim (2019a), "Slingerland, Edward, *Mind and Body in Early China: Beyond Orientalism and the Myth of Holism*," *Dao: A Journal of Comparative Philosophy*, 18 (2): 305–12.

Behuniak, Jim (2019b), "Response to Edward Slingerland," *Dao: A Journal of Comparative Philosophy*, 18 (3): 489–91.

Dennerline, Jerry (1988), *Qian Mu and the World of Seven Mansions*, New Haven, CT: Yale University Press.

Gernet, Jacques (1985), *China and the Christian Impact: A Conflict of Cultures*, trans. J. Lloyd, Cambridge: Cambridge University Press.

Goldin, Paul R. (2008), "The Myth That China Has No Creation Myth," *Monumenta Serica*, 56: 1–22.

Graham, Angus Charles (1990), *Studies in Chinese Philosophy and Philosophical Literature*, Albany, NY: SUNY Press.

Graham, Angus Charles (1991), "Reflections and Replies," in Henry Rosemont Jr. (ed.), *Chinese Texts and Philosophical Contexts: Essays Dedicated to Angus C. Graham*, 267–322, La Salle, IL: Open Court.

Hall, David L., and Roger T. Ames (1995), *Anticipating China: Thinking Through the Narratives of Chinese and Western Culture*, Albany, NY: SUNY Press.

Leibniz, Gottfried Wilhelm (1994), *Writings on China*, trans. Daniel J. Cook and Henry Rosemont Jr., Chicago: Open Court.

Nietzsche, Friedrich (1966), *Beyond Good and Evil*, trans. W. Kaufmann, New York: Vintage.

Puett, Michael (2002), *To Become a God: Cosmology, Sacrifice, and Self-Divinization in Early China*, Cambridge, MA: Harvard University Asia Center.

Putnam, Hilary (1987), *The Many Faces of Realism*, La Salle, IL: Open Court.

Putnam, Hilary (1990), *Realism with a Human Face*, Cambridge, MA: Harvard University Press.

Said, Edward W. (1978), *Orientalism*, New York: Pantheon Books.

Sivin, Nathan (1974), "Foreword," in Manfred Porkert (ed.), *The Theoretical Foundations of Chinese Medicine*, Cambridge, MA: MIT Press.

Slingerland, Edward (2013), "Body and Mind in Early China: An Integrated Humanities–Science Approach," *Journal of the American Academy of Religions*, 81 (1): 6–55.

Slingerland, Edward (2019), *Mind and Body in Early China: Beyond Orientalism and the Myth of Holism*, Oxford: Oxford University Press.

Slingerland, Edward (2019), "Response to Jim Behuniak," *Dao: A Journal of Comparative Philosophy*, 18 (3): 485–8.
Taylor, Charles (1989), *Sources of the Self: The Making of Modern Identity*, Cambridge, UK: Cambridge University Press.
Whitehead, Alfred North (1938), *Modes of Thought*, New York: Free Press.
Williams, Raymond (1976), *Keywords: A Vocabulary of Culture and Society*, New York: Oxford University Press.
Zhang, Longxi (1999), "Translating Cultures: China and the West," in Karl-Heinz Pohl (ed.), *Chinese Thought in a Global Context: A Dialogue between Chinese and Western Philosophical Approaches*, 29–46, Leiden: Brill.

4

From the Écart[1] to the Unfamiliar: Thinking Paths—Reference Points

François Jullien
(trans. Steven Burik)

– An attentive reader: To learn Chinese so as to better read Plato, that is finally over.

Or maybe it starts more radically. One does not stop wanting to go back to what might be at the beginning of one's thinking, one's *arche*. And then, thinking comes only afterward.

– A detour through China, but at the same time a return to philosophy. At the same time, and not afterwards. Or else one never comes back: one specializes, one becomes sinicized. You seem to at least move away from that strategy which has prevailed in your work for so many years. This back and forth is no longer central.

What I don't move away from, in any case, is a certain bareness of thought which I went, from Greece, to seek in China. What happens to thinking if it abandons its grand concepts: Being, God, Truth, Liberty—the grand theoretical four? When one cannot fall back on the history of questions and especially when one abandons the language that carries them. When one abandons the "Europe of the ancient parapets." Or what must thinking undertake if it wants to turn against its heritage and, not so much to uproot itself, but to *get unstuck*? Not to critique a preceding philosophy but to undermine its particular foundation, a foundation that it does not know and that we need to make explicit.

This is the road I always follow.

Sinology?

– Let us reprise this development to its beginning, even if I imagine you are weary to return to it. What is your current relationship to sinology? Still conflicting? Yet you have unmistakably asserted to be a sinologist. We know from interviews that after a first trip to China, you have followed classes, in Hong Kong, with the last of the great Confucians, Xu Fuguan and Mou Zongsan, and even that you were the sole

European in the room (Marchaisse 2000, Martin and Spire 2011). Whoever opens La Valeur Allusive or The Propensity of Things, or Detour and Access, or The Great Image has no Form, etc. can see for themselves the extent of your readings in classical Chinese, and also how closely you have read those texts, that is to say first in their commentaries. For can one read classical Chinese otherwise? Besides, you have contributed to popularize this education in classical Chinese in France, at a time when only Contemporary China was studied, first and foremost at Paris 8, and then in the different departments of Chinese studies in Paris. On that score, you have even assumed administrative or representative functions, as President of the French Association of Chinese Studies or Director of the UFR Oriental Asia at Paris-Diderot for six years. And yet …

One has to first say where one's desire comes from. Or why does one want to study Chinese? I chose to learn Chinese to draw a reflexive use from it when I was at the École Normale, as a young Hellenist, educated by Bollack and Vernant. Because one would often say, "We are the heirs of the Greeks," but what does one know of that heritage? How does one measure it, as long as one hasn't left it? So I decided to go to China to leave the Greek "heritage" and to interrogate it from outside. From *outside* of our history in Europe, and that excluded also the Arabic world, which is so close to our history. As from outside of our language, the European or rather Indo-European language, and that excludes India and parts ways with the great preceding generation, that of Benvéniste and Dumézil who went from Greek to Sanskrit. I wanted to try a different route, at the worst moment in the history of contemporary China (at the very end of the Cultural Revolution). Another entry route into philosophy—from the Chinese *outside*. A way of putting in perspective where I came from or to take a step back, in my mind. That is why I "externed" to study in Beijing.

Another reason added itself, which I sensed from the beginning, but which I have only been able to justify in retrospect. Going to China was a way to avoid having to choose a philosophical specialization: moral philosophy, aesthetics, or political philosophy. Because in the feeling of dispossession experienced while facing the unknown Chinese, such sectorization of thought immediately lost its pertinence. Because from the outset everything in thinking is undermined, and all at once.

– It's from having studied Chinese, without this being a specialization in Chinese for you, for so long, regardless of how slow Sinological learning is, at least without setting it as a goal, that your divorce from Sinology comes, or part of it does at least. Also in China your work is sometimes suspect, because its objective is not to celebrate Chinese culture.

For me, the point has been, from the beginning, to make Chinese thought serve as a source of interrogation *emerging from somewhere else*. From outside of the European filiation, and so cut off from it at the outset. So we are forced to return to European thought to interrogate it from the outside, in its embedded choices, its biases, or, in other words, its "obviousness." That means, in fact, its unthought nature. In short, to make use of Chinese thought as a grand *theoretical operator*. This is what I have said again and again. But who among the Sinologists has effectively understood this choice? One cannot understand it if one does not have even a bit of imagination.

– *Since you do not occupy yourself solely with China, you have been classified as a 'comparativist' (Jullien 2020).*

Which I am evidently not. Because *comparing* is to go through similarities and differences, to remain on the surface. Between China and Europe, either one privileges the differences and one isolates those cultures from one another (so one practices "culturalism"), or one privileges the similarities and sinks into a dull humanism badly concealing its ethnocentrism.

What I do is entirely different: by arranging a face-to-face between Chinese and European thought, I allow them to reflect on one another as well as from one another. That means to search in the other its own theoretical assumptions, the buried choices from which it has thought, in short, to go back to its *unthought*. Each one thereby "de-constructs" itself through the other. What I call the "unthought" is that from which one starts to think but of which one thinks not: that on which one's thinking leans.

– *You have been reproached for saying "Chinese thought," when it is so diverse, first of all due to its history. I know you have already responded a hundred times to this objection. But once more, one last time (Jullien 2007a).*

This is why I say more explicitly: Chinese "language-thought." For me this is rather simple: "Chinese thought" is not some mythical or transhistorical entity but thought which is written (conceived) in Chinese. The same goes for "European" thought. It is not that the language determines the thinking, but it does predispose it and serves as its most primary resource. One cannot neglect the gap between a language which declines its nouns and one that does not, one that conjugates its verbs and one that does not, one that possesses a very elaborate syntactical construction and one that is quasi without grammar (like classical Chinese is), one that possesses the verb "to be" or not, and so on. This I have repeated many times. But if one has not experienced this or has not reflected on it …

– *You have also been reproached for neglecting contexts.*

I do not neglect contexts, but I do not limit myself to them (is the pleasure of showing off one's erudition not somewhat foolish?): context intervenes discretely in the construction of my encounters, because I always start by following a singular thread of coherence (this text, that commentary, of which I clarify the reference)—there is indeed no thought that is not singular. But at the same time, I allow myself to abstract in order to forge, from that basis, concepts and questions.

The concept is not exempt from *context*; one always begins from a certain context, but one's concern about the context does not prohibit the work of the concept. Otherwise this contextualization is an evasion: a heap of footnotes that have an appearance of erudition. Anyway, one has given up from the start on philosophy. We will have nothing in French but a tedious *History of Chinese Thought*, a retelling of the one written by the Chinese themselves; or otherwise one that doesn't question—not having the means to do so, because it hasn't begun such reflective work—the pertinence of the European categories that we import into it underhand.

We can do something so much more useful, and what to me seems urgent: to think with Chinese thought; and to a greater extent, to reconfigure the field of the thinkable through the reflexive relations that take place between languages and ways of thought around the world. For Europeans, this doesn't mean giving up their Reason while leaning toward the thinking of the Far East but to put it back under construction. This is what has seemed to me very interesting to pursue. But it is true that in Orientalism, the more boring one is, the more scholarly one seems. Or else one popularizes.

– *Nevertheless, is excessive generalization not a danger? "Chinese" thought (or "European" thought) is so diverse.*

It is infinitely diverse in all the singular paths that have been opened up in it, and during so many centuries. But we will have to take into account what I call here the *background of understanding* (*fond(s) d'entente*), background (*fond*) as in background noise or music but also stocks (*fonds*) that are a resource: this unspoken background *starting from which* ways of thinking, be it in China or in Europe, can enter into opposition and discussion with each other but which itself stays largely implicit between ways of thinking that are in effect most diverse. As Zhuangzi magnificently says, "In all discussion there is the unspoken." It is this *unspoken implicit* of the Chinese language-thought at the end of Antiquity (between the thinkers of the "Hundred Schools") or in the seventeenth century (Wang Fuzhi) that I have sought to make appear, by putting it in perspective and confrontation with a European language-thought that is exterior to it. This means there is no comparison between these languages and thoughts, but it is *reflection* of the one through the other. Likewise, on the Greek side: this *background of understanding* that constitutes the *logos* or the verb "to be," including in Heraclitus.

The diversity between thoughts is thus even more perceptible when one sees it emerge from this shared unspoken, or let's say from this secret alliance that escapes them for a large part and only lets itself be perceived from outside, and that makes it possible for thinkers who oppose one another to nevertheless understand each other. Rather it is because they can sufficiently understand each other that they can oppose each other.

So what I call *background of understanding* is that common source of thinking from which those who share it, even without knowing they share it, can think and discuss. It always has a particular configuration, but not the one of the *episteme* which Foucault describes, because what one sees *from the outside* between thoughts that have been unaware of each other, like those of China and Europe, is not what one sees *from the inside*, through "archaeology," which is more sensitive to the effects of rupture.

This is why one must read from *as close as possible* (the singularity of a meaning) but also from *as far as possible* (by moving back and putting in perspective: which constitutes its condition of possibility); or *from the inside* ("rupturalism") *and from the outside*, where the old notion of "tradition," which one thought buried, suddenly resumes service.

> – But we sometimes perceive threads of coherence from the Chinese side that, in a minor way, can recall those of the Greeks; and reciprocally (Jullien 2006).

This is most interesting: on one side we perceive outlines of threads of coherence that we see unfold on the other side. For example, with those whom we call the Mohists at the end of Chinese antiquity, we perceive a taste for definition, refutation, or geometry that reminds us of what we know of the Greeks. This is what I call to *glimpse*: those Mohists "glimpsed" elements of logic that are familiar to us, like causality, but which remained marginal, covered up, and undeveloped in Chinese thought. So the question is then to understand why those threads of coherence did not evolve, in China, into a thinking of "truth" such as philosophy developed.

Because cultures are always in relations of power both internally and externally: the prevailing threads of coherence in them bury other possibilities. Consider, the other way around, Heraclitus, whose "mobilism" and coherence of opposites are not dissimilar to what Chinese thought has developed in full but which on the European side remained suppressed for so long under the building of ontology.

> – You have been reproached in this respect for "essentializing" Chinese thought.

Conceptualizing is not essentializing. An *abstract* concept does not define. But it is the definitions that essentialize. A concept serves as a thinking tool. The only question is: is it capable of serving this purpose? I do not define Chinese thought to determine what will be its identity, but I employ it as a resource to produce concepts.

> – And so the reproach of "culturalism"?

I reject simplistic universalism, which is an ethnocentrism unaware of itself, as much as the lazy relativism which encloses cultures in their own world. But I have tried, on the basis of both Chinese thought and European thought, to produce concepts which render them intelligible to one other, exerted as they themselves are by this demand of the universal which is the calling of the concept.

Whoever has read me knows. I am tired of repeating myself. The obstacle is evidently elsewhere. Those who have disseminated such critiques have done so because they haven't read me. Or rather they have done so not to have to read me.

> – These are, however, their best arguments.

You know very well that what is essential is in the unsaid. I have never been able to have a debate with a sinologist opposed to my work. Even the author of a certain *Contre François Jullien* was invited on multiple occasions, and first by myself, but has always recused himself.

– So one moves on.

I don't care anymore. It's in the past.

– You go forward.

The Deconstruction of Ontology

– Your initial concepts were more directly influenced by Chinese thought. It is through them that you have undertaken your deconstruction of ontology from outside.

Because you know this major fact that the Chinese language does not speak of "Being" in the absolute sense of "I am," *to be or not to be*,[2] but only in terms of predication. It is in this opening that I got involved as a young Hellenist: how do we think if we proceed *outside of* Being? In other words, outside of the entrenched opposition between "being" and "non-being," or presence and absence, since "being," according to the Greek (of Heidegger), is "being present." When one thus leaves what appears to me characteristic of the thought of being: the idea of assigning. To "assign" is to confer to each "being" its proper place and, by extension, its "property." So it is the concepts which escape this elementary operation of the Greeks of determination by *assigning*, that I have tried first to elaborate based on the threads of coherence in Chinese thought.

– And first of all that of the "allusive," to which the "evasive" responds (Jullien 1985, 2012a).

The thought of the *allusive* has remained underdeveloped in European thought, limited to the rhetorical figure of allusion, with the exception perhaps of German Romanticism, yet it is a thought which precisely seeks to emancipate itself from the great reign of Being. "Underdeveloped" as opposed to the great unfolding that the *symbolic* has seen in Europe; the symbolic which is inscribed in the ontological structure separating the sensible from the intelligible, becoming its very image. But the relation promoted by the *allusive* is no longer one of resemblance but of reference: the word comes to "play alongside" (the Latin says *ad-ludere*) what would be the object of speech, but here it is precisely no longer an "object" that one can circumscribe and determine, the relation within the allusive remaining weak, implicit, effusive, in short "evasive."

The *evasive* signals the modality of what is (in contrast to the *assigned*) diffused, forceful, and invasive (in China according to the code of the "wind," *feng* 风). But we are too limited in Europe to grasp that. Exactly because there is nothing left there to grasp ontologically, and assigning is lost in it. Proofs of this are to be found in our notions of "air," of "atmosphere" or of "influence," which are so limited and which only serve to indicate that which escapes from the grasp of the subject and, by extension, from its control. Is it not the worst thing for the subject to be "under the influence," deprived of its freedom? But from these perceived threads of coherence in Chinese thought, I have tried to make concepts that can serve in those fields where the heritage of ontology can be an obstacle to their development, like the fields of aesthetics or psychoanalysis.

- *Likewise, you have also taken the Chinese notion of blandness and made it into a concept–the most discreet one maybe—of the deconstruction of ontology. For blandness is not only the most evanescent or evasive flavor, it undoes first of all the distinction between the sensible and non-sensible, that which the Greeks thought as "being," which means as being the "intelligible" (Jullien 2007b).*

In taking shape at the head of flavor or in its retreat, *blandness* is the flavor which does not let itself be assigned, confined, and specified. Because it is indeed a flavor, but it is not pronounced enough to let itself be separated: between sweet *or* sour, salty *or* sugary. It is the flavor which does not allow itself to be chosen, or thereby lost, amongst the indefinite possibilities of savoring.

Blandness makes us thereby go back to the threshold of the sensible, into the *transition* of the perceptible and the imperceptible, without thereby having to introduce a "distinction" between them, as indeed the great platonic founding gesture of ontology did.

- *Hence the concept of availability which you have elaborated from different fields in Chinese culture. Blandness is the flavor that remains available; and the same can be said of bland music, a bland feeling, a bland painting: they let us "move at ease," without imposing anything. One even speaks of blandness as the most important quality of the Sage (Jullien 1998).*

In contrast to the ideal of liberty that has carried European thought, I regard *availability* as a disposition that refuses to have to choose between possibilities so as not to deprive itself of any possibility.

Confucius remains available: he is neither pro nor contra; he does not "dig his heels in"; if he needed to take charge, he took it; if he needed to let it go, he let it go. Availability is keeping one's position open, which means not to have a fixed position: to accommodate all possibilities, to remain in what is otherwise called the *com-possible*. Any determination, as one knows, is at the same time deprivation.

- *This availability applies in art (Jullien 2012b).*

The great image that "has no form" is the one that does not let itself be actualized, determined, reified, in any fixed form, which as such is particular and limiting.

- *But can one not fix a position in politics? Can one not be "against" in a clear-cut manner, when it comes to politics?*

Is this not why the Chinese "literati," those who teach us to think without taking position, were at the same time unable to promote themselves to the position of *intellectuals*? And always stayed in the shadow of the Emperor.

– This is why you contrast Chinese availability to the thought of the ideal, which is founded on the ontological distinction between the sensible and intelligible: the ideal is the ideational abstracted from the sensible, extracted from its impurity and carried over to the absolute of the eidos, but which Plato ingeniously connected to the most passionate desire, eros (Jullien 2009).

"Ideal" is a European term, for one finds it equally in all the European languages: it is a term that has made Europe, which one should not forget now that this notion, which from Plato onward through the Renaissance and culminating in Romanticism has *made tradition* in Europe, is abandoned and has even become suspect. However, it has for so long carried the ambition of art as well as that of politics (revolution). It may even be that Europe cannot be made, today, because it has renounced the "ideal." Actually, we no longer want this rupture between the schemes of the phenomenal and the concrete on one side, and on the other the scheme of ideality separated abstractly—arbitrarily?—from experience, which seems an "escape." But this ontological distinction has nevertheless made possible, by the institution of this scheme of ideality, the promotion of classical European and Galilean science, departing from the empirical to ideally account for it by mathematical modelling.

One also has to consider how this "daring" ideal ("one has to dare," *tolmeteon*, that grand Platonic verb) may have allowed theoretical effects; but also, given that this ideal finds itself connected to desire, the mobilization of wills, as a result of the promotion of subjectivity.

– It is from this ideality that the "beautiful" advanced itself in the classical age in Europe, exerting its hegemony on art for many centuries. Because it is in pursuit of that absolute of the exemplary form, the eidos, detached from the sensible (Jullien 2015).

The "beautiful" is actually perched on this pedestal of ontology, and it is this pedestal that it exposes. That is why it has been the backbone of metaphysics, teaching us to abandon the diversity of the sensible to abstract the unity of the idea from it: the Beautiful/Good (*Le Beau*). But that is also why, in return, it hits us even more violently with "fright"—turmoil—by its absolute bursting into the midst of the sensible.

But the critical Chinese tradition has not isolated—abstracted—the "beautiful/good," and this is expressed, once again, in the binominal, by correlation of opposite and complementary terms: "flourishing/smooth," "limpid/attractive," "secret/elegant," and so on. And since it does not commit the ontological distinction of the sensible and intelligible, the ambition of the artist is to "transmit" a spiritual dimension (*chuan shen* 传神) right through the sensible.

– This modelling of the Beautiful/Good is embodied by the Nude (painting). A Nude is not empirical (Jullien 2007c).

That there was no "Nude" in Chinese art makes us look in return for the buried biases from which the *tradition* of the Nude in Europe proceeds, from sculpture to painting, to photography, strangely interposing itself between the desire of the flesh and the shamefulness of nudity. The Nude emerges in the immediacy of the sensible, while at the same time it is the privileged terrain of modelling, overturning this sensible of the flesh in the form that would be *ideal*: the "canonical" beauty. Based on its impossibility in China and reflecting from it, the Nude discovers as its condition of possibility, apart from geometricization, choices that are after all so singular. Especially the decomposition of the body in parts and their recomposition in a whole: from analysis to synthesis, from anatomy to harmony. Or the incarnation of the being through its presence, *ousia* as *parousia*; just as its elevation into the essence, for example of heroism or the genius: to sculpt Napoleon nude.

In China, however, the body is rather a quasi-formless bag of breath-energy of which one should most carefully follow the circulation (as in acupuncture).

– *This is also why you oppose the European conception of landscape—again a European word or a word that "makes Europe" by its semantic composition which is similar from one language to the other (paesaggio, and* land-schap, Land-schaft, land-scape[3]*)—to the way in which the landscape is expressed (or thought) in Chinese language-thought. On the European side, the horizon is cut out based on the position of the subject. On the Chinese side, the landscape is the great correlation of the "mountain(s)-water(s)," shan-shui* 山水: *of what is high and what is low, or what has form (the mountain) and what has no form (water), of what is immobile (the mountain) and what is mobile (water), or of what one sees (the mountain) and what one hears (water) (Jullien 2014).*

In Europe, landscape is conceived from the position of the subject, from the primacy accorded to visual perception, from the relation between the parts and the whole—choices that are constitutive for European thought.

But the Chinese language-thought thinks not by *composition* ("syntax"), but by *correlation* and dynamic tension. This is also why it could not carry out—or didn't have to—the great ontological distinction of the visible and the invisible-intelligible, the foundation of ontology.

If landscape thinking is so developed in China, it is because it promotes a decanting of the sensible, giving access to the spiritual, *but without abandoning* the sensible. Just as blandness is the "flavor beyond flavor" as the unfolding of flavor because it is no longer confined to the sensible, so landscape is celebrated as "the landscape beyond landscape." "Beyond" by disengaging, in its *aura*, but not by separation and transposition to an ideal plane, as the *meta* of metaphysics has it.

– *All these concepts and these preceding courses are related and even overlapping. That is why they remain active, actual, in your work (cf. David 2016).*

By reflecting between Chinese and European thoughts, between ontology and dis-ontologization, a problematic field has indeed opened itself up and is even becoming immense. We will never finish surveying this field. But we can already begin to make the most of it—on the basis of these anchoring points—toward a *general philosophy*, maybe even more "general" than in its traditional questioning.

Displacements

– Another branch of your concepts is in the strategic range. They have been used in the world of management to think about efficacy. But they equally proceed from a similar dis-ontologization and introduce a displacement with respect to European thought. To displace: (décaler) to move aside (déplacer), but also to remove the hold (la cale)— the hold of ontology (Jullien 1995a, 2004a, 2005).

The most common conception of efficacy in Europe, the one that comes to us from Greek philosophy and is not the archaic *mètis* (wisdom or skill) as embodied by Ulysses, teaches us to come up with a plan and to reason in terms of means and ends (the *business plan*).[4] What we find there is the primacy accorded to the ideal form, to the *eidos* detached from the empirical. But Chinese thought draws our attention to the favorable conditions contained in the situation itself, serving as carrying factors, and which must be taken advantage of to succeed: this is what I have called, from a Chinese term (*shi* 势), its *potential of the situation*. So the "situation" is then no longer this adverse reality, as "circum-stance" (again a European word: *peri-stasis*, *Um-stand*, etc.)[5], a circumstance on which, and against which, must be imposed what we set as goal. Rather it is the resource that one has to know how to develop to one's profit: it is a case, then, no longer of *projecting* (an imperative) but of *detecting* (a propensity); no longer of *modelling* (a plan), but of *maturing* (conditions). This has led to the conceiving of the "great general" as the one who gains "easy" victories because he knew how to discretely cultivate favorable factors and reduce the ones that were not, so that the situation deflects itself as a slope from which the effects flow down and from which he can harvest the ripe fruit without having to go to battle. An understanding that is effectively *strategic*, resting on the processual unwinding, in a long-lasting and consequential relation of condition, rather than *heroic*, by counting on the momentary action where the will is maximally invested in accordance with a concerted plan.

But I nevertheless do not renounce *modelling*, in politics as well as in business. Because one has to model to *mobilize* (willpower): we make plans not so much to apply them (are we so naïve?), but more to publicly propose the direction that we want to go and to establish it as a chosen and shared ideal. This is so that, instead of manipulating others underhand, without them even knowing about it (their troops, their teams), one can treat them as subjects freely giving their assent.

– Which is related to your conception of "silent transformations" (Jullien 2011).

I call *silent transformation* a transformation that proceeds without noise, therefore one that is not spoken of. Silence from two sides. This transformation is silent because it is global and continuous. It does not stand out, so we do not notice it, so to speak. But afterward, we observe its effect. And this effect is even more perceptible, as an *auditory event*, given that we did not perceive the path of the preceding transformation.

– But why "silent" and not invisible, as one would expect?

To understand this we must oppose the sense of hearing to the sense of sight, and to that end, move from Greece to China. *The sense of sight* is a sense of the local (I look here or there) and of the discontinuous (I open or close my eyes): it is the sense that Greek thought has privileged, considering it to be closest to intelligence.

The *sense of hearing* on the other hand is the sense of the global (I hear equally well behind my head) and the continuous (even if I want to close my ears I will still hear). But it is the sense that Chinese thought has privileged. To say "intelligent" one says "hearing-seeing" (*cong-ming* 聪明), hearing before sight. Because sight will search in the world for that which is "thrown" (*jeté*) before it and forms an obstacle to it: its "ob-ject" (*son ob-jet*); but hearing gathers as in a horn—this is why one has to lend an ear to the silent transformations that discretely make their way, continuously and globally, without alerting.

The Chinese strategist operates through silent transformation, this is why she "does not act" but makes (lets) the situation grow or mature: when it has reached maturity, there is nothing more to do than harvest (*li* 利 in Chinese), without there strictly speaking being a "target" or "aim" (*skopos* says Greek) methodically fixing in advance "goals" to attain (*telos*) by detaching them from the processuality of things, even if that means tragically forcing destiny.

– *But this concept of silent transformation is not only strategic. Because what in the world would not arise from silent transformation?*

To this we do not lend any attention, but then it comes back right in our faces even more vociferously. Climate warming is an example, global and continuous as it is. Or even ageing is another example: we do not perceive ourselves ageing because it is everything in us that ages and over a length of time. Until we come across a photo from twenty years ago: only then we realize, with surprise, the result. In short, I scarcely see anything in the world that could escape from this concept. In psychoanalysis, is a cure not a silent transformation? In art, is it not that which video represents? Or would it not equally be the case with dance?

– *This focus on silent transformation presupposes a different approach to what we call "time" (Jullien 2001).*

To the extent that there is no explicit concept of "time" in classical Chinese, that is before the invasion of European thought.

With regards to time the Chinese in fact know neither the physical approach to it (Aristotle), that of the trajectory of a moving body from point A to point B; nor the metaphysical approach (Plato-Plotinus) separating becoming from Being, or time from eternity; nor the linguistic approach via conjugation (past/present/future), as Chinese does not conjugate.

On the other hand, the Chinese language-thought thinks the "season" (the moment-occasion: *shi* 时) and through the recurrence of the seasons, duration (*jiu* 久). The duration of processes, of periods and worlds, and the duration of "maturations." But it does not think the homogenous-abstract time that European thought set up as a framework a priori to experience and thought. At the same time as it continues to recognize an enigma there.

– *The same goes for the concepts of indirectness and obliqueness, which emphasize the processual. They equally displace us from ontological assigning and are not solely strategic (Jullien 2004b).*

In the Chinese strategy of maturing, the *oblique*, as opposed to the *frontal*, makes it possible to operate in the duration, processually and through discreet gestation: rather than attacking head-on, in a dramatic confrontation, I prefer to engage in an exposition that indirectly unsettles my opponent bit by bit, and hence without him having the chance or occasion to retaliate.

But this opposition between the frontal and the indirect is also a political one. The Greek city-state is organized in a frontal way, one camp against the other, on the model of a pitched battle, phalanx against phalanx; and democracy equally demands frontality, to organize itself in a debate: in the *agon* and at the *agora*.

It is the same in philosophy: thesis/antithesis. Because if one discourse can advance one idea, says Protagoras, you need two opposed discourses to prove its truth. And when alone, I think of objections to make to myself.

In fact, the conceptual couple of "frontal" and "indirect" applies in numerous practices: instead of approaching from the front, which risks giving rise to a resistance, proceed from the side to "sidestep" the difficulty. In pedagogy: not to lecture or impose the lesson, against which one can stand up, but to lead to comprehension. We seek not to *persuade*, the grand Greek verb (*peithein*), since the other can refute; but to *influence* by conditioning (*feng-hua* 讽化)—without the other even realizing it and without there being room to resist. We do not say it explicitly, but let the meaning make its way indirectly: the Chinese art of the *allusive*. In either case, it is counting on the efficacy of a processual unwinding rather than on an effort of *imposition* of the subject.

– *This is why the Chinese language-thought, thinking the processual, has not developed the great myth of Creation (Jullien 1989, 2012c).*

There is no beginning of time and no end of time, but a continuous transformation is at work through correlation of the breath-energies, opposed and complementary, the famous *yin* and *yang*. The world dies every day, the world is born every day. Neither the grand opening of the Genesis, nor the grand closing of the apocalypse. China has not thought the position of an exterior God who, through his sovereign action, creates the world and opens time out of eternity.

– *What you say regarding the importance of indirectness, of conditioning, of influence, leads us to ask about the morality of the Chinese. If action is not emphasized, then neither is the choice which decides the action, nor, as a consequence, the freedom which such choice requires. Would it not be the case then, in China, of a social morality, of a regulation of behaviors, or could it nevertheless be established as a prerogative of the subject (Jullien 1995b)?*

What we translate so badly as "rite" or "ritual" (but how to translate otherwise seeing that we do not have any equivalent?) ensures, as a behavioral matrix, the channeling or the "containing" of desires, without thereby requiring their extinction, so without asceticism, at least before the entry of Buddhism in China.

On the other hand, if the Chinese have not thought behavior in terms of "actions" as separable units requiring each time an initiative of the subject, it is because they have conceived behavior in terms of a "course," in its continuity, along the lines or on the model of the course of "Heaven" (天行). Like such a course, behavior should neither deviate nor become obstructed—"evil" or "wrong" (*le Mal*) is itself nothing but such deviation and obstruction.

Or if they have not thought in terms of "will," it is because they have disregarded or overlooked the tragic distinction between what happens "voluntarily" and "involuntarily" (*ekôn/akôn*), from which arises the Aristotelian framework of "deliberation" and "preferential choice," before the rise of Augustin's *voluntas*, understood as the originary capacity of the subject compared to God. But the Chinese have thought behavior in terms of "propensity" (toward the good, in Mencius), of deflection and efficacy: Mencius does not say I "want," but I "do."

> *– In Europe we have constructed an ontology of the subject corresponding to the ontology of Being and presiding over action as the other presides over knowledge. It suffices to recall that the sub-ject is originally (physically) the "under-lying sub-stratum" of change, itself remaining the same, as is the sub-stance as the underlying sup-port of the things. But how can we implement any morality without this anchoring of the subject in Being?*

But it is precisely this insulated position of the "subject" vis-à-vis the world that has led us in Europe to a narrow, paradoxical, and very "mysterious" conception of "sympathy" which is nonetheless so often placed at the "foundation" of morality. Instead, in China, the reaction of "humaneness," when faced with the unbearable as it happens to the other, attests to a radical solidarity of existence to existence (the Confucian *ren* 仁) that can extend itself progressively to the totality of the greater Process of the world. Through this an access is opened to the unconditional, "Heaven," which does not require an ontological distinction, classic to Europe, between a "self" conditioned in the world and another "noumenal" me with a metaphysical status as the subject of freedom.

> *– In classical Europe it is sincerity that has constituted the foundation of a moral subjectivity in its relation with the other and firstly with God who sees into one's heart. What if such a sincerity is not promoted (Jullien 2020)?*

I do not actually translate *xin* 信 by sincerity, as is usually done, but rather by "reliability." From *reliability* follows the "viability" of relations. Not to say what one thinks, but to keep to what one says. Not the transparency of conscience, but confidence. However, confidence is also not a matter of a momentary choice or of a concerted action, it does not proceed from a command, but arises by "progressive accumulation," as virtue does, and over time. It too is *processual*.

> – *Proceeding accordingly through displacements between Chinese and European thought, you inevitably come up against the problem of translation, as one can see here. Or even of its impossibility, as you go against the logic of translation, which is in search of equivalences. You have also been reproached for your literal translations or translations that are not sufficiently "natural" in French, that do not "flow"* (Jullien 2006).

Translating is actually not assimilating. But assimilation is still the naïve, unquestioned, and unconscious ideal in Sinology. Even if this means that the translator then adds a pinch of exoticism to make it appear Chinese or to make it appear poetic. I have given numerous examples of this in my work, even the most recent. Of course, translating is searching for equivalences from one language to another, but at the same time in the translation we should not lose sight of, and even seek to suggest, that which *resists* those equivalences. Which can only be done precisely by deconstruction, and this with a view to reconstruct on that basis a heterotopic framework, as a reflexive counterpart, which would serve as the condition of possibility for this translation. One must then both *de*-categorize and *re*-categorize, that is to say, undo the choices imposed by our language to open it to the possibilities of the other. All the *displacements* that I organize in a network making room for a concerted translatability of Chinese to French serve this purpose.

Translating is then both assimilating and dissimilating: to maintain oneself as long as possible *in between languages* where the possibilities, from one language to the other, are reflected; and in this reflective *in-between*, to re-elaborate the resources of the one with respect to the other, in order to open it up to this in-between on the basis of its own fruitful exigency of which it was unaware.

> – *It is in this operative in-between, opened by the écart (or gap), that a translation becomes possible. Or else* (Jullien 2012c, 2012d)?

See for example the translation of the *Laozi* in French (the editions of Seuil or Gallimard or others). "Being" and "non-being" are added, while the Chinese text talks about the "there is"/"there is not" (yet actualized, *you* 有 and *wu* 无), otherwise said the what "there is" (that is actualized) and the undifferentiated—and thus harmonizing— Foundation of things. Added there is the "subject," whereas in Chinese it is not expressed, thereby obstructing the processuality constantly stated by Chinese thought. We conjugate and (syntactically) construct a sentence, whereas the Chinese neither conjugates nor constructs, but thinks through formulation and correlation, and so on. This then seems well translated, "elegant," makes for good French, and of course there is no "mistake" in translation. But the text so translated signifies *something entirely different* than the original. One has come back home: the translation has arranged the foreign text into our habitus, has conformed it to our expectations. It is no more than the facsimile of our own thought, the moon in relation to the sun.

Notes

1. *Translator's note*: Although the standard meaning of "écart" is gap, Jullien understands this as an opening of betweenness instead of exclusion. We have therefore chosen not to translate "écart" here in the title.
2. *Translator's note*: "*to be or not to be*" is in English and italicized in the original.
3. *Translator's note*: The words "paesaggio," "land-schap," "Land-schaft," and "land-scape" appear in their original languages here.
4. *Translator's note*: *business plan* in English in original.
5. *Translator's note*: *Um-stand* in German in original.

References

David, Pascal (2016), *Penser la Chine: Interroger la philosophie avec François Jullien*, Paris: Hermann.
Jullien, François (1985), *La Valeur allusive*, Paris: Publications de L'Ecole française d'Extrême-Orient.
Jullien, François (1989), *Procès ou Creation, Une introduction à la pensée de letters chinois*, Paris: Seuil.
Jullien, François (1995a), *The Propensity of Things: Toward a History of Efficacy in China*, New York: Zone Books.
Jullien, François (1995b), *Fonder la Morale, Dialogue de Mencius avec un philosophe des Lumières*, Paris: Grasset.
Jullien, François (1998), *Un Sage est Sans Idée, Ou l'Autre de la Philosophie*, Paris: Seuil.
Jullien, François (2001), *Du "temps," éléments d'une philosophie du vivre*, Paris: Grasset.
Jullien, François (2004a), *A Treatise on Efficacy*, Honolulu: University of Hawaii Press.
Jullien, François (2004b), *Detour and Access: Strategies of Meaning in China and Greece*, Cambridge, MA: MIT Press.
Jullien, François (2005), *Conférence sur l'efficacité*, Paris: PUF.
Jullien, François (2006), *Si Parler Va sans Dire, Du Logos et d'Autres Ressources*, Paris: Seuil.
Jullien, François (2007a), *Chemin Faisant, Connaître la Chine, Relancer la Philosophie*, Paris: Seuil.
Jullien, François (2007b), *In Praise of Blandness: Proceeding from Chinese Thought and Aesthetics*, New York: Zone Books.
Jullien, François (2007c), *The Impossible Nude: Chinese Art and Western Aesthetics*, Chicago: University of Chicago Press.
Jullien, François (2009), *L'Invention de l'Ideal et le Destin de l'Europe*, Paris: Seuil.
Jullien, François (2011), *The Silent Transformations*, London: Seagull Books.
Jullien, François (2012a), *Cinq concept proposes à la psychanalyse*, Paris: Grasset.
Jullien, François (2012b), *The Great Image Has No Form, or on the Nonobject through Painting*, Chicago: University of Chicago Press.

Jullien, François (2012c), *Entrer dans une Pensée, Ou des possibles de l'esprit*, Paris: Gallimard.
Jullien, François (2012d), *L'Écart et l'entre*, Paris: Galilée.
Jullien, François (2014), *Vivre de paysage, Ou l'impensé de la raison*, Paris: Gallimard.
Jullien, François (2015), *This Strange Idea of the Beautiful*, London: Seagull Books.
Jullien, François (2020), *From Being to Living: A Euro-Chinese Lexicon of Thought*, trans. Michael Richardson, London: Sage.
Marchaisse, Thierry (2000), *Penser d'un Dehors (la Chine): Entretiens d'Extrême-Occident*, Paris: Seuil.
Martin, Nicolas, and Antoine Spire (2011), *Chine, La Dissidence de François Jullien*, Paris: Seuil.

Constellation III

Translation

5

Translation as Method

Souleymane Bachir Diagne
(trans. Philippe Major)*

There is a letter, addressed to Lucien Lévy-Bruhl by Husserl, that Maurice Merleau-Ponty considered of the utmost importance, to the extent that he wished it would figure prominently in the philosopher's collected works, which were then being published by the *Husserl Archives Leuven*. In this letter dated March 11, 1935, to which Merleau-Ponty alludes in "The Philosopher and Sociology," Husserl responds to the ethnologist Lévy-Bruhl after reading *Primitive Mythology*, a work the latter had sent to Husserl soon after completing it. Commenting on the letter, Merleau-Ponty (1964: 107) begins by noting that "he seems to admit that the philosopher could not possibly have immediate access to the universal by reflection alone," that he must take into account anthropology, since it is impossible for him "to construct what constitutes the meaning of other experiences and civilizations by a purely imaginary variation of his own experiences." One must find the means to "understand how time passes and being is constituted in these cultures." To this end, one must *go see for oneself*, as the expression goes, and recognize, in Husserl's own words, that "historical relativism is incontestably justified as an anthropological fact" (108) and that one must therefore put "evident facts" "in contact with other cultural formations" (100). In a word, one must submit them to "the experience of the foreign" (in accordance with Antoine Berman's title); one must put them to the test of *translation*.

The significance of this letter commented on thusly by Merleau-Ponty is highlighted by the fact that its stance appears, at first glance, to differ radically from what Husserl vigorously argued a few weeks later in the well-known Vienna lecture of May 7, 1935, on "Philosophy and the Crisis of European Humanity."[1] This lecture no longer addresses the need to "understand," to be put "in contact with other cultural formations," or to concern oneself with "what constitutes the meaning of other experiences and civilizations." On the contrary, Husserl (1965: 157) insists, if the other "humanities" (*humanités*), with the various "historicities" that mark them, have good reasons to "Europeanize themselves," Europe, insofar as it possesses an unbiased understanding of itself and its own telos, recognizes that it does not need, for example, to "Indianize" itself in any way. It is true that this is not "bound to the soil of national traditions," and that the philosophical community that first appeared in Greece grew and evolved by welcoming and assimilating all kinds of "foreigners," whom from then on lost their status of foreigners (174). Yet the fact remains that the insertion in the universal posited by the common language renders translation unnecessary: as long as one understands this language, one is a member of the community.

There is, of course, no contradiction between the letter and the lecture; only a shift in their respective perspectives and stakes. Considering anthropological variations does not entail one must rely in all matters on the positive sciences and the empirical. Yet one must nonetheless take into account—and this is the path taken by Merleau-Ponty—the impossibility of a "universal by reflection alone." Which road, or which method—to conjure up the etymology of the latter—leads to the universal? And first and foremost, of which universal do we speak?

In order to clarify these questions, let me cite a passage from an essay entitled "From Mauss to Claude Lévi-Strauss," in which Merleau-Ponty (1964: 119–20) builds on his commentary of the letter from Husserl to Lévy-Bruhl, reflecting on what the philosophical approach can gain by engaging with anthropology:

> The equipment of our social being can be dismantled and reconstructed by the voyage, as we are able to learn to speak other languages. This provides a second way to the universal: no longer the overarching universal of a strictly objective method, but a sort of lateral universal which we acquire through ethnological experience and its incessant testing of the self through the other person and the other person through the self. It is a question of constructing a general system of reference in which the point of view of the native, the point of view of the civilized man, and the mistaken views each has of the other can all find a place—that is, of constituting a more comprehensive experience which becomes in principle accessible to men of a different time and country.

Let us consider the various facets of this important passage. What is at stake here is *translation*. And method, or a mode of access to this universal that no longer relies on "reflection alone," but is uncovered in the midst of an encounter and confrontation with other ways of saying, other languages. This first of all entails that the attempt to unbuild oneself in order to then rebuild oneself is not the result of an introspective meditation on the self. The *Discourse on the Method* reminds us that it is after the time of voyage and experience that the time of meditation occurs; when in solitude, a retreat from which natural light can shine through brightly, the path "to conduct one's reason well and to search for truth in the sciences" comes to be fully exposed. What Merleau-Ponty says here is that it is not after but during and through voyage, and in the experience of speaking other languages, that the second path to the universal opens itself up. Let me reiterate: "to learn to speak other languages" is of no use as long as one is situated in the location of the universal and in the language that speaks it, in contrast to which the various other idioms would be but more or less confused approximations. It is when such location, such (politically or culturally) imperial or (ontologically) "historical" language, no longer exists and when all human tongues are held as equal that learning other languages proves to be a necessity.

The two universals or the two paths toward the universal discussed by Merleau-Ponty are thus representative of an opposition between the path of recentering and introspection on the one hand, and the path of voyage, of learning languages and decentering on the other. After all, translation is first and foremost exactly that: a method of decentering. On this, we must heed the lesson the poet Goethe taught us when he declared that one who does not know a foreign language does not understand one's own in any way. In terms of our inquiry into "another path towards the universal," the German poet's remark tells us that even when attempting to know oneself, and know oneself in one's own language, a detour through a foreign language and more generally through an other proves to be necessary.

Does this entail that regardless of the language spoken and despite the existence of a plurality of languages, the goal is to say, in a different manner, the same thing, the same universal, in each of them? This is indeed an important question, in answer to which I would like to recall a scene that took place in the tenth century, in 932, in the presence of the Seljuk vizier al-Fadl ibn al-Furat, where a verbal contest between the Arabic grammarian Abu Sa'ld al-Sirafi and the philosopher and logician Abu Bishr Matta ibn Yunus took place. The vizier himself had organized this public confrontation which turned out to be, in the history of philosophy in the Islamic world, somewhat of a symbol: a dramatized representation, as it were, of the opposition between those, represented by Matta, who advocated opening the Muslim world to the sciences and the wisdom of the Greeks and those, having for spokesman Sirafi, for whom the Quranic Word and the sciences that had evolved around it—including the grammar of Arabic, the sacred language of revelation—had to be protected from contamination. It is worth noting that although it now takes different shapes, this opposition still exists today.

Sirafi was particularly troubled by two things: first, by the vanity displayed by the new Arab and/or Muslim philosophers who claimed that logic—*Aristotelian* logic, of course—could serve as a universal scale on which the validity of any reasoning could be judged; and second, by the transformations—or *profanations*, according to Sirafi—that beset, in the process of translating Greek philosophy, an Arabic language of which he saw himself as the faithful custodian. In essence, his violent attack against the philosopher Matta puts forth the following question: how can your Aristotle be considered to have brought to light a grammar of human thought that is not the grammar of a particular language? How could he, to summon Merleau-Ponty's terms, have taught a logical universal that looms over (*surplombe*) all contexts, over the diversity of human languages? What he bestowed to his followers, like Matta, as an object of devotion by presenting it as universal, is it not simply the grammar of his own language—that is, Greek? The violence experienced by the *jus et norma loquendi* of the Arabic language at the hands of philosophers/translators who wish to make it conform to Greek ways of saying cannot but highlight that what is at stakes is a confrontation between two different grammars, including a Greek grammar whose claim to universality has no basis, especially not when facing the language of the revealed Word. It is worth noting, for illustrative purposes, that one of the targets of the astringent grammarian is the artificial use of the copula in cases where it is not common usage in Arabic (the language being reknown, like many others, for being one of "zero copula"). Such philosophers will therefore say "Socrates *he* sick" (*Socrate* huwa *marid*: here the personal pronoun functions as a copula) or "Socrates *is found* sick"

(*Socrate* mawjudun *maridan*) in order to properly conform Arabic to the canonical form of the proposition in Aristotelian logic: S is P.

In the event as reported by historians, Matta is mainly concerned with defending himself against the verbal assault led by his adversary, who of course has the audience on his side. He nevertheless manages to put forth an important argument that relies on the notion of "translatability": the definition of truth itself, the marker of universality, is translatability in all languages. What is true is what can be universally translated without loss of meaning. An arithmetic example naturally comes to Matta's mind, as he says to his interlocutor: "The intelligibles are the same for all men. Don't you see that 4 and 4 make 8 for all nations and that it is thus for all that is alike?"

The question, however, is precisely that of knowing what it is that is indeed alike. Can we extrapolate from what is true in terms of the translatability of mathematical intelligibles, given that mathematics is a language of its own and is thus always already translated, to intelligibles carved out from the very stuff of which the language we speak is made?

Many years ago, when commenting on the debate between the grammarian and the logician, I sided with the latter. I still do, although now I am more sensitive to the truth *also* implied in Sirafi's point of view, even if we must of course abhor the attitude of exclusion, insularity, and isolationism that manifests itself in it.

We must also pay attention to the fact that the Arab grammarian had already expressed, at the beginning of the tenth century, what the French linguist Emile Benveniste would say in a 1958 article titled "Categories of Thought and Language." In this article, Benveniste shows how much the Aristotelian logic attributing a predicate to a subject owes to Greek grammar, and in particular to the nature of the copula "to be," not to mention its significance when compared to a language that is "zero copula."

The lesson we can learn from Sirafi's position, of which Benveniste's article reminds us, is the same one as that which was taught by the philosopher Nietzsche, who saw himself first and foremost as a philologist, as we know. This lesson, which was also that of the Sophists, as Nietzsche himself reminds us, states that all human languages have their depth, that our empirical ways of saying cannot be ignored, and that we cannot simply go through them in order to reach the truly essential—that is, the intelligible. Let me cite, on this point, Nietzsche (2002: 20) himself:

> The strange family resemblance of all Indian, Greek, and German philosophizing speaks for itself clearly enough. Where there are linguistic affinities, then because of the common philosophy of grammar (I mean: due to the unconscious domination and direction through similar grammatical functions), it is obvious that everything lies ready from the very start for a similar development and sequence of philosophical systems; on the other hand, the way seems as good as blocked for certain other possibilities of interpreting the world.

For the present purpose, it suffices to conclude, from Nietzsche's observations on the existence of "philosophies of grammar," that translation, especially when taking place from one philosophy of grammar to another, is a genuine *labor*. A labor that is also one of mourning, as Paul Ricoeur maintains. But a labor that does work, and that always ends up accomplishing its objective, for what is not solely "intelligible" but also simply human can always be translated by another human.

Nietzsche's assertion should not be understood as the expression of a determinism according to which a mode of thought would be mechanically produced by language. As such, we should not think of the philosophies of grammar as confining us in a relativism that says: "to each language, or to each family of languages, corresponds a philosophy that is sustained by it." It is important to measure, a posteriori, the extent to which thinking is inclined to take a particular course due to language and its categories. We know, however, that "to incline" is not "to necessitate," in Leibniz's terms. This issue of language and of its ability to incline the way we think is at the heart of "philosophizing in Africa." It is on this point that I would now like to focus my attention to conclude my discussion. I particularly have in mind, regarding this point, the debates relating to what the Rwandan philosopher Father Alexis Kagame called "linguistic philosophy" that took place on the African continent. Two years prior to the publication of the article by Benveniste mentioned above, Kagame put forth the same argument as that of Sirafi to the effect that the Aristotelian onto-logic was but the grammar of the Greek language. From this, he drew the relativistic conclusion that the main task of philosophers speaking the languages that came into existence and evolved on the African continent was to excavate their own categories of language and thought, and thus bring to light the philosophies unique to them. Kagame, in his relativist fervor, went so far as to declare that since, in the Bantu languages, the sole purpose of the verb "to be" was to serve as copula (which entails that it cannot be used in an absolute way, without a predicate), the cartesian formula *I think therefore I am* "does not make sense" in these languages.

To this, one must reply that it is translation itself that will give it a sense. Wolof, Bantu, or any other language can always use its own resources to translate *Discourse on the Method*, including the *cogito* formula that is a fundamental part of it. Since translating is precisely to overcome relativism. It is concerned with the universal, but a lateral universal. Of this, we can say, as Antoine Berman did, that translation entails an "ethical aim," a "humanist aim." This aim reveals that the point is not to barricade ourselves in the "philosophy of grammar," making of each human idiom a philosophico-linguistic insularity. On the contrary, the objective is to position ourselves first and foremost within the encounter in order to examine language through translation. Barbara Cassin, author of the *Dictionary of Untranslatables*, speaks of "philosophizing in languages," while Séverine Kodjo-Grandvaux writes that our task is to "make of the philosopher a translator."

To better grasp the importance of the issue of translation, it is worth comparing Kagame's relativist remarks (there exists different philosophical grammars and therefore some languages have the cogito while others do not) to the pragmatic approach of Ghanaian philosopher Kwasi Wiredu (1996), as understood from his reflections on "The Concept of Truth in the Akan Language." Wiredu explains clearly that when it comes to the word "truth" in its purely cognitive sense (instead of the moral sense of truthfulness), there exists no Akan word for this concept. This observation is not without analogy to Kagame's comments on the verb "to be," although its goal is to show how this fact puts to the test of translation philosophical issues related to the notion of truth, such as the theory of truth as correspondence between statement and reality. "These linguistic contrasts [between Akan and English]," Wiredu (1996: 107) comments, "have some very interesting consequences for the theory of truth."

Generally speaking, the to-and-fro between English and Akan, the process of translation—that is, of putting them in relation to one another, of submitting them to "the experience of the foreign," in the words of Antoine Berman—enables the Ghanaian philosopher to provide an important reflection on the fact that issues have a way of clarifying themselves, in some way, when we simultaneously inquire about them in English and Akan. This then leads one to ask what a philosophical problem is and what it means for a problem to be universally addressed:

> Although it is, I think, correct to say that a problem like the one about the relation between truth and fact arises out of the nature of the vocabulary of English, it does not follow that it is not a genuine philosophical issue in English. The concepts of truth and fact are among the most fundamental concepts of human thought. Without the notion of something being a fact or of a proposition being true thinking is inconceivable unless it be a mere succession of ideas, and even that can be doubted. It seems obvious then, that the relation between the terms "truth" and "fact" is a philosophical issue; for, of course, one cannot give a fundamental clarification of any of these foundational concepts in English without relating them one to the other. Yet, since these terms need not be both present in all natural languages, as the case of Akan shows, this task is not inescapable for the human mind. From which it follows that some philosophical problems are not universal. (Wiredu 1996: 108-9)

The majority of African philosophers consider that the time has come to give their rightful place to African languages in philosophical reflections taking place on the continent. To liberate them, generally speaking, from the realm of private interactions to which they have been confined, in order to make of them a vehicle for modern sciences and creativity. Paulin Hountondji often reiterates that there are two possible ways of conceptualizing this project. It can be thought of as aiming to produce *another* philosophy, one that would remain close to the ways of saying of its language. This is the relativist path of Kagame, as discussed above. This task can also be understood as a means to think philosophically from within translation and the junction of perspectives. This path, which makes of translation a method, is precisely that which an analysis such as the one offered in "The Concept of Truth in the Akan language" opens up. It is a path that makes it possible to accommodate an authentic concern for the universal with an effective consideration for the pluralism of languages and cultures.

Notes

* This text is a translation from the French original: Souleymane Bachir Diagne (2015), "La traduction comme methode," Selected Papers from the XXIII World Congress of Philosophy, Special Supplement, *Journal of Philosophical Research*, 9-15.

1. *Translator's note*: In the French translation of the Vienna lecture, the title is rendered as "The Crisis of European Humanity and Philosophy," while the English translation renders "*europäischen Menschentums*" by "European Man." I have retained the French emphasis on *humanity*, here, as Bachir Diagne uses this term to point out the gap between theoretical universality (humanity) and historical diversity (humanities), one of the main themes of his essay.

References

Husserl, Edmund (1965), "Philosophy and the Crisis of European Man," in Edmund Husserl (ed.), *Phenomenology and the Crisis of Philosophy*, trans. Quentin Lauer, 149–92, New York: Harper Torchbooks.

Merleau-Ponty, Maurice (1964), "The Philosopher and Sociology," in Maurice Merleau-Ponty (ed.), *Signs*, trans. Richard C. McCleary, 98–113, Evanston, IL: Northwestern University Press.

Merleau-Ponty, Maurice (1964), "From Mauss to Claude Lévi-Strauss," in Maurice Merleau-Ponty (ed.), *Signs*, trans. Richard C. McCleary, 114–25, Evanston, IL: Northwestern University Press.

Nietzsche, Friedrich (2002), *Beyond Good and Evil: Prelude to a Philosophy of the Future*, Rolf-Peter Horstmann and Judith Norman (eds.), trans. Judith Norman, Cambridge, MA: Cambridge University Press.

Wiredu, Kwasi (1996), "The Concept of Truth in the Akan Language," in Kwasi Wiredu (ed.), *Cultural Universals and Particulars: An African Perspective*, 105–12, Bloomington: Indiana University Press.

6

Thinking Along with Texts from Afar:
Why One Doesn't Understand Texts without Philosophical Reflection and Can't Do Philosophy without Inspiration

Elisa Freschi

In this chapter, I will argue in favor of doing intercultural philosophy confronting philosophers of the past. I will start by discussing whether at all one needs to engage with other philosophers while doing philosophy and claim that comparisons[1] are just the normal way we think, and that in this sense the real choice is not between comparing and not comparing but between comparing explicitly or implicitly, that is, between comparing while being aware of what one is doing and comparing while being unaware of the way one is accessing a new idea through the lenses of a familiar one. Next, I will argue in favor of the engagement with philosophical texts that are remote in time, space, or other circumstances, in order to challenge our ideas and seeming intuitions. I will then move on to the constructive part of this paper, in which I will promote engaging with great thinkers of the past, since this engagement will sharpen one's understanding of them as well as one's philosophical acumen. The greatness of an author depends on what one is looking for and, for instance, an epistemologist might not recognize the greatness of Martin Buber and vice versa. However, "great thinkers" are in general thinkers who have—I am borrowing from Italo Calvino's definition of "classics"—never ceased to tell us what they have to say. In a philosophical context, I would like to add that great thinkers also need to display some awareness of their philosophical positions and to be able to defend them instead of just upholding them in a dogmatic way. In this sense, great thinkers of the past can still be interrogated today when we try to find out why they defended a certain viewpoint. According to the same definition, Annambhaṭṭa, though interesting, does not count as a "great thinker," since as soon as one asks why he assumed a certain ontological position one does not find any available answer in his *Tarkasaṅgraha*.[2]

Last, I will speak in favor of the very unfashionable topic of translations as a philosophical exercise. I am aware of how translations are seen as a clerical task in today's academia (especially in North America, where they can even be outsourced to research assistants and/or students), but I will argue that they are the real litmus test of one's understanding of a text. Translations, in other words, force one to engage with the text without being able to hide beyond a compelling interpretative narrative.

How do the topic of engaging with philosophers of the past and that of translations hold together? Because the latter is an indicative test of the effectiveness of the former and because both require a close engagement. In both cases, one needs to step out of one's comfort zone and move toward a confrontation with the other thinker.

1. The Unavoidability of Comparison

What to do with comparisons? They are always risky, insofar as one risks styling oneself as an impartial observer while being in fact part of the discussion. Hence, should not one avoid them altogether?

As tempting as this suggestion might be, I do not think it is viable. As I see them, comparisons are hardly avoidable. In fact, learning and understanding are—in my eyes—not different from reducing the unknown to the known, and therefore necessarily involve the comparison of what we know already with what we come to encounter, so as to make place for the latter within the former. This is also the reason which makes it hardly possible to learn something altogether new, for instance, a sentence in a language completely unknown or the way a certain technical procedure works within an engine one knows nothing about. In other words, we learn by means of (implicit) comparisons. If we know Tamil, we'll be able to guess the meaning of a Telugu sentence by comparing it with what we think should be its Tamil counterpart. If we know how a car's engine functions, we will be able to speculate about the way a boat's engine works. At times, we will even do it implicitly, without being aware of the fact that we are understanding by comparing. In such cases, we tend to miss to what extent our understanding of the former case informs our understanding of the latter.

However, implicit assumptions are dangerous, exactly when we are not aware of them. Would it not be better to be straightforwardly aware of what we are doing when learning about, for example, a new theological approach to the problem of theodicy? If we are not aware of the fact that we are tacitly comparing the new theological approach we are reading about with Augustine's approach, we run the risk to oversee their differences and to criticize the former not on its own terms but based on the latter.

Thus, if I am right and comparisons are not really avoidable, should one not rather become aware of one's doing comparisons and of the risks involved in every comparison? As for the risk of tacit comparisons, their risks are akin to the ones of holding implicit assumptions, insofar as one mistakes one's beliefs with facts.[3] This is also the risk run by some scholars who claim that no discussions with thinkers outside their scientific approach are worth undertaking, since whoever is outside that paradigm is just outdated and only of historical interest. Such thinkers, I am afraid, run the risk to mistake a specific approach with the only true one, and to state that other philosophers are not on the same boat in their quest for truth because they do not subscribe to that approach. There are ethical issues at stake here, but even apart from them, this approach makes them close their eyes to any possible criticism in a way akin to the refusal to look in the telescope by Galileo Galilei's judges, who knew a priori that they were right and did not even need to check.[4]

What about the risks of explicit comparisons? The main problem regards the asymmetry of comparisons. If I compare language A with language B while being myself a native speaker of language C and knowing (and appreciating) A and B equally well, I might be in the ideal situation for making a comparison. However, this ideal situation is hardly ever the case. Usually, we compare something we know less with something we know better or, even worse, with something we identify with. That is, the tertium comparationis collapses with one of the two comparanda. This risk is even bigger in case of the process of learning through implicit comparisons. Explicit comparisons force one to at least be explicit as for the two (or more) comparanda and the tertium comparationis.

2. Comparing with Historical Sources

Having established the unavoidability of comparisons in general, let me come to the specific case of comparisons based on historical sources. I will therefore not discuss the parallel case of papers written by authors who are still alive, although geographically or culturally distant. I will also not discuss the case of ideas coming from the past which are not or no longer available in texts composed by their authors. This group would cover lost texts (such as gnostic texts only extant through their opponents' refutations) as well as texts which were never committed to writing, such as important parts of precolonial African philosophy. In both these cases, the effort to reconstruct their positions is much bigger than in the case of fully extant texts, and therefore the methodology which will be discussed below (Section 4) will need to be accordingly adjusted, just like when one plays football with a child and tries most of all to leave her enough space to develop her skills rather than fighting back as hard as one usually would.[5]

I will suggest that engaging with historical sources means entering in a *dialogue* with them. One might object that the paradigm of dialogue is an idealized one, since it does not take into account social and cultural asymmetries. Part of these objections will be discussed below (see Section 4). In a nutshell, I think that they are less salient in the case of historical sources, since history crystallizes the past and makes asymmetries less directly dangerous. Attacking a dead philosopher, for instance, is not as risky as disagreeing with a powerful colleague, who will be responsible for one's career advancements, project evaluations, and peer reviews. Should one suggest the more radical objection that dialogue is altogether impossible and that philosophy is nothing but soliloquy, then I should ask them to stop engaging with this (as well as with any other) article. Dialogue is, like democracy, a fragile tool, but it is the only one available for human beings in their cooperative quest for advancing in depth of critical thinking.

3. Are There Alternatives?

3.1 The Illusion of "Free" Research

There might be philosophers who sit quietly in a corner and think deeply in order to elaborate new theories. In most cases, however, philosophers, like artists or mathematicians, need a starting point, an inspiration. They do not philosophize out of nothing, but rather start with an idea or a problem they want to solve. In many cases, they start with ideas which are prompted by other actual philosophical conversations. In others, they will get ideas from books, TV series, video games,[6] scientific theories, and so on. However, just like in tennis, it is easier to play or to philosophize well, if you have a good partner. Amazing philosophical books have been published taking as their inspiration TV shows or comics, but it takes a philosophical genius to develop a philosophically powerful argument with a philosophically limited inspiration as one's starting point.

3.2 The Illusion of Novelty

One of the things which immediately turn me off when I read a philosophical abstract are phrases such as "In this paper I am offering *for the first time* a solution to the problem of X" or "I present a *novel* approach to X" or "a *completely new* solution to X, *never* attempted by anyone." Why so? Because they are naïve to a point which seems to me unacceptable for a philosopher. Assuming that the philosophical history of humanity encompasses at least thousands of years and covers a number of languages and cultures impossible to master by a single individual, how can one even conceive the thought that one is suggesting something *for the first time*? Even checking all philosophical journals issued in 2018 in the world would possibly take a lifetime.[7]

Thus, the phrases I have emphasized above in fact mean something else, namely *for the first time in what I deem to be relevant*, with the additional aggravating circumstance that one is often not aware of it and mistakes what *one* deems to be relevant with what *is* relevant. And what is it that one deems to be relevant? Usually contemporary philosophical discussions in the jargon one philosophically grew up with, which often means "mainstream" Anglo-American analytical philosophy. While Anglo-American analytical philosophy may have enormous philosophical merits, it would be inherently unphilosophical to consider it the only way one can think philosophically. Why inherently unphilosophical? Because it would consider philosophy just a techné, closing oneself to the possibility of listening even to colleagues who have a different way of doing philosophy. In the following, I will discuss an alternative way of doing philosophy, namely by exposing one's thoughts to the challenge of powerful antagonists: great texts of the past.

In this spirit, I encourage students and colleagues to move away from the conviction that philosophy is best done in an empty space, to realize that engaging with other thinkers is an essential part of the philosophical enterprise and, consequently, to start reading primary sources. One might object that there are enough English-speaking colleagues to engage with and that there is no need to look for further sources in other languages. This is a perfectly fine objection, but only if one is ready to accept that it would be appropriate to say that one engages only with colleagues of one's own university or county, instead of constantly looking for new challenging ideas and for possible objections to one's tenets.

4. "Wrestling with the Angel"

I have discussed above about the unavoidability of comparisons. Still, "comparative philosophy" as such risks to be a controversial enterprise since it rests on the assumption that one compares some philosophical ideas with one's own ones, without leaving one's standpoint, which is usually the politically and sociologically dominant Euro-American academia. How can one move away from these imbalanced comparisons? By stepping away from one's privileged standpoint and trying, instead, to do philosophy in a cross-cultural (or intercultural) way,[8] that is, by enabling a philosophical dialogue among positions instead of having one position compared to another one. Intercultural philosophy is based on a dialogue, that is, not just on a sheer juxtaposition of monologues, since such a juxtaposition would not lead to any new result and both partners would not be able to gain anything out of it. In order to achieve this result, one needs to be able to engage in a real dialogue. This is a less trivial issue than it may look like at first sight and in fact thousands of pages, from Plato to H.-G. Gadamer, have been dedicated only to the topic of how can dialogues and especially philosophical dialogues take place. The situation becomes even more difficult when in addition to the normal boundaries between people one needs to cross the additional bridge of cultures and of time. How can such a dialogue look like?

In order to attempt an answer, I will borrow an enigmatic yet fascinating image from the Genesis.[9] Genesis 32:22–32 contains the strange episode of Jacob wrestling with God. It is a single combat which cannot aim at the destruction of the other combatant, but rather at engaging closely with him. I will claim here that this is a good simile for the kind of dialogue one should look for in intercultural philosophy, especially when dealing with historical sources. In fact, one should not aim at destroying one's philosophical opponent, but also not remain at the superficial level of a peaceful chatting. Even if one is reading someone whose ideas one feels sympathetic with, in order for the encounter to be really fertile, one needs to engage in a real combat, that is, in a strict philosophical confrontation, being ready to have to admit one's defeat and to change at least some of one's assumptions.[10] This means that one is not just staging a combat and in fact holding tight to one's ideas. One is ready to risk one's (philosophical) life, that is, one's beliefs. Conversely, one's philosophical opponent might also end up being defeated insofar as one might find out that they overlooked a possible objection or did not take into account some possible development of their theories. How can this practically occur?

In my experience, again, Jacob's wrestling offers a good clue: one needs to get closer to one's philosophical opponent. It is not enough to just cherry-pick an idea and expand it in a different direction in order to claim that a dialogue had taken place.

Rather, one needs to be able to engage closely with a whole theory, possibly taking into account its context and its consequences. Now, a historical opponent offers in this sense serious disadvantages but also an important advantage. The disadvantages lie in the fact that an opponent who is no longer alive cannot react, reassessing their views, explaining their point better, correcting misunderstandings, and the like. Much more work needs to be done, consequently, by the partner who is alive and able to engage in the discussion. She will need to fill holes, reconstruct partially unexplained views, make implicit points explicit, expand theories to unexpected cases, and so on. She will have to be humble in her attempt, trying to substantiate each claim in the dead opponent's own words. I am in this connection a strong believer in the principle of charity, and I try to reconstruct a theory in the most charitable way (more on this in n. 19). Nothing is gained, I think, by defeating a weak opponent, and it is even offensive to think that great thinkers of the past did not think of attacks which look evident for us.

The advantage of engaging with an opponent of the past lies, conversely, in their being far from the actuality. They do not need to be influenced by extra-philosophical issues, such as their opponent's academical position or country of residence. This is particularly relevant when it comes to asymmetrical power relations, such as a star professor in a well-known university in the Anglo-American world engaging in a dialogue with an opponent coming from a very different background. Our opponents from the past do not need to feel intimidated. They will not be impressed by one's pedigree and remain inflexible on their positions, even if they are out of fashion, such as idealism.

4.1 Fight All Night

I hope that readers will bear with me while I keep on exploiting the metaphor I chose. There are a few more indications, in fact, that we can take out of it. First, Jacob *fights*. He does not just encounter the angel, he fights with him. Similarly, in order for the encounter with another philosopher to be really transformative, one should not just engage with a restatement of one's ideas but rather look for points of difference and not just of harmony. One is not transformed with the encounter of the n-th philosopher who agrees with oneself.

Then, Jacob fights *all night*. He fights while not being completely sure about the strength of his adversary, whom he cannot see. He tests his adversary's and his own strength throughout a long wrestling. Similarly, although a short quote by a Chinese or an Arab philosopher might embellish our articles and impress our readers, this is not what I mean when I am talking about a fruitful transformative encounter. For that, one needs time and ongoing engagement. An easy device in this sense is to engage with a full text, not just an impressive quote. By engaging with the full text, this unleashes its potential for a cross-cultural fertilization, insofar as the same question is given a different answer, or vice versa, or the context is completely different. It is not irrelevant whether the discussion about the existence of free will, for instance, is prompted by the problem of God's omnipotence or, as in Viśiṣṭādvaita Vedānta, by that of the validity of the injunctions of the sacred texts asking one to do something (see Freschi 2015).

By engaging in this way with full texts, one can go beyond a trivial restatement of what one knew with a different voice. It takes time, but we are doing philosophy, not emergency surgery.

One might counter that a single text is not enough and that one should read not just a whole text, but the complete works of a given thinker, including their diaries and letters, and perhaps also those of their pupils and teachers and so on.[11] In this way, the demand to read full texts would expand so much as to become not realizable. It is true that one needs to find a balance between the opposite needs of feasibility and completeness. Pragmatically, this balance will be found again each time by forcing oneself outside the comfort zone of the chapters one already knows out of secondary literature into the wildness of what has not yet been fully researched.[12] More on this topic will be discussed below, Section 5.3.

4.2 Fight with an Angel

Jacob wrestles with an *angel*. Philosophically speaking, we might remember ourselves that little is gained by engaging with opponents of little value. You found out a petty mistake in someone's article? Write them a personal email. You completely disagree with an article written by an alleged philosopher who seems not at all well prepared in their topic? Think well before engaging in writing a rejoinder which will take you months. It is hardly the case that you will learn much out of a weak opponent. You could still decide to engage in a debate for the benefit of the readership, but this is an extra-philosophical concern.

By contrast, fighting with a strong opponent forces one to strengthen one's arguments and dialectical ability. One sees better what one's weak points are and which objections one might have overlooked. The subtlety and depth of one's opponent stimulate one to gain a similar level of depth and accuracy in developing one's arguments. Until …

4.3 Fight to Get a Benediction

In the enigmatic Biblical passage I chose as a metaphor for one's philosophical engagement, Jacob tells to the angel that he will not let him go until he gets his benediction. Defeated after a night-long battle, the angel does even more than that, since he blesses Jacob and also gives him a new name. Out of the metaphor, engaging with a strong philosophical opponent means that one does not only improve one's philosophical skills and conclusions. One also (re)gains her identity. Through confrontation, one discovers what one really cares for and how to fight for it. At the end of the battle, one in this sense gets a new identity (a new name) which is usually closer to oneself than one's independent and unchallenged starting point.[13]

4.4 What about the Angel?

Thus, one is challenged by the encounter and, if one has followed the steps above, one cannot continue to think in the same way after it. In other words, the one who is fighting with the angel will be transformed by the encounter. What does the angel, that is, one's interlocutor, gain out of one's engagement with them? The question could be posed even in the case of a living interlocutor who fights back, since even in that case one risks focusing only on one's side, one's transformation.[14] The situation is, however, worse in the present case. How can one have what Bo Mou calls "constructive engagement" if there is no living interlocutor?

In fact, let me remind the readers once again that this article focuses on an engagement with historical sources who cannot actively join the dialogue and for which it is therefore difficult to imagine that one's engagement with them results in a transformative experience also from their side. Given these circumstances, one can distinguish several cases:

- In the standard case of one's engaging with a philosopher who has no living tradition inspired by him, the encounter may happen to benefit only one side, namely the contemporary scholar's one. Can one still speak of a dialogue, or even of a polylogue,[15] if there is no room for a real transformation on both sides? Not really, given that there is no reciprocity. The gain will be completely on the side of the contemporary scholar, who will achieve a new understanding without modifying their source.
- There is then the case of a contemporary scholar's engagement with a historical source which enjoys a living tradition of interpretation, for example, Śaṅkara or Thomas Aquinas. Even if one cannot modify the source itself, one can accept a real and lively encounter with the contemporary exponents of their school. This is what Daya Krishna attempted within his Saṃvāda project, when he invited Lakshman Joo to discuss his Pratyabhijñā tradition or living sufis to discuss Sufism.[16] In these cases, it is imaginable that one's interactions may modify both interlocutors, although the living tradition does not necessarily correspond to the original author's intentions.
- The last case is the most speculative one, namely the case in which an encounter is deemed to be able to modify both parts although the thinker of the past has not originated an uninterrupted living tradition (e.g., Gadamer's engagement with Plato). Although the historical source cannot be modified, its reception will be enriched by the encounter with a powerful opponent. No historian of philosophy can now look at Plato without thinking of Gadamer's understanding of him, even if one disagrees with it. Similarly, Daya Krishna's understanding of Mīmāṃsā, of Vedānta, of bhakti, or of the *Nyāya Sūtra*s might be criticized, but it undoubtedly shed light on so far neglected aspects of these schools and texts, thus enabling later scholars to engage with them. Incidentally, one might remember A. Raghuramaraju's arguments against comparing "unprepared" Sanskrit philosophers with, for example, contemporary Euro-American ones. Raghuramaraju stresses that such a comparison will end up showing that the former are "weaker," whereas the point is just that they have not benefitted of decades of scholarship strengthening their shoulders (2018, first section). In this sense, by engaging with an "angel" of the past, we are benefitting their philosophical heritage as well, by making it fit for further philosophical confrontations.

Let me now pause a little bit longer on the last case. One can, I surmise, look at a thinker from the past not just as a curiosity to be photographed and reproduced, but as a person with whom it is worth engaging and ask them questions, even if they did not ask or answer them explicitly. At least in the case of great thinkers, one is able to find implicit answers to one's queries hidden in their discussions of related topics. The alternative, namely taking a thinker's word as only valid in the situation for which it was meant, entails the risk of shunning a real engagement.

Thus, one needs for sure to understand what a thinker meant in their own historical terms and for their own audience. One can choose to read more about the history and sociological circumstances of text productions at the time of the author one is reading. All these are valuable enterprises and the work of historians and so on richly enhanced everyone's understanding of authors from the past. However, a historically bound reading, needs to be part of a hermeneutic circle in which a philosophically engaged reading also takes part. Privileging only the first aspect may be legitimate for certain classes of texts (e.g. archival records), but it definitely misses the purpose for which philosophical texts were composed. In other words, one risks misunderstanding the texts one is so keen in accurately understanding. Thus, after having looked at the historical circumstances of a text, one can then continue to engage with the thinker one is working on and ask them further questions, for which one will probably find an answer somewhere in their works, if only one continues their line of reasoning applying it to a different set of circumstances. In this way, one is taking seriously their philosophical ambitions, since hardly anyone of the thinkers one is working on would have claimed that what they wrote only had a value for the decade, the geographical area, and the social group in which they lived.

A connected problem is: How is it ontologically possible to find answers to questions that had not been asked yet in the works of a thinker of the past? A possible answer has been offered by Italo Calvino's (1991) definition of a classic , namely: "A classic is a book that has never finished saying what it has to say." In philosophical terms, a philosophical classic can go beyond what its contemporaries thought it meant and continue to make us engage with it in a fruitful dialogue. Mario Trevi's analysis of the *Book of Job* contains a similar idea insofar as he speaks of an "eccedenza di senso" (surplus of meaning) in the book which makes it possible for all of us to still find new meanings in it (1991: 6).

I purposefully left a question unanswered insofar as I wrote that this strategy works with "great thinkers," but I did not define "great thinkers." The case of systematic thinkers (Kant, Hegel, Vyāsatīrtha or Veṅkaṭanātha, etc.) is easier to deal with since their systems can often be further stretched to meet unforeseen challenges. Still, the exercise of extending a theory may be relevant even in the case of less systematic thinkers. However, in those cases the interpreter might have to supply more than what she is given by the thinkers themselves. Suppose a given thinker has only written about philosophy of language. One might be able to understand what they believed about epistemology and, to some extent, also ontology, out of short remarks in their books on philosophy of language. However, it might be hardly possible to find out what they thought about political philosophy. I am convinced that this would still be a valid philosophical exercise, but it would not be part of the type described as "wrestling with the angel."

5. Pragmatic Considerations

5.1 Litmus Test: Translations as a Way of Philosophically Engaging

In the preceding pages, I spoke about the importance of the closeness of the engagement. In my experience, a litmus test of the accuracy of such close engagement, especially relevant in the case of philosophical texts from the past, are translations. Why are translations relevant? The close engagement described above entails asking additional questions to the text, as Søren Kierkegaard does with Abraham's story in his *Fear and Trembling*. Such additional asking and digging for answers can, however, also lead one too far away from the text. This is where referring back to the text, ideally in its entirety, instead of just cherry-picking a few quotes, becomes a useful test.

As long as one is not translating the text (no matter whether in view of a publication or not) one *can* still disregard inconsistencies or points one has not completely understood. A serious translation, by contrast, forces one to come to terms with the text at the text's own terms.[17] One cannot use the easy way-out of focusing only on what one already understands, likes, or accepts, and one is forced to enter into a real dialogue with the thinker who authored the text.[18] I am aware of the fact that translations are looked down upon in today's academia, especially in North America. Translations (and critical editions), for instance, are generally not counted as "real" philosophical contributions, they generally do not count if one wants to achieve tenure and so on. They are considered a pedestrian exercise, something everyone can do, and not at all a philosophical exercise. According to such unreflected opinion, translating is easy, one only needs to know the source and the target language and the only obstacles may be occasional unclear words or idiomatic expressions. This attitude has disastrous consequences, insofar as it encourages an understanding of philosophy as the work of geniuses who do not dedicate themselves to the generous exercise of making philosophical texts of the past accessible. Moreover, it is, in my opinion, the result of a deep misunderstanding of what is a philosophical enterprise. As a matter of fact, knowing the source language of a given text is not at all enough to translate it, and surely not in the case of a philosophical text. Knowing German will by no means be enough to produce a philosophically sound translation of Martin Heidegger's *Sein und Zeit* or Immanuel Kant's *Critiques*. Instead, it took Gianni Vattimo's genius and efforts to aptly translate *Truth and Method* into Italian already in 1970, or Giovanni Reale's one to translate Plato. Vattimo or Reale were not doing a pedantic exercise while translating, they were not setting the ground for the real philosophical engagement with these texts. By contrast, they could translate them exactly because they had philosophically engaged with them and had been able to make sense of them. In this sense, their translations came both at the beginning and at the end of a hermeneutic circle of philosophical engagement. In order to be able to translate a text, in other words, one needs to be able to rethink it, as if one were its author. One cannot translate a philosophical text unless one has understood it. In the case of philosophical texts, there is nothing like a "merely literal translation." Such a translation is just *not* a translation, but a compilation of dictionary entries, just like a collation of manuscripts is not a critical edition. A translation of a philosophical text, in sum, requires understanding the text, and a philosophical text can only be understood through a philosophical engagement with it. In this sense, a translation is an appropriate test for the thesis presented in the title, namely, that one does not understand philosophical texts without philosophical reflection.[19] Let me take, for instance, the case of Gaṅgeśa's *Tattvacintāmaṇi*, or of Udayana's *Nyāyakusumāñjali*, or of Maṇḍana's *Vidhiviveka*, which are as terse texts as one might possibly imagine. As long as one is just skimming through them, one might find them consistent with one's picture of, respectively, realist epistemology, rational theology, and deontic reductionism. As soon as one is forced to analyze them in detail, however, and to account for each single sentence, one discovers new asperities and problems, but also hidden gems.

5.2 Case Study

I will here discuss a case study, namely the attempt to ask a philosophically relevant question to an author who did not explicitly deal with it. This explanation is needed, because in many, if not most cases, one will not find exact correspondences across philosophical traditions. Therefore, it might be hard to structure a dialogue on a given topic (say, free will), given that the topic is not dealt with explicitly by all participants in our ideal debate. I will here show how I think this can be done nonetheless, namely, by analyzing the topic in its key components. The question will be that of theodicy and the author is Rāmānuja (traditional dates: 1017–1137), the philosopher recognized as the founder of Viśiṣṭādvaita Vedānta.

Did Rāmānuja ever develop a theodicy? From a historical point of view, we are forced to say that he did not, because the word theodicy was coined by Leibniz and has become an unavoidable topic in European philosophy due to the development of rational theology, but not necessarily in all of the world's philosophies. Again, from a historical point of view, Rāmānuja did not develop a theodicy, also because he thought and lived in an environment in which the theory of karman was practically unchallenged and one could assume that all one's readers were acquainted with it and believed in it, so that the problem of evil had a first answer one could refer to and was therefore less of a critical and unsolvable problem. Is one nonetheless allowed to ask what Rāmānuja would have said, had he encountered Leibniz? I think that one is allowed to, and that a thinker like Rāmānuja would have been thrilled to see his theories put into question by such a worthy opponent.

Can one find an answer to the problem of theodicy in the work of Rāmānuja? One will probably fail to find a systematic treatment of it, but one can find again and again topics which have a bearing on the problem of theodicy (such as free will, God's omnipotence and benevolence, the link of karman and God's will, etc.) and which allow one to reconstruct the missing piece through the way it would have influenced the pieces we have. This exercise is surely of immense benefit for the one who undertakes it, and who is "fighting with the angel," insofar as

- one is forced to reconsider one's opinion about what one might have thought was a universal problem,

- one has to deconstruct the question into its basic elements (i.e., the problem of evil, the existence of an omnipotent God, the role of human decisions, etc.), and[20]
- one has to read a lot of Rāmānuja's works, looking for clues in different contexts.

At the same time, the process can benefit the reception and role of Rāmānuja's philosophy too, since it leads to draw out aspects of Rāmānuja's thought one had failed to notice because one had not asked the relevant questions.

5.3 Methodological Problems, Blindspots, and Suggested Solutions

Let me now assume that one is convinced by the above and willing to engage in the transformative experience of a real dialogue. Let me also presuppose that she is willing to engage with historical texts. What should she do?

The answer is easier in case she wants to read, for example, classical Greek philosophy. Most key texts have been edited, translated, and discussed several times. There are thematic as well as historical approaches, studies based on single authors or on trends and one can get as much auxiliary material as one needs. Moreover, one can generally count on the advantage of having been trained in a philosophical milieu which was directly influenced by such philosophy. One is still fighting with an angel, if one is taking the encounter seriously, but perhaps not in a dark night. The situation might gradually change if one looks at, for example, postclassical Latin philosophy; Middle Ages philosophy in Latin or Greek; Arabic philosophy; Sanskrit; Tibetan, or classical Chinese philosophy; Africana philosophy; Maori philosophy; philosophies which one can only reconstruct from an oral lore; and so on. In all these cases one has (in varying degrees) not enough reliable editions nor translations, not to speak of critical studies and further auxiliary materials. It is hard to evaluate how much this will impact one's study but it is crucially important to bear it in mind. Socrates was certainly a genius, but his genius can be appreciated also because it has been spelt out and explained and its consequences have been developed, by his successors, from Plato and Aristotle to his contemporary interpreters. Scholars have investigated about his life and the various sources we have about it, and have reconstructed the atmosphere of the Greek agorā. This is currently not the case with most of the philosophers belonging to the currents and traditions I listed above. This means that while engaging with, for example, Prof. XY (Africana philosopher), one cannot count on the same degree of scholarship on her and on her milieu, sources, and subsequent fortune. One might therefore be uncharitable to her because one does not know what she was reacting to or at least misread some of her positions as superficial, whereas they could have shown their full significance to a deeper reading. I, for one, cannot overlook the fact that my understanding of Plato has been deeply enriched by reading his interpreters and that I can now perceive the importance of some of his dialectical moves only because I read Werner Jaeger's *Paideia*, without which I would have considered them only as narrative aspects within his works. Summing up, in comparing, for instance, Augustine and Yāmunācārya, we are in an intrinsically imbalanced position and must be aware of its risks, namely letting Yāmuna look less clever than Augustine because we and the limited number of scholars who worked on him are more statistically likely to have overlooked a big number of important facets of his contribution than the much larger number of scholars who worked on Augustine have overlooked in his work.[21] One might reply that, for instance, many Sanskrit and Chinese philosophers have been commented upon for centuries within their own tradition. This, however, does not necessarily help today's interpreters trying to engage philosophically with them. Why so? Because an accurate commentary composed in sixteenth-century Andhra Pradesh focuses often on issues relevant for its time and place, which are often irrelevant for the contemporary philosophical discourse, which was—historically speaking— not shaped by such concerns and topics. Socrates has the advantage of having been interpreted again and again in the history of European philosophy, from Plato until Kierkegaard and beyond, and to have, through such an engagement, shaped the philosophical arena. Nothing like that is thinkable for a Chinese, Sanskrit, Tibetan, or other such author, who have been read and commented upon within their respective traditions, but did not have the chance to influence the configuration of Euro-American philosophy. Methodologically speaking, one needs to be deeply aware of such imbalances in order to counter them. For instance, several twentieth-century interpreters have looked at the Mīmāṃsā school of philosophy and distinguished a "philosophical" part of it (the texts or portions of texts dealing with epistemology and philosophy of language) and a "Mīmāṃsā-proper" part (the majority of Mīmāṃsā texts or portions of texts, dealing with exegesis and ritual). In my opinion, considering exegesis and philosophy of ritual (i.e., the attempt to make a consistent and global understanding of the whole deontic lore found in the Vedas) as nonphilosophical is due to one's philosophical blindspots. Methodologically, being unaware of them makes one blind to certain texts and ideas and too favorable toward others, and I recommend students and younger colleagues to continue questioning themselves in order to become aware of their unconscious biases and look for philosophically stimulating ideas wherever they are found.

Another question regards the low prestige factor of intercultural philosophy, which is usually not ranked high among the philosophical subdisciplines. Apart from sociological reasons (such as the conservatism of philosophical institutions), intercultural philosophy has the objective disadvantage that its exponents typically have to engage in a lot of preliminary work besides their philosophical training. For instance, they need to learn the relevant languages and their cultural worlds, and they need to side with colleagues from other departments (say, Classics, Medieval Studies, Asian studies, etc.) and be able to speak with them. Meanwhile, their fellow philosophers will have focused on nothing but improving their skills in "mainstream" philosophy, such that the intercultural philosopher among them might look naïve to them, because she will have not be as skilled in the latest elements of the mainstream philosophical jargon.

A last problem has to do with the accessibility of sources. Since one cannot be expected to be competent in all languages and cultures, should one limit oneself to intra-cultural comparisons? This is usually the rule but entails the disadvantage of unduly taming the potential of comparison. The alternative approach, namely learning the relevant language(s), entails an enormous investment of time and energy. Moreover, one usually comes to appreciate nonmainstream philosophy at a later stage in one's philosophical development, typically after one's BA or even after one's PhD, so that one has less time available for acquiring the needed linguistic skills in full. However, one can access sources as good as one can and then engage in team work by teaming up with experts. A team can thus work like a swarm of bees, which is able to do things (such as avoiding obstacles) better than any individual member of it, displaying a form of collective intelligence.[22] Such a team work, where one who is preeminently a philosopher teams up with an expert of language Z and its cultural history (let us call her a philologist) is usually extremely productive for both parts, so much that I wonder what the reasons for its relative infrequency could be. I mean, apart from the socioeconomic reasons fostering the tendency of academicians in humanities to work on their own because team work is not enough valued and so on.

This brings me back to the issue of reading complete texts (see Section 4.1). How much should one read to find a balance between feasibility and completeness? Personally, I think that reading at least full sections helps, and that more is better. For instance, it is hard to evaluate the role of an argument within the first book of Śālikanātha's *Vākyārthamātṛkā* unless one has read it all. Sure, it would be even better to read also Śālikanātha's other works and then his main sources, such as Prabhākara's *Bṛhatī*. Reading Śālikanātha's successors, such as his opponent Sucarita and his supporter Rāmānujācārya, also clarifies many points. However, I work with the methodological assumption that philosophers of the past were rational beings and did not willfully try to hide their ideas from fellow philosophers.[23] Their texts can be hard because we lack (parts of) the context or because of their intrinsic imperviousness, but one can trust that they can be made sense of—at the end of the fight.

In conclusion, as a rule of thumb, one should constantly push oneself beyond the limit of what one would have read and toward the self-challenging experience of reading (and fighting with the text), especially with texts distant in time (or through other circumstances). A seriously undertaken confrontation with a text is usually a transformative experience for the thinker(s) engaging in it and one that can lead one to think along an author of the past and discover overlooked aspects of their thought.

The depth of one's engagement, I suggest, can be tested through the practice of translation. Why is translation a useful test? Because it forces one to think along the text and its ideas, thus impelling one to engage closely with it in its completeness (and not just with what is easily palatable in it). In this sense, one is able to translate philosophy only once one has rethought the text completely, almost re-authored it. As Uehara writes, "Translation has closer links to philosophy than is usually assumed" (2010: 306).[24] Moreover, like philosophical thinking, philosophical translations are hard to do well, because they involve a self-reflective analysis.[25]

To sum up, working with philosophical texts of the past is a continuous challenge, but also a rewarding enterprise because of its intellectual richness. Like a fight with an angel, it can push one to the limits of one's intellectual possibilities, and it cannot be left unfinished. As a litmus test of such an engagement, I suggest the use of philosophical translations, which force one to think along the text instead or before refuting it.

Notes

1. I am grateful to Ralph Weber for suggesting that when one is comparing something known to something unknown, one is doing an analogy rather than a comparison. Analogical thinking has, in fact, a long history exactly in a field in which one compares the known with the unknown, i.e. in theology. However, I will stick in the following by the use of the term "comparison," since no one has suggested, as far as I know, "analogical philosophy," whereas "comparative philosophy" is an important philosophical approach. I will argue in the following that one of the main problems with comparative philosophy is that it is, in fact, analogical, in the sense that there is no neutral point from which one looks at an even field of comparison.
2. I once presented the topic in class, in connection with Annambhaṭṭa's (unjustified) assumption that bodies made of atoms of fire, of air, or of water exist in various mythical worlds, and a gifted student (Munema Moiz) came up with this very poignant definition: "A great thinker should, presumably, show a level of reflectiveness about her positions that detaches her from her milieu, even if she ends up re-affirming the intuitions of her milieu." Ralph Weber pointed out that I am talking of great thinkers but then borrow a definition about great texts. This is due to the fact that, especially in a situation such as that of Sanskrit philosophy, where almost no information about the personality of the philosophers involved is available, I methodologically suggest focusing on them as they appear through their work without postulating any difference between the two.
3. On implicit assumptions in history, see Mary Fulbrook's (2002: 35–7) remarks: "A-theoretical historians, if provoked sufficiently, may be brought to enunciate the view that Theory Is Not History and historians should get on with The Real Job of Doing History. Now for the bad news. Even those who have no interest in theory are actually operating with implicit paradigms. In fact, the rest of this book is devoted to unpicking the various elements involved even in implicit paradigms. We have just introduced some of these elements, which, if unpacked a little more, include: the constitution and categorization of 'facts'; the selection of which 'facts' to include and exclude; notions about the relationship among elements; the significance and weighting given to each element; the constitution of what might be called a Geschichtsbild, the historical picture of the whole, and the emplotment, the tale told about the combination of selected elements (sometimes called the metanarrative); and the general evaluation and emotive coloring given to the final product, the representation of history (including the use of language through which to write and represent selected aspects and interpretations of the past). ... For example, how should one approach characterization and explanation of the English Civil War—or English Revolution, as Marxist historians (used to) like to call it? ... [I]t is important to note the fact that any historical explanation entails choices about selection and explanation, whether or not it is considered by its proponents to be theoretical. And what satisfies one historian's curiosity (analysis of key meetings, the specific motives or actions of particular individuals) may seem just a matter of irritating or even trivial detail from the perspective of another historian."
4. I am aware that I am simplifying the opinions of Galilei's judges, since these claimed that there was no epistemological warranty of the correct functioning of the telescope. An interesting discussion on the presentist approach took place between Timothy

Williamson and Chakravarthi Ram-Prasad, see Manchanda, Ram-Prasad, and Williamson (2019) and Ram-Prasad's answer (Ram-Prasad 2019).

5. Several interesting ideas about how to deal with texts which were never committed to writing and whose content has to be reconstructed out of archaeological findings and anthropological research have been discussed in the podcast *History of Africana philosophy*, by Peter Adamson and Chike Jeffers.
6. For an instance of videogame-inspired philosophy, see Marcus Arvan's idea that the world is a peer-to-peer simulation (2015) as elaborating on Nick Bostrom's seminal paper (2003). The number of philosophical books inspired by videogames, TV series (e.g. South and Engels 2018), new technologies (e.g. Marino 2019 on the blockchain), etc., is enormously growing.
7. I am grateful to Ralph Weber, who suggested that "novel" or "for the first time" are not meant to indicate absolute novelty, but just "with regard to what is currently discussed." As will be explained in the next paragraph, I tend to be less optimistic about what authors mean when they claim to be the "first" to say X or to offer a "novel" approach to Y.
8. For a short introduction on this terminology, see Kirloskar-Steinbach, Ramana, and Maffie (2014).
9. The following paragraphs are inspired by the fascinating episode of Genesis 32:22–32, that I am here adaptively reusing for a new purpose (on "adaptive reuse" see Freschi and Maas (2017)).
10. This is why in the following I will continue to speak of an "opponent" even in the case of a discussion with one's philosophical predecessors, e.g., H.-G. Gadamer discussing with Plato. My metaphor of wrestling with the angel is also meant to show that one needs to "fight," i.e. closely engage, also when one is involved in a discussion with someone one holds in high esteem.
11. I am grateful to Micaela Latini for a discussion on the need to look into an author's private correspondence.
12. Ralph Weber asked me whether I mean here "researched by oneself" or "researched in general." I do believe in teamwork, as will be discussed below and do not think that one can restart again each time (for instance, writing a dictionary, checking all libraries in search of manuscripts, collating them all etc.). Thus, depending on the work of others is unavoidable, especially when it comes to the groundwork mentioned in the previous sentence. As for secondary literature retelling the philosophical contents of a given text, this is probably more or less reliable according to the various fields of expertise, and be less reliable in historically underresearched fields, such as Africana philosophy.
13. One is reminded of Paul Ricoeur's remarks concerning "Self-understanding in front of the work": "The text is the medium through which we understands ourselves. This … theme … extends the fundamental characteristic of all discourse whereby the later is addressed to someone. But in contrast to dialogue, this *vis-à-vis* is not given in the situation of discourse; it is, if I may say so, created or instituted by the work itself. A work opens up its readers and thus creates its own subjective *vis-à-vis*. … In contrast to the tradition of the *cogito* and to the pretension of the subject to know itself by immediate intuition, it must be said that *we understand ourselves only by the long detour of the signs of humanity deposited in cultural works.* What would we know of love and hate, of moral feelings and, in general, of all that we call the *self*, if these had not been brought to language and articulated by literature? Thus, what seems most contrary to subjectivity, and what structural analysis discloses as the texture of

the text *is the very medium within which we can understand ourselves*" (2016, p. 155, part II, section 7 "Appropriation," emphasis added). I am grateful to Ralph Weber who suggested the parallel with Paul Ricoeur.
14. See Coquereau-Saouma's discussion of François Jullien in Coquereau-Saouma, forthcoming.
15. The term has been coined by Franz Wimmer, who is also the main exponent of "intercultural philosophy" as opposed to "comparative philosophy."
16. On the Saṃvāda project see Mayaram (2014) (and especially B. Bäumer's contribution within it) and Elise Coquereau-Saouma's discussion of the methodology of dialogue in connection with *saṃvāda* in Coquereau-Saouma (2019). For a different example, one can think of von Stosch's (2018) engagement with contemporary Islamic theologians when discussing the Qurʾān's approach to Jesus.
17. Readers should pause on the "can" before pointing out that there are philosophers who have understood, e.g., Plato without having translated him. I am not claiming that no one can thoroughly understand a text unless they translate it, but just that translating is a useful way to bring oneself back to the text and test one's understanding thereof.
18. In this sense, translations also push one beyond the alternative between a charitable and a noncharitable reading (about which see the debate between Schwitzgebel (2017) and Adamson (2016)). One cannot focus only on what looks "sensible and pedestrian" (Schwitzgebel 2017) if one is forced to translate the whole text, instead of producing a succinct summary of it.
19. What about, one might ask, a wrong translation? This counts as a failed test of one's understanding, like a perceptual error is for perception. My argument above relies on the fact that a philosophically able translator will sooner or later become aware of their errors while translating a whole work, because they will note that what they are reading now clashes with what they thought they had understood. I am aware of how this is a hermeneutic circle and is never ended. In this sense, translations are always perfectible, and the practice of translating will nonetheless continue sharpening one's understanding. By contrast, in the case of writing essays about a given author or text, one might avoid, consciously or unconsciously, facing points conflicting with one's interpretation.
20. I discussed this method in Freschi (2018).
21. Many of the problems intrinsic in this imbalanced comparison are discussed by A. Raghumararaju at the beginning of Raghuramaraju (2018).
22. For a discussion of multi-agent systems, see Kaufman (2011).
23. Even Leo Strauss' pioneer essay on censorship (tellingly composed in 1941) discusses the need of encrypting information for laypeople, not for one's fellow philosophers. Thus, censorship might be a factor when philosophers speak to, or can be read by, people in power, and especially when they talk about issues people in power are interested in, such as religious or political topics, less so when they discuss logic or epistemology. Moreover, philosophers are generally bright thinkers and are skilled in communicating with colleagues of their times and of the future. I can therefore imagine Veṅkaṭanātha being less outspoken on a given issue, but I am also convinced he would warn his readers about what was happening, just like his anxiety about the possible reactions of his audience to his inclusion of Pūrva Mīmāṃsā within his school is apparent precisely while he insists on how his authoritative predecessors had already accepted it. For an enjoyable experiment of how could this happen within literary criticism, one might want to read Antonio Manzini's short story *Critica della*

ragione ("Critique of Reason"). More importantly, such point of view, if taken to its extreme consequences, would lead us to a hermeneutical paralysis, suspecting the text instead of entering in dialogue with it in all cases for which we have not enough historical data (a circumstance which covers most of Sanskrit philosophy). By contrast, I completely agree with Strauss's approach when he suggests reading between the lines and with the conclusion of Strauss (1941), namely "The works of the great writers of the past are very beautiful even from without. And yet their visible beauty is sheer ugliness, compared with the beauty of those hidden treasures which disclose themselves only after very long, never easy, but always pleasant work."
I am grateful to Ralph Weber for having raised this objection.
24. In this article, Uehara deals with Japanese philosophy and how translations from Chinese shaped its self-awareness, while the reader is reminded of how translations shaped philosophy in the Latin world, in the Islamic world, and then again during the Renaissance.
25. Also noteworthy in this connection are Ladmiral's reflections on the reflectiveness inherent in translating (and in doing philosophy) in Ladmiral (1994).

References

Adamson, Peter (2016), "Rules for History of Philosophy," *History of Philosophy without Any Gaps*. Available online: https://historyofphilosophy.net/all-20-rules-history-philosophy (accessed April 22, 2021).

Arvan, Marcus (2015), "The Peer-to-Peer Hypothesis and a New Theory of Free Will," *Scientia Salon*. Available online: https://scientiasalon.wordpress.com/2015/01/30/the-peer-to-peer-hypothesis-and-a-new-theory-of-free-will-a-brief-overview/ (accessed April 22, 2021).

Bostrom, Nick (2003), "Are We Living in a Computer Simulation?," *Philosophical Quarterly*, 53 (211): 243–55.

Calvino, Italo (1991), *Why Read the Classics?*, M. L. McLaughlin (ed.), Boston: Mariner Books.

Coquereau-Saouma, Elise (2019), "Intercultural Dialogues and the Creativity of Knowledge: A Study on Daya Krishna," PhD thesis, Charles University, Prague, and University of Vienna.

Coquereau-Saouma, Elise (forthcoming), "François Jullien's Lexicon," in Georg Stenger and François Jullien (eds.), *De l'Être au Vivre: Lexique Euro-Chinois de la pensée*, Stuttgart: Metzler and Springer.

Freschi, Elisa (2015), "Free Will in Viśiṣṭādvaita Vedānta: Rāmānuja, Sudarśana Sūri and Veṅkaṭanātha," *Religion Compass*, 9 (9): 287–96.

Freschi, Elisa (2018), "Alternative Theisms," *The Philosophers' Magazine*, 82: 94–8.

Freschi, Elisa, and Philipp André Maas (2017), "Introduction: Conceptual Reflections on Adaptive Reuse," in Elisa Freschi and Philipp André Maas (eds.), *Adaptive Reuse: Aspects of Creativity in South Asian Cultural History*, 11–25, Wiesbaden: Deutsche Morgenländische Gesellschaft. Harrassowitz.

Fulbrook, Mary (2002), *Historical Theory*, Abingdon, Oxon: Routledge.

Jeffers, Chike, and Peter Adamson, "History of Africana philosophy" (Podcast). Available online: https://podcasts.apple.com/us/podcast/history-of-indian-and-africana-philosophy/id1039976787 (accessed April 22, 2021).

Kaufman, Maike (2011), "Local Decision-Making in Multi-Agent Systems," PhD thesis, University of Oxford.
Kirloskar-Steinbach, Monika, Geeta Ramana, and James Maffie (2014), "Introducing Confluence," *Confluence: Online Journal of World Philosophies*, 1 (1): 7–63.
Ladmiral, Jean-René (1994), *Traduire: théorèmes pour la traduction*, Paris: Tel Gallimard.
Manchanda, Nivi, Chakravarthi Ram-Prasad, and Timothy Williamson (2019), "The Limits of Western Philosophy: With Nivi Manchanda, Chakravarthi Ram-Prasad, Timothy Williamson," *The Institute of Art and Ideas*. Available online: https://www.youtube.com/watch?v=CpIZjKpvM0U (accessed April 22, 2021).
Marino, Francesca (2019), *Blocksophia: La filosofia della blockchain*, Sesto San Giovanni: Mimesis.
Mayaram, Shail (ed.) (2014), *Philosophy as Saṃvāda and Svarāj. Dialogical Meditations on Daya Krishna and Ramchandra Gandhi*, New Delhi: Sage.
Mou, Bo (2010), "On Constructive-Engagement Strategy of Comparative Philosophy," *Comparative Philosophy*, 1 (1): 1–32.
Raghuramaraju, A. (2018), "Bending Deleuze and Guattari for India: Re-Examining the Relation between Art and Politics in Europe and India," in Elise Coquereau-Saouma and Elisa Freschi (eds.) *The Challenge of Postcolonial Philosophy in India: Too Alien for Contemporary Philosophers, Too Modern for Sanskritists?*, 475–87, special issue of *Sophia: International Journal of Philosophy and Traditions*, 57 (3).
Ram-Prasad, Chakravarthi (2019), "What's Philosophy If It Isn't Western?," in *Multicultural Philosophy Conference*, Manchester. Available online: https://www.youtube.com/watch?v=davqrJU97Ck (accessed October 8, 2021).
Ricoeur, Paul ([1981] 2016), *Hermeneutics and the Human Sciences: Essays on Language, Action and Interpretation*, John B. Thompson (ed.), 3rd ed., Cambridge, MA: Cambridge University Press.
Schwitzgebel, Eric (2017), "Against Charity in the History of Philosophy," *The Splintered Mind: Reflections in Philosophy of Psychology, Broadly Construed*. Available online: http://schwitzsplinters.blogspot.com/2017/01/against-charity-in-history-of-philosophy.html (accessed April 22, 2021).
South, James, and Kimberly Engels (eds.) (2018), *Westworld and Philosophy*, Oxford: Wiley-Blackwell.
Stosch, Klaus von (2018), "Reflecting on Approaches to Jesus in the Qur'ān from the Perspective of Comparative Theology," in Francis Xavier Clooney and Klaus von Stosch (eds.), *How to Do Comparative Theology*, 36–58, New York: Fordham University Press.
Strauss, Leo (1941), "Persecution and the Art of Writing," *Social Research: An International Quarterly of Political and Social Science*, 8 (4): 488–504.
Trevi, Mario (1991), "Giobbe: dolore e interrogazione," in Amos Luzzatto (ed.), *Il libro di Giobbe*, 5–52, Milan: Feltrinelli.
Uehara, Mayuko (2010), "The Philosophy of Translation: From Nishida Kitarō to Ogyū Sorai," in James W. Heisig and Rein Raud (eds.), *Frontiers of Japanese Philosophy: Origins and Possibilities*, 305–19, Nagoya: Nanzan Institute for Religion & Culture.

Constellation IV

Postcolonialism and Globalization

7

Reflections for Comparative Method from a Latin American Philosophical Perspective

Gabriel Soldatenko

Graham Parkes (1991: 3) in his important work *Nietzsche and Asian Thought* opens the introduction with the following epigraph:

> I imagine future thinkers in whom European-American indefatigability is combined with the hundredfold-inherited contemplativeness of the Asians: such a combination will bring the riddle of the world to a solution. In the meantime the reflective free spirits have their mission: they are to remove all barriers that stand in the way of a coalescence of human beings.

In this brief thought, Nietzsche offers a useful general starting point for framing a conversation between comparative and Latin American philosophy, and thinking about the ambitious possibilities and some of the conceptual knots such a conversation raises for comparative method. Nietzsche then, provides a novel description for philosophy that gives us a glimpse of a philosophical practice that allows us to recognize a comparative spirit, but one infused by a purpose and horizon that is more akin to a Latin American philosophical sensibility. Thus, Nietzsche asserts that there is a species of "reflective spirits," "free spirits," or philosophers,[1] free of the baggage of the disciplinary herd, which in the context of Latin American and comparative thought, could simply mean the capacity to think outside of, if not beyond, Western philosophic universality. In addition, these free spirits can be further fleshed out in the "Preface" to the *Genealogy of Morals* (1969), where Nietzsche refers to "we men of knowledge" as "honey-gatherers of the spirit," which can be taken to mean something like gatherers of concepts and their genealogies. Again, for comparativists, we could take this simply to mean the effort to identify, collect, and understand a diversity of philosophic concepts and traditions. Lastly, Nietzsche also tells us that these reflective spirits have a unique vocation or calling, to remove all obstacles to the "coalescence of human beings." Taken together, Nietzsche seems to sketch a radical new vision for the practice of philosophy. Here, neither epistemology nor metaphysics enjoy the status of first philosophy, rather, the notorious critic of the herd, offers us a rare vision of the philosopher as shepherd or gatherer, as an agent in the formation of a collective and cooperative humanity. To wit, Nietzsche seems to suggest that some of the barriers to overcome are regional and cultural, in this case the difference between Asian and Euro-American or Western culture. It is also interesting to note that there is no suggestion of overt struggle for primacy, of some ultimate victory for either East or West, rather that the melding, fusion, or coalescence of these distinct cultural forms "will bring the riddle of the world to a solution," and in this respect comes close to a Latin American sensibility that would insist that philosophy ought to have a practical connection to the project of improving human existence.

In this untimely reflection, Nietzsche in broad brushstrokes, anticipates and marks some lofty stakes for the comparative project: the bringing together of humanity and the existential goal of resolving the riddle of the world. Admittedly, the latter is cryptic, but, for our purposes, it serves the purpose of setting an ambitious horizon, one which we could loosely describe as aiming to improve human existence. Consequently, from this Nietzschean reading, comparativists seek to identify and bring to light concepts from other regions and cultural contexts in order to, not only improve and enrich philosophical practice, but more importantly to improve the efficacy of philosophy as a tool for humanity. Put another way, it cannot be the case that comparative philosophy is exhausted by geographic and cultural expansion alone, that is, comparative philosophy does more than simply multiply objects of study, revealing and investigating non-Western concepts *ad infinitum*. Furthermore, to say that such an expansion is for the purposes of improving philosophy as such, also seems like half an answer. To be sure, the creation of a philosophy no longer bound to a provincial eurocentrism is an important first step, but there is a complementary methodological question that follows from this that contemporary comparative philosophy seems to leave understated and in the background, and that is, *why*? Why engage in such a philosophical project? To what end? Latin American philosophy, for its part, has had to consider this meta-philosophical question from its inception, and can perhaps offer some insight for how to think of a contemporary comparative response.

Ironically then, and still from within this Nietzschean perspective, comparative philosophy names a subfield of Western philosophy that heralds the overcoming and realization of the same. Put another way, it is through the investigation and inclusion of non-Western sources that philosophy, as such, is necessarily expanded and remade. In this sense, comparative philosophy has always been committed to the growth of philosophy, so much so that it inevitably entails a constant unease or dissatisfaction with what we take the practice of philosophy to be, and it is the existence of modes of thought outside the West that have provided the contrasting difference necessary for the comparative task of rethinking, remaking, and ultimately improving philosophy. As a result, comparative "free spirits" comb through and study the richness of human thought regardless of geographical, political, cultural, or disciplinary borders in the interest of creating philosophy anew. Thought of in this light, the subfield of comparative philosophy has always carried the radical doubt that Western philosophy alone is insufficient, and hence the project of identifying and understanding non-Western traditions was always, at least implicitly, for the purposes of transforming philosophy, and this has meant, at least in the short term, to overcome the barrier of Western-philosophic universality, and as a result, to make the richness of human thought accessible to all, and again, at least implicitly, for the purposes of improving human existence. Similarly, albeit for distinct historical reasons, Latin American philosophy also shares the goal of critiquing, challenging, and ultimately undoing Western universality, which in turn, also means the creation of a new philosophical discourse. Therefore, comparative and Latin American philosophy share a critical relation with Western philosophy, which by extension is connected to a mutual project of remaking philosophy, and for both subfields, such an orientation is inspired and grounded in a shared interest and commitment to the value of non-Western thought, which together offer us a foundation for a productive reflection on comparative method by way of Latin American philosophy.

These insights notwithstanding, Nietzsche's intuition also highlights the pitfall or limit of a comparativism that would think only in terms of an East–West binary. Certainly, the classical locus of comparative philosophy—"East–West"—had its important initial value in opening and taking seriously forms of thought outside the West, but that was only the first step for a subfield with a much broader project. Indeed, comparativism is the only recognized subfield of Western philosophy that dedicates itself to the study of non-Western philosophical traditions, and for that reason, fairly or not, comparative philosophy has the burden of identifying and attending to *all* non-Western traditions. Hence, the need to temper and be critically self-aware of the potentially exclusionary effect of holding too strongly to a comparativism that is exhausted by East and West.

In fairness, this initial orientation of comparative philosophy was more a historical reflection of Western philosophy's understanding of non-Western thought, rather than any intentional exclusion by comparativists themselves. That is, for much of the history of Western philosophy there were only a handful of traditions that were even acknowledged as being a species of human thought, and Asian philosophies were among these. In the case of the indigenous knowledge systems of the "New World," they were dismissed as satanic and idolatrous by the late scholasticism of the Spanish empire, and in the case of Africa, its thought was either lumped in as part of the Islamic tradition or also dismissed out of hand due to their suspect humanity, chattel slavery being the empirical proof of this Western opinion. To underscore the point, we ought to keep in mind that none of these understandings of non-Western thought were based on mutual dialogue or rational debate between the different philosophies, but simply the expression of a historical geopolitical reality that the West has enjoyed primacy over the rest of the world since roughly 1500. As a result, the classical East–West binary was not a comparative invention, but a holdover geographic sense of what Western philosophy had always already assumed about the history of human thought. Nietzsche then, as that sharp and insightful critic of Western philosophy, stands as an important caution, insofar as *even he* still fell prey to at least one of Western philosophy's prejudices. And, it is also here, to the demolition of this barrier and the broadening of comparative philosophy's scope, that Latin American philosophy can offer some small contribution.

In addition, we can note a second complication for comparative work through Nietzsche, and that is the danger of cultural essentialism, the idea that cultures are static monoliths that can be effectively represented by broad generalizations, like the ones Nietzsche offers between an "indefatigable" Western culture and a "contemplative"

Asian one. Such a distinction is reminiscent of a Hegelian conception of "Spirit," which he went so far as to hierarchize and historicize. While it is certainly the case that contemporary comparativists are acutely aware of this danger and are careful to frame any discussion of Asian thought in its proper cultural and sociohistorical context, the conceptual knot of culture remains. Indeed, it may be the case that the most obvious cultural and philosophical comparisons to make are precisely between those traditions that are completely distinct from one other, but this way of thinking of cross-cultural comparison is complicated by the historical reality that in some parts of the non-Western world local cultures were unable to maintain their integrity and difference as sharply as in the Asian case. In such a context then, any possibility or desire to achieve a culturally authentic understanding is more difficult, if not impossible, to attain.

This contrast, between non-Western traditions and their varied cultural contexts, highlights possible ways that comparative philosophy could expand and complicate how we understand culture and cross-cultural analysis. Stated differently, if it is the case that comparative philosophy has the responsibility of stewardship of non-Western philosophies broadly, then one of the corollaries of such an expansion of the comparative project beyond East–West would also necessarily mean the inclusion of new ways of thinking about culture. For example, in the case of Latin America and the Caribbean, the following terms have been variously deployed for thinking of culture *there*: mestizaje, hybridity, transculturation, and créolité.[2] By extension, and not surprisingly, the methods by which cross-cultural comparison has been undertaken in the Asian contexts may not easily translate to a Latin American one, this in turn reopens an important field for philosophical reflection by comparativists on precisely that conceptual terrain that, perhaps for an East–West orientation, was already settled, and that is, the concept of culture.

It is by way of contrast that Latin American philosophy offers comparative thought a distinct cultural milieu along with new modes and problems for cross-cultural analysis. Ultimately, the goal here is to expand and complicate avenues of cultural analysis rather than set a universal methodological model for all comparativists. In this regard, comparative philosophy is home to a plurality of models of cross-cultural work, in which each region and culture requires a subtly distinct approach, but still share a common goal, the enrichment of philosophical thought and the improvement of human existence. This brief introduction through Nietzsche gives us a general frame through which to take up and look more closely at the conceptual points where comparative and Latin American philosophy intersect; more specifically, through the concept of culture and cross-cultural method; secondly, by way of the related and corollary goal of pushing back against Western philosophic universality and creating philosophy anew; and thirdly, through the meta-philosophical question of the overarching goal and purpose of philosophy. To that end, this chapter is divided into three sections: the first two offering close readings of essays that were foundational to Latin American philosophy and how they relate and contribute to thinking about comparative thought; and the third offering a brief review of useful signposts that Latin American philosophy offers for further reflection on comparative method.

Introducing Latin American Philosophy, Leopoldo Zea (1912–2004), and the Problem of Culture

In introducing Latin American thought to the comparative project, and for the sake of clarity, it is important to distinguish between "philosophy in Latin America" and "Latin American philosophy," that is, Latin American philosophy names a specific and relatively recent philosophical movement within the long history of philosophy in Latin America. Thus, philosophy in Latin America names the general history of philosophy in the region, which can be divided into two general moments: pre-Columbian indigenous thought and Western philosophy. Latin American philosophy then, appears as a localized and critical reaction to a philosophical context where Western philosophical discourse, from 1500 on, was the only perspective that mattered. Beyond this general dissatisfaction with Western philosophy, however, it is a somewhat unsettled question what Latin American philosophy names, and many philosophers in Latin America today would not readily identify themselves as such. This is both a reflection of the newness and ambiguity of Latin American philosophy, and of the powerful grip Western culture, and by extension Western philosophy, has enjoyed in Latin America. In this sense, and as will be made clear in the following pages, the differential relations between Latin American and Asian philosophies to Western philosophy may only be a matter of degrees, but that difference had a profound philosophical effect locally. In short, Latin America represents the most extreme case of the effects of colonization and the concomitant establishment of Western cultural universality, which had a necessary and dramatic effect on philosophical discourse there, which offers comparative philosophers an important and contrasting context for the development of non-Western thought and cross-cultural contact.

Latin American philosophy then, has as one of its defining problematics the following meta-philosophical question: "What has philosophy been taken to *be* and *do* in Latin America?" To unpack this a bit, there is, on the one hand, the *historical* question of the forms that philosophy has taken in Latin America and, on the other, the *practical* question of the purpose philosophy has served in Latin America. As a result, answering the question "what is Latin American philosophy?" is one of the central sites of debate and development of contemporary Latin American philosophy. In this regard, even though Latin American philosophy, the way it is being presented here, is a small part of the history of philosophy in Latin America, it does represent a concentration of contemporary Latin American thinkers who are devoted to the task of critiquing and highlighting the limits of Western philosophy broadly, its specific shortcomings in the Latin American sociohistorical context, and with an eye toward recreating philosophy, such that, it not only includes voices and perspectives from Latin America but can also speak to Latin American's experience and circumstances.[3]

There are two essays that are typically used as benchmarks for the foundation of Latin American philosophy: the first, and older of the two, is by Mexican philosopher Leopoldo Zea, "The Actual Function of Philosophy in Latin America,"[4] where one finds the question of the status and value of a Latin American philosophy posited for the first time. In this sense, and as remarked earlier, Latin American philosophy is unique because its birth is marked by paradoxically posing the question of the status of its own existence. Zea (1986: 220) expresses the problem this way;

> Now, there is one particular issue that concerns not only a few men in our continent, but the Latin American man in general. This issue concerns the possibility or impossibility of Latin American culture, and, as an aspect of the same issue, the possibility or impossibility of Latin American philosophy.

For Zea, it was the cultural context of the World Wars that provoked him to ask about Latin American philosophy; Zea argued that the wars had exposed a crisis in Western culture and by extension Western philosophy, and that this crisis had opened a novel opportunity for Latin American philosophy to both distinguish itself from Western philosophy, and to contribute to philosophical discourse from a Latin American perspective. Zea (1986: 220) explains,

> A Latin American culture, a culture proper to the Latin American man, was considered to be an irrelevant issue; Latin America lived comfortably under the shadow of European culture. However, the latter culture has been shaken (or is in crisis) today ... The man who had lived with so much confidence under a tree he had not planted now finds himself in the open when the planter cuts down the tree and throws it into the fire as useless. The man now has to plant his own cultural tree, create his own ideas.

Zea (1986: 222) puts the problem more concretely a little further on,

> This is the heart of our problem: we do not feel heirs of an autochthonous [Amerindian] culture, because that culture has no meaning for us; and that which has meaning for us, like the European, does not feel as our own ... The malaise is that we want to adjust the Latin American circumstance to a conception of the world inherited from Europe, rather than adjusting that conception to the Latin American circumstance.

There are two crucial points that we can make here relative to comparative philosophy: first, it is revealing that Zea frames Latin American thought as being disconnected from an autochthonous culture and of therefore being completely dependent on European or Western culture. In other words, the way Zea introduces Latin American philosophy is as a subfield of Western philosophy, *not* as a standalone non-Western tradition. Zea then, is walking a fine line between acknowledging a Latin American difference in terms of its "circumstance," but still only having the cultural tools and resources of Western philosophy through which to make sense of that circumstance. Such a situation may perhaps run afoul with a more traditional comparative position that would look suspiciously on Latin American philosophy for not being culturally distinct enough to qualify as a species of non-Western thought. However, such a judgment would be an error because what Zea is attempting to do is mark and establish a specific Latin American difference that could serve as the starting point for the development of Latin American philosophy. That is, although at the moment of Zea's writing a Latin American philosophy did not formally exist, by raising the point that it should and could, he created the ground for the unfolding of a new species of Latin American philosophy that would be dedicated to creating a voice of its own after being smothered and muted since the colonial period. Zea's position is also revealing for his understanding of Latin America's cultural circumstance, such that, Latin American philosophy's birth is more profoundly marked by its complex entanglement with Western culture and philosophy than an attempt to recuperate and reclaim Amerindian modes of thought.

To put this in more explicit comparative terms, what Latin American philosophy offers is a reversal of the order of relations that historically brought non-Western thought to the attention of Western philosophers. For example, with respect to Asian philosophy, the West from an early date had tacitly accepted, in a backhanded way, that some species of religious or mystical thought existed in "the East," and as a result there had been a steady curiosity from more generous Western philosophers who were willing to take up and investigate Asian thought more seriously, Leibniz being perhaps the most famous early example of this tendency. In general, what we can say about the historical route of reception of Asian philosophy is that it was predominantly Western philosophers with a genuine curiosity and interest in understanding the thought of other regions and cultures that took up the task. In contrast, in the case of Latin America and the Caribbean, what we find is the demand by non-Western philosophers that they be recognized as philosophically distinct from Western philosophy. In the case of these non-Western philosophers we find an effort to distinguish a new species of non-Western thought, where Western philosophy had dominated for centuries. Thus, whereas in the Asian cases one finds a relative isolation and independence from Western philosophy, in Latin America there is a complex historical and cultural relation at play, such that, Latin American philosophers had to remind not only Western philosophers, but Latin Americans as well, that they had the capacity to contribute philosophically and that Latin American social life, culture, and history were worth philosophizing about. Zea, to his credit, was among the first to raise the possibility of this move toward a Latin American philosophical independence; and, although Zea did not take the leap himself, he did make it possible for Latin American philosophers who followed to both take a more critical position toward the monopoly of Western culture in Latin America, and more clearly understand themselves as non-Western philosophers.

The second comparative point worth making, is of Zea's own description of the cultural context of Latin America, and here we can return to his claim that Latin Americans "do not feel as heirs" to Amerindian culture. Although it is true that in the context of academic philosophy such a thing as a Latin American tradition did not exist, it is a much grander claim to say that effectively *only* Western culture existed in Latin America, and it is in this latter sense that Zea seems to overstep. We can explain this slip in two ways and both are linked to the complex problem of culture in Latin America. The first cause, we could describe as the problem of *cultural dependence*, and a horizon that Zea did not seem to be able to see beyond. Thus, Zea would write: "The Latin American man knows himself to be the heir of Western culture and now demands a place in it. The place that he demands is that of collaborator. As son of that culture he no longer wants to live off it but work for it" (1986: 225). Or again, "Latin America finds itself at a vantage point in time—which may not last long—but that must be used to initiate the task that belongs to it as an adult member of Western culture" (229). Unfortunately, for Zea, this position hinged on the naïve hope that Latin American thought would be accepted as properly part of the Western patrimony, a concession that Western philosophy had never made. From Zea's perspective, if Latin America was essentially culturally Western, then it ought to be seen as an equal contributing member to Western philosophy, since it is the only philosophical voice the region had. After all, by the late nineteenth century the transcendentalists and pragmatists had achieved that status for North America, why not Latin America? It is telling that a Latin American philosopher could not anticipate this rejection given the history of the West and its treatment of non-Western peoples, but it was precisely Zea's commitment and dependence on Western culture that blinded him.

The second cause for Zea's oversight could be named the problem of *cultural exclusion*, that is, for as much as Zea's framing of Latin American culture raised the complex issues that accompanied Latin American philosophy, it also dismissed wholesale the important cultural inheritance and residue of the pre-Columbian societies of the Western hemisphere. In effect, for as much as Zea may have gotten right in terms of highlighting the cultural tension between Latin America and the West, he also flattened the differences by not attending to the inescapable indigenous cultural influence that is part of Latin American history and identity. In fairness, it is important that we do not think of Zea's stance here as an expression of his racism, but rather as a kind of general Latin American ethnocentric common sense with historic roots in the colonial period where societies in the Americas were universally organized according to a strict racial and cultural hierarchy. Thus, it should not be surprising that after four hundred years of living in such a context, Latin Americans, particularly those in larger urban centers and in the middle and upper classes, were inculcated to develop a certain prejudice and sense of identity where they often rejected and dismissed any relation to indigeneity and aspired, and imagined themselves, to be Western. To underscore this point, we can think of the similar racial experiences of French Caribbean colonial subjects like Aimé Césaire and Frantz Fanon, who had to live in France to understand that black folks from the colonies were never really accepted as "Frenchmen," even though their school text books in Martinique taught them to say "I am a Gaul." It is therefore the historical roots, sociopolitical effects, and cultural trauma of Latin America that Zea helped to open up to philosophical reflection, and which constitute the cornerstones of Latin American philosophy today.

As a result, and with respect to comparative philosophy, what Latin America presents us with is a non-Western context with a unique cultural knot where Latin America represents a cultural example that does not conform to a neat distinction between Western and non-Western cultures in relative isolation. That is, by highlighting the specific problems of cultural dependence and cultural exclusion Zea identifies the complex character of cultural analysis in Latin America, where what it means to be Latin American involves the tripartite relation between an indigenous past, Western colonialism, and the varied ways that they have mixed over time and created a distinct

Latin American cultural context. Further, and in a strictly philosophical sense, Latin America's cultural situation also offers a further complication where the relation between Western and non-Western is marked by the historical effort to quash and stamp out indigenous thought and replace it with Western modes. In this regard, the history of Latin American philosophy since 1500, presents us with the reality that philosophy in Latin America is necessarily caught in an agonistic comparative situation where multiple traditions are in a tense and sometimes hostile relation to one another, and this is a direct result of the colonial relation. In general, and since Zea, the effort to establish a novel Latin American philosophical sensibility has required work along the following three trajectories: first, the creation of a new decolonized framework for thinking of the Western–non-Western philosophic relationship, such that the colonial judgment that only Western philosophy mattered was jettisoned. Secondly, an effort to clearly mark out the concepts, questions, and themes that would constitute the field of investigation for Latin American philosophy. And thirdly, the hard work of recuperating and sketching out pre-Columbian systems of thought that had been nearly wiped out and still live on within the various indigenous communities of the continent.

Augusto Salazar Bondy (1927–1974) and the Sociopolitical Character of Latin American Philosophy

Building on Zea, the second essay that forms the bookend to the initial formation of Latin American philosophy, is Peruvian philosopher Augusto Salazar Bondy's "Can There be a Latin American Philosophy?"[5] This essay, like Zea's, was also written in a time of crisis, which equally influenced the philosophical argument. However, there was a key difference between the two crises: for Zea, the World Wars had created a *cultural* crisis that conditioned the possibility for a Latin American philosophy, and for Bondy, the crisis was of a distinctively *political* nature. Globally, and most acutely across the non-Western world, revolution and decolonization were in the air, from Latin America to Algeria and Vietnam. Thus, Latin America during the late 1960s, like much of the non-Wester world, was deep in the throes of social unrest and upheaval. For instance, the success of the Cuban Revolution in 1959 had, for better or worse, inspired the desire for radical change across the continent, and student activism was commonplace throughout the region and was punctuated by the massacre in Tlatelolco in 1968. It was also during this period that the influential social movement that would eventually bring Salvador Allende to power in Chile was organizing and roiling. And lastly, it was also during these years that the radical and novel Latin American interpretation of Christianity known as "Liberation Theology" took shape. Bondy's essay then, has some of this political fire without ever being explicitly committed to any ideological position. That is, Bondy managed to present a withering critique of both philosophy in Latin America and its sociopolitical context, without overstating and claiming to have a solution. Thus, the essay reads more like a manifesto and call to philosophical action, or rather a call for a philosophy of action.

As a result, Bondy answers the title of his essay in the affirmative, but only suggests the basic criteria that constitute the point of departure and goal of a Latin American philosophy. In addition, Bondy does not write his essay as a response to Zea, nor does he cite him, but he does accept the same general account of a Latin American cultural and philosophical context dominated by Western norms. Bondy (1986: 233) puts it succinctly,

> To review the process of Hispanic American philosophy is to relate the passing of Western philosophy through our countries, or to narrate European philosophy *in* Hispanic America. It is not to tell the history of a natural philosophy *of* Hispanic America ... there are no creative figures to found and nurture their own peculiar tradition, nor native philosophic "*isms*."

Unlike Zea, however, Bondy does offer a harsh appraisal of philosophy in Latin America and delivers a full-throated call for the meta-philosophical task of creating a distinct non-Western Latin American philosophy. With respect to Bondy's assessment of philosophy in Latin America, and for the sake of brevity, we will highlight only two of his sharpest criticisms: the first, is what he calls an "imitative sense of thought," which he describes as a mode of thinking "done according to theoretical molds already shaped in the pattern of Western thought—mainly European—imported in the form of currents, schools, and systems totally defined in their content and orientation" (Bondy 1986: 234). In contrast to Zea, then, who took a relatively neutral position and understood this situation simply as the context of philosophy in Latin America, Bondy problematizes it; that is, he understood it as a limiting and debilitating factor that demanded the creation of an entirely *new* philosophical mode for Latin America. Thus, Bondy was critiquing what philosophy in Latin America was, and that it was inadequate to a Latin American context, because of its reliance on Western philosophy, and as a result called for the meta-philosophical task of creating a new and "authentic" Latin American philosophy.

The second criticism, Bondy describes as a permanent feature of philosophy in Latin America, and that is, "the great distance between those who practice philosophy and the whole of the community." Bondy (1986: 235) goes on,

> There is no way to consider our philosophies as national thought, with a differential seal, as one speaks of a German, French, English, or Greek philosophy. It is also impossible for the community to recognize itself in these philosophies, precisely because we are dealing with transplanted thought, the spiritual products of other men and cultures.

In total then, Bondy paints a bleak picture of philosophy in Latin American and sets the stage for his radical call for not only a new Latin American philosophy, but a philosophy with the added responsibility of having an immediate and practical value to the community and locus that calls it into being. In this respect, Bondy completes the idea that appears still half-formed in Zea, and understands the project of a Latin American philosophy as a form of philosophical independence. Consequently, the birth of Latin American philosophy amounts to the creation of a species of non-Western thought, and this is because it is linked to the Latin American *social* need for liberation. For Bondy (1986: 240–1) then, Latin American philosophy is brought into existence as a result, and in the midst of, a sociopolitical problematic:

> If we are aware that this cultural and philosophical condition is not peculiar to Hispanic American countries, but is largely similar to that of other countries and regional groups of nations, belonging to what today is called the Third World, then it is clear that, to explain it, we must utilize the concept of underdevelopment, with the correlative concepts of domination.

Bondy therefore adds a dimension to the project of Latin American philosophy that Zea had not raised, and clearly lays the sociopolitical ground of a non-Western Latin American philosophy whose primary purpose is to push back against "domination." For Bondy then, Latin American philosophy at once *emerges* from within a cultural and philosophical context of Western domination but also *exists and works against* a related and corollary sociopolitical context of domination, and therefore has a necessary and practical responsibility in effecting liberation. Bondy (1986: 242) puts all this in philosophical terms:

> Hegel said that the owl of Minerva took flight at dusk, thus giving philosophy the character of a theory that elucidates the meaning of facts already accomplished. It is not always so. Contrary to what Hegel thought, we feel that philosophy can be, and on more than one historic occasion has had to be, the messenger of the dawn, the beginning of historic change through a radical awareness of existence projected toward the future.

In short, Bondy argues for a Latin American philosophy that is meant to contribute to "historic change," by way of a critique of the present, and with an eye toward a Latin American horizon free of domination.

From a comparative perspective, what is worth highlighting here is that it is the turn to sociopolitical philosophy that firmly establishes the non-Western character of Latin American philosophy. That is, what allows Bondy to decisively break with Western philosophy in a way that Zea could not was the demand that Latin American philosophy must be linked in some way to the local situation and community. Through Bondy then, Latin American philosophy becomes a clearer example of non-Western thought not because it presents a self-contained tradition that developed in isolation, but rather because it is a philosophical discourse that emerges and takes shape as it tackles the unique complexity of the Latin American cultural, social, and political context of domination. Thus, Latin American philosophy is non-Western because it generates a set of ideas and themes that are called into being by the specificity of Latin American circumstances. In contrast to Zea then, who argued that Latin American philosophy be a junior partner to Western philosophy and thought of the Latin American philosophical project as primarily reflecting on the cultural knot of Latin American identity, and its complex relation to the West; Bondy offered a vision for

Latin American philosophy that, in addition to the problem of identity, would also play an important role in the improvement of Latin American social life. In this sense, Bondy was suggesting nothing less than a revolution in philosophy in Latin America, where the discipline of philosophy was to be remade according to the demands of the Latin American context and for its liberation.

To be clear, even for Bondy, this did not mean the wholesale dismissal of Western philosophy, but a careful, creative, and critical parsing out of those concepts that could be useful to the task of creating Latin America anew. Bondy (1986: 243–4) explains the relation to Western philosophy this way,

> Consequently, those who heed the call of reflexive thought in Hispanic America cannot dispense with the acquisition of the techniques developed by [Western] philosophy in its long history, nor can they cast aside all those concepts capable of serving as support of a solid national cultural base. But all the while they must keep in mind their provisional and instrumental character and not take them as models and contents to be imitated and repeated as if they were absolute. Rather, they must be taken as tools to be utilized as long as there are no others more effective and more adequate to the discovery and expression of our anthropological essence.

Consequently, even though Latin American philosophy may be distinct and independent from Western philosophy, it may still keep and use those concepts that are efficacious to the end of producing liberation in Latin America. This is a pragmatic concern for those pieces of Western philosophy, or any tradition for that matter, that may be of use in the Latin American context, and, for Bondy, it is the task of Latin American philosophers to parse out and determine what those may be. In the end, the species of Latin American philosophy that Bondy proposes is one that is a response to a Latin American circumstance where philosophy in Latin America was no longer sufficient for the task required, and this in turn meant that Latin American philosophers had to take seriously the meta-philosophical questions of what philosophy ought to *be* here, along with the corollary question of what philosophy ought to *do* here? In this general way, Latin American philosophy offers a rich meta-philosophical discourse that could serve comparative philosophers with similar, if understated concerns, well.

Three Signposts for Comparative Reflection

To this point, we have traced the general conceptual ground that Latin American and comparative philosophy share through a brief reflection on one of Nietzsche's suggestive visions for a philosophy of the future. In addition, we have taken a close look at two of the foundational texts of Latin American philosophy and highlighted the unique historical circumstances, cultural knots, and political characteristics of this relatively new species of non-Western thought. Taken together, what this brief review of Latin American philosophy was meant to provide a comparative audience was a contrasting non-Western example that does not fit within the standard East–West framework, and can offer some ways in which to expand and complicate what we take comparative philosophy to be. By way of conclusion then, we can briefly take up three upshots that can function as the basis for further conversation between Latin American and comparative philosophy.

1. Colonialism: In a previous article, I made the case that the most salient set of concepts that Latin American philosophy offers comparative thought are colonialism, coloniality, and decolonization.[6] I argued that for Latin American philosophy there is no more important and formative historical event than colonialism, and it is that basic idea that also has some value for comparative philosophy broadly. For example, the possibility and creation of sustained cultural contact between the West and much of the non-Western world was precisely through colonial expansion. In this sense, colonialism was the basic setting and backdrop for cross-cultural contact between West and non-West, and this is equally true for Latin America and Asia. Moreover, Latin America represents the first and conditioning instance of cross-cultural engagement during the period, and it was fundamentally marked by violence, exploitation, and racism. Further, it was this same mode of colonialism and its attendant practices, with varying degrees of success, that would also make its way to Asia. Thus, it is no coincidence that the first Western efforts to engage in linguistic study and translation, along with engaging non-Western thought broadly, in both Latin American and Asia, were undertaken by missionaries. Furthermore, and in both cases, the motivation for such work was the same, as an extension of cultural domination generally, and for the project of Christian conversion specifically.

In this respect, the colonial experience, and its differential effects, is one way that Latin American and Asian philosophy are part of a common conversation. We could go so far as to say that it is precisely the colonial period that creates the need for a Western–non-Western distinction, and this was especially the case for philosophy. More specifically, for Western philosophy the years between 1500–1800 were central to the formal establishment of Western universality, such that, all other non-Western traditions were judged to not meet the bar of Western rationality. Relatedly, and as Peter Park convincingly shows in *Africa, Asia, and the History of Philosophy* (2013), it was also in the late eighteenth and early nineteenth centuries that philosophy took its disciplinary shape as a field of study wholly monopolized by Western philosophy. For non-Western philosophy, on the other hand, this period meant at best exclusion and dismissal, and at worst wholesale destruction and erasure. Perhaps a more accurate way of describing this historical period and the forms of cross-cultural contact it produced, is to instead think of it as one that inaugurated and invented *borders*. That is, "contact" in the context of colonialism was patently negative and harmful for non-Western people and their cultures. Thus, certainly the borders between West and non-West were drawn, and correlatively the borders between modern and primitive, civilized and savage, and, in at least the case of Africans and Amerindians, human and non-human. It is for these general reasons that the concept of colonialism and the centrality it plays in Latin American philosophy may offer a further avenue for comparative reflection and the study of cross-cultural contact.

To offer just one concrete example of how colonialism can supplement comparative work, we can look at the introduction to *Comparative Philosophy Without Borders* (2015), where Arindam Chakrabarti and Ralph Weber offer a detailed picture of the moving parts that constitute comparative method: first, there is the individual making the comparison and their particular philosophical disposition, their area of specialization and regional interests for example; second, there are the two *relata* that are to be compared; third, the concepts or traditions to be compared are placed in relation to some *tertium*, that through which the *comparanda* are being compared. Lastly, they note a "pre-comparative *tertium*," what they refer to as the "clothes" of the comparer. So, for Chakrabarti and Weber, there is an important distinction between an individual's preferred philosophical position, and the broader philosophical context within which they happen to be working. Taking this description and pairing it with the concept of colonialism we get a fuller and more accurate sense of the comparative situation, where colonialism had a formative effect both on that which is typically compared, West versus non-West, and, more importantly, on the grid of intelligibility within which philosophers do their work. That is, Western philosophic universality is still the common sense that holds when philosophers define or describe the history and purpose of philosophy. In short, and from a Latin American philosophical perspective, colonialism and its historical impact provides a useful and supplementary concept that calibrates and gives a more accurate sense of comparative philosophy relative to Western philosophy broadly, where the pre-comparative *tertium* is not value neutral, but at some times indifferent and at others hostile to the comparative project, and more suspicious and skeptical of non-Western philosophy as such.

2. Language in the Study of non-Western Philosophy: As suggested earlier in the chapter, if it is the case that comparative philosophy has a responsibility to non-Western philosophies in general, then one of the points that follow from this is a necessary expansion of how we understand and practice comparison. There is no doubt that one of the primary routes of development of cross-cultural philosophy in the Asian context has been through philology and the difficult task of translating and making Asian philosophical texts accessible and understandable to Westerners. In the case of Latin America, however, philology has had a minimal role to play and is exclusively confined to the study of pre-Columbian thought. That is, the use of philology as an arm of Latin American philosophy, or as a tool for cross-cultural analysis *there*, has been almost entirely absent, and it has been scholars outside of philosophy who have taken up that work, namely anthropologists, historians, and art historians. It is only until quite recently that one finds philology and the investigation of pre-Columbian thought being conducted by Latin American philosophers themselves.

This, however, is not to say that language and its investigation is not an important part of Latin American philosophy. Rather, the philosophical value of language in the Latin American context exists on a different register outside of the problem of translation. In this respect, it is worth mentioning that Latin America has a rich literary history that in many ways anticipates and runs parallel to Latin American philosophy. Indeed, it is through literature that one finds a sustained conversation on Latin American identity and experience that predates the formal development of Latin American philosophy. To expand this point, it was the case that for much of the history of Latin America, those thinkers who had the desire to reflect on and treat Latin American experience and identity could not use philosophical discourse because of the limiting "imitative" character of the discipline and its commitment to

Western philosophical norms, and thus literature became the primary outlet. To give an example of this phenomenon, we can think of the Martinician thinker Aimé Césaire who spurned philosophical discourse and relied instead on surrealism and poetry as his main tools for the construction of the Negritude Movement. There are two points worth underscoring here: the first is the anemic character of philosophy through the twentieth century in Latin America and the Caribbean, such that, literature was the more attractive option for those interested in working and reflecting on the experience and value of non-Western subjects and places. Second, is the specific role of language here, where the philosophical value of Latin American and Caribbean languages is not in the first place in translation, but in creative writing.

By way of contrast then, if one of the classic problems of translation for an East–West comparative approach is how to convey, as authentically as possible, a non-Western cultural concept in Western terms, then in Latin America the philosophical problem of language is one where Western cultural forms were imposed by force, and it is through those same cultural resources that Latin Americans accounted for the specificity of a non-Western context and experience. In the Latin American case then, the question is not so much of translation since the languages are already Western, whether Spanish, French, English, Dutch, or Portuguese, but its creative use, such that it can effectively express and describe the context on which it was imposed. To drive this point home, we can turn to the words of James Baldwin in a short editorial, "If Black English Isn't a Language, Then Tell Me, What Is?," where he writes, "People evolve a language to describe and thus control their circumstances, or in order not to be submerged by a reality that they cannot articulate. (And, if they cannot articulate it, they *are* submerged" (1998: 780). Baldwin (1998: 781) continues a little further on,

> It goes without saying, then, that language is also a political instrument, means, and proof of power. It is the most vivid and crucial key to identity ... There have been, and are, times, and places, when to speak a certain language could be dangerous and even fatal. Or, one may speak the same language, but in such a way that one's antecedents are revealed, or (one hopes) hidden.

Thus, Baldwin claims that "a language comes into existence by means of brutal necessity, and the rules of the language are dictated by what the language must convey" (782). It is language thought of in this sense, that in the Latin American philosophical context, must be added alongside the philology and translation of pre-Columbian texts and ideas, and it is both uses of language that together make up the ground for cross-cultural work, but which at the same time opens other possibilities for how to think more broadly of the philosophical value of language in comparative work.

3. The Purpose of Comparative Philosophy: In closing this chapter, we can briefly take up one of the most influential Latin American philosophers of the last several decades, Enrique Dussel and his essay "A New Age in the History of Philosophy" (2008) where he sketches out his own vision for a philosophy of the future. We can frame the essay as being written from a Latin American philosophical perspective but addressing themes that are important to comparative thought, the project of remaking philosophy and embracing an inclusive and global philosophical sensibility. In short, this essay is

important because it is one of the rare instances where a Latin American philosopher clearly touches on concerns that are at the heart of comparative work. That is, a broad consideration for non-Western philosophies and the related concern of how such a global diversity can be accounted for and included within the discipline of philosophy. Furthermore, we can highlight how Dussel tempers Bondy's political framing, such that, the project for philosophy is not overtly revolutionary but is framed as a tool for attending to the needs of humanity, what Dussel describes as "core universal problems." Indeed, Dussel argues for a polycentric history of philosophy that does not begin with any single thinker or tradition, but rather traces the varied responses to these problems. In the earliest stages of this history of philosophy the kind of core universal problems he suggests are in response to the thrownness of human existence and its common "bewilderment in the face of the real." More concretely, this bewilderment produces two general lines of questioning: one, attempting to account for external reality, and the other attempting to offer some explanation and justification for human existence and behavior. Thus, for Dussel, every region and culture, according to its specific rationality, produced answers and coherent systems of understanding that respond to the core universal problems.

Not surprisingly, Dussel argues that the independent development of all these philosophical traditions underwent a jarring interruption with the colonial moment such that their independence was universally challenged and, at some instances, whole traditions erased. Thus, the previous diversity of human thought, before the colonial period, was flattened by the insistence and judgment that the West had the only mode of philosophizing or reasoning that could "correctly" respond to the core universal problems. The title of the essay then, in speaking to a "new age" in philosophy, is asserting the idea that philosophical discourse today, and in the future, cannot accept the ethnocentric judgment of the past. Furthermore, it is Dussel's description of what this new philosophic practice ought to look like that is of most interest to comparativists, because he offers an account of the process for producing and maintaining a globally inclusive philosophy. In the most general sense, Dussel's purpose is to expand philosophy, such that it more explicitly includes non-Western traditions and through such an expansion enriches the available resources for humanity's effort to resolve today's core universal problems, which are no longer the same as in the ancient past, but now include problems like: poverty and the environment.

In this respect, Dussel is proposing an encyclopedic project where a necessary step in a philosophy of the future is an inclusive and thorough accounting of all traditions, in order to expand the philosophical resources available to all. Thus, according to this account, no tradition has priority; instead according to the context and problem, people can use and borrow those philosophical resources that are most useful for their resolution. Consequently, Dussel can imagine instances where concepts from Asian traditions may be of use in a Latin American context, and vice versa. Ultimately, Dussel's aim here is not to declare winners and losers, or to identify the "best" or "most true" tradition, but rather to put all traditions at the same table so that they can actually have a conversation. Again, the similarities with the comparative project are clear here.

For Dussel, this philosophical project is at once critical, recuperative, and creative. Critical, in the sense that Dussel understands the creation of this new philosophy as being built, at least in part, through an important and necessary philosophical dialogue. One which Dussel describes as being a "North-South" dialogue, where the traditions of the global South address the philosophy of the global North, or Western philosophy, to critique and correct the various ways in which Western philosophy historically made errors in its assessment, treatment, and description of non-Western places and people. The point in such an exercise is not to dismiss Western philosophy, but to calibrate and correct its missteps, such that expressions of ethnocentrism, racism, misogyny, and homophobia are clearly marked, tempered, and challenged. In addition, Dussel also posits a complementary South–South dialogue between non-Western traditions, for the purpose of recuperating and rediscovering non-Western modes of thought and traditions that were formerly dismissed or forgotten. Further, a South–South dialogue is also important because it would foster dialogue and reflection between traditions that have almost solely relied on Western philosophy as their only interlocutor. Lastly, these dialogues offer a rich and creative vein for fruitful cross-cultural dialogues, particularly for the purpose of expanding our philosophical imagination, both in terms of what philosophy is, and what philosophy does.

The kind of philosophic project Dussel proposes is not one aimed toward a new universal meta-philosophy that everyone ought to subscribe to, and where all regional distinctions fall away. Rather, the emphasis here is in keeping particularity and pluralism, precisely because it is these differences that enrich human thought. Moreover, Dussel seems to underscore that for such an anarchic philosophy to work, it requires cooperation and dialogue across traditions, not for the purposes of fixing philosophy but for realizing philosophy as a practical tool for humanity. Indeed, there is a strain within the history of comparative thought that understands the project as intending to strengthen or fix problems in Western philosophy. I wonder, though, if such a framing misses the forest for the trees; that precisely such an emphasis on aiding or fixing the West misses the bigger opportunity to create philosophy anew. To demand that philosophy ought not to have the distinction of West and non-West and that philosophy is not so much about aiding or fixing any tradition, but aiding and fixing human existence.

Notes

1. The use of "reflective spirits" is suggestive of Nietzsche's frequent use of "free spirits" as an equivalent term for the "philosopher of the future," or as the philosopher who is the creator and practitioner of the "philosophy of the future." E.g., part 2: "The Free Spirit" in Nietzsche (1966).
2. Briefly, just to name a representative thinker for each term see the following: with respect to mestizaje, José Vasconcelos, *La Raza Cosmica* (2012); with respect to hybridity, Néstor García Canclini, *Hybrid Cultures* (1995); with respect to transculturation, Fernando Ortiz, *Cuban Counterpoint* (1995); and with respect to créolité, Edouard Glissant, *Caribbean Discourse* (1989).
3. To name just a few of the major figures of contemporary Latin American philosophy: Enrique Dussel, Nelson Maldonado-Torres, Walter Mignolo, Maria

Lugones, Linda Alcoff, Catherine Walsh, Santiago Castro-Gomez, and Eduardo Mendietta.
4. Originally published as Leopoldo Zea (1942), "En torno a la filosofía americana," in *Cuadernos Americanos*.
5. Originally published in John P. Augelli, ed. (1969), *The Meaning and Problem of Hispanic American Thought*. Additionally, this essay was an abridged summary of a longer treatment published the year before, *¿Existe una filosofía de nuestra América?*. Also, note that the publication of this essay was in an anthology by a Latin American studies department rather than philosophy, highlighting the ambiguous value of Latin American thought for Western philosophy.
6. See Gabriel Soldatenko (2015).

References

Baldwin, James (1998), "If Black English Isn't a Language, Then Tell Me, What Is?," in Toni Morrison (ed.), *James Baldwin Collected Essays*, 780–3, New York: Literary Classics of the United States.

Bondy, Augusto Salazar (1968), *¿Existe una filosofía de nuestra América?*, Mexico: Siglo XXI.

Bondy, Augusto Salazar (1986), "Can There be a Latin American Philosophy?," in Jorge Gracia (ed.), *Latin American Philosophy in the Twentieth Century*, 233–44, Amherst: Prometheus Books. Originally published in John P. Augelli (ed.) (1969), *The Meaning and Problem of Hispanic American Thought*, Lawrence: Center of Latin American Studies University of Kansas.

Chakrabarti, Arindam, and Ralph Weber (2015), "Introduction," in Arindam Chakrabarti and Ralph Weber (eds.), *Comparative Philosophy without Borders*, 1–33, New York: Bloomsbury.

Dussel, Enrique (2008), "A New Age in the History of Philosophy: The World Dialogue between Philosophical Traditions," *Prajna Vihara: The Journal of Philosophy and Religion*, 9 (1): 1–22.

García Canclini, Néstor (1995), *Hybrid Cultures: Strategies for Entering and Leaving Modernity*, Minneapolis: University of Minnesota Press.

Glissant, Edouard (1989), *Caribbean Discourse: Selected Essays*, Charlottesville: University Press of Virginia.

Nietzsche, Friedrich (1966), "The Free Spirit," in Friedrich Nietzsche, *Beyond Good and Evil: Prelude to a Philosophy of the Future*, trans. Walter Kaufmann, 33–56, New York: Vintage Books.

Nietzsche, Friedrich (1969), "Preface," in Friedrich Nietzsche, *On the Genealogy of Morals*, trans. Walter Kaufmann, 15–23, New York: Vintage Books.

Ortiz, Fernando ([1940] 1995), *Cuban Counterpoint, Tobacco and Sugar*, Durham, NC: Duke University Press.

Park, Peter (2013), *Africa, Asia, and the History of Philosophy: Racism in the Formation of the Philosophical Canon, 1780–1830*, Albany, NY: SUNY Press.

Parkes, Graham (1991), "Introduction," in Graham Parkes (ed.), *Nietzsche and Asian Thought*, 3–19, Chicago: University of Chicago Press.

Soldatenko, Gabriel (2015), "A Contribution toward the Decolonization of Philosophy: Asserting the Coloniality of Power in the Study of Non-western Philosophical Traditions," *Comparative and Continental Philosophy*, 7 (2): 138–56.

Vasconcelos, José ([1925] 2012), *La Raza Cosmica*, 6th ed., México: Editorial Porrúa.

Zea, Leopoldo (1986), "The Actual Function of Philosophy in Latin America," in Jorge Gracia (ed.), *Latin American Philosophy in the Twentieth Century*, 219–30, Amherst, MA: Prometheus Books. Originally published as Leopoldo Zea (1942), "En torno a la filosofia americana," *Cuadernos Americanos*, 3: 63–78.

8

Why Philosophy Needs Sanskrit, Now More than Ever

Jonardon Ganeri

It is becoming increasingly apparent that philosophy, in the institutionalized form it takes in the contemporary academy and most especially in the way it is practiced in the dispersed anglophone academy, faces a range of serious structural issues, for instance, in its ranking mechanisms, journal publication instruments and citational practices, and culture of intolerance and disinclusion. The problem I want to focus on here is philosophy's problem with diversity. In comparison with other disciplines in the humanities such as literature, theatre, political science, and history, there is a marked absence of diversity in the syllabi of philosophy curricula at undergraduate and graduate levels, and there is an equally marked lack of diversity in the ethnic and gender composition of philosophy student bodies and faculty.

I believe that the single primary cause of philosophy's diversity problem is that the profession remains deeply implicated in a legacy of colonial patterns of thought and organization, institutional models that really only took root in the nineteenth century. The urgent need of philosophy now is to decolonize, and that means to globalize, to embrace and incorporate a diverse plurality of philosophical traditions and practices, including both literary and oral cultures beyond the European tradition.

There have been times in the past when philosophy has recognized the need about which I shall speak: in Baghdad in the seventh century, with the Bactrian Barmakid translation project from Sanskrit to Arabic even before the better-known project to translate into Arabic from Greek (van Bladel 2011); in Lhasa in the ninth century, transmitting Buddhist philosophical Sanskrit into Tibet; and even in London early in the nineteenthth century, when Henry Colebrooke promoted Sanskrit mathematics and philosophy to his colleagues at the Royal Society (Rocher and Rocher 2011).

This is, I believe, a time when the same need arises again, and even more urgently so. Let me begin by trying to identify the sources of the doctrine that European philosophical tradition, its classics and its canon, occupies a privileged position in the global intellectual history of humanity. I'll then review a different, Sanskritic, conception of classicity, and go on to describe the critique of European exceptionalism by anti-colonial thinkers from the first half of the twentieth century. That part of the chapter will be diagnostic, but I also want to say something constructive, and I'll move in the final third of the chapter to sketch an alternative model for philosophical practice to that which currently prevails, one grounded in a defense of pluralism, a pluralism about ways of interrogating the single reality we share, and a model itself retrieved from Sanskrit thinkers.

The Myth of European Exceptionalism

There is an old joke about the classics. A "classic" is a work that everyone likes to refer to but nobody wants to read. That's actually a good definition for our purposes because it can easily be globalized. Still we might hope for a more concrete analysis of the function of the notion of the classic, and I will review two more substantive recent proposals. For the latest thinking about the idea that there is something exceptional and unique about the Greek classics I'll turn to Edith Hall, who spoke about this very topic in her Gaisford Lecture at the University of Oxford on June 4, 2015. Hall laments the fact that the provision of education in the classics in Britain is now highly polarized, with the classics (i.e., the Greek classics) exhalted in private schools and elite colleges but utterly ignored in the state system and in the majority of universities outside Oxbridge. Hall argues that the classics are too special to be ghettoized, but she is more than conscious that the topic of the exceptionalism of Greek classicism is deeply tendentious. She says:

> The question has become painfully politicized. Critics of colonialism and racism tend to play down the specialness of the ancient Greeks. Those who maintain that there was something identifiably different and even superior about the Greeks, on the other hand, are often die-hard conservatives who have a vested interest in proving the superiority of "Western" ideals and in making evaluative judgements of culture. My problem is that I fit into neither camp. I am certainly opposed to colonialism and racism, and have investigated reactionary abuses of the classical tradition in colonial India and by apologists of slavery all the way through to the American Civil War. But my constant engagement with the ancient Greeks and their culture has made me more, rather than less, convinced that they asked a series of questions which are difficult to identify in combination amongst any of the other cultures of the ancient Mediterranean or North Eastern antiquity.

One might think that in order to reach the conviction that the Greeks are this special Hall would have had to spend time engaging with the non-Greek classical civilizations of India and China, about which there is not a single word in her entire lecture, although she feels confident enough to venture that "none of these peoples produced anything quite equivalent to Athenian democracy, comic theatre, philosophical logic, or Aristotle's *Nicomachean Ethics*." Let me let that pass, though, because what she does say is more interesting. Hall acknowledges that many recent advances in scholarship about the cultures of the Ancient Near East have called into question the idea that the ancient Greeks were special. These advances "have revealed how much the Greeks shared with and absorbed from their predecessors and neighbors … they reveal the Greek 'miracle' to have been one constituent in a continuous process of intercultural exchange." She accepts that "taken singly, most Greek achievements can be paralleled in the culture of at least one of their neighbors": the Babylonians knew Pythagoras' theorem, the Phoenicians created the phonetic alphabet, the Hittites, also highly literate, developed chariot technology, and the Egyptians medicinal knowledge based on empirical experience, and so on for Mesopotamia, the Levant, Persia, and Asia Minor. Summing up the situation, she says:

> Some scholars have gone so far as to ask whether the Greeks came up with anything new at all, or whether they merely acted as a conduit through which the combined wisdom of all the civilizations of the eastern Mediterranean was disseminated across the territories conquered by Alexander the Great, before arriving at Rome and posterity. Others have seen sinister racist motives at work [and have] claimed, with some justification, that northern Europeans have systematically distorted and concealed the evidence showing how much the ancient Greeks owed to Semitic and African peoples rather than to Indo-European "Aryan' traditions."

Then in what does the specialness of the Greeks consist? Hall's answer is this:

> I do not deny that the Greeks acted as a conduit for other ancient peoples' achievements. But to function successfully as a conduit, channel, or intermediary is in itself to perform an exceptional role ... Taking over someone else's technical knowledge requires an opportunistic ability to identify a serendipitous find or encounter, excellent communicative skills, and the imagination to seek how a technique, story or object could be adapted to a different linguistic and cultural milieu ... Of course the Greeks were not by nature or in potential superior to any other human beings, either physically or intellectually ... But that does not mean they were not the right people, in the right place, at the right time, to take up the human baton of intellectual progress for several hundred years.

There is, again in this comment, a certain blindness to the relay races already being run in China and India. But what I find fascinating is that the best efforts of contemporary classical scholarship to unearth that unique feature which made Greek civilization special has ended up concluding that their exceptionalism was in how well they made use of the ideas and innovations of others. Hardly exceptional enough, one would have thought, to justify Thomas Macaulay infamously declaring in 1835, that "a single shelf of a good European library was worth the whole native literature of India and Arabia."

The Sanskrit Cosmopolis

Let me turn now to a second recent discussion of the idea of the classical. Sheldon Pollock recently published an enchanting essay entitled "The Alternative Classicism of Classical India" (2015). Pollock, like Hall, begins by stressing processes and interactions with the Kushans, Scythians, and with Mesopotamia, from where India derived the seven-day calendar and even the names of the days. Unlike Hall, Pollock is not blind to interactions between India and Greece. He records the available evidence that the other people's achievements successfully channeled by ancient Greece include Indian intellectual achievements such as epistemological skepticism and theories about the nature of the self. India, though, was no less exceptional in its opportunism than Greece, and channeled ideas from Greek theatre and drama into a South and South-East Asian intellectual space by no means less vast or enduring than the run of the Greece baton in the West. While Hall echoes the somewhat clichéd claim that "the Greeks [meaning obviously Socrates] show us how to question received opinion and authority," without specifying who this "us" is meant to be, Pollock distances himself from Johannes Bronkhorst's recent argument that "the very conditions of possibility of Indian philosophy are found in interactions with Indo-Greeks," and indeed that "Indians learned the art of rational discussion from the Greeks in public debate, where people defend their opinions against others who disagree with them but are obliged to listen to arguments." Pollock makes the more telling point that in this complex picture of interactions, it is "no longer clear why we should care [who was first]—we are not after all being asked to judge intellectual property rights—except to the degree the question of origins of such cultural goods enables us to assess the transformations introduced by people in each sphere according to their own particular needs and interests."

Yet it is not Pollock's point to argue, against the claim of Greek exceptionalism, that channeling and transforming the ideas of others is a global achievement. What he tries instead to do is to identify the specialness of India, that is, the

> civilizational products and inventions in India that seem, if not unique, at least defining of its cultural formation, both for their distinctiveness and their durability ... —both those that are explicitly enunciated in the tradition and those that, more elusively, are embodied in practice—[and] that constitute a certain alternative classicity.

Pollock identifies four. The first two are explicitly enunciated:

1. Transcendental Paradigmatism: "The whole of dramaturgy and especially the theory of aesthetic response (*rasa* is the Sanskrit term), which represents one of the defining traits of Indian classicism, pivots on the paradigmatic: what is always going to be true of human beings. Indian drama sought to explore ... the nature of both civic and emotional *typicality*."
2. Argumentative Pluralism: "The classicity of Indian philosophy lies precisely in the development of reasoned argument in the face of wholesale conceptual assaults—of the sort that never occurred in the Greek world since Greeks never philosophized with those, above all non-Greeks, who could have delivered such assaults. For classical India, pluralism itself became something of an ultimate value. A verse composed by the great eleventh-century philosopher king, Bhoja of Dhar, offers a perfect encapsulation: 'Learn Buddhism, behave like a Jain, follow Vedic norms, and meditate on Shiva.'"

Then also two that are implicit, embodied in practice:

3. Non-Coercive Cosmopolitanism: "A form of broad cultural participation which knew nothing of the tyranny to 'be like' us that marks western cosmopolitanism from Romanization to modern western globalization ... Unlike Greek literary culture, in which non-Greeks could, typically, not participate, Sanskrit literary culture was open to adoption by everyone everywhere. This cosmopolitanism consisted of a certain vision of culture and power. First, power was always thought of as something that was to be dispersed and shared, a decentralization that should be judged as a victory and not a defeat. Second, culture served to ennoble rather than merely to 'legitimate' power. ... Last, [Sanskrit], the language that expressed both culture and power was one that, wherever it was adopted, was adopted freely and never under coercion."
4. Voluntary Vernacularism: "Classical Sanskrit cosmopolitanism existed in a uniquely advantageous relationship with local ways of being. According to Indian classicity, you could be cosmopolitan while staying at home ... At the same time, the notion of staying home, of being local, in this classical world was unlike anything seen elsewhere. It was a voluntary vernacularity, which knew nothing of the compulsions of ethnicity."

So we have "a particularism that never expressed itself as an exclusion, and a universalism that never objectified, let alone, enforced, its universalism." Pollock is of course aware that not everything was rosy about Indian classicism, with its extreme hierarchies and sometimes inhuman forms of social inequality. Yet, he says, "what the study of the Indian classical past offers in the main, however, are instances of how to be human that seem all but inconceivable in the contemporary world." India too is exceptional, but differently so.

My own studies of the intellectual practice of philosophy in classical India bear out many of these claims. They have led me to see that there is a fundamental contrast between two styles of reasoning, that of abstract syllogistic and formal deduction and that of particularist, case-based, "blueprint+adaptation" extrapolation. The latter model—whose origins in India lie as much in the ritual reasoning of the Mīmāṃsā exegetes and the jurisprudence of the Dharmaśāstra as in explorations in the science of prediction in the medical treatises and, most especially, in early Nyāya logic—developed into a general theory of ethical and normative reasoning.[1] This mode of intellectual inquiry is typical of the age when sūtras were compiled and first commented upon, and philosophers in the "Age of the Sūtra" exhibit exactly the traits of argumentative pluralism and paradigmatism which for Pollock constitute Indian classicity. All the participants co-opted, reused, and adapted the innovations of others, and this is the hallmark of a pluralism that is distinct from the uniqueness of Greek channeling highlighted by Edith Hall only in that everyone was up to it. Application of the Sanskrit idea of the *pūrvapakṣa* (an opponent imaginatively considered by the author of a philosophical work) lends a dialogical (but non-Socratic) texture to these texts. And, I might add in disagreement with Johannes Bronkhorst, we can trace the origins of this open-textured and dialogical model of rational inquiry to well before the arrival of Alexander. When Sanskrit philosophers talk about the general character of the sūtras, they are mostly concerned to draw parallels with the defining grammar of Sanskrit language, Pāṇini's *Aṣṭādhyāyī*, which exploits a range of brevity-enabling devices to compose what has often been described as the tersest and yet most complete grammar of any language. If his was a complete generative explanation of grammar, then the *Vaiśeṣika-sūtra* should be a complete generative explanation of the ontological structure of the cosmos and the *Nyāya-sūtra* a complete generative explanation of the epistemological foundations of knowledge. The sūtras achieve compactness by making sequence significant, by letting one item stand for or range over many, and by using lexicon artificially. More important than even the sūtras themselves were the initial commentaries written on them. These commentaries—the technical designation of which is *bhāṣya*—had as their explicit aim the construction of a systematic body of concepts, a weaving of the threads into a single unified fabric of philosophy.

Thus there is a model of intellectual inquiry whose application is widespread in the classical age, an age which came to an end when the brilliant Buddhist Dignāga (*c.* 480–540 CE) introduced quite new models of reasoning and philosophical analysis. An emerging consensus agrees in identifying Dignāga as marking the beginning of a new postclassical era in Indian philosophical thought, some scholars emphasizing his theoretical innovations and others his transformation of discursive practice. As important as these shifts in doctrinal formulation and discursive practice was the transformation Dignāga achieved in the nature of intellectual endeavor, with a movement away from an epistemic localism to a rule-based universalism. The classical Age of the Sūtra, distinguished by its use of a model of rationality grounded in adaptation and projection from locally normative paradigms, was over. Now too the precise formulation of definitions of key philosophical concepts takes center stage as constitutive of philosophical practice, rival definitions of what purports to be a single concept locking horns in contexts of philosophical debate. Rapidly this became the hallmark of philosophical activity in a broad Sanskrit cosmopolis that was to endure for centuries and whose geographical borders spread well beyond the subcontinent. During this period of dialogue between Buddhist, Jaina, and Hindu astonishing theoretical advances were made in understanding the working of the human mind's properties, processes, and powers—in analyses of selfhood, consciousness, moral psychology, and agency.

K. C. Bhattacharya's Critique of European Philology

Despite their many differences, both Pollock and Hall are in search of some unique historical feature or cluster of features that is the hallmark or defining trait of the classical tradition they write about, India in one case and Greece in the other. The brilliant pre-independence philosopher Krishnachandra Bhattacharyya (1875–1949) argued powerfully for freedom from the intellectual slavery brought by a coercive colonial occupation of India. Bhattacharyya was also, like Pollock, keen on provincializing Greek classicism, which in the early twentieth century was being forced down the throats of educated Indians at the expense of indigenous learning. For Bhattacharyya, unlike Hall, this was not simply an unfortunate but localized abuse of the classics, it was symptomatic of a deeply symbiotic relationship between European classical scholarship and colonialism. He called on philosophers to show reverence for the Indian classical traditions and not to let themselves be brainwashed into thinking that Greek classicism was the only classicism in town. Yet he was more aware than were many of his peers of the dangers involved in a nativist and uncritical return to the past. Reverence for him meant an attitude of aesthetic sympathy for the living fabric of a philosophical world. This formed the basis of an Indian notion of the classical, to be held against and so to provincialize European classicism. In fact it was not so much the abstract idea of the classical which concerned him as the nature and role of the classicist, and what he tries to provide was an alternative Indian understanding of the classicist's duties, methodologies, and responsibilities. In particular he argues that the import of positivist scientific philology into the study of India's classical heritage is profoundly mistaken, indeed that it is itself another manifestation of intellectual colonization.

The clearest example of the way in which the notion of an Indian classic is drawn on to serve the purpose of intellectual decolonization is in his series of brilliant interpretations of the classical sūtra-systems of Yoga, Sāṃkhya, Alaṃkāra, and Vedānta. In an extremely informative "Introduction" to his 1907 *Studies in Vedāntism*, Bhattacharyya ([1907] 1958) explains his methodology. He first tenders a deeply insightful critique of the kind of text-historical philology exemplified by the Indologist George Thibaut. Thibaut no doubt believed himself to be bringing all the scholarly apparatus used to study the Greek classics to bear on the Sanskrit classics, and thought of himself therefore as doing something that showed respect to the Indian past; he would have agreed with Hermann Oldenberg's ([1906] 1967) claim that "from purely formal perspective, methodologically, the tasks of that the Indologist has to solve are in every way comparable to those of the classical philologists." Yet Bhattacharyya saw in this nothing other than another reflex of the colonial mentality, and as an imposition of the "mechanical rationality" he would criticize elsewhere. He argues that the Indian classics deserve a quite different sort of respect and require a quite different kind of approach. The phrase he uses for this is "aesthetic sympathy":

> To contemplate with something of an aesthetic sympathy an ancient life-ideal animating an organized body of ancient thought, just to quicken, it may be for a moment, the consciousness, always very torpid, that the dominating ideal of the day is only one among many possibles ... a true philosophical system is not to be looked upon as a soulless jointing of hypotheses; it is a living fabric which, with all its endeavor to be objective, must have a well-marked individuality. Hence it is not to be regarded as the special property of academic philosophy-mongers, to be hacked up by them into technical views, but is to be regarded as a form of life and is to be treated as a theme of literature of infinite interest to humanity.

"A theme of literature of infinite interest to humanity" is as good a definition of the classical as any, but what distinguishes Indian classicity is that it is also "a form of life" and "a living fabric." Phenomenological immersion replaces analytical detachment as the right way to respect the classics.

Bhattacharyya now analyses the respective tasks of the classical and the contemporary Indian philosopher, demonstrating that neither has the same ambition as the scientific philologist. The task which Śaṅkara set himself "is not that of the critical historian, it is the task of piecing together the several texts [i.e., the Upaniṣads] into a philosophical system, of developing a hypothesis on a necessary basis which will cover all the texts." In this attempt "to systemize all the texts into a well-rounded philosophy" it may be that some passages are left out as embodying false speculations. The existence of outliers, false readings, is no problem for the classical philosopher, though it would be for a philologist following a positivist methodology. Philosophical systematization has, in Bhattacharyya's words, a greater degree of *latitude* than text-historical philology.

A contemporary Indian philosopher should not confuse their task with that of the philological positivist either. Rather, "the attitude ... should be neither that of the apologist nor that of the academic compiler but that of the interpreter which involves, to a certain extent, that of the constructor too," but where "the work of construction has been subordinated to the work of interpretation." Bhattacharyya anticipates the all-too-familiar counterresponse that in this "there is a danger, no doubt, of too easily reading one's philosophic creed into the history," but he observes that there is an opposite and more severe danger, "the danger of taking the philosophic type studied as a historic curiosity rather than a recipe for the human soul." And finally Bhattacharyya elegantly turns the tables on another of the philologist's favorite arguments that text-critical historical reconstruction must be prior to philosophical interpretation. In fact, just the reverse, for "the historian cannot begin his work at all unless he can live in sympathy into the details of an apparently outworn creed and recognize the truth in the first imperfect adumbrations of it." A historian of philosophy must exchange an attitude of mere documentation for one of sympathetic interpretation if the project of historical reconstruction is to begin at all.

Bhattacharyya's own commentaries on the Indian classics are perfect exercises in this art of sympathetic interpretation, or aesthetic sympathy. In these immersive commentaries a space is opened between the modern Indian reception of Sanskrit classicism and the European reception of Greek classicism. Whereas a Greek classic is a text of which one seeks accurate historical knowledge in order to be able to use it as a norm, a reliable standard of judgment, a Sanskrit classic is a work whose world one enters as a living fabric. While the form of reverence or respect that Europeans show to their ancient texts is one of historicizing a discrete past age and using its values as a standard on which to rest their own judgment, the reverence that is due an Indian classic is quite different. It is, rather, an atemporal relationship with a form of life, a relation of phenomenological immersion combined with reconstructive interpretation. European philology has not only been provincialized, that is, shown not to be providing a universal account of the classical but merely a parochial one, but also made to seem just a little lifeless.

Bhattacharyya composed a series of brilliant interpretive commentaries on a series of the classical Indian philosophical systems, including Yoga, Sāṃkhya, Vedānta, and even Jainism.[2] Unsurprisingly, given what we have said so far, he also examined with great care the classical Indian account of aesthetic response in the form of the theory of *rasa*.³ In each case he brought his distinct philosophical technique, of aesthetic sympathy, of imagination combined with humility, to bear. The fact that he did not restrict himself to just one classical Indian worldview is, I think, telling: *within* the Indian tradition, he himself was a pluralist. In other words, he was perfectly aware that the aesthetic methodology of Indian classicism sustains a pluralist rather than an exclusionary outlook.

Anti-colonial Critique

The idea is developed further in a paper entitled "Svarāj in Ideas," a talk delivered in Candranagar in October 1931 but not published in his lifetime. At a time when calls for India's political independence from British colonial rule were gathering momentum, Bhattacharyya issued a plea for freedom from what he called "cultural subjection," a deeply insidious and almost invisible intellectual slavery. In a clear reference to colonial rule, he says that

> cultural subjection is ordinarily of an unconscious character and it implies slavery from the very start … There is cultural subjection only when one's traditional cast of ideas and sentiments is superseded without comparison or competition by a new cast representing an alien culture which possesses one like a ghost.

Bhattacharyya's clear understanding of the pernicious effects of intellectual colonization is echoed by two other anti-colonial thinkers from the period. In what sense of the term "need" does the discipline of philosophy need Sanskrit? One sense is described in the 1940s by Simone Weil when she said in the course of her sustained and brilliant study of colonialism, that "it seems that Europe periodically requires genuine contacts with the East, in order to maintain spiritually alive." "European civilization," she argues, "is a combination of the Oriental spirit with its opposite, and in that combination there *needs to* be a high proportion of the former." "The proportion today," she says, speaking in 1943, "is not nearly high enough. We *need* an injection of the Oriental spirit." For past antecedents Weil mentions—limited as she was by the historical knowledge of the day—the Egyptian and Phoenician influence on Hellenism, the eastern origins of Christianity, and the importance of Arabic and Persian to the philosophical culture of the Middle Ages. Weil (1962: 204–5) is acutely conscious of the racial politics in play when she continues that

> At the present day, when the American, the Englishman, and the Hindu are together, the two former will fraternize on the surface, each of them secretly thinking himself much superior to the other, and the Hindu will be left out. To recreate by degrees an atmosphere in which the reactions of the three will be different may well be, from the spiritual point of view, a matter of life and death for Europe.

There is a clear early acknowledgment here of a phenomenon I will return to, the manner in which colonialism creates false fraternities, and nowhere more so than within the white academia. For as Weil noted, the British saw the colonies simply as business, but the French carried with them the principles of 1789 wherever they went, and this had one of two possible outcomes: "Either the natives regard these principles as an affront to their own traditions, or else they become sincere converts to them and are indignant at being excluded from their application."

The imperial philosophers' false claim to universality catches the excluded outsider in a vicious dilemma: make your use of reason like ours (in which case what extra value does your philosophy bring to the table?) or admit that you are outside reason and not actually engaged in philosophy at all. The dilemma is false because the neutrality of colonial reason it presupposes is a phoney mixture of two myths: the first that the colonial will to universality is impartial; the second that the existence of the outsider's will to universality is to be denied. In denying outsiders a will to universality the colonizer denied them their humanity, and the various ignominious philosophical rationalizations of colonial rule were but corollaries of this basic double move. Simone Weil would observe it in the intrinsic absurdity of children in French Polynesia being made to recite "Our ancestors the Gauls had blond hair and blue eyes … " while forbidden from their indigenous custom, language, and tradition, forbidden from even accessing the libraries containing documentation relating to it. So colonial philosophers took what was in fact itself a local way of using reason (one contextually entangled with the history of the colonial project), falsely promoted it as a uniquely acontextual methodology, and denied that outsiders had so much as a concept of the general application of reason on the grounds that they did not share its parochial epistemic practices.

Simone Weil's essay was written in 1943 but the same sentiment about cultural rejuvenation was identified earlier by Sarvepalli Radhakrishnan, in his inaugural lecture delivered before the University of Oxford in 1936, on becoming the first Spalding Professor of Eastern Religions and Ethics. Writing on the eve of the Second World War, at a time when the world for the first time in its history could be described as a single global economic and geopolitical community and yet when populist forces threatened to tear it apart, Radhakrishnan identified a profound malaise in the spirit of the West. The old order of medieval Christendom was in its death throws and nothing but uncertainty replaced it. Every civilization is an experiment in living, but the European experiment had reached a dead end. For Radhakrishnan, what was vitally needed, if Europe was to find its spirit, was revitalization from the East. "The great periods of human history," he noted, "are marked by a wide-spread access of spiritual vitality derived from the fusion of national cultures with foreign influences." Radhakrishnan offers as examples, the influence of Egypt on Judaism and Greece, and of Arabic culture in the medieval world, before continuing,

> In times of trouble we draw the profoundest inspiration from sources outside us, from the newly recovered past or the achievement of men under different skies. So, perhaps, the civilizations of the East, their religions and ethics, may offer us some help in negotiating difficulties we are up against. The only past known to the Europeans emerging from the Middle Ages was the Biblical, and the Graeco-Roman and their classics happen to be the subjects studied in the great universities

founded in that period. Now that we have the whole world for our cultural base, the process of recovery and training in classics cannot cease with listening to the voices of Isaiah and Paul, Socrates and Cicero. That would be an academic error, a failure of perspective. There are others also who have participated in the supreme adventure of the ages, the prophets of Egypt, the sages of China, and the seers of India, who are guide-posts disclosing to us the course of the trail.

Radhakrishnan goes on to say something about the Oxford chair which had been created for him:

> The institution of the Chair by the far-sighted generosity of Mr. and Mrs. Spalding, and the unprecedented appointment of an Asiatic to an Oxford Chair, are motivated, I take it, by a desire to lift Eastern thought from its sheltered remoteness and indicate its enduring value as a living force in shaping the soul of the modern man.

Radhakrishnan is here quite prescient in explicitly raising issues about diversity both in the curricular content of university education and in the ethnic composition of the faculty body. He may have been disappointed to learn that nearly a century later, the very same structural issues would continue to haunt and hamper university education in the West. The hopes of the Spaldings for the Chair, I may note, were to be only partially fulfilled before the Oxford establishment claimed it and transformed it into a conventional position in Indo-European philology of just the sort K. C. Bhattacharyya had long before criticized.

Radhakrishnan, Weil, and Bhattacharyya had higher ambitions for philosophy than contemporary philosophers have for the discipline. Their view was that philosophy had the potential, if it expanded its horizons, to resolve the great clash of values—between cosmopolitanism and localism, between a commonwealth of nations and the forces of popularism. Contemporary academic philosophers have mostly surrendered any conception of themselves as playing such a role in global politics or even in public life, and that may or may not be a bad thing. But this shrinking in the ambitions the discipline has set for itself is surely correlated with the restriction of its horizons. You will be hard pressed to find in a standard course on ethics, for example, any discussion of the ethical principles and values that informs the lives of billions of Chinese or Muslims or Buddhists, and in their absence it is evident that a course on ethics will offer nothing in the greater rapprochement of humanity philosophers like Radhakrishnan imagined.

A New Model for Philosophy: Stance Pluralism

I have commented on the absence of diversity in academic philosophy, and I have traced its origins to philosophy's ongoing implication with colonial intellectual practices. Those of us who work with extra-European philosophical traditions in the international philosophical academy today can feel a certain sympathy with Weil's remark about "the spirit of 1789." There is an almost missionary zeal with which a certain set of philosophical principles and a particular philosophical methodology is promoted in the academy. I want to conclude my chapter, though, in a more constructive vein.

I will briefly sketch a more inclusive and pluralistic future for philosophy, and I will do so by retrieving and repurposing meta-philosophical ideas from a group of Sanskrit philosophers, the Jaina philosophers of India.[4]

In my own work, I have sought to inhabit the elusive ground that respects pluralism but denies social constructivism. I have investigated the plurality of classical Indian philosophical *śāstras*, a *śāstra* being not merely a systematic representation of a network of ideas but a fluid disciplinary practice for the production of knowledge of a certain sort in a certain domain. They have been described as "Sanskrit knowledge systems," and since their concern is not only with the manufacture of a body of belief but with how such beliefs are warranted—how beliefs are argued for and what kinds of evidence can be provided—it seems entirely correct to describe them also as "epistemic cultures" in the sense the phrase has been used recently by Karin Cetina. Although the world of Sanskritic India supported a plurality of Sanskrit epistemic cultures, they did not exist in isolation from one another but were in constant mutual dialogue and often very vociferous conflict. The Buddhists were concerned not only about the truth for Buddhists but about the truth, and that is why Buddhists spared no intellectual energy in devising refutations of opponent views. The Vaiśeṣikas, the Naiyāyikas, the Cārvākas, were concerned not only about truth for Vaiśeṣikas, for Naiyāyikas, for Cārvākas, but vociferously engaged each other in philosophical argument often of the highest order of sophistication and complexity. Disagreement of this sort implied a shared commitment to there being data that all agree grounds claims to knowledge and of there being mutually acknowledged instruments for the warranting of beliefs. There was precious little agreement about what that data is or about the nature and proper characterization of the epistemic instruments, that is about what the Indians called *prameya* and *pramāṇa*, but there was agreement that there must be some correct characterization of both.

Space for this pluralistic realism, though, seems to vanish in the oscillation between two views that have largely shaped contemporary discussion: the view, on the one hand, that that science is a single, unified, discipline that discovers a single objective world according to a uniquely valid set of objective epistemic procedures; and the view, to the contrary, that truth is relative to the interests, perceptions, background commitments, and values of disparate communal groups. Perhaps the clearest articulation of the first view, and with it the contemporary philosophers' "spirit of 1789," is in Paul Boghossian's 2006 book entitled *Fear of Knowledge*. Boghossian meticulously constructs an argument against epistemic pluralism. The target of his argument is the view that there are many "epistemic systems," a view that would seem to "give immediate support to the idea that there are many radically different, yet equally valid *ways* of knowing the world." Here, the notion of an epistemic system is that of a collection of epistemic principles, "general normative propositions which specify under which conditions a particular type of belief is justified" (Boghossian 2006: 85). There are "generation" principles, which generate a justified belief on the basis of something that is not itself a belief, and there are "transmission" principles, which prescribe how to move from some justified beliefs to other justified beliefs (65). Again, there are "fundamental" epistemic principles, principles "whose correctness cannot be derived from the correctness of other epistemic principles," and "derived" epistemic principles, whose correctness can be so derived. The way of fixing beliefs that we call "science," Boghossian suggests, is but a rigorous application of certain "ordinary, familiar" fundamental epistemic principles, Observation, Deduction, and Inference to the Best Explanation.

Boghossian (2006: 73) defines epistemic relativism as the conjunction of three claims:

A. There are no absolute facts about what belief a particular item of information justifies (epistemic non-absolutism).
B. If a person, S's, epistemic judgments are to have any prospect of being true, we must not construe his utterances of the form "E justifies belief B" as expressing the claim *E justifies belief B* but rather as expressing the claim *According to the epistemic system C, that I, S, accept, information E justifies belief B* (epistemic relationism).
C. There are many fundamentally different, genuinely alternative epistemic systems, but no facts by virtue of which one of these systems is more correct than any of the others (epistemic pluralism).

His objection to (B) is that propositions of the form *E justifies belief B* are normative, they make claims about what one should believe given certain evidence, whereas propositions of the form *According to the epistemic system C, E justifies belief B* are purely descriptive, they merely document the logical implications of a given epistemic system (75). A purely factual remark about what an epistemic system requires has come to replace a normative claim. The view I want to defend affirms pluralism but rejects relativism, and I can thus agree with Boghossian about this. His objection to (C) is this. Let us suppose that one epistemic system, C1, employs epistemic principles that imply *if E, B is justified*, while another epistemic system, C2, employs epistemic principles that imply *it is not the case that if E, B is justified*. How can it be, in this circumstance, that there are no facts by virtue of which one system is more correct than the other, Boghossian asks. If there are no absolute facts about justification, then C1 makes a false claim, and C2 claims something true. More generally, if we take any contradictory pair of epistemic systems, "if one of them is deemed to say something false, the other will have been deemed to say something true. Under those circumstances, it's hard to see how it could be right to say that there are no facts by virtue of which one epistemic system could be more correct than any other" (91). Boghossian's target is the thesis he terms "Equal Validity": "There are many radically different, yet 'equally valid' ways of knowing the world, with science being just one of them" (2). His argument is that the very idea of a plurality of epistemic systems, each encoding a particular conception of epistemic justification, is incoherent.

Boghossian, however, mischaracterizes the view of an epistemic pluralist. He is wrong when he says that that pluralism about epistemic cultures is reducible to a pluralism about epistemic *systems*, namely sets of general normative propositions which specify under which conditions a particular type of belief is justified. Reflection on the Sanskrit knowledge systems makes it evident that the proper characterization of epistemic pluralism is not as consisting in pluralism about epistemic systems. Indian epistemology in general is an analysis of *pramāṇas*, methods for interrogating reality and sources of warranted belief. A *pramāṇa* is, more or less, what Boghossian means by an epistemic principle. The Indians were perfectly aware of the distinction between generative principles and transmission principles and would have chastised Boghossian for failing to mention an important transmission principle, Testimony. Their names for Observation, Deduction, Inference to the Best Explanation, and Testimony are *pratyakṣa*, *anumāna*, *arthāpatti*, and *śabda*. Yet they may have forgiven him, because they also discussed and disagreed among themselves whether Testimony is a fundamental or a derived epistemic principle, and they were, in general, fully cognizant of the importance of establishing a basic set of underived epistemic principles. Other putative epistemic principles, *pramāṇas*, were entertained, and much discussion took place around the question of their status, for example, whether they are derivable from more basic epistemic principles and whether they ought to count as epistemic principles at all. Yet, the important point is that although the different Sanskrit epistemic cultures disagreed with each other about what the underived epistemic principles are, they agreed that there is just one correct set of such principles. That is, they agreed about there being just one epistemic system, even though they disagreed about what constitutes it. So the epistemic pluralism that the Indian tradition displays cannot correctly be characterized as a pluralism about epistemic systems.

In fact, the proper way to formulate epistemic pluralism has already been provided for us, and by the Sanskrit tradition itself. The remarkable Jaina philosophers make a distinction of fundamental epistemological significance when they say that as well as and in addition to *pramāṇas*, epistemic principles, there are also *nayas*, epistemic *standpoints* or *stances*, and that both are essential constituents of an epistemic culture.[5] A *naya* is not a proposition but a practical attitude, a *strategy* or *policy* which guides inquiry: it is an *approach* to the problem of producing knowledge, not a thesis about the sources of justification.[6] One such policy might be to attend only to what is immediately present in experience, another might be to enumerate everything one encounters without making any categorial distinctions, another to attend to stasis rather than flux, or vice versa. To see that stances are not propositions, we need only reflect on the epistemic stance adopted by Nāgārjuna, the Buddhist Mādhyamika, who denied that there is any way to say what nature is *in itself* (*svabhāva*). Nāgārjuna was accused of refuting himself, for if his epistemic proposition is that everything is thus empty then that proposition should be itself empty, that is, without meaning *in itself*. His response was that he held no proposition that emptiness is not a proposition, indeed that it would be a fatal error to mistake adopting emptiness as a philosophical position for belief in any philosophical proposition.[7] And this might remind one immediately of van Fraassen's (2002) argument that, as a position in the philosophy of science, empiricism is not a propositional thesis, for it if were then, since it claims that every thesis is open to empirical confirmation or disconfirmation, it would itself be open to empirical confirmation or disconfirmation. The idea is helpfully elaborated by Anjan Chakravartty (2004: 175), who says,

> A stance is a strategy, or a combination of strategies, for generating factual beliefs. A stance makes no claim about reality, at least directly, It is rather a sort of epistemic "policy" concerning which methodologies should be adopted in the generation of

factual beliefs ... Stances are not themselves propositional; they are guidelines for ways of acting. One does not believe a stance in the way one believes a fact. Rather one commits to a stance, or adopts it.

So, for instance, "physicalism is not so much a factual thesis, but a deference to the claims of basic science." To adopt a stance is to resolve or commit oneself to acting or making decisions as described by it. Stances are open-ended, in terms of how they are interpreted and applied; their application requires discretion and judgment. They express and implement values, much as the policy of not lying implements a positive valuation of the truth (Teller 2004: 166). Let me therefore say that a stance is a policy adopted toward the employment of epistemic principles. Correctly understood, epistemic pluralism is thus a commitment to pluralism about epistemic stances, not to a pluralism of epistemic systems in Boghossian's sense.

Boghossian's (2006: 91) argument against pluralism about epistemic systems was that "if one of them is deemed to say something false, the other will have been deemed to say something true. Under those circumstances, it's hard to see how it could be right to say that there are no facts by virtue of which one epistemic system could be more correct than any other." This argument does not apply to epistemic stances, for it is possible for there to be pairs of genuinely alternative epistemic stances and no facts by virtue of which one is more correct than the other. We can see this most clearly if we remember that stances are action-guiding policies governing the application of epistemic principles. One can analogously think of a route as a guide to performing the action of reaching the summit of a mountain: there can be different routes up the mountain, perhaps with different benefits and drawbacks, but equally good for reaching the top. Here it is absurd to say that deeming one of the approaches "true" necessitates deeming the other "false," both because truth and falsity are not the norms according to which plans for action are evaluated, and because whatever that norm is, both approaches may satisfy it equally well. To give another example: it is often the case that a given mathematical theorem can be proved in two different ways, adopting in each case a different proof strategy, yet both equally "correct," that is, sound as proofs of the theorem in question. Although stances are normatively evaluable, the appropriate norm of evaluation is not truth or falsity. Rather, a stance is "evaluated as being well or ill advised, conducive to certain ends, easy or difficult to administer, and in many other practical respects" (Teller 2004: 166). One path up the mountain may be steeper but shorter, another more scenic, another better served with tea shops. So one can order stances, if only partially. There can also be bogus pseudo-stances (*nayābhāsa*), just as there can be bogus pseudo-principles (*pramāṇābhāsa*); for example, the ad hoc policy of being an empiricist on Mondays, a rationalist on Tuesdays, a Mādhyamika on Wednesdays, and so on.

The Jaina distinction between principles and stances is enough to diffuse Boghossian's argument against epistemic pluralism. I have said that distinct stances may sometimes apply with equal correctness to an investigation. The Jainas argue that this does not entail that the distinct deliverances of stances are necessarily contradictory. Rejecting the idea that things have a single unique essence, the Jainas instead say—and this is their third theoretical innovation—that reality is in some sense manifold or multifaceted: the Jaina term is *anekānta*. Metaphysics tends to treat objects, qua targets of inquiry, as if they are simple points, like the peak of a mountain. Yet the mountain itself is metaphysically more complex, its variously shaped sides offering different aspects to the climber and so different potential routes to the top. So, to quote Siddhasena, "The real thing, whose essence is multiplex (*anekānta*), [forms] the domain of all acts of awareness; an object qualified by one facet (*ekadeśa*) is known as the province of the standpoint (*naya*)" NA 29 (Balcerowicz 2002: 83, modified). Siddharṣigaṇi elaborates, adding that "the real thing, both external and internal, endowed with a form that is under the sway of *muliplex essential natures* not separate from each other, unfolds itself to all epistemic principles (*pramāṇa*)" NAV 29.1 (84). Mountaineers, whichever route they select, have the same tools and techniques available to them, but the mountain unfolds itself differently to each, and each aspect thus presented has as much of a claim to be the essence of the mountain as any other. Likewise, each nondogmatic epistemic stance is an approach to some one aspect of the world. Different stances are policies for warranting beliefs about different aspects of the world. That is, we might think that there is a plurality of special sciences, each special science having as its provenance some particular domain or level of properties, no such domain being reducible to any other. To say this is to deny that there is a single way the world is *in itself*, that there is some uniquely objective description of the world viewed *sub species aeternitatis*, from nowhere; rather, the multiplicity of different approaches collectively constitute a "view from everywhere."

A pluralism about epistemic cultures, practices, or stances is compatible with the idea that there is a single reality to be explored, a multi-aspectual, multidimensional, multiply essenced one. That is the lesson I have learned from my study of India's profound tradition of intellectual pluralism. It is deeply encouraging to me that contemporary thinkers, some, like Karin Cetina, through empirical analysis of actual scientific practices; some, like Geoffrey Lloyd, through cross-cultural historical explorations of the contrasts between ancient Greece and China; and others, like Hubert Dreyfus and Charles Taylor in their book *Retrieving Realism* (2015), through a philosophical wish to escape the horns of the oscillation between scientism and subjectivism, have begun to converge on some version of exactly the solution first touted by the Jainas of India, namely that epistemic cultures are practical policies to be adopted, not sets of propositions to be believed, and that reality is manifold so that no one epistemic culture can claim privileged access to nature as it is in itself. So a pluralism about epistemic stances, not about epistemic systems, is what we need to defeat "the spirit of 1789." K. C. Bhattacharyya's further move—in fusing Jaina *anekāntavāda* with Indian *rasa* theory—was to associate the adoption of distinct stances with distinct proprietary phenomenologies, and so with the subjective question "what is it like to adopt an epistemic stance?"

Conclusion

My argument has been that academic philosophy is in something of a state of crisis. Evidence of this crisis include heightened appreciation of the value of world philosophies, the internationalization of the student body, the philosophical pluralism which interaction and migration in new global movements make salient, growing concerns about diversity within a still too-white faculty body and curricular canon, and identification of a range of deep structural problems with the contemporary philosophical academy in its discursive, citational, refereeing, and ranking practices. What is needed is a fresh start in which a plurality of pre- and de-colonial intellectual stances are brought together in new forms of institutional arrangement. Philosophies from every region of the world, locally grounded in lived experience and reflection upon it, need to find new autonomous and authentic forms of articulation. Academic philosophy needs to become polycentric: the philosophical world must transform itself into diverse network of productive sites. Europe and other colonial powers will have been provincialized, no longer mandatory conversation partners or points of comparison but rather unprivileged participants in global dialogue. And, finally, philosophers within the largely anglophone international academy need to begin to acknowledge their responsibility so to arrange international institutions as to enable wide and open participation; that is, acknowledge that their present governance of the academy is a fallout from colonialism rather than an entitlement derived from the exceptional intellectual superiority of Greek classicism and its legacy. I have drawn on ideas that were worked out in detail in Sanskrit to develop an inclusive and pluralistic model of philosophical practice, and that is one way in which philosophy today needs Sanskrit. A practice of epistemic pluralism brings together ways of interrogating reality from many of the world's philosophical traditions, including the Sanskritic, and that is a second way in which academic philosophy today needs Sanskrit. Indeed John Dewey, the great American educationalist, called the last lecture he delivered to his graduate students, "The Idea of Pluralism." He said there that

> pluralism is the greatest philosophical idea of our times. How are we going to make the most of the new values we set on variety, difference, and individuality—how are we going to realize their possibilities in every field, and at the same time not sacrifice that plurality to the cooperation we need so much? How can we bring things together as we must without losing sight of plurality? (Dewey 1959: 102)

For Dewey education has to do with the insightful reorganization of experience, and yet the sources of experience are plural, and the challenge for education is to bring diverse sources of experience into cooperation, without falling into either the traps of scientism or relativism. In my opinion the Sanskrit philosophical traditions teach us exactly how to do this.

Notes

1. For details, see my "Reasoning through Cases" (2000).
2. "Studies in Yoga Philosophy," "Studies in Sāṃkhya Philosophy," "The Jaina Theory of Anekānta," "Studies in Vedāntism," in K. C. Bhattacharyya (1958), *Studies in Philosophy*, vol. 1, essays 1, 4, 5, and 8.
3. "The Concept of Rasa," in K. C. Bhattacharyya (1958), *Studies in Philosophy*, vol. 1, essay 7.

4. For a longer version of the discussion in this section, see my "Epistemic Pluralism: From Systems to Stances" (2019).
5. TS 1.6; see Tatia, Nathmal (1994). NAV 29.28; see Piotr Balcerowicz (2002: 124).
6. "Among these, the [general] definition is as follows: 'The reflection of one facet of an object recognized by a *pramāṇa* is the standpoint,' because this [general definition] pertains to all particular standpoints and because it is capable of distinguishing [among standpoints of] different forms." NAV 29.12 (Balcerowicz 2001: 97).
7. Nāgārjuna, VV 29; see Kamaleswar Bhattacharya et al. (1978: 113).

References

Balcerowicz, Piotr (2002), *Jaina Epistemology in Historical and Comparative Perspective. Critical Edition and English Translation of Logical-Epistemological Treatises: Nyāyāvatāra, Nyāyāvatāra-vivṛti and Nyāyāvatāra-ṭippana*, Stuttgart: Franz Steiner Verlag.

Bhattacharya, Kamaleswar, Elgin H. Johnston, and Arnold Kunst (1978), *The Dialectical Method of Nāgārjuna: Vigrahavyāvartanī*, New Delhi: Motilal Banarsidass.

Bhattacharyya, K. C. (1907), *Studies in Vedāntism*, reprinted in K. C. Bhattacharyya (1958), *Studies in Philosophy*, 1–6, Gopinath Bhattacharyya (ed.), Calcutta: Progressive Publishers.

Bhattacharyya, K. C. (1931), "Swaraj in Ideas," Sir Asutosh Memorial Lecture delivered at Candranagar in October 1931, organized by Charu Chandra Roy, *Visvabharati Quarterly*, 20 (1954): 103–14.

Bhattacharyya, K. C. (1958), *Studies in Philosophy*, ed. Gopinath Bhattacharyya, Calcutta: Progressive Publishers.

Bladel, Kevin van (2011), "The Bactrian Background of the Barmakids," in A. Akasoy, C. Burnett, and R. Yoeli-Tlalim (eds.), *Islam and Tibet: Interactions along the Musk Routes*, 43–88, London: Ashgate.

Boghossian, Paul (2006), *Fear of Knowledge: Against Relativism and Constructivism*, Oxford: Oxford University Press.

Chakravartty, Anjan (2004), "Stance Relativism: Empiricism versus Metaphysics," *Studies in the History and Philosophy of Science*, 35: 173–84.

Dewey, John (1959), *Dictionary of Education*, New York: Philosophical Library.

Dreyfus, Hubert, and Charles Taylor (2015), *Retrieving Realism*, Cambridge, MA.: Harvard University Press.

Fraassen, B. C. van (2002), *The Empirical Stance*, New Haven, CT: Yale University Press.

Ganeri, Jonardon (2000), "Reasoning Through Cases." Available online: https://www.academia.edu/15523158/Reasoning_Through_Cases (accessed April 29, 2021).

Ganeri, Jonardon (2019), "Epistemic Pluralism: From Systems to Stances," *Journal of the American Philosophical Association*, 1–21.

Hall, Edith (2015), "Pearls before Swine? Citizens' Classics for the 21st Century," *Gaisford Lecture*, University of Oxford, June 4, 2015. Available online: http://www.podcasts.ox.ac.uk/gaisford-2015-lecture-pearls-swine-past-future-greek (accessed April 29, 2021).

Oldenberg, Hermann (1906), *Indische und klassische Philologie*, reprinted in Hermann Oldenberg (1967), *Kleine Schriften*, vol. 2, 1515–23, Klaus Janert (ed.), Wiesbaden: Fritz Steiner Verlag.

Pollock, Sheldon (2015), "The Alternative Classicism of Classical India," *Seminar*, vol. 671 (July 2015). Available online: https://www.india-seminar.com/2015/671/671_sheldon_pollock.htm (accessed April 29, 2021).
Radhakrishnan, Sarvepalli (1936), *The World's Unborn Soul*, Oxford: Oxford University Press.
Rocher, Rosane, and Ludo Rocher (2011), *The Making of Western Indology: Henry Thomas Colebrooke and the East India Company*, London: Routledge.
Teller, Paul (2004), "What Is a Stance?," *Philosophical Studies*, 121: 159–70.
Weil, Simone (1962), "East and West: Thoughts on the Colonial Problem," in *Selected Essays 1934–43*, trans. Richard Rees, 195–210. Eugene, OR: Wipf & Stock.
Tatia, Nathmal (1994), *That Which Is: A Classic Jain Manual for Understanding the True Nature of Reality: A Translation of Umāsvāti's Tattvārtha-sūtra*, New Haven, CT: Yale University Press.

9

Global Post-Comparative Philosophy as Just Philosophy

Arindam Chakrabarti and Ralph Weber

Comparative philosophy occupies but a niche in most philosophy departments around the world. Yet, there have been some important advances in the last decade or so that its practitioners rightly celebrate. There is a growing market for journals and books on the topic, as many up-and-coming young philosophers take a different attitude toward the ambiguously labeled field of "non-European philosophy." In an important sense, their interest is a mirror image of changed life circumstances. Multiculturalism, cosmopolitanism, globalization, the climate crisis alongside debates on how to mend past wrongs, persisting structural injustices, and the tension between identity and planetary politics have entered the general consciousness at an unprecedented level and largely in tandem with the new realities of a world bound together and made highly accessible through digital communication technology. These new realities have brought about significant changes in the way a young student would encounter and learn about "non-European philosophy," regardless of where in the world this student lives. At the same time, it seems considerably harder to ignore the diversity of philosophical traditions around the globe as easy as it was possible to ignore them throughout much of the second half of the twentieth century, in which large parts of philosophy increasingly turned into an ever more specialized discipline, much of it more analytical and more in tune with cognitive sciences.

"Non-European philosophy" has also become harder to ignore because of debates in disciplines other than philosophy. Scholars in history, anthropology, literature, parts of sociology and political science, and in many of the more recent disciplines from new area and global studies to feminist and queer studies have emphasized the importance of positionality in ways more susceptible to valuing difference and hybridity across the globe. Discourses on world systems theory, postcolonialism, and decolonialism have brought important perspective to the problem of Eurocentrism, epistemic injustice, and the power-knowledge nexus that underlies global knowledge production. Admittedly, mainstream philosophy has by no standard figured at the forefront of these developments. Today, however, even the most insular philosophers will have heard of them. While some mainstream philosophers have shown admirable and sustained interest, there are also many who have simply come to accept the unavoidability of allowing some space to these viewpoints even within the centers of institutionalized philosophy. And thus we see the occasional filling of a new position by someone with a specialization in comparative philosophy. And so it might happen that a specialist in comparative philosophy comes to occupy a room next door to a mainstream philosopher and the occasional conversation over dog walking in cities or the trouble or joys of teaching might lead to an interest in each other, finally touching upon philosophical topics.

Perhaps, therefore, it is simply a question of time until comparative philosophy will no longer be a niche, but more firmly integrated into philosophy departments. Yet, perhaps, the issue is not so much about whether but rather about how comparative philosophy will be integrated. And, perhaps, the manner in which integration occurs is directly related to the reason for the integration. It seems to differ much whether the integration is a mere political concession or based on some acknowledged philosophical value, and there is a large realm where political and philosophical motivations can and do concur. One way of integration often representing a political concession is an exclusionary inclusion, which sometimes shows in the establishment of special sections and panels for "non-European philosophy" at the annual conferences of philosophy associations or in the added chapter or two, like an appendix, in a volume otherwise and mainly dedicated to problem-oriented philosophy. Exclusionary inclusion acknowledges, say, "African philosophy" as philosophy, and thus is inclusive, but it labels it at the same time as something other than philosophy proper and therefore also excludes it. These labeling practices are widely constitutive of the contemporary comparative philosophy landscape, but partly come at the cost of a host of othering issues. Then again, surely not all claim toward difference amounts to othering, and some practitioners of comparative philosophy will argue fervently for real philosophical difference between culturally coded philosophical traditions or endorse a kind of strategic essentialism or emancipatory power behind labels such as "African philosophy." There are also some more pragmatic concerns that might underscore the idea of special sections at conferences, as the expertise and language competency might be as deterring for a mainstream philosopher on a panel about Chinese philosophy as it is on a panel about ancient Greek philosophy or German idealism. Olberding (2017), however, has pointed out that non-European languages often face more particular skepticism.

This chapter revisits some recent controversies around the apparent difficulty of integrating comparative and "non-European philosophy" into philosophy departments in an attempt at distinguishing political from philosophical concerns. How to frame and label the philosophical concerns is important for the political discussion and crucial for achieving a more just philosophy. We argue for a global post-comparative approach, similar to what is also called fusion philosophy. But the results of such an approach should also constitute just—and nothing more than—philosophy, that is, amount to nothing qualitatively different from philosophy. The gist of the matter has to do with methodology, that is, with how to do philosophy. In this spirit, we offer two brief methodological arguments, one pertaining to a weak historicism, the other to the philosophical value of polyglotism, hopefully working toward facilitating the non-exclusionary inclusion of "non-European philosophy," no longer deserving of the label, in a future globally decentered philosophy.

Political Barriers and Philosophical Issues of a More Global Philosophy

From its beginnings, arguably in the nineteenth century, comparative philosophy has most often been a philosophical as well as a political enterprise. In recent years, important voices in the discipline have vented their frustration about the lack of recognition received within philosophy departments, based on the conviction that they have put forward their persuasive arguments over and again, but that the other side simply refuses to listen. Bryan W. Van Norden and Jay Garfield's op-ed, "If Philosophy Won't Diversify, Let's Call It What It Really Is" (2016), published in the *New York Times* triggered an enormous amount of comments and responses. Given that their main point was one about renaming philosophy departments as "departments of Anglo-European philosophy," the amount of xenophobic and racist comments that the piece apparently received revealed a political underside that stands in stark contrast to the diminishing social prestige of academic philosophy in most societies. Van Norden later doubled down with a volume called *Taking Back Philosophy: A Multicultural Manifesto* (2017), in which Garfield offers a short Foreword. There, Garfield (2017: xviii–xix) registers the oddity of a situation in which leagues of mainstream philosophers know for a fact, but somehow miraculously, that there is nothing to be gained from "non-European philosophy" *without* ever having looked at a single text, let alone context (see Van Norden 2017: 13–16, for a concrete example, and p. 28 for Eric Schwitzgebel's point how existing ignorance comes to justify continued ignorance). Those who have made "non-European philosophy" their specialty, in turn, are convinced that not only is there something valuable, but it also directly speaks to the interests of what mainstream philosophers are concerned with, even if perhaps only in part (as it should be assumed that such cross-engagement would also bring to the table new topics and interests).

Garfield in his Foreword and Van Norden in the text itself offer plenty of political arguments for a more structural and institutional inclusion of non-European philosophy, pointing out problems of structural racism, ethnocentrism, and Orientalism. Beyond these heavyweight "moral" (and political) issues, Garfield (2017: xix) mentions the "epistemic" (and therefore philosophical) side of the problem as one of ignorance, of "arguments, positions, and perspectives," that is eventually rooted in a kind of inverse argument from authority: because so-and-so said it, it cannot be relevant. Since this would quite obviously be a bad argument, it is often reduced to another one, which simply refuses to see these "arguments, positions, and perspectives" as being about the same subject matter, not even close, it could be added, just superficially related. This is as such a philosophically serious point, but it is unclear how any two positions, including those "within European philosophy" can ever be claimed to be on the same subject matter conclusively. Whether they are, and in what respect they are, is a comparative question itself and presumably the result of an inquiry and an agreement rather than a matter of straightforward evidence. Such agreement, in turn, as well as disagreement, is more often than not a key feature and indeed the most exciting part of any philosophical debate.

Perhaps less publicly noted, but no less interesting, is the 2017 exchange between Carine Defoort and Tim Heysse in the journal *Philosophy East and West*. Initially, Defoort (2017a; but see also 2017b) published an article on "Chinese Philosophy at European Universities," which she opened by bemoaning the "futility of rational arguments" in this matter, pointing out the role of emotional ties to the institutions in which one is philosophically socialized. She reads recent attempts at inclusion of "non-Western content" as exclusionary inclusions, being "well meant ad hoc corrections that actually allow the dominant framework to persist" (Defoort 2017a: 1049). Defoort's (2017a: 1066) article deliberately focuses on the institutional side of the question, explicitly bracketing out the "philosophical arguments for the acceptance of Chinese (or any other non-Western) philosophy." In his "polemical response," Heysse (2017) makes it clear that he would have loved instead to hear the philosophical arguments since it is eventually only those that can ensure inclusion into the philosophical conversation. The mere political imposition of philosophical content is in his view utterly ineffective. Heysse (2017: 1084) fashions philosophy as an Oakeshottian conversation and seems to think of the inclusion of "non-European philosophy" as a matter of time only, as sometimes, he writes, it "takes a generation or two."

Heysse (2017: 1083) is explicitly not defending a conception of philosophy as separated from politics because the former is somehow based on "Universal Reason," but because the former is and should be independent from politics. What counts as philosophy is decided by the philosophical audience on the basis of internal criteria. Heysse has of course a point, since the alternative that takes everything to be simply and only an expression of politics is also singularly unattractive. But this is ideal theory, which becomes clear when Heysse (2017: 1084) emphasizes that true conversation knows no hierarchy, which makes it a realm almost completely immunized from politics. Almost, but not entirely, because Heysse (2017: 1084)—even in this clearly ideal setting—has to insist that "most conversations" are for insiders only. He is of course aware that this is not how the conversation has taken place in our nonideal world:

> To understand the history of philosophy as a conversation is therefore not to deny that philosophy is political or that it is shaped by gatekeeping practices, institutional resistance, and other manifestations of power. It is, however, to insist that it is only by virtue of capturing the interest of philosophers that a subject matter may contribute to and become part of the conversation of philosophy. (Heysse 2017: 1084)

Heysse's statement is telling. The conditions he lays out are such as that there is no other way to gain entry into "the conversation of philosophy" as by the successful capturing of "the interest of philosophers." Who are these philosophers? It seems to be an existing and defined group that is already in conversation with one another, indeed, constituting the conversation of the very discipline itself. Hence, if their interest is captured, one can join the conversation; if it is not, then it seems that one's contribution was just not topical enough, not capturing enough interest, and therefore rightfully excluded. It is a thin line that separates this attempt to focus only on the philosophical merit of a contribution from just another and only slightly disguised gatekeeping practice.

From the point of view of those pursuing a more global philosophy, the word "philosophers" in the abovementioned quote can only be read as meaning those practicing "European philosophy" or "meta-philosophy in the European tradition." The coincidence of "European philosophy" with "mainstream philosophy" makes it problematic to have the mainstream decide over what constitutes and what does not constitute a philosophically interesting contribution. Yet, the idea of "mainstream philosophers" and a "mainstream philosophy" is not just a gross abstraction of limited use, it is also deeply perspectival. A philosopher working on or with Heidegger might think quite differently about what constitutes the current mainstream than an analytic philosopher does, and individuals across the spectrum might have more inclusive or exclusive understandings regardless of the respective tradition they stand in. Heysse's mention of "the conversation of philosophy" must hence be taken with a grain of salt. That conversation might resemble more the kind that Gadamer had—or did not have … —with Derrida in Paris in April 1981 (Bernstein 2008). Heysse's criterion for inclusion, that is, the capturing of the philosophers' interest, smacks also of an overly empirical approach. The emphasis seems to be on what those philosophers actually do find interesting, not what they should find interesting. Inversely, both Garfield and Van Norden as well as Defoort make the point that whereas philosophers should find these contributions from "non-European philosophy" interesting, they apparently do not find them interesting. While the empirical side is doubtlessly of major importance, it cannot be avoided to ask the question of what philosophy is also normatively (see Gassmann et al., 2018). Heysse (2017: 1084) acknowledges this dimension by referring to "the normativity of conversation," but grounds it on the "normativity of interest," which alone can ensure "the independence of conversation from power."

The notion of capturing one's interest is highly ambivalent. In ordinary conversation, we often use the word "interesting" with a certain intonation (something like "iiiiiiinnnteresting") to be polite, but it precisely does not mean that we are interested to the degree of wanting to engage. For something to be genuinely interesting, it needs to be arousing, perhaps challenging, but just to the right degree. If someone simply parrots one's own views, then that might be psychologically or sociologically interesting in and for itself, but it is hardly philosophically interesting. If someone speaks about something that one finds has nothing to do with what oneself is interested in, then one might still acknowledge that the matter seems interesting in and so far as it obviously has captured the interest of that person, but it is not philosophically interesting for oneself. The tension of being too close or too distant is familiar to many in the field of comparative philosophy and we have discussed it in relation to the vocabulary that one uses to describe the "non-European" philosophical position (Chakrabarti and Weber 2015a: 17–18).

The ambivalence in the notion of interest lies in that it might make a difference whether Heysse's "philosophers" are interested in terms of "iiiiiiinnnteresting," of acknowledging that others are interested or of finding it themselves philosophically interesting. For the latter, which is what Heysse seems to have in mind, the condition of possibility would require a considerable effort. Imagine if someone at a philosophy conference comes across as mainly talking about drinking tea, even if he or she does so in the most sophisticated manner, then one might simply go along and believe that person or ask the person to demonstrate that this is philosophically interesting in terms of what one takes the "conversation of philosophy" to be. The question is how much one would have to learn and know about the unfamiliar subject matter to come to judge whether it is philosophically interesting or not. Imagine the presentation at that conference is about the Japanese way of tea combining the structural phenomenology of Heinrich Rombach, Zen Buddhist scholar Shin'ichi Hisamatsu and the historically dubious, semilegendary figure of the Laozi (Heubel 2014) or seemingly simply on the background of Spinoza's argument in the *Tractatus Theologico Politicus*. On the one hand, a similar situation might pertain with an Ancient-Greek-loaded presentation about the philosophical value of Aristophanes' plays, where nonspecialized "philosophers" might simply deny the philosophical value and categorize the contribution, say, as an exercise in philology. On the other hand, as mentioned above, the distance to travel might appear even longer (for Europeans) when it comes to non-European languages, cultures, and philosophies. The point is that positionality is crucial in all of this. There is a risk of judging something as being outside "the conversation of philosophy" as meaning no more than that it is not part of "my conversation of philosophy" or "my group's conversation of philosophy." The more effort it would be required to get to a position of judging the philosophical merit of a contribution from outside one's own specialization and one's own group, the more likely it seems to take the easy route and reject the contribution as uninteresting or as interesting but not topical and so forth.

Heysse is aware of these difficulties. For one thing, he makes his own ignorance a topic from the beginning, adding to this admission that "my ignorance is, therefore, in a sense unjustifiable but also, to my mind, unavoidable" (Heysse 2017: 1082). This shifts the discussion to the question of what to do with this unavoidable ignorance—that of course exists on all sides. Heysse (2017: 1082) himself comes to assert philosophical merit against his own criterion when he expresses his wish to know more "about the Chinese authors Defoort provides in her long list of names ('there is a total absence of expertise on Confucius, Mozi, Mencius … [etc.]')," adding that "surely, we should not define 'philosophy' in a way that excludes these authors." How would he know that these authors warranted inclusion? Has Defoort or someone else made him find an interest in these authors? Defoort, in the quoted passage, lists the names of more than fifty Chinese authors from across two and a half millennia.[1] It seems highly unlikely that Heysse has learned about the philosophical merit of all these figures and on that basis has come to show interest in them.[2] Notwithstanding, in this passage, Heysse displays admirable openness giving advance credit to a list of authors he is admittedly ignorant about. As such, this inclusion based on ignorance does not invalidate his larger point that, eventually and ideally, the main trigger for interest should be philosophical, but it perhaps emphasizes that politics may play a crucial role with regard of creating the conditions of possibility for "the conversation" of global philosophy.

To some extent, everyone operating from within a niche wishes to have one's own niche finding more institutional acceptance and moving from a niche to the center. But with comparative philosophy, it is not just a question of specialization or philosophical preference, like a Hegelian would want all philosophers to understand the utmost relevance of Hegelianism or a philosopher of food would want more philosophers to join in and comprehend the topic's centrality. It is more like there is a suspicion about bias in the very sociological and political setting of philosophy, similar to issues of gender, class, and race that constitutes political barriers to a more global philosophy. Removing some of these barriers and becoming as superficially conversant with "non-European philosophy" like most "philosophers" are with ancient Greek philosophy or the topic of nominalism in medieval European philosophy might pave the way toward a levelheaded discussion about philosophical merit. Whether or not something has philosophical merit, it seems, cannot be decided solely by whether it captures the interest of one specific, let alone the established, insider group. It appears that one would have to find a constructive middle ground between Heysse's "philosophers" and those who continue to seek their acknowledgment. This middle ground, we assert, can be found in and through questions of methodology, that is, of what it means and how to do philosophy.

Argument for a Weak Historicism and an Instrumentally Unrealistic Idea of History

The first middle ground that can be established concerns the utility of the history of philosophy for the purposes of seeking transhistorical or contemporary philosophical insight. Such insight is often said to lie at the heart of efforts within analytic philosophy, which is then confronted with the charge of being ahistorical. Hans-Johann Glock (2008: ch. 4), searching for a definition of analytic philosophy (he eventually argues for a family resemblance account), examines the idea whether or not the discipline's alleged ahistoricity, which would seem to include a rejection of historicism, constitutes a defining characteristic. He defines historicism as "any position that promotes historical thinking in philosophy and warns against ignoring or distorting the past" (89). Glock introduces three variants of such historicism:

(1) Intrinsic Historicism: Proper philosophy is ipso facto historical, all philosophical insights are historical in nature, and there is thus no distinction between philosophy and the history of philosophy.
(2) Instrumental Historicism: Studying the past is necessary, but only as a means for achieving philosophical, not historical ends; doing the history of philosophy is not doing philosophy, but the former is indispensable for doing the latter.
(3) Weak Historicism: Studying the past is useful, but not indispensable.

Glock is unequivocal in his conclusion. He judges intrinsic historicism to be "misguided" and instrumental historicism "unproven." Most analytic philosophers, however, he asserts, accept weak historicism (90). If a majority of analytic philosophers rejects intrinsic and instrumental historicism, then weak historicism might be the best candidate for a middle ground. For those analytic philosophers who embrace what the majority among them rejects, no middle ground would have to be established.

But would a recognition of the general utility of the history of philosophy for doing philosophy in any way mean that comparative philosophy would have to be included? There are two sides to this question. On the one hand, there might be a similar split between those who do comparative philosophy with a historical interest and those who pursue it decidedly philosophically. As we will see, some such debate has occurred not long ago within comparative philosophy. On the other hand, the utility could simply be extended to the history of "European philosophy" and not include the history of "non-European philosophy." Indeed, it is possible to imagine that the utility is conceived as restricted to one's own or direct precursors, or some such notion. Even more subtly, utility could be admitted as a concession without consequence. Since it is only useful but not instrumental or intrinsic and since many things are useful, it would follow that no systematic or institutional inclusion is particularly warranted. This would amount to an inclusionary exclusion yet again. So the questions to answer are what exactly "useful" means in weak historicism, whether the history of philosophy is particularly useful and whether "non-European" philosophy is included in all of this.

It might well be the case that quite a sizable number of analytic philosophers who embrace weak historicism would think first and foremost of the "European history of philosophy" as the relevant history. Glock, to be sure, does not seem to share such a narrow outlook. In one passage, he speaks of the possibility of learning from "a foreign text or culture," but adds that this is a lesson that analytic philosophers should adopt from the hermeneutic tradition (113).[3] In just any case, the issue cannot be settled by turning to whether analytic philosophers would include "non-European history of philosophy" as part of the relevant history of philosophy. We would be back at Heysse's "philosophers" and "the conversation of philosophy." Fortunately, there is a host of arguments for such inclusion, ranging from ancient near eastern influences on early Greek philosophy by an older Babylonian philosophy in its own right (Van de Mieroop 2017) to various ancient and modern Asian conceptions of philosophy (Steineck and Weber 2018). A perhaps even more effective line of argument, however, comes from efforts to expose global connections and entanglements of the "European history of philosophy," as for example Gopnik (2009) showcases with regard to whether David Hume might have known about Buddhism. Surely, even the crudest Eurocentric view that only sees European philosophy as valid and valuable could not deny the fact that this philosophy has traveled the world and found a reception in many places that would have to be counted as part of its history, as, for example, Seidel (2010) relates with regard to the reception of Kant's philosophy in Teheran. In view of all this and a globally institutionalized philosophy, it is hard to imagine how a hermetic account of a European history of philosophy could stand any ground. From this point of view, philosophy, even if most narrowly conceived as historically a European phenomenon, has always had a global history.

So the real issue comes down to the relation between philosophy and its history. That it comes down to this is quite clear since we find similarly opposed camps on this specific question within comparative philosophy. A few years back, a short exchange (rather than a debate) between Michael Levine and Mark Siderits took place. Levine (2016) had criticized Siderits (2003, 2015) and his conception of fusion philosophy, particularly the latter's claim that "fusion philosophy is meant to be a successor to the practice of what has been called comparative philosophy" (Siderits 2003: xi). Fusion philosophy, according to Siderits (2003: xi), combines two particular positions, namely that problem-solving is central to philosophy and that the "counterpoising of distinct traditions can yield useful results in this endeavor." To what extent this "counterpoising of distinct traditions" should be historically informed became an explicit issue when Michael Nylan (and Martin Verhoeven) leaned in on the exchange. Nylan joined Levine's criticism from the viewpoint of a historian who among else is specialized on the philosophy of early China. Following Levine's account of Siderits, she comes to charge Siderits and fusion philosophy with being ahistorical.

Nylan, summing up Levine's criticism, depicts Siderits's fusion philosophy as "denying the utility of *long* training in non-Western cultures and sustained reflections upon methodological problems, resting content with isolating ideas from their embedded contexts" (Nylan and Verhoeven 2016: 120). Polemicizing the matter further, she then asks how, "without *any* training in context and method," can one be sure "that one has even understood the extracted bits, their logics, their rhetorical strategies, or their inherent appeals, then and now?" (120). Nylan's concern is obvious and as such legitimate, as one can certainly never be completely sure. Since this is so, one could also not possibly be sure even after the longest and most arduous training that is humanly imaginable. Nylan (2016: 121) seems to agree, since she shows skepticism even with regard to Siderits's idea that historical texts could be "sufficiently well understood" to use them for addressing a philosophical problem: "Complex and subtle texts with layers of meaning" always have many meanings, not one. The picture that emerges from this is that fusion philosophy's uses of historical texts for attempts at tackling currently debated problems in contemporary philosophy amount to nothing more than scholarly irresponsible "cherry-picking" of dilettantes (without any training); a "skeptic," Nylan (2016: 120) adds, "might even argue that fusion philosophy risks becoming yet a new form of neocolonial extraction of resources (ideas and arguments)."

The exchange allows us to make two points. The first point is a telling irony. Those who charge Siderits for his presumed ahistorical, untrained philosophical extractivism might well have chosen the wrong scholar. Siderits is particularly well trained in the context and method of the Buddhist texts that he draws on for his fusion philosophy. In his "Response to Levine" (Siderits 2016), he tries to set the record straight in this regard, highlighting his lifelong training in Buddhism and his more philological, historical scholarship. Yet even when after looking at this record one would come to the (impressively self-certain) conclusion that Siderits is simply too little trained, still cherry-picking, then certainly one would have to abstain oneself from such practices. The relativist implications would be radical and it would become hard to say anything much at all. Surely, when debating the approach of fusion philosophy as to its virtues over against comparative philosophy, one engages in discussion of a contemporary problem, perhaps a philosophical problem, that even if it is not one that one finds particularly relevant oneself, one would have to concede that it is a problem that some find relevant enough to think about, write about, and publish. Taking a position such as rejecting Siderits's fusion philosophy would then certainly have to do justice to Siderits's texts, their context, and method. It is thus not without irony that the critics cherry-pick themselves considerably when passing judgment on Siderits. Is the recent past comprising Siderits's texts since at least the 1970s not yet past enough to warrant the historical approach thought appropriate for other figures in the more distant past? Who is the careless fusion philosopher here? What is more, to argue in the present discussion that "problem-solving" might be a fundamentally mistaken view, Nylan (2016: 120) draws on a quote from Zhuangzi quite in the way that a fusion philosopher would. Perhaps, after all, fusion philosophers are not as ahistorical as their critics might think.

The second point has to do with the exact worry beyond polemics that historians such as Nylan have with use of historical sources for philosophical argument in the present. She highlights "the dangers of ignoring the historical settings for pronouncements in the early literature, while glossing over the implications of vocabulary nuances and changes within a given culture" (120). Siderits, by the way, is in full agreement. He addresses several possible pitfalls of fusion philosophy, which he sees as variants of the problem of "superimposition" and leading to "a failure to see deeper differences and thus obscured important lessons" (Siderits 2015). More importantly, however, Nylan's emphasis on "vocabulary nuances and changes within a given culture" hits the nail on its head. There are many ways how the history of philosophy might be thought useful for the practice of philosophy. Glock (2008: 103) writes:

> The community of ideas relevant to our contemporary philosophical problems is not exhausted by contemporaries. The problems, methods and theories of the past have not simply been superseded by empirical progress. As a result the endeavors of past thinkers remain a valuable source of inspiration, both positively and negatively.

Besides inspiration, which is still very broad, Glock (2008: 103) also mentions the knowledge of philosophical positions and their evolution, and then adds that "if we are to profit from the philosophical reflections of the past, we must recognize conceptual differences and shifts concerning key terms." It is not far-fetched to argue that Glock's "conceptual differences and shifts" are not so different from Nylan's "vocabulary nuances and changes within a given culture." What is different are the interests that go with finding such nuances and conceptual differences. In a caricatured view of historians being interested in the past and philosophers being interested in the present, these interests come to stand at opposite ends. Historians might or might not believe to recapture the past and many would think of their discipline as very much being about the present, not the past. Even if recapturing the past might be a mere ideal, it constitutes a legitimate scholarly interest. There is nothing wrong with trying to find out what Wittgenstein was doing by writing the *Tractatus*, even trying to find out what he was thinking when doing it. A scholar might be genuinely and intrinsically interested in this. Fusion philosophers as much as post-comparative global philosophers will not share such an interest, but their interest will of necessity be instrumental. There is a large difference between superficial and intrinsic-like instrumental interest. The former would amount to what Nylan and Levine both rightly dismiss as quick and hasty self-confirmation of one's own presuppositions (Levine 2016: 219, Nylan 2016: 120). And fusion philosophy at worst would indeed be that. At its best, however, fusion philosophy would try to approximate intrinsic scholarship, even instrumentally upholding an unrealistic idea of history as capable of recapturing the past, in their attempt to retrieve nuances and conceptual differences. It stands to reason that learning about all sorts of new and presumably different contexts, including learning languages, is not only a wonderful way to refine one's conceptual thinking, but also of challenging one's own presuppositions. The more historical inquiry, the better, it would seem. But an instrumental interest also sets limits, as philosophers tackling a problem by recourse to two or more philosophical traditions have to juggle a set of questions that do not add up to a unified marching order, but make for hard choices: "How much history of ideas will be necessary or sufficient for good fusion thinking? How much text-interpretation will be required? How much a-historical original conceptual creativity will be necessary? How much resemblance-discovery should be aimed for? How much contrast-discovery is essential? How to achieve a balance between giving rigorous clear arguments and being contemplatively authentic and phenomenologically descriptive?" (Chakrabarti and Weber 2015b: 234).

From Unflaunted Polyglotism to Just Philosophy

As delineated in our edited volume (Chakrabarti & Weber 2015a, 20–2), before it came to occupy a more or less secure "niche" in the mainstream curriculum (at least in the UK and USA if not yet in Europe)—perhaps through an exclusionary inclusion—comparative philosophy passed through at least three stages. Of course, we should not forget that at least in the case of eighteenth-century German Indological enthusiasm, which started with the "romantic" zeal of Schlegel, Holtzmann, Garbe, and Jacobi, and culminated in Max Muller's monumental translations of RgVeda, the intellectual politics was profoundly evangelical, Christianizing, and Aryan-supremacist (see Adluri and Bagchee 2014).[4] The first wave of translations of "oriental" texts into German, English, and other European languages ushered in, at best, giddy universalism. It chanted slogans like "Neo-Platonists like Plotinus and Indian Monists like Shankara were giving similar non-dualistic solutions to the same problems of metaphysic, let's find the same empiricism and anti-Self arguments in Buddhists and David Hume," and so on. This first wave generated, among the colonized Asian intellectuals, a revivalism and "we-said-all-this-long-ago" cultural chauvinism that has not yet disappeared totally. A second wave came when more caution and deeper textual analysis in the original languages came to be practiced in Chinese, Sanskrit, Pali, and Arabic. The total neglect of Africa in the arena of philosophy was registered and diagnosed. Thus, some measure of politically self-critical "historical contextualism" brought in the period of contrast: "The Chinese, Indian, Islamic, Akan religious and political backgrounds being incommensurably different from, Aristotelian, Judeo-Christian as well as European scientific genealogy of rationality, it is their differences from Euro-American philosophy that should be studied and highlighted"—became the spirit of the comparative fringe of continental and analytic philosophers. Both Western-style philologists/Indologists as well as "native" Indians, Chinese, Africans were happy to discover that questions like the problem of evil or the free will versus determinism debate or notions like apriori knowledge or logical deductive necessity were missing from the practical, spiritual, animistic, dynamically naturalistic Chinese, Indian, or African cultures of thought. More recently in the twenty-first century, came the turn to reverse the gaze, where the search for traces of recognizably Western problems in Eastern texts was replaced by the reverse search for recognizably Eastern philosophical problems in Western philosophy. Instead of asking whether there are idealists and realists, individualists or communitarians in Indian or Chinese philosophy, the questions were more like: "Where are the Confucian concepts of *ren* and *li*, the Bhagavadgita concepts of *dharma* and *yoga*, the Bantu concept of *Ubuntu* in ancient Greek or modern European or British social moral political thought?" A fourth wave is beginning to show up in the twenty-first century, which is sometimes critically theorized as fusion philosophy, which we have referred to above as global post-comparative philosophy. In this fourth phase, contemporary ground-level live issues in different branches of philosophy, such as the mind–body problem, the problem of relative priority of liberty versus equality in politics, the problem of our knowledge of other minds, or, the question of the distinction between sense and reference of a word, or the problem of self-deception and weakness of the will started to be discussed by drawing freely from old and new, European or "non-European," Greek or sub-Saharan, Islamic or Hindu, phenomenological, hermeneutic or analytic or Wittgensteinian resources that happen to be randomly accessible by the original philosopher (not a mere chronicler of regional histories of philosophy) who was cooking the fusion.

Of course the worldwide awakening of increased sensitivity to the—as yet far from complete—process of decolonization and refashioning of cultural identities by demands of reparation profoundly impacted each stage of this broadly three-plus-one stage history of comparative philosophy.

Indeed, the fourth phase is only beginning. In this chapter we are expressing the new hope that fusion philosophy when done well will be "just philosophy." It will be "just" in two senses. It will do away with the epistemological triple injustice done to "theories" from the Global South

(a) by excluding the story of the millennia of debates within Indian, Chinese and Arab, and African philosophies from the allegedly global history of human thought,
(b) by openly or insidiously marking off Asian or African philosophies as not "philosophical" in the same sense in which Greco-Roman-European philosophies, for all their internal differences, are considered "philosophical," and
(c) by de-modernizing (often under the garb of veneration or cultural Otherness) all non-Western philosophy as prescientific, ancient, and—in effect—dead museum items for philological and anthropological research.

But this future post-fusion philosophy would be "just" also in the simpler sense, of being mere or sheer philosophy. What should strike us while conceptualizing this second sense of "just" is the significant redundancy of this adjective: just philosophy is philosophy, period, without any qualifiers or adjectives. In this, the adjective "just" is similar to the adjective "true." To assert the proposition that coal is black is true, is to assert that coal is black. When a post-fusion philosopher, keeping Kant's categorical imperative as well as Hindu and Buddhist ethics in mind, considers what is the source of normativity in the imperative prohibition "You should not kill or be cruel to another human being or yourself," they would be doing just philosophy, hopefully tapping into more than one philosophical tradition for their intuition pumps.

Such philosophy simpliciter would require, of course, knowledge of diverse traditions, and ideally of many languages. But comparative philology should not take over the task of spontaneously comparative philosophy. Both the methodological polyglotism as well as the (implicitly historically politically self-aware) commitment to staying in between languages and cultures must remain unflaunted and unclaimed. If people do not need to alert us when they mix Foucault, Hobbes, and Gramsci in solving the problem of, say, power without hegemony, as a live contemporary human political problem, why must the (still exclusionary) adjective "fusion" be retained when people would use resources from the Mahabharata, St. Augustine, or the Buddha while crafting a position of soft-determinism or neutral monism or anti-realism about aesthetic values?

In our earlier volume in praise of borderless philosophy, we said that eventually the epithet "comparative" should be dropped in the fourth phase, as we do global post-comparative fusion philosophy. The same is of course true of "post-comparative," "fusion," and so on, so if the fourth phase is successful we will eventually arrive at just philosophy (as shown above, in both senses of the term), the final and fifth phase of epithetless philosophy. Such just philosophy will presuppose but not consist in scholarly textual historical erudition about "who said what and when" in Chinese, German, Swahili, Sanskrit, Spanish, Arabic, Greek, Latin, Japanese, French, Hawaiian, Korean, Khmer, and so on, and in what sense. Encyclopedic histories of world philosophies have their own perspectival blind spots. Kant opens his *Die Religion innerhalb der Grenzen der bloßen Vernunft* (Religion within the Limits of Bare Reason) with a ridiculously garbled allusion to Hindu cosmogony, making Lord Shiva (whose name is the Sanskrit word for "Good") sound like radical evil because he is the cosmic destroyer! Hegel's world histories of philosophy are notoriously skewed with grand culturally myopic biases. Bertrand Russell says somewhere that Hegel's encyclopedic story of the progress of the world mind—inevitably reaching its destination in Germany of course—goes like this: Indian philosophy of Brahman only captured pure static changeless Being—and since Hegel knew next to nothing about Chinese thought, so the Chinese mind represented its antithesis; pure Nothing. It is only in the European enlightenment that we have the pinnacle of synthesis: dynamic Becoming! Russell's own representation of Hegel was unabashedly cartoon-like, even in the deservedly celebrated and carefully titled *History of Western Philosophy*:

> This illustration might also be used to illustrate the dialectic, which consists of thesis, antithesis, and synthesis. First we say: "Reality is an uncle." This is the thesis. But the existence of an uncle implies that of a nephew. Since nothing really exists except the Absolute, and we are now committed to the existence of a nephew, we must conclude: "The Absolute is a nephew." This is the antithesis. But there is the

same objection to this as to the view that the Absolute is an uncle; therefore we are driven to the view that the Absolute is the whole composed of uncle and nephew. This is the synthesis. But this synthesis is still unsatisfactory, because a man can be an uncle only if he has a brother or sister who is a parent of the nephew. Hence we are driven to enlarge our universe to include the brother or sister, with his wife or her husband. In this sort of way, so it is contended, we can be driven on, by the mere force of logic, from any suggested predicate of the Absolute to the final conclusion of the dialectic, which is called the "Absolute Idea." Throughout the whole process, there is an underlying assumption that nothing can be really true unless it is about Reality as a whole. (Russell 1946: 759)

Even when more or less textually accurate and erudite, such historical bird's-eye views or "doxographic" accounts of philosophical opinions of the predecessors have, in the past, tended to push ground-level real philosophy to the background. Studying, reporting, and cataloguing ancient and modern views of people and thinkers from different parts of the world is no substitute for doing philosophy first hand, paying logical and phenomenological attention to one's own life and thought, which Souleymane Bachir Diagne (2016) beautifully puts as "putting concepts to work." Constantly updating the preparatory multilingual, multicultural and methodologically vigilant work, a "just philosopher" would put those dialogically distilled concepts to work by grappling with ground-level ever-fresh problems of philosophy, by asking questions such as these:

- How did the universe begin?
- Are time and tense differences, past and future real?
- What purpose/s should human beings—individual persons and the human species as such—live for?
- Should a geographically spread out people (of a country) govern themselves or should they be governed by a ruler or ruling elite who has more power/knowledge than the average citizen?
- Are material objects perceived by many viewers as existing independently of perceptions really out there or are they cooked up by our individual or intersubjective thought and experience and language?
- Is it the maxim or principle for the sake of which an action is intentionally done or the actual consequence of the action for a large number of people's happiness or suffering that determines whether the action is good or bad, right or wrong?
- Are we free to choose the kind of life we shall have, the thoughts we shall think and the actions we shall perform, or are we (in a hard or soft way) determined by natural, biological, karmic forces?

Take the first or the last question. If philosophers spend all or most of their time investigating what the ancient Egyptians or ancient Indians or current scientists in Europe and North America thought or think about the origin of the universe and the free will versus determinism question, such intellectual history, however comparatively done, will keep postponing the (post-comparative) project of putting to work, in our own lives and thinking, those basic human concepts—concepts precariously placed in the middle space of meaning between two distinct languages as one attempts the nearly impossible but cultural-politically obligatory task of translation. We have to ask questions such as, is truth reducible to justification or verification or does it belong to some "eternal thoughts" or propositions independently of human capacity to prove or disprove? And we have to ask, should future suffering of others be eliminated just because it is empathically feelable as if it is one's own suffering or simply because it is suffering? A nineteenth-century John Stuart Mill, the ninth-century Buddhist monastic master Shantideva, and Sidgewick from early-twentieth-century Cambridge would join that anachronistic debate "in our head." Differences of historical contexts, layers of meaning, and translational difficulties would be remembered and struggled with, methodologies would be examined and reexamined. But the debates would be directly about truth and pain, about freedom and the self, about the badness of exploitation and inequality.

This very discussion of ours of course is not conducted in any cosmopolitan language. In so far as we are writing (and thinking) in English, we are unavoidably valorizing certain grammatical "universals"—such as counterfactual-conditional form or the subject-predicate form. The language in which we conduct philosophy does determine—though less deeply than we sometimes tend to think in a postmodernist deconstructionist vein—which questions make sense and which do not. Yet, the language of *just philosophy* cannot afford to be some artificially egalitarian philosophical Esperanto. How to find the right language for cosmopolitan thought then? The only apt response to this pertinent query seems to be this. We have to be vigilant and try to think always at least bilingually straining to occupy and stay in a translational middle ground of conceptual content, as it were!

A deeper tension between alertness about any kind of methodological and linguistic-political egalitarianism and practicing just ground-level philosophy consists in the fact that the latter—doing sheer philosophy of the ground-level issues of metaphysics, ethics, epistemology, political philosophy, and aesthetics (why does aesthetics always come last?)—requires a certain kind of indifference, unstudied innocence, or unselfconsciousness about these methodological issues of knowledge politics. Such a tension can be productive, instead of being an obstacle to the feasibility of just philosophy. Let us try to illustrate it with the early writings of K. C. Bhattacharyya who starts off as a typical comparative philosopher but ends up doing philosophy in the most unlikely synthesis of contemplativeness and analytic rigor. K. C. Bhattacharyya, in a sense, was way ahead of his time.

Writing in early-twentieth-century colonial times, with a triple master's degree in English, Sanskrit, and philosophy, and reacting sharply against the typical marginalization of Indian philosophy in the English-European academic philosophy curriculum, he started his career by practicing unapologetic comparative philosophy interspersed with what we are calling "just philosophy," simply breaking his own "new" philosophical ground in matters of self, consciousness, and self-consciousness. In 1907, a method-conscious 32-year-old K. C. Bhattacharyya (1907: 2) wrote:

> The very name of philosophy has sometimes been denied to Indian speculation on the ground, *apparently established historically*, that the Oriental intellect is not

sufficient dry and has not masculine virility enough to rise to anything higher than grotesque imaginative cosmogonies. *When history thus sits in judgment on philosophy*, an Indian student of Vedanta may well be excused if to him a reproduction of the philosophy, such as *may bring it into contact with modern problems*, appears far more important than any *mere historical dissertation.* (our emphasis)

Both in this early book as well as in his mature masterpiece *Subject as Freedom* (1930), K. C. Bhattacharyya approached the topic of self and subjectivity "through psychology" which reads like phenomenology in Husserl's or even Merleau-Ponty's sense (note the two chapters on bodily subjectivity he included in this utterly non-expository ahistorical monograph on the grades of self-awareness), though he never refers to them and most certainly could not have read the latter. But even while interpreting Vedanta psychology creatively, his immediate interlocutors were Kant and Hegel. Witness these passages from the youthful *Studies in Vedantism* (1907):

> The difference between Hegel and Vedānta is connected with a fundamental difference regarding the conception of self between Kant's synthetic unity of apperception and the Vedāntic ātman or caitanya. They are generally regarded as the same, and in fact there is a good deal of similarity between them. Kant's self, though transcending empirical consciousness, is individualized in a sense, for it is this which becomes practical as well, emerging as a postulate directly implied by morality ... whether individualized or not, it is still *agent*, the form of *knowing* rather than that of knowledge. In Vedānta, however, the self is the breath of this knowledge, the light of consciousness, something eternally accomplished rather than being accomplished. (Bhattacharyya 1907: 22)

After these explicitly comparative contrastive exercises, the text takes flight into *doing* borderless philosophy by proposing a scintillatingly new and post-comparative argument about the logic of conceivability:

> Who knows that even this cohesion may not break down with further experience? That it cannot be conceived is no argument, for the moment something is said to be inconceivable, it is pronounced to be conceivable by implication. The subject of the proposition, "this cannot be conceived" is in fact a *conceived* inconceivability. This is only a negative conceivability, however. It is only an "indefinable sense of the Beyond," mere *matter* of knowledge without positive form. In the very humility of accepting absolute skepticism as a possible view, there is the transcendence of it, in which, however, there is no differenced self to enjoy the triumph. (Bhattacharyya 1907: 22)

This is just philosophy at its best, and it presupposes but does not flaunt a multicultural confrontation of cultures in one's open yet culturally rooted mind.

Conclusions

Comparative philosophy has cleared some ground toward finding institutional acceptance in philosophy departments. The question of our time is how comparative philosophy will be integrated. Will it be as a political concession or as an acknowledgment of philosophical value? If it is to be included as just philosophy—in both senses of the term—then a mere political success on philosophical terrain (just philosophy) would seriously impair acknowledgment as being philosophy proper (just philosophy). Inversely, the inclusion of "non-European" philosophy on purely philosophical terms runs the risk of buying into a power-free conception of philosophy that goes against its own history as much as against any common sense about the realities of institutional power. Put differently, if one argues for an unpretentious inclusion of "non-European" philosophy into mainstream philosophy, then that unpretentiousness is easily disturbed by knowledge politics, which it is wrong to ignore. Yet, doing philosophy as the kind of ground work we have described can only be done effectively if and when it proceeds in a distance from knowledge politics, which therefore it is imperative to ignore. Is there a way out of this dilemma?

We would like to suggest that similar to our argument about the instrumental utility of history, by which more quasi-intrinsically motivated historical investigation is helpful for pursuing philosophical interests that are not invested with historical authority, but stand by themselves, an argument can and should be made about a maximally politically concerned practice of doing philosophy in order to advance philosophical arguments that are precisely not reducible to mere politics. Garfield (2012) responds in an interview:

> Western philosophers gained access to Asian and African traditions initially by noting similarities and differences. But that, as A. C. Mukerji, of Allahabad, was to note in 1932, is not to do philosophy, but is at best a preparation. To take philosophy seriously is to engage with it philosophically. We take Aristotle seriously not when we write about his ideas, but when we take his ideas as part of our discussions. Similarly, we take Nāgārjuna seriously not when we talk about how similar his ideas are to Hume's, but when we take him as an interlocutor.

At first glance, this might look like classical *philosophia perennis*. But in our view it could not be more different, since the historical consciousness that also weak historicism presupposes and cultivates and the awareness of knowledge politics foreground positionality in a way that forces those interested in doing global post-comparative or simply just philosophy to own the question in quite a fundamental manner, that is not pointing toward a solipsism, but to a hermeneutics of suspicion that questions whether we are ever talking about the same matter in a dialogue. It is also not a plea for classical *philosophia perennis* because the stock of questions that motivates philosophers is itself subjected to change. New questions about the ethics of artificial intelligence are asked today, as other questions, say, about transubstantiation have retreated into more specialized quarters. And in this sense, one would have to expect that the non-exclusionary inclusion of "non-European" philosophy into the philosophical mainstream would shift "the conversation of philosophy," perhaps not radically, but twitching it here and there, bringing in new questions and even new conceptions of philosophy.

Polyglotism has a similar nuance-crafting philosophical capacity as weak historicism and awareness for knowledge politics have. To occupy a translational middle point and putting concepts to work from there might constitute just philosophy exactly in the unpretentious manner that we have advocated in this chapter. English might be the philosophical lingua franca these days, but it bears mentioning that this designation implies people communicating with each other whose native language is different. The point about the philosophical value of polyglotism is that this plurality of languages is not a deplorable state of affairs to overcome but a resource to be exploited philosophically, be it German–English, ancient Greek–French, but also Arabic–Czech, or indeed, Pali–Japanese.

For all the excitement about decentering philosophy, decolonizing the curriculum, and ensuring that philosophical traditions from across the world find the recognition that they justly deserve, there is a risk of a flaunted intercultural comparative philosophy that mistakes a philological and historicist study of philosophy for all that philosophy should be about. While a useful instrument, it should not be confused with the end of philosophy itself. Siderits's claim that "fusion philosophy is meant to be a successor to the practice of what has been called comparative philosophy" is well aligned with an epithet-free philosophy that is global and post-comparative, that is just philosophy, but that knows how to make conscious, informed, and unpretentious use of comparative philosophy in all or some of its historical, linguistic, and cross- and transcultural diversity.

Notes

1. "Confucius, Mozi, Mencius, Laozi, Zhuangzi, Xunzi, Shang Yang, Shen Buhai, Shen Dao, Han Feizi, Guanzi, Heguanzi, Huainanzi, Shizi, Wang Chong, Lu Jia, Jia Yi, Huan Tan, Liu Xin, Dong Zhongshu, Yang Xiong, Liezi, Lu Sheng, Han Yu, Li Ao, Liu Zongyuan, Luo Yin, Zhou Dunyi, Zhang Zai, Cheng Yi, Cheng Hao, Zhu Xi, Wang Yangming, Li Zhi, Fu Shan, Wang Gen, He Xinyin, Wang Fuzhi, Wang Zhong, Fang Dongshu, Weng Fanggang, Gu Yanwu, Zhang Xuecheng, Huang Zongxi, Kang Youwei, Liang Qichao, Zhang Taiyan, Wu Yu, Hu Shi, Feng Youlan, Fu Sinian, Liang Shuming, Xiong Shili, Mou Zongsan, Qiang Zhongshu, Tang Junyi, and Li Zehou …," see Defoort (2017a: 1059).
2. Heysse (2017: 1085) is also somewhat contradictory when he asks Defoort for the philosophical arguments because "more specific arguments in favor of non-Western philosophy are required if we are to kindle the interest of philosophers," just to add that "such arguments are certainly being made" and giving himself two examples.
3. Glock (2008: 113) adds: "That is one lesson of the hermeneutic tradition which its analytic admirers have yet to assimilate. But it is a lesson which chimes with the dominant attitudes and practices of analytic historians: we should learn from a text by taking it seriously as raising issues and evincing claims of substantive interest."
4. A certain philosopher-Sanskritist of our times, in response to a draft of this chapter, has naturally endorsed our futuristic idea of comparative philosophers doing just or

sheer philosophy but reacted to our indictment of the nineteenth-century German Sanskritists in the following words:

> Surely everyone working in the 19th and early 20th c. looks "racist" to us (just like people of the future will censure us in similar ways) and surely they were all too convinced of the truth of the religion they were educated in. But is there anything "distinctive" about German indologists in this respect? If they are just like any other intellectual of their age, then I am not sure it makes sense to single them out.

An immediate response that we would like to make is this. "Everyone" working in those early years on the Upanishads or Mahabharata does not look racist at all, only those whose interest in the "critical historical scientific hermeneutic method" was majorly driven by colonial and evangelical motive do. Surely the Indian Sanskrit-speaking pandits who not only taught those texts but also wrote newer commentaries in the nineteenth and early twentieth centuries do not "look like racists" to us. For all their Brahminical casteism, many of them were not only preserving but re-enlivening those texts, until European Sanskritists came and claimed to understand the original Gita or original Upanishads better than those who believed in the contents of those texts, simply because they had the scientific distance of disbelief in the content and spiritual significance of their Vedic-Puranic-Tantric wisdom.

References

Adluri, Vishwa, and Joydeep Bagchee (2014), *The Nay Science: A History of German Indology*, New York: Oxford University Press.
Bernstein, Richard J. (2008), "The Conversation That Never Happened (Gadamer/Derrida)," *Review of Metaphysics*, 61 (3): 577–603.
Bhattacharyya, Krishna Chandra (1907), *Studies in Vedāntism*, reprinted in Krishna Chandra Bhattacharyya (1983), *Studies in Philosophy*, Vols. I and II bound together, Gopinath Bhattacharyya (ed.), New Delhi: Motilal Banarsidass.
Chakrabarti, Arindam, and Ralph Weber (2015a), "Introduction," in Arindam Chakrabarti and Ralph Weber (eds.), *Comparative Philosophy without Borders*, 1–33, New York: Bloomsbury.
Chakrabarti, Arindam, and Ralph Weber (2015b), "Afterword/Afterwards," in Arindam Chakrabarti and Ralph Weber (eds.), *Comparative Philosophy without Borders*, 227–39, New York: Bloomsbury.
Defoort, Carine (2017a), "Chinese Philosophy' at European Universities: A Threefold Utopia," *Philosophy East and West*, 67 (4): 1049–80.
Defoort, Carine (2017b), "Outrageously Irrelevant Remarks of a Girl in a Closed Conversation: A Reply to Tim Heysse," *Philosophy East and West*, 67 (4): 1086–91.
Diagne, Souleymane Bachir (2016), "Edward Said Memorial Lecture: Philosophy in Africa," lecture given at the American University in Cairo AUC, School of Humanities and Social Sciences (SHSS), November 5. Available online: https://www.youtube.com/watch?v=n2EBVDm8bRg (accessed May 21. 2021).
Garfield, Jay L. (2012), "Buddhist Howls," 3:16. Available online: https://www.3-16am.co.uk/articles/buddhist-howls (accessed May 21, 2021).

Garfield, Jay L., and Bryan W. Van Norden (2016), "If Philosophy Won't Diversify, Let's Call It What It Really Is," *New York Times*. Available online: https://www.nytimes.com/2016/05/11/opinion/if-philosophy-wont-diversify-lets-call-it-what-it-really-is.html (accessed May 21, 2021).

Garfield, Jay L. (2017), "Foreword," in Bryan W. Van Norden (ed.), *Taking Back Philosophy: A Multicultural Manifesto*, xi–xxi, New York: Columbia University Press.

Gassmann, Robert H., Elena Louisa Lange, Angelika Malinar, Ulrich Rudolph, Raji C. Steineck, and Ralph Weber (2018), "Introduction: The Concept of Philosophy in Asia and the Islamic World," in Raji C. Steineck and Ralph Weber (eds.), *Concepts of Philosophy in Asia and the Islamic World*, vol. 1: China and Japan. Leiden: Brill, 1–49.

Glock, Hans-Johann (2008), *What Is Analytic Philosophy?*, Cambridge, UK: Cambridge University Press.

Gopnik, Alison (2009), "Could David Hume Have Known about Buddhism? Charles François Dolu, the Royal College of La Flèche, and the Global Jesuit Intellectual Network," *Hume Studies*, 35 (1, 2): 5–28.

Heubel, Volker (2014), *Wegmomente. Aspekte einer Philosophie des Tee-Weges in der Konstellation von Rombach, Hisamatsu und Laozi*, Bochum: Projektverlag.

Heysse, Tim (2017), "The Conversation of Philosophy: A Polemical Response to Carine Defoort," *Philosophy East and West*, 67 (4): 1081–6.

Levine, Michael (2016), "Does Comparative Philosophy Have a Fusion Future?," *Confluence: Online Journal of World Philosophies*, 4: 208–37.

Nylan, Michael, and Martin Verhoeven (2016), "Fusion, Comparative, 'Constructive Engagement Comparative', or What? Third Thoughts on Levine's Critique of Siderits," *Journal of World Philosophies*, 1 (1): 119–27.

Olberding, Amy (2017), "Philosophical Exclusion and Conversational Practices," *Philosophy East and West*, 67 (4): 1023–38.

Russell, Bertrand (1946), *History of Western Philosophy*, London: George Allen and Unwin.

Seidel, Roman (2010), "Reading Kant in Teheran: Towards a Reception of the Iranian Reception of European Philosophy," *Asiatische Studien/Études Asiatiques*, 64 (3): 681–705.

Siderits, Mark (2003), *Personal Identity and Buddhist Philosophy: Empty Persons*, Burlington, VT: Ashgate.

Siderits, Mark (2015), "Comparison or Confluence Philosophy?," in Jonardon Ganeri (ed.), *The Oxford Handbook of Indian Philosophy*, Oxford: Oxford University Press. Available online: https://www.oxfordhandbooks.com/view/10.1093/oxfordhb/9780199314621.001.0001/oxfordhb-9780199314621-e-5 (accessed May 21, 2021).

Siderits, Mark (2016), "Response to Levine," *Journal of World Philosophies*, 1 (1): 128–30.

Steineck, Raji C., and Ralph Weber (eds.) (2018), *Concepts of Philosophy in Asia and the Islamic World*, vol. 1: China and Japan. Leiden: Brill.

Van de Mieroop, Marc (2017), *Philosophy before the Greeks: The Pursuit of Truth in Ancient Babylonia*, Princeton, NJ: Princeton University Press.

Constellation V

Plurality, Neutrality, and Method

10

On the Taming of Comparison: Methodological Myopathy, Plurality, and Creativity

Robert Smid

In his seminal essay, "In Comparison a Magic Dwells," Jonathan Z. Smith (1982: 21) wrote that, "borrowing Edmundo O'Gorman's historiographic distinction between discovery as the finding of something one has set out to look for and invention as the subsequent realization of novelty one has not intended to find, we must label comparison an invention." For Smith, this association with invention was a negative ascription, rendering comparison susceptible to subjective associations that are not only unfounded among the objects of comparison but which also gloss over important differences. It was such spurious connections that he had in mind when he likened the process to "magic" rather than science. In his assessment, this susceptibility was due to the lack of any established "rules for the production of comparisons." Comparison, he argued, should be more like discovery, where what is found is a direct methodological result of the search itself.

Smith's critique was well-founded for its time, as there had been relatively little in the way of second-order reflection on comparative method—relative, at least, to the significant growth in the practice of comparison. In the many years since, countless comparativists and critics of comparison have seized on his analysis, employing it to argue for all manner of conclusions ranging from the inherent futility of comparison to its subsequent coming of age. In this chapter, I aim to do something different. It seems to me that the distinction he draws on between discovery and invention remains centrally relevant to the challenges facing comparison today, though not for the reasons he expressed. In this chapter, I will argue that what comparison needs now is actually *less* discovery and *more* invention.

This reversal of Smith's earlier diagnosis will require a careful defense, but some preliminary observations may help to convey what I have in mind. The first is the enduring value of his essay for underscoring the importance of method in comparison. This is attested to by the fact that, while originally written for an audience of fellow scholars in religious studies, it has become a landmark publication for comparative methodology in multiple disciplines, including and especially philosophy.[1] In comparison a magic did indeed dwell, and it was not limited to comparisons within religious studies. Yet while Smith's critique of the lack of methodological rigor was among the most trenchant of his time, he remained committed to the necessity and significance of comparison and to the possibility of overcoming the challenges that he himself raised. These twin characteristics have made his essay a consistently productive point of reference for comparativists across the disciplines. This chapter continues in that tradition, seeing in Smith's work not so much a foil as a conversation partner.[2] As will be seen in what follows, his broader corpus provides many clues for the development of my argument.

The second observation—almost too obvious to note—is that much has changed since the publication of Smith's essay almost forty years ago. There are now a wide variety of carefully crafted and rigorous comparative methods available to the would-be comparativist, methods that have taken critiques like Smith's seriously and have taken great pains to minimize and/or acknowledge subjective biases. The careful attention paid to these issues provides good reason to believe that comparison is no longer so easily rendered invention, but can now stake a credible claim for discovery.[3] Smith's own work has also continued to develop since that time, both building on and perhaps also challenging his position in this essay. In fact, he expressed his frustration that he was so often "arrested" by interpreters at about the time that the essay in question was published (Smith 2004: ix). This essay will seek to avoid this by treating the distinction between discovery and invention not as definitive of Smith's thought more generally but as the diagnosis-in-passing that it was. It will also highlight his later work that follows up on and perhaps challenges that distinction.

At the same time, subsequent scholars have also challenged some of his earlier claims. Most notable are those that have further problematized the distinction between objectivity and subjectivity, which complicates any sharp distinction between invention and discovery.[4] Comparisons, like any interpretations, are now taken to be a gnarly mix of both objectivity and subjectivity, and attempts to eliminate the latter have proven to be ungrounded at best and deceptive at worst. The current consensus is that the best that can be done is to acknowledge—which entails at least admitting, if not also celebrating—the more subjective dimensions of comparison and strive diligently to ensure that they do not eclipse, or become eclipsed by, the more objective dimensions. If the current consensus is accurate, then invention cannot be exorcised from the comparative process, nor should it be. The relevant question is thus what role it should have within that process.

In arguing for more invention in comparative philosophy, then, I am not arguing against the merits of discovery-oriented approaches, or against any of the impressive work that has been accomplished over the last few decades in acknowledging and minimizing biases. Nor am I ignoring the dangers of invention-oriented approaches, which include increased susceptibility to Orientalism, colonialism, racism, and a host of other unwanted influences. To the contrary, my argument is premised on the claim that, while there is always room for further improvement, there has now been sufficient scholarly response to Smith's concerns—both in theory and in practice—to allow for a broader reconsideration of the role that invention can play in comparative methodology. Indeed, I contend that discovery-oriented approaches have become so well-established that the greater danger for comparativists is no longer that they will realize some novelty that they have "not intended to find" but rather that they will so constrain themselves methodologically as to find—and thus to find consistently—*only* what they "set out to look for" in the first place. Bound in this way, comparison becomes a dry, reiterative exercise, such that the results of comparison speak more to the interests informing the method than to the objects of comparison themselves.

In an attempt to push back against this development, I argue that invention can and should play a more active role in comparison than Smith's essay seems to allow. My argument proceeds in three steps. In the first section, I offer a definition of comparison that underscores the role of difference in the comparative encounter and links the negotiation of that encounter with interest. While neither difference nor interest are novel concepts in comparison, they are usually only addressed at the level of discrete comparisons (i.e., at the point that differences can be interpreted within a larger context and interest has been made conscious and articulated). Yet both concepts have roots that go much deeper than that, reaching as far back as the initial encounter with difference, and the interests that inform that encounter can continue to affect the comparative process in often unacknowledged ways. In the second section, then, I identify two seams in the comparative process that provide an indication of some of these interests: namely, the question of what makes a comparison "interesting" and the close relation between philosophical commitments and comparative method. Both of these seams point to the need to address the role of method in framing, reinforcing, and justifying interests in comparison—a need that has not received enough consideration in comparative philosophy to date. In the third section, then, I offer three recommendations for becoming more critically aware of the interests driving method, each of which seeks to provide critical distance between comparativists and their methodological choices. The end result is an embrace of a provisional methodological pluralism, which represents not an underlying philosophical commitment but rather a methodological stance. Embracing methodological pluralism in this way, I argue, amounts to the reintroduction of invention at the level of methodology. In the conclusion, I offer some observations regarding the role of creativity in comparison and its relation to the methodological interests highlighted in this chapter.

A Provisional Definition of Comparison

Self-critical methodological studies of comparison often begin with a definition of their subject matter, since how comparison is defined will have implications for how it is practiced. Unfortunately, such definitions are so limited that, while they usually share some common features with other such definitions, they consistently fail to attain any broader assent. This is attested to by the persistent lack of agreement about what comparison is, let alone how it should be practiced. Yet the necessity of providing a definition persists, so I offer the following definition with the foreknowledge that it will be deemed imperfect and incomplete. It does, however, serve the interests of this chapter, an acknowledgment that will prove to be of foremost significance.

Comparison, I argue, is an interpretive response to the encounter with difference at the most basic level. Stated in these terms, the definition appears to fall into the "similarities and differences" model of comparison that has been appropriately critiqued as too reductive over the last several decades. However, the "difference" to which this definition refers does not pertain to any identifiable similarities or differences; it precedes even the most basic of such articulations. Instead, it refers to the raw encounter of difference itself. It is the recognition that two items are related in some unidentified way and that the contours of that relation require further interpretation. In this respect, "difference" as described here is not unlike what Levinas meant by "alterity" or "otherness," and a similar theory could perhaps have been developed with reference to subsequent continental philosophers.[5] Given my background and interests, however, I have found it more productive to develop the concept in relation to the work of the American philosopher Charles Sanders Peirce. At the heart of his philosophy is a trichotomy of Firstness, Secondness, and Thirdness that, taken together, are meant to account for all of the relations that might exist among any possible things and which, I maintain, provide a useful framework for thinking about comparison.

For Peirce, "Firstness" is a purely abstract notion, referring to how an object or event is in and of itself, independent of its relation to any other thing. It is purely abstract because, while it is possible to conceive of such relationless existence as a logical possibility, it is impossible to conceive of it as anything other than such a possibility, "for as long as things do not act upon one another there is no sense or meaning in saying that they have any being" (1931–58: 1.25).[6] In terms of comparison, this would be akin to an item that had never been encountered, and thus never been conceptualized in relation to other things.[7]

"Secondness," by contrast, refers to the resistance that is entailed in the very relationality of an object or an event with other objects or events. This resistance occurs not because those objects or events are fundamentally distinct from one another but rather because they are related to one another in whatever ways that they are, and that relationality constrains their possibilities relative to one another as well as their possibilities for interpretation. Secondness does not entail any indication of what those constraints are or what kind of relation they represent; it only acknowledges the brute actuality of an object or event—"brute" because of the unspecified but steadfast resistance it asserts on that with which it is in relation. This is the encounter with difference referred to earlier—brute, unspecified difference—and it is with this encounter that comparison begins. In the context of inquiry, Peirce (1931–58: 5.375 and 5.394) described this moment as the "irritation of doubt," which initiated the formation of new beliefs, but in the context of comparison it is better understood as the intrusion of the unfamiliar, the demand for attention, and the sparking of an interest that would lead to comparison.

It is only in "Thirdness" that the relations asserted in Secondness are given any specification. Thirdness represents all of relations that can be specified among any of the objects or events that can be said to exist. These relations are myriad, as objects and events can be related in multiple ways simultaneously, those relations can be further specified in multiple ways, the relations themselves can be related in multiple ways, and so on. Thirdness represents the rich diversity and interrelatedness of all that exists and all that can be known, and interpretation consists in the specification of those relations. In terms of comparison, this means that all interpretation is comparative, as all interpretations are always made in reference to something else. Furthermore, in the same way that comparison always occurs in Thirdness (by virtue of its relationality), so it also *only* occurs in Thirdness (since it is only at that point that such relations can be articulated).

The entirety of comparison, then, occurs within Thirdness. While this is factually accurate (according to the theory), I think it is a mistake to define comparison solely in terms of Thirdness. This makes it seem that objects of comparison present themselves in whole cloth, as though their relations are already prepared for articulation and the comparativist needs only register them. It is dinner without the hunger, marriage without the attraction, publication without the inspiration. What is missing is the shock to the system that is Secondness, that moment so brief that it is almost timeless but upon which the entire process of comparison gets its footing.[8] Of course, no sooner is difference registered than the hounds are off in the hunt for specification of that relation, but the chase is not the whole of the hunt; the hunt begins with an unexpected sound, a flash of color, the scent of something wild in the air. It is in an effort to foreground this often forgotten aspect that I defined comparison in terms of Secondness rather than Thirdness alone: comparison may be the response, but it is only half the story if it forgets that to which it is a response.

The difference that this makes for comparison is that it challenges the limits of academic comparison (i.e., comparison that takes place within the relatively controlled environment of academic scrutiny) by highlighting the extent to which comparison is initiated long before it is subjected to academic scrutiny. The initial impulse to compare has a wildness to it: it grasps at the connections most ready at hand to provide some resolution—any resolution—to the unanticipated interruption. More careful considerations follow, of course, and reach their greatest refinement through academic scrutiny, but that cultivation has a history—often a very long one—that is not fully erased by any such efforts at domestication.[9] At the same time, however, there is little about academic comparison, at least as currently practiced, that alerts the comparativist to the lingering effects of such primordial influences. By the time it has found its way through to academic scrutiny, everything appears to be "above board," emerging seamlessly from the refined gaze of the comparativist and cultivated for consideration within the broader academic community.[10]

What this means is that there are residual interests stemming back as far as the initial encounter with difference that go on to influence the academic process of comparison. Comparativists are, especially more recently, attuned to the influence of interests on the process of comparison, but this awareness tends to be restricted to the academic context of comparison alone. What Peirce's trichotomy helps to highlight are the less commonly addressed influences that precede that context—interests that can influence how the objects of comparison are defined, the method one is drawn toward, and the resolution that one seeks in comparison. For his part, Peirce was very aware of the pervasive interplay of interests in human inquiry, including both their positive role in initiating inquiry and their negative role in suppressing it. His comments about interest are thus many and varied; indeed, he underscores the importance and inevitability of interests while also warning against their power to obstruct or distort.[11]

A careful reading of his work, however, can provide at least some measure of guidance about the role of interests at the outset of interpretation. Consider, for example, his tripartite semiotics, which consists of an object of interpretation, the sign that represents it, and the interpretant that identifies the respect in which the sign stands for its object. While his semiotics does not correspond directly with his trichotomy, the two run roughly parallel such that there are important intersections between them. Peirce touches on the question of interest when considering how logical interpretants—arguably the closest semiotic counterpart to Thirdness—are initially formed. He writes that this will require "a specification of what [the inquirer's] *interest* in the question is supposed to be. ... [U]nless our hypothesis be rendered specific as to that interest, it will be impossible to trace out its logical consequences, since the way that the interpreter will conduct the inquiry will greatly depend on the nature of his interest in it" (Peirce 1931–58: 5.489).[12] In other words, one cannot understand the process of inquiry—whether understood in terms of interpretation more generally or comparison in particular—without understanding the interests that inform that process. And, as Peirce (1931–58: 7.277) points out, such interests extend back as far as the "first impulse" of thought.[13]

Peirce's comments provide some indication of the role of interest in interpretation, but subsequent scholars have made this connection more clearly. For example, Smith (2004: 51) writes that "the statement of comparison is never dyadic, but always triadic; there is always an implicit 'more than,' and there is always a 'with respect to.' In the case of an academic comparison, the 'with respect to' is most frequently the scholar's interest." Ralph Weber (2013: 593–603, esp. 595–6; and 2014: 151–71, esp. 166) has developed this relation substantially in his description of the need for a third term, or *tertium comparationis,* in relating two or more *comparata,* also highlighting the significance of interest for selecting the *tertium.* While the triad employed by both Smith and Weber is significantly different than the one developed by Peirce, they all seem to agree on the importance of interest for comparison, and that interest stems back to the earliest impulse to interpret/compare.

When one looks at the initial impetus for comparison, then, one should see not only difference but also interest. It is the interest of the comparativist through which the relation to that difference is negotiated through interpretation; it is there from the very outset of Thirdness. This sounds fine, but it actually presents a significant problem for comparison: if interest has roots going back that far, then it will be difficult, if not impossible, to become aware of and fully acknowledge one's interests. In this sense, the established academic ritual of announcing one's interests at the outset of comparison misses the mark by half: it only acknowledges the interests that are already conscious, and leaves aside any interest that may not be conscious but still influence the process and outcomes of comparison.

Two Seams of Interest

Fortunately, there are at least two seams in this process that reveal the ongoing influence of these initial interests in academic comparison. The first pertains to the question of what makes a given comparison "interesting." Obviously, this will be a largely subjective determination, but this doesn't take away from its relevance or significance even in an academic context and so it is worth considering at least some of the dimensions that inform it. One of the foremost of these will be the interests of the comparativist, as shaped by their expertise (e.g., their academic training, research interests, history of publications) and their situatedness more generally (e.g., their personal, social, political, economic, and cultural context). The significance of such interests is now generally acknowledged, and as a result it is increasingly customary to acknowledge such interests at the outset of the comparative process; however, it is notably less common for comparativists to link these interests directly to why they found the comparison interesting in the first place. Whether the cultivated interests of the comparativist are, in fact, "interesting" in any broader sense is generally taken to be the jurisdiction of the discipline as a whole, as negotiated through the discursive community of scholars at conferences, through peer review, and through further consideration in subsequent publications.

At first glance, this may seem to be the outworking of an efficient process, whereby comparisons of possible interest are first passed through the filter of individual comparativists and then through the filter of the broader academic community such that only the most interesting comparisons tend to make their way through.[14] Yet this process elides the issue of initial interest altogether, as it assesses interest only when the academic process has been followed through to completion. It is thus better equipped to gauge *whether* a given comparison turns out to have been interesting to a reasonable subset of the academic community than to assess *why* it is so. Why is one comparison deemed interesting while another is not? Why is "this" chosen and not "that" as the category for comparison? What do the prevalence of such interests say about the comparativist or the broader academic community? While it is entirely acceptable to allow that comparativists will find interesting what they find interesting and to resist any attempts to dictate what they *should* find interesting, it is another matter entirely to suggest that comparativists need not concern themselves with the peculiarity of their interests. Comparativists are trained to be attuned to the partiality of their perspectives, both individually and collectively, so the relative lack of attention paid to why comparativists choose the subject matter they do should raise some red flags.[15]

As it turns out, Smith is one of the few comparativists to directly address this facet of interest directly.[16] Comparison, he writes, "is, at base, never identity. Comparison requires the postulation of differences as the grounds of its being interesting (rather than tautological) and a methodical manipulation of difference, a playing across the 'gap' in the service of some useful end" (Smith 1982: 35).[17] Note that it is the postulation of difference—the "gap"—that serves as "the grounds of its [i.e., the comparison] being interesting." If this is the case, then what makes a comparison interesting (or not) has roots that go back as far as the initial encounter itself. Potential objects of comparison are not interesting, in and of themselves, such that they are simply found by the comparativist; they are *made interesting* by the comparativist through their encounter with difference, and the ongoing influence of this initial encounter must be accounted for. "For the most part," he writes, "the scholar has not set out to make comparisons. Indeed, he has been most frequently attracted to a particular datum by a sense of its uniqueness. ... This experience [of making initial connections], this unintended consequence of research, must then be accorded significance and provided with an explanation" (Smith 1982: 22). To date, neither has the significance of these initial connections been acknowledged nor has an adequate explanation of its relation to the academic process of comparison been provided.

A second but related seam pertains to the relation between these interests and method. It is an awkward but generally accepted feature of comparative methodology that one's choice of method is likely to be aligned with if not explicitly drawn from the philosophical tradition(s) with which one most closely identifies. This is awkward because it makes it easier for the assumptions of the comparativist to make their way into the comparison and present themselves as part of the outcomes of comparison. It is generally accepted because there is no alternative; there is no view from nowhere, no neutral place for the comparativist to stand, and one's own philosophical commitments typically provide the most productive non-neutral ground.[18] Comparison thus proceeds on the trust that comparativists will work diligently to police their interests, which is really a Reaganesque "trust, but verify" (where verification is meant to occur via peer review). Such policing appears to be reasonably effective at the level of individual comparisons; there is, at least, a lot of handwringing about the extent to which such interests unduly affect the comparisons themselves. There has been much less reflection, however, about the ways in which interests inform comparative methods in particular. As a result, important methodological considerations remain unaddressed. How does a given method shape the interests driving a comparison, and to what extent is it shaped by pre-comparative (and perhaps even pre-philosophical) interests? What kinds of connections is a given method prone to find, and what kinds does it tend to overlook?

Again, Smith turns out to be a thought-provoking conversation partner on this issue. He was a fierce critic of the assumptions running through the work of the most seasoned comparativists and was effective at showing how those assumptions distorted its outcomes. His work was particularly notable for its ability to track these interests across multiple works in the discipline to show how they reflected not merely the peculiar interests of individual comparativists but shared interests in the field or discipline more generally.[19] Yet here Smith found himself with a conundrum: on the one hand, he knew that such interests could never be fully eliminated from comparison; on the other hand, it seemed clear that some interests occluded, distorted, or otherwise obstructed the process more than others. On what basis, then, is one to choose among the interests that might drive comparison?

For Smith, there was only one justifiable answer to this question: it should be the interests associated with the ongoing development of the discipline. This conclusion is premised on two interrelated commitments. The first, expressed in relation to religious studies, is that there is no such thing as religion apart from the discipline that imagines it.[20] He makes this claim in one of his most controversial and frequently cited passages:

> While there is a staggering amount of data, of phenomena, of human experiences and expressions that might be characterized in one culture or another, by one criterion or another, as religious—*there is no data for religion*. Religion is solely the creation of the scholar's study. It is created for the scholar's analytic purposes by his imaginative acts of comparison and generalization.[21] (Smith 1982: xi)

Although Smith expresses this commitment in terms of religious studies, its implications for philosophy should be clear: the data does not self-identify as being philosophical or non-philosophical; philosophers decide—both individually and collectively (and often contentiously)—what "counts" as philosophy, and they do this through comparison and generalization.[22] Scholars should thus be "relentlessly self-conscious" of the relation between their work within the discipline and the imaginative construction of that discipline. Again, writing in terms of religious studies, Smith (1982: xi) concludes that, "for the self-conscious student of religion, no datum possesses intrinsic interest. It is of value only insofar as it can serve as exempli gratia of some fundamental issue in the imagination of religion." The only valuable data, the only data worthy of interest, is thus the data that serves the purpose of the ongoing development of the discipline.

The second commitment is a consequence of the first: if there is no data that is intrinsically interesting, then there is nothing to recommend any possible connections among the data over any others. Both the collection of data and any comparisons of it by scholars in the discipline are derivative of the discipline more generally. "Comparison does not necessarily tell us how things 'are,'" he writes; rather,

> comparison tells us how things might be conceived, how they might be "redescribed." ... *A comparison is a disciplined exaggeration in the service of knowledge*. It lifts out and strongly marks certain features within difference as being of possible intellectual significance, expressed in the rhetoric of their being "like" in some stipulated fashion. Comparison provides the means by which *we* "re-vision" phenomena as *our* data in order to solve *our* theoretical problems.[23] (Smith 1990: 52)

"Disciplined," in this context, implies something like "carefully regulated," but it is clear that, for Smith, the knowledge in service of which the exaggeration (i.e., the comparison) is made is defined by the ongoing development of the discipline that it is meant to contribute to.

If there is no discipline apart from the continual imagining of it by its constitutive scholars, and if comparisons are valuable within that discipline only insofar as they contribute to its ongoing development, then the only interests that should be operative in comparisons within a given discipline should be those that pertain to that development.[24] But which interests are these, specifically? On this point, Smith was an avowed pluralist: they are whatever interests drive scholars in the ongoing development of their discipline.[25] The discipline should thus regard comparison as an act of redescription, which deconstructs accepted relations and reconstitutes them in new ways "so that we may see things in a new, and frequently unexpected, light" (Smith 1982: 36).[26] This is not to say that any redescription will do; many, perhaps most possible redescriptions will not be useful, helpful, or interesting, but they all provide the comparativist with "a shifting set of characteristics with which to negotiate the relations between his or her theoretical interests and data stipulated as exemplary" (Smith 1990: 53). This openness to redescription not only aids in the alignment of comparisons with the interests of the comparativist—which, the reader will recall, is the "grounds of its being interesting" (Smith 1982: 35)—but it also unsettles persistent residual interests that might otherwise obstruct further understanding. The best redescriptions will actively undermine the sacred cows of the tradition, allowing the discipline to continue its creative advance in new and interesting ways.[27]

The Value of Invention

As the last lines of the previous section suggest, there is a dimension in Smith's own work that resists the elimination of invention from the process of comparison. Redescription is nothing if not a creative process, and appears designed to allow for precisely "the subsequent realization of novelty one has not intended to find" (Smith 1982: 21). Smith's advocacy for more discovery in comparison thus appears to be less an "either-or" distinction than a recognition that, at that time, lack of methodological rigor was the greater challenge for comparison. As I argued in the introduction, the situation for comparison has changed, such that there are now a number of rigorous methods that can stake a credible claim to discovery. At the same time, however, it is these very successes that now occlude the interests laden in each method, insofar as they threaten to confuse what a given method finds in its comparisons with what is there to be found. The best remedy for this, I argue, is a revalorization of invention at the level of methodology.

Smith's work has provided significant guidance thus far, so the first question should be whether his work provides an adequate response to the problem at hand. I find that, while he may address the problem at the level of method, he does not do so at the level of methodology. Specifically, his method of redescription arguably meets the requirements of "discovery," and does so without sacrificing the openness to unexpected novelty otherwise associated with invention. It is simultaneously disciplined and pluralistic, which is no mean feat. The problem is that his method is pluralistic in itself but not pluralistic with respect to method, which makes it of little use in trying to navigate the plurality of interests informing method itself. Consider, for example, his framing of religious studies as an imagined construct: many scholars in the discipline would not follow him in that framing of their subject matter, and so would not be able to follow him through to the conclusion that comparison is only a "disciplined exaggeration in service of knowledge." That claim would be no less controversial in the context of philosophy, and so is unlikely to provide compelling guidance for the discipline on how best to address the issue of interest in comparison at the level of method. If the problem attending the successful development of discovery-oriented methods is that they now so constrain themselves methodologically as to find—and thus to find consistently—*only* what they set out to look for in the first place, then the solution cannot simply be another method.

While it is necessary to move beyond Smith's work at this point, he does offer one final piece of advice at the close of his last monograph:

> The disciplined study of any subject is, among other things, an assault on self-evidence, on matters taken for granted. ... The future of our increasingly diverse societies will call on all our skills at critical translation; all our abilities to occupy

the contested space between the near and the far; all our capacities for the dual project of making familiar what, at first encounter, seems strange, and making strange what we have come to think of as all-too-familiar. Each of these endeavors needs to be practiced and refined in the service of an urgent civic and academic agendum: that difference be negotiated but never overcome. (Smith 2004: 389)

This is the right idea, I think, but it needs to be applied at the level of methodology. How is it possible to avoid matters being taken for granted—from becoming all too familiar—in the application of method, and to remember that differences are only ever "negotiated but never overcome?" As should be clear from the first section of this chapter, I take the negotiation of difference—much as Smith did—to be a matter of the interests attending its encounter, so delivering on this obligation methodologically will require becoming more aware of the interests informing comparison via the many methods through which it is practiced.

In what follows, then, I offer three recommendations that will assist comparativists in uncovering these interests. Each recommendation builds upon the previous one, and thus demands more of comparativists as a result. None of them is entirely unprecedented, but they become less and less common as they progress. Organizing them here is thus an attempt to push comparative philosophy further along in this direction. To both explain each recommendation and justify its push, I have framed each one as an analogy to what comparative philosophers have demanded of philosophy more generally. Effectively, then, I am arguing that the task of contending with the methodological interests driving comparative philosophy is only an extension of the comparative task more generally, and therefore one which comparativists must be more intentional and proactive in addressing. The payoff will be in a greater critical awareness of one's own methodological choices as well as a greater appreciation for the alternative choices made by others.

The first recommendation is simply to be familiar with the variety of methods available in comparative philosophy. At first glance, this seems like a relatively easy recommendation to follow, and is admittedly the lowest possible bar. And yet, it is a bar that philosophy has often failed to clear even when it has had the resources necessary to do so. For most of the modern period, it was exceptional—exotic, even—for Western philosophers to be familiar in any significant way with non-Western traditions that might reasonably be considered philosophical. This has been increasingly apparent over the last hundred years as critical translations of key texts have become increasingly available. This trend continues into the present, where—as Bryan Van Norden and others have pointed out—many philosophy departments in the United States don't value familiarity with non-Western philosophy enough to even offer courses on its many traditions (let alone hire specialists).[28] As most comparativists would agree, such negligence is no longer excusable, and only undermines the credibility of departmental claims to represent "philosophy" as such.

Fortunately, comparativists have been more successful in this regard, not only with respect to familiarity with multiple philosophical traditions but also—as is the focus of this chapter—familiarity with multiple methods of comparison. Comparativists of very different methodological commitments present at many of the same conferences and publish in many of the same journals, which not only provides a ready means for comparativists to become familiar with these methods but also for there to be some degree of debate about them (more on this anon). At the same time, however, these same institutional structures also impede the process. The aforementioned presentations are typically discrete events, providing only disjointed exposure to the full array of available methods. This is exacerbated by issues like disparities in financial resources and the tribalism that sometimes attends professional organizations, which further restrict the access that comparativists have to alternate methods. As noted in the introduction, one of the primary purposes of this book is to facilitate this process by providing a centralized resource for contemporary comparative method in philosophy, and in this respect it should facilitate the cross-methodological familiarity that comparative philosophy already strives to foster.

Gaining familiarity with more methods than one is certainly a worthwhile goal for comparativists, and comparative philosophy should be commended for effectiveness in this respect; but this, in and of itself, will do little to reveal the most basic interests informing any given method let alone provide guidance for which method a comparativist should choose. A second recommendation, then, is that comparativists seek to engage the diversity of methods directly. Engagement requires familiarity, but it also requires investment. In terms of the history of Western philosophy's engagement with comparative philosophy, this is akin to asking Western philosophers to know more about non-Western traditions than can be learned in an introductory undergraduate course before weighing in on their meaning, value, or relevance for philosophy. For example, while many Western philosophers have rejected the status of non-Western traditions as "properly philosophical" on poorly conceived and incomplete evidence, very few of those who have engaged these traditions in the depth they deserve—engaging them as peers and equal partners in the engagement—have come to a similar conclusion. This should provide at least some indication that substantive engagement is an effective corrective for exclusivist categories of comparison.

As it pertains to method, comparative philosophers have been somewhat successful in the pursuit of such engagement, but its successes have been limited. Beyond merely gaining familiarity, the primary form of cross-methodological engagement has been critique. Comparative philosophy has a rich history of such exchanges, both at conferences and in publications, which now reaches back over seventy years. The most productive forms of critique have been those that critique methods from within the context of that method (i.e., consistent with its terms, commitments, etc.); such critiques serve to strengthen methods by making them clearer and more consistent. Critiques from outside of that context can also be productive, but often simply run up against the differences that divide them. The least productive forms of critique are those that have as their primary agenda demonstrating the superiority of another method (typically, one's own), although even these can at least gesture toward a landscape for further engagement. What all of these forms of critiques fail to do, however, is to account for the persistent plurality of methodological options. Intra-methodological critiques fail to acknowledge the relevance of other methodological options to the critique, while extra-methodological critiques fail to acknowledge the underlying differences among methods that check the effectiveness of any such critique. In short, they do not address the connection between methods and their respective interests, and so are only marginally effective at engaging other methods or their adherents.

It is instructive to look again to the history of comparative philosophy here for further clues. What the varieties of critique above amount to in this analogy is the attempt to only engage philosophical traditions from within the context of the tradition itself (intra-methodological) or to critique it from the context of another tradition (extra-methodological). Neither approach is consistent with the broader goal of comparative philosophy, which—insofar as it is comparative—seeks to engage traditions across whatever differences, distances, or divisions may exist among them. If comparative philosophy's engagement with methods is to be consistent with its engagement of philosophical traditions, then it must begin to pursue more substantive means of cross-methodological engagement. Any such means must begin with the acknowledgment that, while critique performs a significant and often constructive role in the cultivation of methods, it must be balanced by a readiness to engage those methods on their own terms. A central facet of this must be the recognition that different methods will have different interests, and that any critique that fails to recognize this will fail to hit its mark. At the same time, those differences in interests, along with the categories and commitments that attend them, should themselves be a relevant topic for critique.

What such engagement calls for is large-scale studies across methods, which seek to describe each method on its own terms, to document its successes and failures at attaining its own stated goals, and to take note of the concerns of other methods that that method does not register. Something like this can be found in the work of taxonomists like Walter Watson ([1985] 1993) and David Dilworth (1989): each sought to classify philosophical traditions according to their characteristics according to several metrics simultaneously; the purpose was to provide an overview of all of philosophy, such that the component traditions could be better understood with respect both to each other and to philosophy more generally. The taxonomic approach has fallen out of favor, in large part because the taxonomies themselves were suspiciously mathematical (see, e.g., their mutual predilection for sets of four) but also because both struggled to do justice to the full diversity of the traditions they sought to categorize. This is not surprising, as taxonomy is a fundamentally reductive exercise: component parts must ultimately find their place within the grid, even if the categories themselves have to be adjusted to allow this for this. Philosophers comparative and otherwise have found Wittgenstein's concept of family resemblance a more effective model for accounting for such plurality.

This notwithstanding, such taxonomic theories had two features to commend them: the first is that they sought to describe philosophical traditions in their own terms, and the second is that they sought a way to understand each of them relative to one another. These are the necessary starting points for a more substantive approach to cross-methodological engagement, as they put each tradition in relief against the others and can thus highlight the relativity of each one relative to its aims and concerns. I know of no extensive study like Watson's or Dilworth's that pertains to comparative methods in particular, but there have been at least some partial attempts. For example, in *Methodologies* (2009), I sought to present some of the foremost methods in the

American pragmatist and process traditions, presenting each on its own terms and attempting to document—in as impartial a manner as possible—the strengths and weaknesses of each relative to their stated aims and shared interests.

The limitations to such an approach are clear. It can only be imperfect, since if it is impossible to eliminate interests from a comparison or a method, it will also be impossible to eliminate them from a comparison of methods. It will also be subject to abuse, as it can be used to pigeonhole methods or backhandedly argue for the superiority of just one of them; as is the case with interests, this can be done not only intentionally but unintentionally as well. The most constraining limitation, however, will be the very practical one of time and resources: it is simply too difficult for one scholar to complete such a monumental task, and institutional structures make it difficult for multiple scholars to take on such a task together. But none of these limitations should be prohibitive—not even the third—if cross-methodological critique is to be, itself, genuinely comparative. Comparative philosophers need to find ways to make more headway on this front.

The third recommendation takes this one step further and entails actually applying methods other than one's own to the comparative task. This recommendation almost certainly requires delivery on the second one as a precondition, as no one is likely to apply a method other than their own unless they have some understanding of what advantages other methods have relative to their stated interests. In terms of Western philosophy's engagement with comparative philosophy, this is akin to asking Western philosophers to not only learn about but also to *do* non-Western philosophy—at least in part, and at least occasionally. This is, historically, the equivalent of what Western philosophers have demanded of their non-Western counterparts in order to be treated as legitimate philosophers. The difference for Western philosophers is that, because of the power dynamics working in their favor, most have not felt obliged to invest the effort required to reciprocate. It is for this reason that philosophy in the West remains a largely parochial affair.

Most comparativists would probably agree that this is a failure on the part of Western philosophers, but the task is admittedly monumental. There is always more work to be done in one's own tradition/method, and professional obligations typically require that one make as much headway in one's specialty as possible. Any time one might spend on other traditions/methods thus falls into the category of luxury: one might want to invest it, but it is usually in short supply. How many comparativists have carefully employed a method other than the method with which they are most familiar and/or prefer? To be clear, this does not include initial shopping for a method or applying a method just long enough to show that it is inferior to one's own; it means accomplished comparativists immersing themselves in other methods, adopting their interests and concerns, and following them wherever they lead.[29] Examples of this are rare and speak to the difficulty of the task. However, if one is to take methodology seriously, then one must be willing to put other methods into practice—at least in part, and at least occasionally. It is only then that one can understand one's own method as anything more than a parochial concern.

But the advantage is greater than this. Even more than engaging other methods (as noted earlier), employing them should provide further clarification not only about the interests informing them, insofar as they differ from one's own, they should also—by the same measure—provide clarification about the interests operative in one's own method. Furthermore, if those interests are able to be further identified, then being able to apply multiple methods should provide the comparativist with a much greater array of options. For example, this could include the use of counterfactuals as part of the comparative process: what would the result of comparison be if method B were applied rather than method A? What is registered well with the use of one method that is occluded in another, and what tradeoffs exist as a result? This should result in a more comprehensive rationale for the method one adopts, which acknowledges the aims and interests of the comparativist(s) and is transparent with respect to the alignment of those interests and the anticipated outcomes of comparison. It would also allow for more pointed critiques, such as that another method might have better served the aims and interests of the comparativist(s) than the method that was actually employed.

The best method, then, is not necessarily any single method, but rather the method best aligned with the aims and interests of a particular comparison. If the interests of a given comparativist are such that a single method consistently serves as the best method for their work, then so be it, but ideally the comparativist should have applied alternative methods enough to be able to articulate that connection. The language of methodological justification thus shifts from "my" (i.e., parochial) or "the best" (imperialist) to "best for these purposes" (pluralist). Significantly, this does not necessarily commit the comparativist to pluralism more generally; there may be one method that is, in fact, better than all of the others. If there is, however, this will have to be determined empirically, and the current plurality of methods within comparative philosophy provides a clear indication that no such determination has yet been reached. Faced with this plurality, I am arguing for methodological pluralism as a methodological commitment in itself—perhaps a meta-methodological commitment—on the grounds that it is the most effective way to register the interests informing each method and to choose among those methods in an informed way.

The three recommendations above—commending familiarity, engagement, and application, respectively—entail increasingly extensive demands on the comparativist. It is thus no surprise that, while the larger part of Western philosophy has failed on all three fronts relative to comparative engagement, comparativists have only done modestly better relative to method. While there is reasonable familiarity across methods, engagement has been largely limited to critique and application has been exceedingly rare. One of the purposes of this essay is to push comparativists on this issue, arguing that developing and applying methods in relative isolation from one another runs counter to the comparative task in which it is otherwise involved. There is no expectation that comparativists will be able to fulfill all of the ideal conditions for cross-methodological engagement (at least not within the conditions of finitude), but this essay at least aims to point in the direction that such engagement should be headed.

All of this brings us back, at last, to the value of invention. Isn't it the case that even the most robust methodological pluralism amounts to little more than applying multiple methods of discovery? What has any of this to do with invention? The key here is that, while pursuing comparison within one method alone leads to a constrained and perhaps controlled array of possible results, applying alternate methods not only helps to reveal the particularity of each method but also opens up new possibilities for unanticipated outcomes (i.e., "realization[s] of novelty one has not intended to find"). In this way, it underscores the unpredictability of genuine inquiry, and reestablishes both the challenge and the reward of the comparative endeavor. At the risk of pushing the point too far, it acknowledges the persistent wildness of comparison and highlights the peculiarity of our various attempts to tame it with method. In this respect, the initial interest provoking comparison is not that far removed from the interests driving the many methodological options available.

Conclusion

"There is nothing easier than the making of patterns," writes Smith (1982: 35), "but the 'how' and the 'why' and, above all, the 'so what' remain most refractory." To answer the "so what" question, a comparison must retain its link to the interest manifested in the initial comparative impulse. This is what makes the comparison worth undertaking in the first place, rather than being merely a dry, rote exercise. If that interest is significantly transformed over the course of inquiry—as is often the case—that transformed interest effectively becomes the new interest driving the comparison.[30] Yet, as noted above, the methods by which such comparisons are undertaken have their own interests as well, and those interests can also shape the comparison. If these two interests—or, perhaps, sets of interests—are not carefully negotiated, they can undermine the comparative process as a whole.

Negotiating these interests, however, does not necessarily mean aligning them; in fact, aligning them may be among the worst possible settlement of interests. As noted at the outset of this chapter, the greater part of the significance of Smith's "In Comparison a Magic Dwells" lies in its warning about how "recollections of similarity" can gloss over potentially relevant differences when not constrained by an appropriately rigorous method. Such an approach is "more a matter of memory than a project for inquiry" and is thus more akin to magic than science (in his use of those terms). Such "magic" persists even in the case of reasonably rigorous methods if they are not able to register and interrogate those interests.

I have argued that a further danger exists when the interests of method are so aligned with the interests of a comparison that they only reinforce their own shared interests. Such an alignment not only fails to interrogate the interests initially informing a comparison but also reinforces them through the process of comparison. This is, effectively, confirmation bias as applied to comparison. In such a situation, the supposed results of comparison are more a reflection of the commitments of the method than they are of whatever it was that was supposedly compared. The relationship becomes particularly degenerate when the interests of method go on to inform which comparisons will be entertained, thus creating an insular cycle that appears to both produce consistent results over time while also reinforcing the validity and effectiveness of the method.

In the contemporary context of comparative philosophy, punctuated as it is with regular opportunities for cross-methodological engagement, it is difficult for any method to reach such a level of insularity. Yet any methodologically self-reflective comparativist must be aware of the danger, and I think that the danger is more prevalent than most would like to admit. It manifests itself in the relative siloes that persist among methodological options, organized within various professional societies, academic journals, and lineages of education and publication. The danger is not with these institutions or lineages in themselves—for a variety of complex reasons, they are the primary venues within which comparison takes place at all—but rather in the extent, or to the extent, that they privilege a limited set of methodological options in the practice of comparison.

In this chapter, I have argued for a methodological pluralism that encourages familiarity, engagement, and application of diverse methods in comparative philosophy. The term "methodological pluralism" is intended in two senses: first, it implies a pluralistic approach to the diversity of methods, on the grounds that—while one may believe a certain method to be superior to others—it is by no means clear which method is in fact superior in one respect or another or as a whole; second, it implies a merely methodological commitment to such pluralism, as it is born of an acknowledgment of the currently unsettled state of methodological deliberations rather than a commitment to its intractability. In encouraging familiarity, engagement, and application of methods, I am not advocating for ambivalence about the relative value of any particular method or about the value of method as a whole, but rather for an increase in the breadth of methodological options considered in any comparative context as a corrective to the relatively unregulated and potentially excessive influences of particular methodological interests in a localized environment. Of course, this will not be enough to correct for all of the influences that emerge from the interests driving individual comparisons and/or the method(s) by which they are interrogated, but attending to these interests and their intersection should at least provide a helpful corrective.

More broadly, it also repositions the frame by which comparative methods are evaluated. Smith's argument in favor of method as "discovery" was meant to protect against spurious comparative claims, and the greater share of comparative methodology for the last several decades has been focused toward that end. It manifests itself in the ability to undertake a comparison through rigorous application of a particular method, yet without much if any reflection on the part of the comparativist about the implications of that particular methodological choice. The methodological pluralism for which I have argued presses back on this trajectory by injecting "invention" back into methodological consideration, thus reopening the comparative process to possibilities beyond the purview of any particular method. This corrective implicitly relies on the increased rigor of individual methods in a manner consistent with the move toward "discovery," and thus avoids the dangers associated with "invention" by operating at the meta-methodological level. This balance acknowledges both the initial wildness of comparison and the dangers of unilinear attempts to tame it, and settles for a multi-perspectival space within which to pursue it. If what is compared is to continue to resemble anything like what is initially encountered, this is arguably a necessary compromise.

Notes

1. It should be acknowledged that the disciplinary context of Smith's work does present some challenges for application in the context of comparative philosophy, but as it pertains to method these challenges are not particularly prohibitive. In this chapter, I draw only on those aspects of his work that have relevance across the two disciplines.
2. "Conversation partner" might seem a bit much, given that Smith can no longer answer back, but this was hardly a problem for Smith in his own work: "That's what a historian does," he writes. "They run back and forth to make both sides of a conversation happen" (Sinhababu 2008).
3. Consider, for example, Smith's own assessment of the Comparative Religious Ideas Project in his preface to its second published volume; see Robert Cummings Neville (2001: xi–xii). Smith describes the project there as having an "articulate theory of comparison" that is worthy of its readers' trust. This is hardly the only method to be appropriately rigorous, but it provides at least some indication that Smith himself saw significant progress on the concerns he raised in the essay in question.
4. An excellent example of this can be seen in the more recent collection of essays on Smith's contributions to comparative religion; see Kimberley C. Patton and Benjamin C. Ray (2000). While generally appreciative of Smith's work, this collection also highlights some of the challenges it faces.
5. See Emmanuel Levinas ([1947] 1987); see also Giles Deleuze (1968) and Jacques Derrida ([1967] 1978).
6. References to Peirce's collected papers are traditionally cited by volume and paragraph, and I will follow those conventions here.
7. This is an epistemological rendering; a metaphysical rendering would frame Firstness in terms of an object or event that, in fact, had no relation with any other object or event. Peirce renders the Trichotomy in both ways at various points.
8. Incidentally, see Smith's ([1978] 1993: 293) comment to this effect in his play on Paul Ricœur's famous quip that it is the symbol that gives rise to thought: he revises it to state that "it is the perception of incongruity that gives rise to thought." While Ricœur's statement is generally consistent with Peirce's semiotics, Smith's revision—which pushes back from Thirdness to Secondness—is arguably more consistent.
9. It should be noted that the distinction drawn between initial interests and academic comparison is a heuristic one, not an analytic one. There can be no hard and fast distinction between the two, as it is not only unclear when an interest becomes "academic" but also quite clear that academic scrutiny at least aspires to reach as far back into the process as possible. Nonetheless, insofar as the term "academic" has any meaning at all, it must be possible for there to be nonacademic interests, and these are arguably the wellspring from which academic interests are subsequently drawn.
10. Incidentally, this tendency was not lost on Smith. He writes that "it is as if, unbidden and unearned by work and interpretation, a connection simply 'chooses' to make itself manifest, to display its presence on our conceptual wall with a clear round hand"; (Smith 1982: 53). Magic, indeed.
11. See, e.g., Peirce (1931–58: 2.750, 7.436, 7.489, 6.100, 6.406, 7.186, 7.277, and 7.396) to get a sense of the variety of ways that Peirce addresses the issue of interest.
12. Bold and italics original.
13. See also Peirce (1931–58: 7.433).

14. Obviously, "interest" is not the only criteria of good comparisons; they must also be executed in an informed, clear, and methodologically rigorous way. In this section, however, I am only concerned with the cultivation of interest.
15. See Oliver Freiberger (2019: 96–101) for a rare example of a comparativist reflecting at length on why his interests in a given comparison are what they are. See also Peirce's *Collected Papers* (1931–58: 7.186) for his recognition of the link between interests and what one finds interesting (as it applies in the context of the natural sciences); see also Peirce (1931–58: 7.499).
16. Smith's contributions in this respect are both acknowledged and further developed in Hugh Urban (2004). But, see also John W. Parish (2009).
17. See also Smith (1987: 14). The connections with Peirce's trichotomy should be evident here: the postulation of difference—the "gap"—is a pretty apt description of Secondness, while the "methodical manipulation of difference" is a reasonable stand-in for Thirdness.
18. The language of "not having a place to stand" echoes Smith's claims about the challenges of being an historian; see for example Smith ([1978] 1993: 129; 289). I suggest here that the same challenges apply to the comparativist, insofar as any "new" comparison is already built on an interminable history of previous comparisons. See Weber (2014: 169) for more on this point.
19. Smith's *Drudgery Divine: On the Comparison of Early Christianities and the Religions of Late Antiquity* (1990) provides an excellent example of this, detailing how the apologetic interests of Protestant comparativists precluded an accurate understanding of the relationship between early Christianity the so-called "mystery" religions that surrounded it. In the closing page of that monograph, Smith (1990: 143) is very explicit that both the problem and the solution pertain directly to the question of interests.
20. This might also be expressed, in a turn on Shakespeare's quip in *Hamlet,* by saying that there is nothing either religious or nonreligious but the imagination of scholars makes it so. "Imagination," in this sense, does not indicate illusoriness or falseness; it instead refers to the second-order, reflective thought by which the idea—in this case, the discipline of religious studies—is constructed.
21. Italics original; see also Smith (1990: 51, 143).
22. These implications arguably extend to all disciplines in the humanities and social sciences, and perhaps to all disciplines as such, but I cannot address those broader implications here. I note that there are important differences between philosophy and religious studies that may mitigate these implications as well. As I will argue further anon, however, it is not productive to follow Smith on this rendering of the interests that should drive comparison, so arguments about the extent to which these implications carry over is moot for the purposes at hand.
23. Italicization of the second sentence added.
24. If comparison is, as noted earlier, "playing across the 'gap' in the service of some useful end," then the discursive life of the discipline appears to be the most useful end—and perhaps the only possible end—that Smith (1982: 35) deemed relevant.
25. I find Smith to be somewhat unclear on this point: it is clear that the interests he is critiquing are not conducive to the discipline, but it is not clear what interests should take their place. See Sam Gill (1998) and Hugh Urban (2000) for two contrasting accounts of this ambiguity in Smith's work.
26. See also Smith (1990: 53).

27. This is an admittedly unsatisfactory account of comparison as redescription, but Smith's work in this area is also arguably inadequately developed. For example, while interpreters like Parrish and Urban disagree widely on how to understand this aspect of his work, this is one point upon which they both agree.
28. See Bryan Van Norden's "Letter to the Editor" (1996) and *Taking Back Philosophy: A Multicultural Manifesto* (2017).
29. This is something I attempted to do, for example, with respect to David Hall and Roger Ames's method of using bridge traditions; see Smid (2012).
30. This is not an exact science and requires no determination of "how much change in interest is enough change to merit being considered a new interest." It is simply an admonition that one must keep one's interests in view.

References

Deleuze, Giles (1968), *Différence et Répétition*, trans. Paul R. Patton, New York: Columbia University Press.

Derrida, Jacques ([1967] 1978), *Writing and Difference*, trans. Alan Bass, Chicago: University of Chicago Press.

Dilworth, David A (1989), *Philosophy in World Perspective: A Comparative Hermeneutic of the Major Theories*, New Haven, CT: Yale University Press.

Freiberger, Oliver (2019), *Considering Comparison: A Method for Religious Studies*, New York: Oxford University Press.

Gill, Sam (1998), "No Place to Stand: Jonathan Z. Smith as Homo Ludens, the Academic Study of Religion *Sub Specie Ludi*," *Journal of the American Academy of Religion*, 66 (2): 283–312.

Levinas, Emmanuel ([1947] 1987), *Time and the Other*, trans. Richard A. Cohen, Pittsburgh, PA: Duquesne University Press.

Norden, Bryan Van (1996), "Letter to the Editor," *Proceedings and Addresses of the American Philosophical Association*, 70 (2): 161–3.

Norden, Bryan Van (2017), *Taking Back Philosophy: A Multicultural Manifesto*, New York: Columbia University Press.

Parish, John W. (2009), "You Show Your Smith and I'll Show Mine: Selection, Exegesis, and the Politics of Citation," *Method and Theory in the Study of Religion*, 21 (4): 437–59.

Patton, Kimberley C., and Benjamin C. Ray (2000), *A Magic Still Dwells: Comparative Religion in the Postmodern Age*, Los Angeles: University of California Press.

Peirce, Charles Sanders (1931–58), *The Collected Papers of Charles S. Peirce*, 8 vols., Charles Hartshorne, Paul Weiss, and Arthur W. Burks (eds.), Cambridge, MA: Harvard University Press.

Sinhababu, Supriya (2008), "Interview with J. Z. Smith," *Chicago Maroon*. Available online: https://www.chicagomaroon.com/2008/06/02/full-j-z-smith-interview/ (accessed April 22, 2021).

Smid, Robert W. (2009), *Methodologies of Comparative Philosophy: The Pragmatist and Process Traditions*, Albany, NY: SUNY Press.

Smid, Robert W. (2012), "The Responsible Society as Social Harmony: Walter G. Muelder's Communitarian Social Ethics as Bridge Tradition for Confucian Economics," in Roger T. Ames and Peter D. Hershock (eds.), *Value and Values: Economics and Justice in an Age of Global Interdependence*, 241–58, Honolulu: University of Hawaii Press.

Smith, Jonathan Z. ([1978] 1993), *Map Is Not Territory: Studies in the History of Religions*, Chicago: University of Chicago Press.
Smith, Jonathan Z. (1982), *Imagining Religion: From Babylon to Jonestown*, Chicago: University of Chicago Press.
Smith, Jonathan Z. (1987), *To Take Place: Toward a Theory in Ritual*, Chicago: University of Chicago Press.
Smith, Jonathan Z. (1990), *Drudgery Divine: On the Comparison of Early Christianities and the Religions of Late Antiquity*, Chicago: University of Chicago Press.
Smith, Jonathan Z. (2001), "Foreword," in Robert Cummings Neville (ed.), *Religious Truth*, xi–xii, Albany, NY: SUNY Press.
Smith, Jonathan Z. (2004), *Relating Religion: Essays in the Study of Religion*, Chicago: University of Chicago Press.
Urban, Hugh (2000), "Making a Place to Take a Stand: Jonathan Z. Smith and the Politics and Poetics of Comparison," *Method and Theory in the Study of Religion*, 12 (1): 339–78.
Urban, Hugh (2004), "Power Still Dwells: The Ethics and Politics of Comparison in 'A Magic Still Dwells,'" *Method and Theory in the Study of Religion*, 26 (1): 24–35.
Watson, Walter ([1985] 1993), *The Architectonics of Meaning: Foundations of the New Pluralism*, reprint edition, with a new preface, Chicago: University of Chicago Press.
Weber, Ralph (2013), "How to Compare?," *Philosophy Compass*, 8 (7): 593–603.
Weber, Ralph (2014), "Comparative Philosophy and the *Tertium*: Comparing What with What, and in What Respect?," *Dao: A Journal of Comparative Philosophy*, 13: 151–71.

11

Comparative Philosophy without Method: A Plea for Minimal Constraints

Steven Burik

When Robert, Ralph, and I first met to discuss this project, my first impression was that I would write a paper on what I thought was the methodology of comparative philosophy. Then I realized that what I thought was the method that I would employ in my work would only be one of the various possible methods. Then I thought that if this was the case, there may virtually be no limit to the number of methods of comparative philosophy. And that informs my claim here: that methodological constraints on comparative philosophy should be minimal and kept minimal.

My position is based on two ideas. The first is tied to the well-known story of G. E. Moore being asked what philosophy was. He famously pointed to the wall of books behind him and said philosophy was "what these are about." Moore of course referred to an entire history of thinking with its own categories, demands, and interests, but more importantly to the impossibility of narrowing down philosophy to *one* definition or to *one* particular method or to *one* way of doing philosophy. The second idea has to do with the definitions of method and methodology. Method, as most dictionaries will tell us, is "a particular procedure for accomplishing or approaching something, especially a systematic or established one" (*Oxford English Dictionary Online*). A method is a framework applicable to different instances, a blueprint to be used again and again. But to think of method in this way goes against the very idea of comparative philosophy. Methods are culturally bound. Chinese philosophy has certain methods, Western philosophy has certain methods, and within Western philosophy analytic philosophy and continental philosophy have different methods. Even singular thinkers such as Heidegger or Zhuangzi may themselves employ different methods within their philosophical works to achieve different goals.

Thinking of method as blueprint assumes that we can then apply that method to other intercultural encounters in philosophy as well. But every single encounter will have different overlaps based on different methods, and this suggests that every different comparison should be based on these differences. In terms of methodology this leaves us very little substance to work with. Beyond saying such minimally obvious things as comparative philosophy should be an open dialogue or based on the search for similarities and differences, it seems that very little can be said a priori about the *actual* method needed in any particular instance of comparative philosophy. So while we may be able to discuss different methods on a micro-level, it seems unhelpful to think on a macro-level about the Method of comparative philosophy.

But method and methodology are two different things. In the Oxford dictionary of philosophy "methodology" has the following entry, quoted in full:

> The general study of method in particular fields of enquiry: science, history, mathematics, psychology, philosophy, ethics. Obviously any field can be approached more or less successfully and more or less intelligently. It is tempting, then, to suppose that there is one right mode of enquiry logically guaranteed to find the truth if any method can. The task of the philosopher of a discipline would then be to reveal the correct method and to unmask counterfeits. Although this belief lay behind much positivist philosophy of science, few philosophers now subscribe to it. It places too great a confidence in the possibility of a purely *a priori* "first philosophy," or standpoint beyond that of the working practitioners, from which their best efforts can be measured as good or bad. This standpoint now seems to many philosophers to be a fantasy. The more modest task of methodology is to investigate the methods that are actually adopted at various historical stages of investigation into different areas, with the aim not so much of criticizing but more of systematizing the presuppositions of a particular field at a particular time (see also naturalized epistemology). There is still a role for local methodological disputes within the community of investigators of some phenomenon, with one approach charging that another is unsound or unscientific, but logic and philosophy will not, on the modern view, provide an independent arsenal of weapons for such battles, which indeed often come to seem more like political bids for ascendancy within a discipline. (Blackburn 2016)

The last sentence of this definition is of particular importance to comparative philosophy and to my argument. We have no view from nowhere with which to analyse different methods or judge them. We only do that from particular backgrounds. We always enter the field from some place, from some position. We look down from up on the river Hao. Methodology can then only mean we survey the methods employed and take heed to not impose one method to the detriment of other viable methods, and stay aware of *our own situatedness not only in our comparative efforts themselves, but also in surveying other approaches, that is, in our methodological considerations.*

Although I do not propose an "anything goes" attitude where everybody gets to assert his or her method against the rest, I do firmly believe that there is a great variety of possible methods which can be fruitfully employed in comparative philosophy, as this volume is testimony to. Hence, I disagree with the statement in the above definition that says: "The task of the philosopher of a discipline would then be to reveal the correct method and to unmask counterfeits." In fact, the dictionary entry itself continues to say that few philosophers still subscribe to that statement. In my view, any methodology of comparative philosophy would need to limit itself to sketching out only the minimum requirements necessary to effectively do comparative philosophy, and these are really heuristics any philosopher should be following. Although we may still "unmask" those interpretations that are by any standard far off the mark, this "revealing" should not lead us to dismiss the large variety of plausible interpretations. There is no essence to comparative philosophy, but rather a fundamental plurality that should be our inherent guideline. Instead of an attempt to fix the methods and methodology of comparative philosophy, which risks becoming methodolatry,[1] I propose to leave comparative philosophy as open as possible, to account for its inevitable elements of plurality and interpretation.

My argument is decidedly postmodern and Zhuangzian. I do not believe in the values of absolutes or objectivity in comparative philosophy, I do not believe in a purely rational and disinterested way of thought, and I do not believe in the inherent value of building a philosophical system or taking a systematic approach to comparative philosophy. Deconstruction (and this should hold for comparative philosophy too) is about questioning such systematic approaches in order to open philosophy up to what is traditionally considered its outside, its other. There is no a priori or first philosophy, no grand Hegelian system incorporating all the differences. If the system building period of Western philosophy has shown us anything, it is that such building tends either to exclude what cannot be incorporated within the system's own categories or to distort it so as to fit those categories.

Philosophers have motives and interests, and their philosophies are influenced and limited by these and other factors. One important aspect of philosophy itself lies in uncovering such motives and presuppositions behind supposedly purely rational pursuits. That is one of the crucial insights that postmodern philosophy (itself well aware of its own motives and interests, as Zhuangzi was of his own perspectives) seeks to convey. So my contribution is inspired by an anti-essentialist rejection of overarching metanarratives. I do not think, for example, that we can ever actually know exactly what Zhuangzi thought, but I also do not think this is important. Richard Kearney argues that every piece of work has some kind of *"narrative flexibility*: every story can be told and retold from a plurality of perspectives." (Kearney 2019: 7, italics in original). The vast historical, cultural, and linguistic distance between us, here and now, and (for example) the classical Chinese thinkers should rather make us guarded against facile claims to knowing what they were about. We simply have no access to the "real" Zhuangzi.

The reasons for my claim to maximum diversity in comparative philosophy and its methodologies are spelled out in the "Reasons for Diversity of Approaches" section, where I hope to convince the reader that this diversity is both a necessary consequence of, and prerequisite for, the idea of comparative philosophy itself and philosophy in general. Then in the "Comparative Philosophy as Philosophy" section, I claim that comparative philosophy is in the process of ending itself. With ever finer comparisons and ever less generalizations (although such generalizations are of course to a certain extent necessary), it will become so specific that it will lose any overarching identity it ever pretended to have. The end of comparative philosophy in this sense is not a negative thing, it suggests a merging of comparative philosophy into philosophy "proper." Based on this, the "On Method and Methodology in Comparative Philosophy" section proposes that we do not need one specific method or methodology for comparative philosophy. It has been claimed that any philosophy is comparative philosophy, and although of course comparative philosophy focuses specifically on comparisons between different cultures, this does not mean that comparative philosophy needs to have any special method or methodology. Instead it may rely on both Western and non-Western sources in different circumstances.

This does not mean that the current work is useless. There is a great deal of value in understanding how various scholars understand their profession, how they see engagement with other cultures as being most fruitful, and what in general to look out for and pay specific attention to when doing intercultural or comparative philosophy. But this is unlikely (and in my view undesirable) to lead to one of even a few preferred methods. Why would we need to limit ourselves in this way? It is better to have the fullest range of methods available so methodology can only spell out the minimum rules of engagement, a version of which I will attempt in the "Criteria and Explanations" section.

Reasons for Diversity of Approaches

Historically, comparative philosophy has moved from comparing East and West to gradually understanding comparisons more and more in micro fashion. Nobody in her right mind would nowadays claim to be comparing "Eastern" and "Western" thought. Even when, for example, comparing Mencius and Aristotle, we would have to choose which parts of Mencius to highlight and which parts of Aristotle, and such choices may differ with different scholars and diverse interests. Of course, such micro comparisons will be based on perceived similarities or interesting differences in thought on certain subjects. Yet again, this only shows that every comparison would have to be fine-tuned to fit the occasion as it actually happens.

A large number of comparative scholars seem to agree (at least to a certain extent) with my stance, most are aware of the impossibility of imposing one interpretation or methodology over others. For example, Ma and van Brakel say, "Underdetermination implies that there is no such thing as *the* correct interpretation. There is an indefinite manifold of more or less plausible interpretations—the degree of plausibility primarily depends on epistemic virtues that are favored" (2016: 257, italics in original). This suggests that the "correctness" of an interpretation is dependent to a large extent on the perspective of the interpreter. They also say that "for the humanities and interpretation in intercultural philosophy, that there are alternative theories is not only a possibility, but is a reality" (89). Comparisons come with a multitude of contextual and ever-changing circumstances, which it would be unwise not to heed. Youru Wang puts this in the following way: "It is impossible to be fixed, since meaning is always context-bound, and context is always on the move in the continuing process of signification and communication" (2003: 146). We must, like Zhuangzi, learn to affirm the multitude of different possible explanations and interpretations, even when those do not fit what we think the text says. There are multiple plausible interpretations of a text, as there are multiple plausible ways of doing comparative philosophy. There is a real danger of reifying comparative philosophy if we seek to detail too much how it should go about.

Philosophical texts are nothing without interpretations. The reader always reads something "into it." Zhuangzi and Derrida actively welcome such participation in the process. Interpretive participation is the very thing that makes a work what it is. As Derrida says:

> The so-called original is in a position of demand with regard to the translation. The original is not a plenitude which would come to be translated by accident. The original is in the situation of demand, that is, of a lack or exile. The original is indebted a priori to the translation. Its survival is a demand and a desire for translation. (1985: 152)

There is no such thing as complete or objective understanding. There is no such thing as an "original" text without interpretations, without its *Wirkungsgeschichte*. In the words of Tim Connolly: "To demand that comparative philosophy be completely independent of one tradition or another, or isolated from any particular historical era, is to demand the impossible" (2015: 25). Or as David Jones has argued, there is no such thing as objectively approaching a text from another culture. We each bring our own interests and ideas into any comparison, and hermeneutics recognizes this: "the idea of an 'open mind' beyond our colloquial expression of 'being open-minded' is a fantasy, an impossible reality" (Jones 2016: 247). While we should make every effort to avoid distorting the meaning of a text, this should come together with the equal awareness of the fact that we always interpret and that we can never find *the* meaning anyway. A double bind such as Derrida suggests. Or in the words of Gadamer: "To try to escape from one's own concepts in interpretation is not only impossible but manifestly absurd. To interpret means precisely to bring one's own preconceptions into play so that the text's meaning can really be made to speak for us" (1989: 398). Good (comparative) philosophy is interpretation that leads to something new, a new take on an issue or new understanding of a philosopher or a school of thought, exactly through comparison with something else. As Arindram Chakrabarti and Ralph Weber say, "What makes it 'right' *philosophically* is not the scholarly accuracy of the history of ideas or the 'scientific historical' correctness in discovering who said what first, or who influenced whom across the cultures, but 'the motivation, the intended next step'— where one wants to go with the comparison" (2015: 28).

As translation is a major issue in comparative philosophy, we realize that when writing in one language we are unable to do full justice to a different culture, yet I argue this does not need to commit one to an ideal-language scenario, as Ma and van Brakel suggest. Contrary to their claims,[2] reporting an attempted comparison of similarities and differences between thinkers from vastly different cultures and language spheres in one language does not necessarily mean one endorses or believes in the ideal-language paradigm. Ma and van Brakel themselves acknowledge that we may never be able to escape writing in one natural language, as "one cannot completely sever oneself from the language in which one addresses contemporaneous scholars" (2019: 25), and "no matter how familiar an interpreter is with the relevant embedding concepts of an older or dead language, he or she remains tied to a modern language" (10). Yet we may, while being tied to a modern language, be critical of the ideal-language paradigm, as the work of Ma and van Brakel itself shows in comparative philosophy, or as, for example, Heidegger and Derrida have shown with regards to the language of Western metaphysics.

It is inevitable to write in a certain language, but one can both acknowledge its shortcomings *and* its necessity. Writing in one language can also be understood as a commitment to acknowledge perspectivism and interpretation as the necessary loci of comparative philosophy. No natural language can fulfil the promise of objectivity. But natural languages are all we have. There is no universal language to appeal to. This does not mean anything goes, but it means we should by right be wary of any attempt to think in terms of one literal or precise meaning, since, "strictly speaking, there is no such thing as explanation (or understanding, letting speak, etc.) *on its own terms*" (Ma & van Brakel 2019: 9, italics in original). Phenomenologically, we know that we cannot know things as they are, but only as they show themselves *to us*, and this *to us* constantly changes. We always interpret, and this is not a bad thing, it is not (only) betrayal, it is reality. In the words of Kearney:

> *Traditore, tradutore*: to translate is always in some sense to betray; for one can never do one's guest true justice. And this means accepting that we all live East of Eden and after Babel—and this is a good thing. Our linguistic fallenness is also our linguistic finitude: a reminder of human limits that saves us from the delusion of sufficiency, the fantasy of restoring some prelapsarian *logos*. (Kearney 2019: 2)

There is of course a lot we can say with relative certainty about the cultural, philosophical, historical, and linguistic background of, for example, Zhuangzi or the book that bears his name, or of Heidegger or Derrida for that matter, so interpretations that clearly contradict such background knowledge are obviously less interesting. But this should not confuse us into thinking we can get it objectively right. Rather, "getting it right" consists of the entire history of *Zhuangzi* reception and criticism, in short of the entire (Eastern and Western and other) engagement with the *Zhuangzi*. Of course, there are better and worse engagements. But it is exactly the continuing history of engagement which makes for the "real" Zhuangzi. It is in new and interesting interpretations that the classics stay alive. Comparative philosophy is, or should be, based on what Chakrabarti and Weber call "the conscious attempt of filling one's mind in an almost terribly unsystematic manner with whatever one gets out of the study of different styles and traditions" (2015: 231). While as comparative philosophers we should make efforts not to distort the ideas coming from other cultural backgrounds, such ideas can only be useful if placed in our current context and, for that, historical considerations are less important than what we think we can achieve in our times by looking at the tradition in new ways.

In short, there are many reasons for why comparative philosophy should be able to employ the full range of methods that philosophy has at its disposal, and even more if we start counting methods from non-Western sources. Comparative philosophy's very essence seems to revolve around decentering rather than providing it with a center.

Comparative Philosophy as Philosophy

There are a number of definitions of comparative philosophy, and there are offshoots or similar enterprises with slightly different names, such as intercultural or world philosophy. Comparative philosophy clearly starts from one culture or conceptual scheme and seeks most often to understand a text from another culture within the interpreter's own conceptual scheme. It seeks to learn something new from a comparison of one (set of) thinker(s) or school of thought to another from a culturally distinct background. Intercultural philosophy attempts to go a step further by exploring how a philosophy in-between different languages, conceptual schemes, or cultures, could exist. World philosophy argues that such an intercultural philosophy will take on a sort of global form alternatively consisting of a mix of different cultures or of a new way of thinking. While the above are oversimplifications, and there are indeed differences, sometimes the names are used interchangeably, and for my purposes and for convenience in this chapter all can be subsumed under the general name "Comparative Philosophy."

If the goal of a certain comparison is to make non-Western ways of thinking understandable for a Western audience, then there is no other option than using at least some Western categories. This also holds the other way around: for example, if Nietzsche needs to be made understandable to a Japanese audience, then Nietzsche should be explained via Japanese categories, if such exist. But the danger of distortion that lies in using indigenous categories to explain a foreign way of thinking is hereby evident. It is in fact impossible not to distort, since we have to write in one language with one audience in mind. It does no good to try to circumvent this problem, as Ma and van Brakel try to do,[3] by publishing the "results" of a comparison in two different languages, since the problem of translation then just resurfaces at another level, which they seem to admit when writing that the two accounts of the "results" in the two different languages "are not expected to be identical" (2016: 201). Translation is always interpretation, even if a comparison is produced in more than one language.

To do comparative philosophy successfully nonetheless, I think that we need to be complicating our own simplifications in much the same way as comparative philosophy has complicated the simplifications and presuppositions of Western philosophy. I base this on the notion of transformation and postmodern views on stability and purity. In Daoist fashion, I think that the inability to arrest meaning permanently is what comparative philosophy should be based on. I am Daoist in the sense that I want comparative philosophy to be an open practice as much as is possible rather than being curtailed by methodological restrictions more than necessary, and in the sense that we want to stand in the open context and judge (mirror) from there what the situation demands, without having to adhere to expectations of preconceived methods.

As a postmodernist, I welcome the impossibility of full presence as an imperative to thought. Instead of understanding comparative philosophy in an essentialist fashion as having a center, a structure, I turn to the notion of infrastructure. Rodolphe Gasché has developed this notion of infrastructure based on his reading of Derrida. An infrastructure is first of all opposed to the idea of structure or system: "What the notion of structure shares with all these concepts is closure. … The concept of structure has always been thought with regard to a point of presence or fixed origin which turns its borders into the circumference of a totality" (Gasché 1986: 144). A structure (or in our context read "a method or methodology") is a term of metaphysics and Western philosophy concerned with substance, closure, and reification. It is essentialist in its core. Closure as a concept seems diametrically opposed to comparative philosophy. The notion of infrastructure might be more helpful here. As Gasché says:

> An infrastructure ... is not an essence, since it is not dependent on any category of that which is present or absent. Nor is it a supraessentiality beyond the finite categories of essence and existence. It does not call any higher, inconceivable, or ineffable mode of being its own. Is has no stable character, no autonomy, no ideal identity. (149–50)

Infrastructures break new paths open, and they do so often by overlaying or disregarding or overriding the rules of the old paths. They do weave different things together, but they do so while not reducing them to homogeneity but by keeping the heterogeneity of those differences intact. Infrastructures are based on the context they find themselves in. There seems little value for comparative philosophy to seek to incorporate differences in any way into a oneness, even if that oneness is "only" methodological. Methods are roads, ways (from *hodos*), but infrastructures are not *one* road or way, or *the* road or way. They are the web(s) of all different ways. As paths they link different thinkers or philosophies together, but they keep those things in their different places. And the linkages can very well be different (e.g., think of roads vs. air routes). We are then reminded by Zhuangzi to "let both alternatives proceed" (Graham 2001: 54). There is no such thing as the Dao. Like *dao*, infrastructure "maintains contradiction and resists its sublation into a higher unity" (Gasché 1986: 151). Infrastructures should not be read in Hegelian fashion as forging a metanarrative tying all the different narratives together, but as plural "instances of an intermediary discourse, concerned with a middle in which the differends are suspended and preserved, but which is not simply a dialectical middle" (151).

I employ the notion of infrastructure to question this need for an overarching metanarrative. Narratives should rather be local, singular, and minimally generalizing: "Infrastructures fulfil the economic principle of successful explanation by accounting for a maximum of phenomena with a minimum of concepts and logical traits" (153). An infrastructure is indeed something that brings, in our context, narratives from different cultures together, but in Derrida's words, "the kind of bringing-together proposed here has the structure of an interlacing, a weaving, or a web, which would allow the different threads and different lines of sense or force to separate again, as well as being ready to bind others together" (1973: 132). Infrastructure, since it is not a ground or overarching idea, has no depth, it is not a metaphysical ground or methodological principle: "Nor ... are the infrastructures deep, as opposed to surface, structures; there is nothing *profound* about them. They are not, strictly speaking, *deeper* grounds" (Gasché 1986: 155, italics in original). An infrastructure, then, is just ever new paths leading from one site to another, ever new sites explored from other sites, but without a clearly defined essence or center. To sum up, I propose that what Saul Newman says of this infrastructure should hold for comparative philosophy:

> The infrastructure is a weave, an unordered combination of differences and antagonisms. It is a system, moreover, whose very nature is that of a non-system: the

differences that constitute it are not dissolved by the infrastructure, nor are they ordered into a dialectical framework in which their differences become only a binary relation of opposites. ... It does not have a stable or autonomous identity, nor is it governed by an ordering principle or authority, it is a "place" that eschews essence, authority and centrality: it is characterized by its very inability to constitute an identity, to form a place. Moreover, its structural inability to establish a stable identity is a threat to the authority of identity. (2001: 9–10)

Comparative philosophy is (like Moore's "definition" of philosophy) part of a history of interpretation, it is just a wider history and an ongoing infrastructure that builds new roads and bridges, and in the process breaks some of the older roads and bridges down. In the terminology of Ma and van Brakel, like philosophy, I understand comparative philosophy to be a family-resemblance-concept, or as I prefer, an infrastructural concept. It covers, and should cover, a wide variety of practices linked together in different methodological ways and linking together diverse styles of thinking in varied ways.

What all this means is again that comparative philosophy should be afforded the methodological width and variety that we accord to philosophy in general. The usual answer given by comparative thinkers to defend against the claim that comparative philosophy is just philosophy is unsatisfactory. To answer this claim, many have argued that what makes comparative philosophy special is that it focuses exactly on the comparison itself, instead of just merely employing comparisons. But the only thing that this does is give it a name, it does not give it a strict or single method or methodology. Connolly mentions that comparative philosophy "gives rise to a unique set of problems: issues concerning incommensurability, one-sidedness, and cultural generalizations, to name a few" (2015: 24). But is this set of problems facing comparative philosophers really that unique? One can equally discuss the incommensurability of analytic and continental philosophy, the perceived one-sidedness of analytic philosophers, or the cultural generalizations we employ when studying Plato. Comparative philosophers do have a distinct approach, which is to explicitly compare culturally different ways of thought to learn something from those comparisons. But this is consistent with my argument that such an approach can admit of a large variety of methods. In terms of methodology, we can indeed point to some generalities and overlapping interests, or minimal criteria, such as openness to diversity, a willingness to engage with the other, a commitment to further understanding beyond the confines of what some consider to be the only "real" philosophy, and an attempt to produce interesting insights based on the comparisons. But these criteria should really hold for *all* philosophy.

In terms of methodology, we could suggest that those methods of comparison that do not take account of the fact that they are coming from one perspective, and that make no effort to minimize distortions, are unlikely to yield good comparisons (but I will have more to say about that in the next section). The fact that some comparative philosophers, such as the ones featured in this volume, specifically think about the methods and methodologies used in various forms of comparative thinking just represents a form of meta-philosophical concern not uncommon in other branches of philosophy. Although indeed very helpful in understanding the field, as this book hopefully shows, such a meta-philosophical concern should not lead to a separate idea or methodology of comparative philosophy or to the strict separation of comparative philosophy from other forms of philosophy. In this sense, I am in agreement with Chakrabarti and Weber when they say that comparative philosophy should "eventually drop its epithet 'comparative'" and that "good creative philosophy in a globalized world should spontaneously straddle geographic areas and cultures, temperaments and time-periods (mixing classical, medieval, modern, and postmodern), styles and subdisciplines of philosophy, as well as mix methods." In short, what they call "fusion philosophy" amounts to "just doing philosophy as one thinks fit for getting to the truth about an issue or set of issues, by appropriating elements from all philosophical views and traditions one knows of but making no claim of 'correct exposition'" (Chakrabarti and Weber 2015: 22).

Since my claim is that comparative philosophy can be done in many different ways, I will focus on my own way to support that claim. I employ the Heideggerian notion of *Auseinandersetzung*, the Derridean idea of a challenge to dominant readings and the search for essences, and the Zhuangzian proposal to not take things too seriously, to be playful and open to different possible approaches. I try to avoid "affirming some things as right and negating others as wrong" (Ziporyn 2009: 38).[4] As soon as we start affirming and denying, we lose the openness to the richness of the sources we work with. That is why this chapter is called "Comparative Philosophy without Method." Zhuangzi talks about allowing "each alternative to proceed" (12) and going by circumstance as staying at the axis of *dao* to respond equally to all (12). He urges us to embrace the "radiance of drift and doubt" (15), and argues that the *dao* has never had "boundaries" (16). Zhuangzi realises that our understanding is based on something "peculiarly unfixed" (11, 39) and wants us to "roam outside the (guide-)lines" (46). He tells us not to set store by "plans and schemes" (54), as "the Consummate Person uses his mind like a mirror, rejecting nothing, welcoming nothing: responding but not storing." And from chapter 20, comparative philosophy should learn that it should be "unwilling to keep to any exclusive course of action" (84).

In short, Zhuangzi urges us not to value only certain interpretations, but to equally entertain all options. Perspectives may be considered right from some point of view but wrong from another point of view. But that other point of view may also be wrong. There is no overarching way of deciding which methods should be considered correct, we have to "go by the circumstances" and "walk two roads," guided by the idea of not imposing (*wuwei*) one way of understanding them as correct, but keeping open as many resources for as many different perspectives as possible, within certain limits. Comparative philosophy needs a "perpetual unease," it cannot rest in dominant readings, the greatest part of its mission is to open these dominant readings of both Eastern and Western works up to novel interpretations. The dominance of certain readings is really reminiscent of the dominance of certain forms of philosophy over others (Shepherd 2007: 235–6). This awareness creates an ethical demand to openness to other traditions.

My continental background is evident in Heidegger's idea of *Auseinandersetzung*, or confrontation, engagement. I believe that comparative philosophy as infrastructure should be thought of in terms of such an *Auseinandersetzung*, a confrontation which not only seeks to bring together, but also to separate what is essentially one. What Heidegger is looking for is another way of seeing *polemos* which he identifies as *Auseinandersetzung*. This German word is hard to translate adequately. It means a variety of things, including "argument," "debate," "analysis," "engagement," "examination," "involvement," "contention." What Heidegger means with it is usually translated as "con-frontation." Another possibility is "engagement." Although superficially understood as a negative term in the sense of a clash between two identities unwilling to change, if we read "con-frontation" more carefully we find the implication that we expose ourselves to the Other, we engage the other, and vice versa, which to Heidegger means that we enter any engagement as much as possible without prejudice, or at least aware of our prejudices and open to different ways of thinking, and we create an atmosphere of mutual coming together in difference (Heidegger equally stresses the "con-" in *con*-frontation), in which things can show themselves as they are. But we know this "as they are" is only based on our position, as they are "to us."

At the same time "con-frontation" or "engagement" also means that we position ourselves as different from the Other. The *Auseinandersetzung* is an encounter between the Self and the Other, yet we must let go of the assertively polemic connotations which often accompany the word "confrontation," or rather, read them in a different way. That really sums up my argument that comparative philosophy is (or should be) philosophy, as it should consist of the combined recognition of interesting philosophical thinkers or schools together with the critical engagement between those and thinkers or schools from other cultural backgrounds.

On Method and Methodology in Comparative Philosophy

For comparative philosophy to have any kind of methodological identity, it would have to deny its own essence. In other words, its essence lies in denying it has an essence. For example, compare comparative philosophy to continental philosophy. It is absurd to think that such diverse ways of thought as Hegel, Nietzsche, Heidegger, Derrida, Habermas, and the like could fit into one method or would adhere to a standard methodology, yet they are known as "continental." Trying to fit these diverse thinkers into one method or methodology would lead to unacceptable generalizations and leave out important idiosyncrasies, something that comparative philosophy is adamantly against by its very nature. We may of course identify certain overlapping interests between certain figures in the continental traditions, but even then, we would not be talking about essential features but more of a web or infrastructure, or as family-resemblance-concepts in the sense espoused by Ma and van Brakel.[5] I therefore believe that comparative philosophy can in principle employ any philosophical method the comparer sees fit given the actual comparison going on and given the interests and motives of those engaged in the practice. In short, by seeking for a separate method or methodology, are we not asking too much of/for comparative philosophy? Robert

Smid's general definition of comparative philosophy is "the attempt to better understand each of the world's philosophical traditions by understanding them relative to each other" (2009: 216). While this is a good and concise definition, he concedes right after this that "what comparative philosophy consists of beyond this—that is, *how* better understanding is to be achieved—differs significantly from method to method" (216).

Again I take my inspiration from Zhuangzi, who often mentions (although implicitly) that there is no "method" to get to *dao*, there is no one "way" to get the "way." "The Genuine Human Beings of old … were not partisan to any one course" (Ziporyn 2009: 41). *Dao* "has its own tendency and consistency, but without any deliberate activity or definite form. It can be transmitted but not received, attained but not shown" (43). But we can also think of the following passages: "The Great Course is unproclaimed … when the Course becomes explicit, it ceases to be the Course" (16). The sage "does not follow any specific course" (18). And in chapter 33 of the *Zhuangzi*, it is more explicitly argued that "within yourself, no fixed positions: Things as they take shape disclose themselves. Moving, be like water, Still, be like a mirror" (Graham 2001: 281). This means that "there are many in the world who apply themselves to some method or technique, and they all believe that what they possess is unimprovable. But in the end where among them is what the ancients called 'the art of the Course'? I say, there is nowhere it is not" (Ziporyn 2009: 117). Again, what the *Zhuangzi* seems to be arguing here, is not that having a method for yourself is necessarily wrong, but thinking that this method should be extended to be considered *the* method is wrong. The last sentence of the last passage suggests exactly what I and the last chapter of the *Zhuangzi* argue: that there is some value in all the different methods and that the last thing we should do or want is to see one method as being superior to others. While we could say that a certain method may be good in a certain case of comparison, we should even then not discourage other attempts to make comparisons via other methods. For if we do, are we not like the "nook and corner scholars" (119), or like the little birds of chapter 1 of the *Zhuangzi* who think they are the only ones who are right, without realizing that they may only hold one piece of the puzzle, and that the puzzle is really quite infinite? Elsewhere in the *Zhuangzi* it is said that one should "transform together with the times. And never consent to be one thing alone. Now up, now down, you take as your measure the degree which is in harmony" (Graham 2001: 121).

A question that follows on from this is whether it should not be the case that the very diversity of the cultures and their even greater diversity in thinking is a fact that should be reflected exactly in the greatest possible diversity in methodology in comparative philosophy? Can we really talk in terms of only Western philosophical methods or methodologies when discussing intercultural or comparative philosophy? Is that not a remnant of the Socratic preoccupation with essence and definition? Should we then not also include methodologies *from* other cultures, such as, for example, the "correlative" or "relational" thinking in classical China, and is this not clearly an ad infinitum enterprise? Leigh Jenco, for example, has made a compelling case for including such methods from other cultures.[6]

An even larger issue, not unknown to comparative philosophers in other contexts, is whether we are able to actually recognize *methodology* or *methods* of other cultures if they do not fit into our preconceived definitions of what a method or methodology is. Should we then go in the same direction as we are trying to do with philosophy, broadening the scope of the concepts of "method" and "methodology"? But how far can we do that with methodology, and why can't we just say then that there is an (almost) infinite variety of methods for comparison of thinking from different cultures? The concept "methodology" is itself a Western concept fraught with presuppositions that may not be shared by different cultures. Are there even family-resemblance-concepts from other cultures for the concept of "methodology"? And even if there are, should we not be open for ways of comparing and practicing intercultural encounters of philosophical traditions that are not based on (preassigned) "methods"?

Of course, in terms of methodology none of this means that we cannot discourse on the use of certain methods in certain circumstances, and we should. I take the task of this book to be exactly that. We can discourse about the appropriateness of methods used in *particular* comparative works, and about the possibilities and desirability of using this method rather than that one in this case, and how one can justify using this method for this particular setting. But to go from there to asserting that comparative philosophy should have a method, or some preferred methods, or even an identifiable methodology, is both asking too much and undesirable. Comparative philosophy should be like Ziporyn's wild card, which

> goes by the rightness of whatever perspective is present as "this" … , which enhances, develops, and breathes life into each of these viewpoints with its responsiveness, fully following along with each alternate arbitrary perspective and thereby further maintaining its own arbitrary perspective, and opening each of them up for interconnection with one another.[7]

Not aiming for a higher perspective, but recognizing the possibility of different perspectives. Not aiming to resolve the conflicts between different methods but merely noticing that different methods are possible. Not looking for a transcendental guiding principle beyond the surface expressions but seeing the different surfaces/methods as "all there is."

The fact that philosophy is probably most fruitfully considered as an infrastructural concept and not as a concept with a clear essence, and the fact that comparative philosophy should clearly not be limited to any kind of philosophy, but should be encouraged to employ the widest variety of what methods and methodology "philosophy" in general has to offer, both support my view that different methodologies will be needed to mediate between the different aspects of various forms of philosophy. If all we can find is an infrastructure, then the quest for one methodology reveals itself as a remainder of the Western obsession with essences, and something that thus should be let go off in favor of more encompassing forms of different methods.

Again, all of this needs to be balanced to guard against the "anything goes" accusation. A family-resemblance-concept of say, liberty, will still need a certain rigor and it is not the case that in exploring this concept we can just say anything. I make a case for pluralism, not for relativism. A "family" also cannot meaningfully be extended indefinitely or randomly. And although an infrastructure can in principle be extended indefinitely, infrastructural concepts cannot be meaningfully extended indefinitely *from any single place* within the web. In this sense we should think of Derrida's call for opening up philosophy while remaining both critical of it *and* critical against attacks to its "fundamentals": On the one hand, "We stand opposed to whatever would prohibit philosophy from … opening itself up to new objects in a way that knows no limit of principle, from recalling that it was already present there where no one wanted to acknowledge it" (2004: 170). On the other hand, while constantly questioning philosophy, deconstruction also affirms it and defends philosophy against "anything that might come along to threaten this integrity, dissolve, dissect, or disperse the identity of the philosophical as such" (170). This is an example of Derrida's double bind, and while this call may sound contradictory, I believe it is correct in asking both for a responsible opening up of philosophy to its other, while at the same time resisting that such opening leads to an "anything goes." The double bind is not infinite license.

Having said that, I do believe that even what are considered "misunderstandings" in comparative philosophy could be very productive. Although the idea of comparative philosophy entails calling out what are patently false interpretations, there is a section of comparative philosophy where "productive misunderstandings" can make for very interesting projects and philosophies. Take, for example, Heidegger's understanding of Daoism. This understanding was arguably one-sided, ill-informed, projecting his own thoughts on Daoism and thereby distorting it in some important ways. Yet it was exactly this misunderstanding itself which contributed to the development of Heidegger's own unique and (in my opinion at least) highly original and important philosophy. So this leads us to perceive comparative philosophy in two ways: for those trying to do objective justice to the Daoists, Heidegger fails on all accounts. But for those more concerned with the possible *Wirkungsgeschichte* of classical Chinese works in a global setting, who acknowledge that their interpretation should not be seen as trying to get Daoism right, misinterpretation may not be that much of an issue. Of course, this would come with the caveat that again, not anything goes. There seems to be a particular reluctance to what are considered "misinterpretations" or "misreadings" of classical texts or resources from other cultures, but I think this has more to do with either cultural chauvinism or historical interest, and should arguably be less pronounced in comparative philosophy. If a certain "misreading" can lead to original and philosophically rich work, then why be so opposed to it? Of course one can and should point out that a misreading has occurred, but such misreading may still lead to interesting philosophy.

This may sound controversial, but in fact misreadings and their productiveness are really nothing new. In fact, one could say that the Chinese commentarial tradition is at least also in part based on misreadings. For example, it is quite certain that Guo Xiang "mis"interpreted some of Zhuangzi's words to suit his own project, but that is part of the *Wirkungsgeschichte* of the *Zhuangzi*. Wang Bi's reading of the *Daodejing* could be considered a "misreading" to those not inclined to see the *Daodejing* as a work of metaphysics comparable to Western metaphysics. And it is quite certain that the medieval Western philosophers tried too hard to fit the Greek thinkers into their Christian ways of thought. Misreadings have occurred throughout history in both "Eastern" and "Western" philosophy, yet they have often led to interesting new approaches and philosophies.

Since there is no original to go back to, there is no correct answer. There are only interpretations. As Connolly puts it: "A thing that doesn't fit well in one domain can have a perfect place in some other, a material that is of no value to one person can lead another to riches. If it seems of little worth to us, it is the result of our own failure of imagination" (2015: 170). I suggest there is (also) an important place for the imagination (read: misinterpretations or misreadings) in comparative philosophy. This also fits in with Zhuangzi's idea of infinite transformation. The world is not static, there are no fixed meanings, and everything changes, and this is good. Goblet words adapt to change. And big gourds can be used for something they are not meant for. Kearney, quoted before on narrative flexibility, also argues for "*narrative transfiguration*: the historical past can be revisited in terms of unexperienced or unexplored 'possibilities,' thereby giving a future to the past" (2019: 7).

Those who look for universals have different concerns from those who focus on differences. Do we need to choose between the two approaches? Can we not "walk two roads," each road with its own concerns and own methods? If one of those sides accuses the other of getting it wrong, is that not a bit like analytic philosophers accusing continental philosophers of not adhering to analytic standards? To which the standard continental reply is of course: we do not need to adhere to your standards, because what we are doing is different and not meant to fit your paradigms. Those paradigms are restrictive, and while they may be valuable to the work you are doing, they form an obstacle to kind of things we want to do. That is why comparative philosophy should be considered an infrastructural concept, in that multiple and sometimes incompatible methods and ways of doing comparative philosophy have to be included into its maze. Like *dao*, we could name it but then we lose its essence, and even saying it has an essence only works in a world of metaphysics not exactly conducive to comparative philosophy. Like Zhuangzi's Hundun, the more we try to define it, the more comparative philosophy dies.

Criteria and Explanations

This short section offers my checklist of minimal requirements for comparative philosophy, mostly in the form of questions:

A. Questions to ask of the "other":

- Does the other (thinker, text, tradition) have a minimal semblance of internal debate, consistently, around topics that are considered philosophical? In other words, are at least a number of the diverse topics that make up the family-resemblance-concept philosophy discussed and argued over by that other?
- Are arguments given by the other, or is it just cultural wisdom pronounced and asserted? It does not matter if we consider the arguments good by our standards, but if there are only assertions, I would not count that as philosophy. It would fit better under religion or cultural wisdom.
- Is there minimal recognition of differences of opinion? In general, do opponents engage with each other, or do they just dismiss each other?

- Is the status quo in thinking either taken for granted, or actively challenged or defended? The sense of critique and critical distance is vital for something to be considered philosophy.

These are really the criteria which I believe distinguish philosophy from other disciplines. The internal criteria for argumentation may of course vary widely in different traditions, but if things are merely asserted, or asserted against the background of a belief system that is never questioned (as in religion), and there is never an attempt at justification of views, then something is surely not philosophy. *Auseinandersetzung* as engagement is both commitment to something shared but also a setting apart. One cannot engage alone, there must be another. That other is recognized as both other and the same, and the engagement comes with a responsibility in the form of a commitment to bring together, but also in the forms of an exposition. Engagement means infiltration but also disagreement, struggle. The lion and the lamb do not always lie peacefully together, in fact they never do unless they are dead. Struggle, *polemos*, is as much part of it, and this is reflected in the critical questioning of traditions.[8] There is nothing inherent in comparative thinking that demands we need to celebrate the other ways of thinking, at least not indefinitely or totally. Openness to and recognition of different philosophical traditions neither equates to endorsement nor precludes criticism. The piety of thinking lies in the harshest deconstruction. One can show no more respect to a philosophy than to see it as worthy of questioning.

B. Questions to ask of the interpreter:

- Does the interpreter recognize in the other's way of thought a form of philosophy? As mentioned, this recognition may be shown by harsh criticism and deconstruction, by *Auseinandersetzung*.
- Has the interpreter been careful in choosing terminology, tried to avoid imposing cultural norms and ideas where possible, or at least explained her choices in interpretation?
- Has the interpreter thought about all her assumptions going into the encounter? Have these assumptions been clarified to the audience?
- Has the interpreter put forward her stance and acknowledged that this is a partial stance?
- And if it fails on any one of these criteria, is it at least interesting as philosophy?

Of course, these lists are hopelessly inadequate. Practitioners of comparative philosophy must always be aware of their own position, their own presuppositions, and their own goals. But we need not deny those, as I have argued throughout this chapter. If we acknowledge and defend our stance, then readers are forewarned. And even in the nowadays unlikely case that the interpreter has not made any effort to fulfil such minimum requirements, we should not automatically dismiss, but rather critically engage her philosophically, while pointing out the shortcomings of her comparative efforts.

Conclusion

How to see the future of comparative philosophy? Practically, there seems a demand for more consistency if we are to make a politically stronger case for comparative philosophy to be included into the curriculum. If we cannot point to a core of what comparative philosophy is, then how could we even teach it? But if it is the fragmentation that comes with infrastructure that defines us, then how can we turn that fragmentation to our advantage? My position is closest to the idea of "fusion philosophy" as advocated by Chakrabarti and Weber, whose main claim is that comparative philosophy is to end and be superseded by a thinking that is "unapologetically, and, eventually, unselfconsciously, comparative and culturally hybrid" (2015: 237). But I am unsure whether we should do this unselfconsciously or whether culturally hybrid fusions are always to be preferred. I would prefer comparative philosophy to have at least the option not only of entertaining but also of rejecting certain points of view on issues, but I believe that Chakrabarti and Weber would agree, as their fusion philosophy includes the idea that "tensions have to be indicated and upheld if they cannot be dissolved, or the opposing views have to be weighed against each other" (232). I am also unclear and therefore uncomfortable with what they consider the standards for "good" comparative philosophy? It seems those standards are largely based along the traditional lines of Western standards of argumentation. It may be better to spell those standards out, but my argument has been that this needs to be done by including standards from non-Western sources.

Importantly, the realization of the impossibility of one methodology or one method should lead to an intellectual humility or awareness of the always already embedded presuppositions of whoever is doing comparative philosophy. We cannot be objective. We should not try, and one of our strengths lies in acknowledging the fundamental limitations of what we do. There are better and worse efforts, but all efforts suffer from incompleteness (never having the entire context available), lack of access to the sources (the impossibility of knowing exactly what Zhuangzi was about), interpretive limitations (where we come from and what our goals are and the language that we use), and, not the least, philosophical limitations (we cannot and should not include everything into philosophy). We may of course seek to widen the philosophical discourses, and that is completely justified, but we cannot ultimately escape such discourses altogether and neither can they be widened indefinitely. Heidegger and Derrida were well aware of the fact they could not escape metaphysics altogether, as Zhuangzi was of his position above the river Hao. Choices that may ultimately not be defensible or justifiable are made at various stages in our comparative process, in terms of what to compare, under which assumptions, which words or characters to translate and how, and for every one of those choices there is usually another possible choice available. While maybe indefensible, we must still demand that such choices be defended. That is the double bind comparative philosophy is in. And that spills over into methods and methodology. They are choices that we make according to a number of factors such as interest, goal, background, education, willingness to expand idiom, jargon, and vocabulary in general, to name a few. To keep those options as wide open as possible, while at the same time open to scrutiny, is what comparative philosophy should aim for.

Notes

1. Methodolatry has been variously defined as "the privileging of methodological concerns over other considerations in qualitative research," or as "a preoccupation with selecting and defending methods to the exclusion of the actual substance of the story being told." Note that I do not say that we should not be concerned with methods and methodology, but I will claim that being overly concerned with these will be detrimental to comparative philosophy.
2. See, for example. Ma and van Brakel (2016: 48).
3. See, for example, Ma and van Brakel (2016: 121).
4. All quotations from the *Zhuangzi* refer to the pages in Ziporyn (2009), unless otherwise indicated.
5. Ma and van Brakel (2016, especially 93–119).
6. Leigh Jenco (2016: 273–88).
7. https://www.hackettpublishing.com/zhuangziphil, accessed April 22, 2021.
8. See my "Polemos and Dao: Conflict and Harmony in Heidegger and Zhuangzi."

References

Blackburn, Simon (2016), "Methodology," in *The Oxford Dictionary of Philosophy*, 3rd ed., Oxford: Oxford University Press. Available online: https://www.oxfordreference.com/view/10.1093/acref/9780198735304.001.0001/acref-9780198735304-e-2017 (accessed April 22, 2021).

Burik, Steven (2015), "Polemos and Dao: Conflict and Harmony in Heidegger and Zhuangzi." (in: *Conflict and Harmony in Comparative Philosophy: Selected Works from the 2013 Joint Meeting of the Society for Asian and Comparative Philosophy and the Australasian Society for Asian and Comparative Philosophy*. Aaron Creller (ed.), Cambridge Scholars Publishing, 2015).

Chakrabarti, Arindram, and Ralph Weber (eds.) (2015), *Comparative Philosophy without Borders*, London: Bloomsbury Academic.

Connolly, Tim (2015), *Doing Philosophy Comparatively*, London: Bloomsbury Academic.

Derrida, Jacques (1973), *Speech and Phenomena*, trans. D. B. Allison, Evanston, IL: Northwestern University Press.

Derrida, Jacques (1985), *The Ear of the Other*, Christie McDonald (ed.), trans. Peggy Kamuf, Lincoln: University of Nebraska Press.

Derrida, Jacques (2004), *Eyes of the University: Right to Philosophy II*, Stanford, CA: Stanford University Press.

Gadamer, Hans-Georg (1989), *Truth and Method*, New York: Crossroad.

Gasché, Rodolphe (1986), *The Tain of the Mirror: Derrida and the Philosophy of Reflection*, Harvard: Harvard University Press.

Graham, Angus C. (2001), *Chuang-Tzu: The Inner Chapters*, Indianapolis: Hackett Publishing Company.

Jenco, Leigh (2016), "Methods from within the Chinese Tradition," in Tan Sor-hoon (ed.), *The Bloomsbury Research Handbook of Chinese Philosophy Methodologies*, 273–88, London: Bloomsbury Academic.

Jones, David (2016), "Traveling around the Threshold: Continental Philosophy and the Comparative Project," in Tan Sor-hoon (ed.), *The Bloomsbury Research Handbook of Chinese Philosophy Methodologies*, 245–56, London: Bloomsbury Academic.

Kearney, Richard (2019), "Linguistic Hospitality—the Risk of Translation," *Research in Phenomenology*, 49: 1–8.

Ma, Lin, and Jaap van Brakel (2016), *Fundamentals of Comparative and Intercultural Philosophy*, Albany, NY: SUNY Press.

Ma, Lin, and Jaap van Brakel (2019), *Beyond the Troubled Waters of ShiFei: From Disputation to Walking-Two-Roads in the Zhuangzi*, Albany, NY: SUNY Press.

Newman, Saul (2001), "Derrida's Deconstruction of Authority," *Philosophy and Social Criticism*, 27 (3): 1–20.

Shepherd, Robert J. (2007), "Perpetual Unease or Being at Ease?—Derrida, Daoism, and the 'Metaphysics of Presence,'" *Philosophy East & West*, 57 (2): 227–43.

Smid, Robert W. (2009), *Methodologies of Comparative Philosophy: The Pragmatist and Process Traditions*, Albany, NY: SUNY Press.

Tan, Sor-hoon, ed. (2016), *The Bloomsbury Research Handbook of Chinese Philosophy Methodologies*, London: Bloomsbury Academic.

Wang, Youru (2003), *Linguistic Strategies in Daoist Zhuangzi and Chan Buddhism: The Other Way of Speaking*, London: Routledge.

Ziporyn, Brook (2009), *Zhuangzi: The Essential Writings with Selections from Traditional Commentaries*, Indianapolis: Hackett Publishing Company.

12

Two Problems of Comparative Philosophy: Why Conversational Thinking Is a Veritable Methodological Option

Jonathan O. Chimakonam and Amara E. Chimakonam

If there is something one could point at and say, here is the most urgent problem confronting comparative philosophy, it would be the problem of method. If we ask a presumably simple question, what is the method of comparative philosophy?, opinions are likely to be divided among practitioners. If, again, we ask whether we can do comparative philosophy with any method in any philosophical tradition, we may likely have more yeas than nays. But why is that? It is probably because it is easier to venture into comparative philosophy with a method one is already familiar with than undertake the difficult task of formulating not only a new but a neutral method for the discipline. This is not surprising. After all, philosophers can be hesitant when it comes to breaking away from convention. But how can we deploy a method from a specific tradition in doing comparative philosophy and expect to be objective and balanced in our study? By its nature, as a discipline that crosses cultural borders of different philosophical traditions, a reasonable, if not a minimal expectation, should be the imperative for neutral methods. One objection to the preceding argument can be that comparative philosophy is not exhausted in cross-cultural encounters; that it can be undertaken within a given tradition (Mou 2010: 1). For example, when the ideas of Kwasi Wiredu and Ngugi wa Thiong'o are compared in the African tradition. We do not hold a hard line against the reasoning that comparative philosophy can be an intracultural exercise, but neither do we promote such a view. Our thinking is that even though one can set out to compare the ideas of G. E. Moore and Bertrand Russell, the "comparative" in comparative philosophy as a discipline should not be trivialized in a literal sense of comparison done in the first-order disciplines. The stakes are higher when borders are involved, and there should be governing rules to regulate the crossing of such borders.

In a later section, we will spell out what we consider to be the proper comparative philosophy tasks and methodological requirements, which may not be relevant in an intracultural exercise. The need for the proper mapping of the field must have been what inspired *the International Society for Comparative Studies of Chinese and Western Philosophy (ISCWP)* to organize its 2008 conference on the theme, "Comparative

Philosophy Methodology." In that conference, we are told that the Chinese philosopher Dunhua Zhao, in his presentation, "challenged the conference's participants to put forward a minimal definition of 'comparative philosophy' and a statement of its methods" (Angle 2010: 106).

More than ten years after Zhao's call, not much has been accomplished, especially in terms of comparative philosophy methodology. Besides Bo Mou's methodological contribution called "constructive engagement," which had been in the making in some essays he published in the first decade of the twenty-first century, the other things that one can find in the literature on methodology are mainly debates. Mou's research crystallized in his 2010, 2013, and 2018 essays, representing the more developed formulations of his method.

This chapter will investigate what we take to be two of the most urgent comparative philosophy problems. These preceding discussions will pave the way for our proposal of conversational thinking as a veritable methodological option for comparative philosophy. Part of our goal will be to offer "conversational thinking," a bourgeoning cross-cultural method, as another veritable option besides Mou's proposal. Another goal would be to produce a conception of comparative philosophy that clearly delineates its boundary. And then, in aligning both our conception and the method of conversational thinking, we will plot a new but clear trajectory for the field of comparative philosophy.

Two Problems in Comparative Philosophy

A common problem of all philosophies[1] that bid to cross borders is that of "method." In the area of comparative philosophy, there may be two such problems: method and conception. We will discuss the two problems simultaneously. Regarding conception, Zhao, cited earlier in Stephen Angle (2010) and Robert Smid (2009), indicates that comparative philosophers have yet to delineate their discipline's scope by producing not really a widely accepted conception but a minimal one that is clear enough. We will investigate this claim. Concerning method, some have assumed that "comparison" is *the* method of comparative philosophy (see, e.g., Wolff 1981; Panikkar 1988; Burik 2009; Smid 2009). Ralph Weber (2013: 593) corroborated when he stated that "much of the disagreement arguably has to do with methodological problems related to the concept of comparison and with the widely prevailing but unwarranted assumption that comparative philosophy should be about comparing 'culturally different philosophies.'" On his part, Wolff set this assumption up with his presentation of the ideas of *comparata* and *tertium comparationis* as two important categories in any comparative exercise, thus assuming comparison itself to be a method.

Weber (2014) provides a conception of comparative philosophy that extends Wolff's proposal. Wolff's proposal includes two aspects, namely, *comparata* (the two ideas/theories being compared) and *tertium comparationis* (the respect in which ideas are being compared) (Wolff 1981, cited in Weber 2014: 152). Weber surveyed ideas in current literature and found additional two aspects, which, when added to Wolff's initial two, gives a total of four aspects covered in standard discussions on comparative philosophy. These other two include the ideas that "a comparison is always done by someone" and "the result of a comparison is a relation between the *comparata* on the basis of the chosen respect" (Weber 2014: 152). Further, Weber puts forward a fifth aspect, his own idea, which he argues should be one of the core aspects covered in comparative philosophy. He calls it "pre-comparative" *tertium,* which for him, "is at work in the setting up of the comparison, that is, in the determination of the *comparata*" (162). These are, for Weber, the five aspects which a conception of comparative philosophy covers. As broad as this conception might be, it appears to circle around the idea of comparison as a method of comparative philosophy.

Raimundo Panikkar (1988: 128–9, 135) equally made the same assumption despite having discussed the notion of "comparative" to include the ideas of "contrasting" and what he describes as "imparative," a form of self-critical and broad-based dimension. He appeared to have joggled the notions of comparative, compared, and comparing philosophies to find the one that best serves the purpose of methodology that goes beyond mere "conventional notions of comparison used by all systematic thinkers" (Panikkar 1988: 117). In the end, he arrived not quite far from where he began. The idea of "comparative" in comparative philosophy, for him, extends beyond the search for common lines; it involves a lot of critical examinations and a special kind of hermeneutics. It is a kind of "imparative," "diatopical hermeneutics" that produces ideas from a dialogue of two traditions (128–31). Yet, even this method does not seem to be completely divorced from the idea of comparison. In other words, it is not exactly clear what is contained in diatropical hermeneutics that is not already contained in the idea of comparison. Comparison can be a critical and interpretive dialogue of two distinct cultures. And such critical and interpretive dialogues produce understanding and new ideas. Ronnie Littlejohn (IEP Online), Steven Burik (2009: 4) and Smid (2009: 2), in their conceptions of comparative philosophy, highlight much of what Panikkar stresses as consisting their idea of comparison. For example, while Burik talks about "hermeneutics" "in-between" "cultural perspectives," Smid talks about "comparison of what lies on either side of the boundary." These views are very much the same as those of Panikkar. Panikkar's (1988: 122) definition of comparative philosophy as "the philosophical study of one or some problems in the light of more than one tradition," clearly indicates satisfaction with and an allusion to comparison as the method of comparative philosophy. His introduction of diatopical hermeneutics, for us, is only a mere change in nomenclature. We will go beyond this assumption that comparison is the method of comparative philosophy. We argue that the "comparative" in comparative philosophy is an attribute that qualifies that brand of philosophy. It may even describe the "style" but only in the sense of "what" it primarily does and not in the sense of "how" it does that or "how" it should do that. Talk about the method of comparative philosophy, for us, should be about the latter and not the former. We will revisit this argument later.

The idea of "contrast" is also reechoed by Daya Krishna (1986: 58–69), who argued that comparative philosophy may be widely conceived to be a search for similarities, but what it ought to search for are differences. For Krishna (1986: 69), "the differences are philosophically interesting only when they are articulated not in terms of the doctrines held, but in terms of the problems perceived and the solutions attempted." Ultimately, like Wolff, Burik, Smid, and Panikkar, Krishna took it for granted that comparison is somehow a or even *the* method of comparative philosophy. In his words, "comparative studies are ... comparisons between societies, culture and civilisations" (59). But even if comparison as a way of identifying similarities and differences and comparing such whether critically or otherwise across cultural boundaries can pose as a method at all, is it fitting for a comparative philosophical exercise?

This is not an easy question. Nothing, indeed, is easy in comparative philosophy, not even its existence. That is why Panikkar (1988: 116) was tempted to suggest that a discipline called comparative philosophy might have been impossible if not for the recognition of its impossibility. Rather than the comparison in a simple sense, both Panikkar and Krishna insist on the incorporation of a critical dimension to the idea of comparison as a method. But "criticality" alone is hardly sufficient in making a discourse philosophy. Scholars in the ancillary sciences are also critical in their views. It is a misplaced assumption to think that once the idea of criticality is sprinkled in, a philosophy of the second-order type is present. If being critical can be said to be the only trademark of philosophy, then the first other disciplines would be indistinguishable from philosophy. This is because through the idea of the centrifugal movement of philosophy, that is, philosophy's divestiture of itself into what is commonly referred to as infrastructural philosophies, all first other disciplines received the anointing of criticality from the mother discipline. So, both Panikkar and Krishna, despite the nuances they have made to the notion of comparison, may not have done enough to totally distinguish the interpretation they have given to comparison as a philosophical method.

Instead of comparative, compared and comparing philosophies, as Panikkar (1988) says, can we talk about "comparative thinking"? The idea of comparative thinking should not be understood in the way Burik (2009) used it. Burik curiously titled his book *The End of Comparative Philosophy and the Task of Comparative Thinking*, in which he argues that comparative philosophy should not stop at comparing similarities and differences in the thinking of various traditions but must locate itself between such differences. This location is what Burik describes as the task of comparative thinking. In his words, "To accommodate different ways of thinking into one discourse without that discourse favoring one of these ways above the other, and thus to make productive meetings possible, should be one of the main tasks of comparative philosophy" (2009: 2). The justification which Burik provides for this line of argument is that the tendency of one, perhaps, dominant philosophical tradition imposing its particularities on the rest as universals, thereby shaping the discourse, is a serious challenge to the true practice of comparative philosophy. For Burik (2009: 3), overcoming such a problem of cultural bias and providing a plain field for all epistemologies in which none is shortchanged or residualized consist in comparative thinking and, thus, a real task of comparative philosophy.

We agree with Burik in his characterization of the problem of cultural marginalization and even the task he has identified for comparative philosophy, but our idea of comparative thinking is slightly different. To explain our understanding, one can begin by shuffling the two concepts in order to create two ideas, namely, comparative thinking (which can mean to fairly compare ways of thinking) and thinking comparatively (which can mean a type of thinking that crosses cultural borders). While Burik's understanding of the concept is closer to the first, ours is closer to the second.

The latter idea has the power to set our imagination on another path. A path that reminds us of what we should be doing as philosophers venturing into a second-order discipline. As comparative philosophers, we are not out to compare in the same fashion as scholars in the first-order disciplines. Comparative philosophers must have tasks, not just a task, to which they must follow a well-articulated procedure to undertake. Such a procedure, it must be stated, should be one grounded in a logic that has a massive expressive power so as to be able to maintain cultural neutrality.

Burik has argued that a neutral method for comparative philosophy is unnecessary if not impossible (2009: 5). But where will the objectivity or the "thinking in-between" come from if we are free to source our methods from within our own traditions? There is clearly a need for a neutral method if we must do comparative philosophy sincerely. Comparative thinking, therefore, gives us an idea of a type of thinking *for* comparative philosophy. What then, we must ask, enables us to do this type of thinking or, should we say, philosophizing? At this point, it becomes clear that we are dealing with a methodological issue all along shrouded in the murky conceptual waters.

We want to discuss "thinking" using the 3D model in geometry in which space is represented in three dimensions: breadth, height, and depth. Deploying the 3D in philosophical thinking, we have breath (doctrine of thought or the philosophical subject matter), height (structure of thought or the methodological issues), and depth (foundation of thought or the logical matters). We want to argue that whereas "thinking" in most second-order philosophies can be done in a two-dimensional range of structure and doctrine, all meta-discourses like cross-cultural philosophies can fully be done in three-dimensional thinking that includes a foundational analysis. These three dimensions can be broken down into two spheres representing, what for us, are the six tasks of comparative philosophy: the discursive sphere (philosophical, methodological, and logical tasks) and the meta-sphere (meta-philosophical, meta-methodological, and metalogical tasks). Thus, it can be stated that the five aspects of comparative philosophy gazetted by Weber, which cover most of the views in current literature, only represent the dimensions of structure and doctrine. Here, our effort is to add depth of foundation to that conception and make a new structural/methodological proposal in the mold of the conversational method.

The structural and foundational dimensions of thinking in comparative philosophy often elude some theories in the field. When one typically thinks of philosophy, whether comparative or otherwise, they get an immediate impression that there are some *thinkings* going on inside. This initial but strong impression in the specific fields of cross-cultural philosophies tends to overshadow the hovering and crucial type of meta-spheric thinkings—structural or meta-methodological and foundational or metalogical types that are mainly found in cross-cultural philosophies. At such a level, philosophy deals not just with concepts but with concept of concepts. It demands not only a method but a method of methods. Moving to the foundation, we encounter logic. Here, we must not just clarify the laws that govern our reasoning; we must question them as well, partly to ensure that they have been well-formulated but mostly to determine the scope of their expressive powers. The demand for justification of thought will vindicate reason only by unmasking logic, which often remains invisible. In thought, logic is mostly invisible until a principle of thought is violated. What this implies is that in cross-cultural philosophies, any attempt at crossing the border must be done carefully, first, in deference to the logics of the philosophical traditions involved, and second, in deference to the logic that subsumes the logics of the *comparata*. A rash and insensitive move can trigger the alarm of the logic of one of the traditions. When this happens, we have a typical case of orientalist tendencies that Burik (2009: 2–3; see also Said 1978, 1993) talks about as a residual treatment of one epistemic formation by another. But it is really a logical problem that can be avoided by employing a neutral method in a comparative study.

From the foregoing, we argue that comparative philosophy goes beyond the study of similar or different subject matter across cultures; it also transcends the question of method to involve logic at its foundational level. Thus, we conceive comparative philosophy as "a discursive and meta-spheric study of the doctrines, structures and foundations of more than one philosophical tradition, using a neutral method."

It does not appear to us practicable to ignore these three dimensions of thinking and still do authentic comparative philosophy. We must remember that the mere fact that one has christened their work "comparative philosophy" does not make it so. A literal understanding of the "comparative" in comparative philosophy will most likely distort the discourse. We are not claiming the final word yet in the nature of comparative philosophy. We are not even claiming that our conception is the best or correct, for that matter. But there is something anybody can claim: it is the fact that a minimum standard can be determined if not axiomatically, at least, empirically. If, for example, we grant that comparative philosophy is a comparison of similarities and differences with some critical orientation, then all philosophies are comparative philosophy.[2] We can all go home!

However, because we have such a minimum bar, which can be determined empirically, no wakeful philosopher requires an axiom system to determine whether the notion of comparative philosophy should be formulated at a level higher than a mere critical comparison of similar and different ideas. Our conception in the above scales this bar, and so do the conceptions by some others. What is at issue all along is what we have discussed above as the 3D thinking required in cross-cultural philosophies like comparative philosophy. Granted that some of the conceptions we have treated in the above cover the first two dimensions, our conception provides more in terms of depth, as we have shown.

Even though some scholars assert that "there is hence no consensus on what it is that comparative philosophy is comparing" (Weber 2013: 596; see also Panikkar 1988), we want to argue that the meaning attached to the word "compare" should be understood in terms of "thinking." Comparative philosophy is not a mere doctrine in philosophy; it is a meta-philosophical discipline in its own right. It is not a method, but it is meta-methodological. It does not only seek to identify and understand the logic of justification in each philosophical tradition; it is also metalogical.

There is something about this process that is worth noting. While we may casually discuss any idea or concept in our various philosophical traditions, comparative philosophy obliges practitioners to carefully note the three aims of comparative thinking. First, they must consider an idea or concept from the purview of methods and the logic of the specific tradition it emanates. Second, they have to cross the border to gauge it against an idea or concept in another tradition, not merely to establish similarities and differences, but a fortiori, to see what new ideas and concepts could be birthed. If, for example, authentic existence for Heidegger in the Western tradition consists in self-discovery and Menkiti in the African tradition says it consists in solidarity with others, comparative philosophers should not simply aim at showing the lines of difference and similarity; that would be a simplistic conception of comparative philosophy. Burik (2009: 2) also argues in support of this view that "comparative philosophy cannot stop at the finding and explanation of similarities and differences between thinking from different cultures, however valuable these findings are. As a discipline, it should locate itself between these differences, while aware of the impossibility of a purely neutral viewpoint." As a rule, they must strive to pit the two ideas against each other to generate new ideas and concepts of existence. The latter consists of progressive thinking to extend the frontiers of knowledge. Third, and this should be the pinnacle of comparative philosophizing, they have to pit the methods and logics of the traditions. Here, once again, the aim must transcend the establishment of similarity and difference to include the ascertainment of the capacity of those methods and the expressive powers of such logics. These aims can be broken down into a number of rubrics that compose the six tasks of comparative philosophy. On the discursive side, we have the philosophical, methodological and logical; and on the meta-spheric angle, we have the meta-philosophical, meta-methodological and metalogical.

But to do all of these tasks we have set aside for comparative philosophers creditably, a neutral method is required. How do we study methods from different traditions grounded in separate logics? And how do we study the expressive powers of systems of logic from different traditions? These are beyond the capacity of any method that is not neutral. Insofar as comparative philosophy involves crossing borders, there appears to be an inevitable need for a neutral method. As Fleming, citing A. G. Larson, argues, "It is no more difficult to cross the boundary from one culture or tradition to another than it is to cross boundaries in ordinary conversation (where misunderstanding is always already rife but which we do with some success" (2003: 269).

We are not contesting the fact that philosophical borders can and should be crossed; our contention is that only neutral methods can marshal discourses at that level creditably. Both the analytical and phenomenological methods are grounded in Western philosophy's bivalent logic and are thus not neutral in that they both deny the intermediate value. Also, both the complementary reflection and the communitarian methods are grounded in the multivalent logic of African philosophy and are thus not neutral enough in that, even though they both have the capacity for bridge building, they accept conjunctive reasoning and reject disjunctive reasoning.[3] The foregoing opens up the playing field for new methods that are neutral. In the next section, we will offer a proposal for a methodological shift in comparative philosophy.

How Else Should We Do Comparative Philosophy? A Call for a Methodological Shift

The "how" question is obviously a question of method. What is not so obvious is what, if any, method can be described as suitable for comparative philosophy. We use the word "suitable" because it is perfectly possible for any philosopher to make claims. Claims are easy to make, probably the easiest part of the philosophical endeavor. What is not so easy is justifying claims. A careful reader would have noticed our choice of verb in the title of this section. We consciously did not ask, "How else 'can' we ... ?" We asked, "How else 'should' we do comparative philosophy?" In the preceding, we assume that some philosophers can straightforwardly delve into comparative philosophy with methods they are familiar with or that are popular in their respective philosophical traditions. But before any industry is dispensed in comparative philosophy, we must cautiously ask, can methods cross borders?[4] It is important to begin with this question because methods have origins in logic, and if the methods and doctrines of various philosophical traditions are grounded in different systems of logic, then it poses a challenge of a fundamental kind to ascertain just how methods can cross borders. Methods are shy when faced with the challenge of crossing a border. They are shy because logic has made them so.

Contemporary comparative philosophers should, among others, concern themselves with the methodological issue of how we should do comparative philosophy as the philosophical study of the various approaches in more than one tradition. We are saying that philosophies A, B, C, D, and so on, are different in that they are varying traditions. What then makes them different from one another to warrant the idea of varying traditions? And what makes them similar to warrant the idea of philosophy? These are the two natural questions that should arise when we entertain the first thought on comparative philosophy. The "comparative" in comparative philosophy must be construed as "thinking" and should be interested, at the initial stage, in the how and where questions of comparative thinking and not immediately in the what and why questions of specific traditions. Concerning the "how" and "where" questions, it should ask about methods of varying philosophical traditions and how methods are generated and where their cultural inspirations come from. The idea of comparative study is inspired by our understanding that knowledge is culturally embedded. So, different approaches have their roots in different cultures. When we ask about how philosophy is done in a given culture, it leads us to "method." And when we ask how methods are generated in a given philosophical tradition, it leads us to logic. Attempts to understand the logical and methodological peculiarities of more than one philosophical tradition should constitute part of comparative philosophy's aims. It is not just to compare what philosophers in diverse traditions say that are either similar or different, correct or incorrect, and so on.

What else have philosophers been saying in the last millennium? Issues like those should concern scholars in the area of comparative intellectual history more than those in comparative philosophy.

Three Requirements for Methodological Neutrality

From the foregoing, a fairly suitable method of comparative philosophy has to fulfil three requirements: *neutral*, so as to be logically and methodologically unbiased; *interpretive*, so as to consider the merit of each within the cultural domain that inspired it; and *conversational*, so as to establish how well each fares in crossing the border. It is in the latter requirement that we can locate the meta-philosophical, meta-methodological, and metalogical tasks of comparative thinking. In this meta-sphere, the goal is not to see what each has to say about the same problem or concept; it is to study the "veracity," "capacity," and "expressive power" of each tradition's doctrine, method, and logic, respectively. So, the truly difficult question of comparative philosophy is, can we have a method that can marshal, on the one hand, the philosophical, methodological, and logical paraphernalia (discursive sphere) of more than one philosophical tradition and, on the other hand, also marshal their meta-philosophical, meta-methodological, and metalogical (meta-sphere) concerns without bias?

It seems, therefore, that one question which is impossible for comparative philosophers to ignore is that of the nature of its method. Should the method of comparative philosophy be neutral or not? By neutrality is meant non-restriction (in terms of its logical background) to a specific philosophical tradition. We had engaged this issue briefly in an earlier passage and will not belabour it again. Our position is that a neutral method is imperative if the border crossing is to be objective and balanced. But there are scarcely enough proposals out there at the moment. In fact, the only neutral method that has come to our knowledge is Bo Mou's "constructive engagement" (2006, 2010, 2013, and 2018).

The Method of Constructive Engagement

In his very lengthy essay (Mou 2010: 18), he identifies three orientations in comparative philosophy, "the interpretation-concerned orientation, the philosophical-issue-engagement orientation, and the historical-description-concerned orientation." These orientations contrast with what we have laid out above as the three requirements of a suitable method for comparative philosophy. In formulating the orientations, Mou appears to focus on the doctrinal aspect of comparative philosophy while we focus on its methodological aspect. Mou's focus, therefore, constrains his analysis only to two dimensions: structure and doctrine. His third orientation, which is "the historical," is surplus to requirement since philosophy and ideas cannot be ahistorical. His second, which is "the philosophical issue" is trivial since the subject matter of comparative philosophy must be philosophical issues. This leaves his first orientation, that is, "the interpretation concern" which is methodological as the only genuine orientation. The first concern of comparative philosophy is methodological, and that is the focus of the three requirements we articulated.

On the orientation of methodology, which was really the only one Mou found inspiration to develop, he formulated what he called the "constructive engagement" strategy. We shall consider this method momentarily to ascertain whether it fulfils our three requirements. According to Mou, constructive engagement as a methodological strategy of comparative philosophy has the following goal:

> To inquire into how, via reflective criticism and self-criticism, distinct modes of thinking, methodological approaches, visions, insights, substantial points of view, or conceptual and explanatory resources from different philosophical traditions and/or different styles/orientations of doing philosophy (within one tradition or from different traditions) can learn from each other and jointly contribute to our understanding and treatment of a series of issue, themes or topics of philosophical significance, which can be jointly concerned through appropriate philosophical interpretation and/or from a broader philosophical vantage point. (1–2)

The above is quite dense to be dissected in a few sentences. But the key features of the method of constructive engagement, it appears, would include an allusion to critical inquiry into how philosophy is done in different traditions, mutual engagement, the possibility of cross-cultural exchanges, and a philosophical joint venture that can lead to new and important outcomes. Mou also indicated that this process could be hermeneutical or even from an approach that is broader in scope.

We find Mou's approach interesting, fresh, and promising. However, one can see that going by our three-dimensional model for comparative thinking; constructive engagement suffers a limitation in the third dimension. It covers the dimensions of doctrine and structure but not the foundation, as we shall point out later. This makes Mou's constructive engagement method two-dimensional. As much as Mou may think that his method can do justice to all the demands of comparative thinking, he is clearly mistaken when viewed from the lenses of three-dimensional thinking. Take, for example, his application of the method in the comparative study of the analytic and continental sub-traditions in Western philosophy. In it, Mou (2013: 152–62) promulgates what he calls eight conditions for adequate methodological guiding principles. Recently (Mou 2018: 11–30), he increased the conditions to ten with extensive discussions added to a new set of guides that he describes as the four fronts in his comparative study. These principles largely cover two of the three dimensions. Unfortunately, as laid out in those work, Mou's method did not indicate that it was designed to cover the dimension of "foundation." So, constructive engagement fulfils the requirements of neutrality and interpretation but not that of conversation, where conversation is a technical term for an encounter that is critical, innovative, creative, and structural and foundational.[5] This is the main weakness of the method of constructive engagement. It was a promising, carefully articulated method, and one which fulfils the test of neutrality, but for its deficiency in depth.

Constructive engagement has recently been compared with conversational thinking by Paul Dottin (2019), who claims that the two methods share some traits in common. As he put it:

Despite their similar philosophical inclinations, the conversational movement and the constructive-engagement movement seem virtually unaware of each other. They do share features in common, however. First, they are contemporaneous movements with both having originated around the turn of the twenty-first century. Second, both perhaps have found some inspiration in the remarkable economic growth China and several African countries have experienced over the last quarter century. From these trends, a rise in confidence that their traditions would have to be heard and perhaps heeded more may have arisen. Third, both movements seek critical yet civil, creative but accountable dialogue with traditions beyond their own regions. (Dottin 2019: 55)

In fact, much of what the two methods share in common may be superficial. The important point is that they both represent advances in comparative thinking from a methodological angle.

The Method of Conversational Thinking as a Veritable Option for Comparative Philosophy

Here, we propose conversational thinking[6] as a more comprehensive method for comparative philosophy. Its capacity covers the three dimensions of thought and two spheres of engagement which account for the six tasks we have identified for comparative philosophy. But there are two things that make the method different and desirable; namely, it fulfils our requirements for a suitable comparative methodology, and its background logic has broad expressive powers.

First, the conversational method fulfils our three requirements for a suitable comparative philosophical method. It is neutral in the sense of not being logically constrained to any specific tradition. It is also interpretive in the sense of promoting critical, creative, and objective engagement. And it is conversational in the sense of opening new vistas of thought and asking questions that stem from the realization of the limitations of the traditions under study.

Second, the logic that grounds conversational method has broad expressive power. It is called Ezumezu logic.[7] This system might be trivalent, but it is a truth-glut and not a truth-gap, like Jan Lukasiewicz's (1970) trivalent system that has an indeterminate (truth-gap) reading of the third value. Ezumezu does not reject the three classical laws of two-valued logic (identity, contradiction, and excluded-middle) but mitigates their absolute identity and difference, which make variables mutually exclusive. This way, additional three laws (njikọka, nmekọka, and ọnọna-etiti) are incorporated to provide the legal bases for complementary inferences that the system of Ezumezu supports. So, instead of unequal binaries (binary contradiction), which two-valued logic engenders in thought, Ezumezu engenders binary complementarity and contextual consideration of variables and propositions. This is what ensures the neutrality of the method of conversational thinking when deployed in any cross-cultural philosophy. The formulation of the three supplementary laws is as mentioned below:

- Njikọka: An arumaristic proposition is true if and only if it is true in a given context and can be false in another context.

   (T) Ax $\updownarrow$ [(T) Ax | → (F) Ax], which reads that Ax is true in a given context if and only if Ax is true in that context wedges that Ax is false in another. The notation | → called wedged-arrow functions only as a context indicator here.

- Nmekọka: If an arumaristic proposition is true in a given context, then it cannot be false in the same context.

   (T) Ax | → ~(F) Ax, which reads that if Ax is true in a given context, then Ax cannot be false in the same context. The notation wedged-arrow functions both as a material implication and a context indicator here.

- Ọnọna-etiti: An ohakaristic proposition is both true and false in a complementary mode of thought.

   [(T) Ax ∧ (F) Ax] $\updownarrow$ (C) (Ax ∧ ~Ax), which reads that Ax is true and Ax is false if and only if Ax and not Ax are complements.

Unlike the two-valued logic that deals with categorical propositions that are analytic, synthetic, and synthetic-a priori, the Ezumezu variant of three-valued logic in addition, deals with arumaristic and ohakaristic propositions that are a species of synthetic proposition. The first are propositions that express one thought but which truth-value could vary in two different contexts. The second are propositions that express more than one thought which can both be affirmed in a complementary mode. An arumaristic proposition or statement affirms **or** denies that *in a given context* all or some of the members of one category (the subject term) are included in another (the predicate term). An ohakaristic proposition or statement affirms **and** denies *in a complementary mode* that all or some of the members of one category (the subject term) are included in another (the predicate term).

Examples of arumaristic and ohakaristic propositions are "you need to drink water to stay alive," and "ụzụ na-amaghị akpụ egbe, nere egbe anya nòdụ,"[8] respectively. For the first proposition, there can be different values in two contexts. For instance, someone stranded in the middle of Sahara Dessert in a hot afternoon, and someone drowning in the River Niger. The Boolean value of the proposition would be 1 and 0 in the two contexts, respectively. This proposition is axiomatized in the laws of njikọka and nmekọka stated in the above that mitigate on the absolute identity/difference in the laws of identity and contradiction. The second proposition expresses two thoughts: first, "that the tail of a kite can serve as a model to a blacksmith who does not know how to fashion rifle butts"; and second, "that a perennial failure can learn from the successes of others." In Ezumezu logic, two variables can be asserted as binary complementarity with the value "C." Here, the law of ọnọna-etiti that mitigates on the mutual exclusivity of the law of excluded-middle, and the absolute difference of the law of contradiction axiomatizes the complementary inference as captured in its formulation above.

The neutrality of the method of conversational thinking is therefore insured by the principles of Context-dependence of Values (CdV) and complementarism that characterize the propositional logic exposition of Ezumezu. The first is stated as "credible value judgements are the ones based on contexts" with the extension that truth-values "may not always be dependent on the collection of facts which a proposition asserts but rather, on the context in which that proposition is asserted" (Chimakonam 2019: 119). The second can be stated as saying that a statement can be both necessary and possible in a complementary mode (109). Thus, with the idea of context analysis conversational method maintains fairness and objectivity in a comparative philosophical discourse of various traditions. Also, with the idea of binary complementation, the method maintains balance and respect in its comparative discourse of traditions.[9]

Thus, conversational method is context-sensitive, objective, balanced, and complementary in its three dimensions. In its doctrinal scope, conversational thinking considers philosophical and meta-philosophical tasks, in that questions are raised about issues and concepts in comparative philosophy, and about the nature of philosophy in specific traditions. In structure, conversational thinking accommodates discussions in both methodological and meta-methodological tasks in that questions are asked not just about how to do comparative philosophy but also about the nature of its methods and the methods of specific traditions. And in terms of foundation, it also considers both logical and metalogical tasks in that besides the investigations into logical issues, questions are raised about the nature of the logic that undergirds comparative thinking and the logics of other traditions. Its questions are ultimately geared toward opening of a collective vista from the realization of mutual self-insufficiency and the need for mutual complementarity of the philosophical traditions.

As a neutral method, conversational thinking is equipped for cross-cultural and interdisciplinary applications, which has been demonstrated in published research. For example, the method has variously been applied in philosophy generally (Chimakonam 2017d; Enyimba 2021, etc.), African philosophy specifically (Nweke 2015, 2016; Egbai 2018, etc.), comparative philosophy (Dottin 2019), intercultural philosophy (Chimakonam 2017b; Egabi and Chimakonam 2019), and interdisciplinary studies (Tavernaro-Haidarian 2018; Enyimba 2019, etc.). The high point of conversational method lies in its capacity to cover the three dimension of thinking discussed above.

In confronting headlong, the six comparative philosophy tasks, actors shoulder the responsibilities of questioning, criticizing, and creating new ideas at both the discursive and meta-spheric levels. There is equal room for both the critical and the creative components. What conversational thinking does not have any room for is the omission of any of the two components. The motto is "criticize but create, where one cannot create, there they must be silent." In other words, conversational thinking promotes constructive criticism as the type that leads to new ideas. So, where there is constructive criticism, creativity naturally follows. One is, therefore, cautioned to be silent instead of providing a destructive criticism.

The creation of new ideas and concepts is cardinal to the goal of comparative philosophy. Those using the method of conversational thinking have an obligation to honour their debts and duties to the places in which the questions they grapple with arise by creating new ideas. But creating a new idea is not the completion of a philosophical exercise undertaken with the mechanism of conversational thinking. There is an equally important demand to present the new idea clearly, justify or falsify, realize the limitations of each tradition so as to open new vistas by asking questions that can extend the frontiers of knowledge.

Conclusion

In this chapter, we have argued that questions about method and logic should be paramount in delineating the conception of comparative philosophy. Jesse Fleming (2003: 260) had clarified this much when he stated that in a comparative exercise, "After first identifying what we take to be similarities between the two philosophical theories (or systems, concepts, or traditions), we naturally move on to identifying significant differences: similarities and differences in regard to logic and method of proof, in regard to values, assumptions, and aims." The task of comparative philosophers must not be limited to the consideration of subject matter, there must be methodological and logical tasks as well. Whilst logic grounds method; it is actually method that directly shapes subject matter. And at the level of comparative thinking, we must search for methods that fulfil the requirements of neutrality, interpretation, and conversation. Our submission in this chapter for conversational thinking as a veritable option, grounded in a trivalent logic system with massive expressive power, should be seen as a proposal to be further examined.

Acknowledgments

Jonathan O. Chimakonam acknowledges that "this work is based on the research supported in part by the National Research Foundation of South Africa (Grant Numbers 132057)." Opinions expressed in this research are those of the authors; the NRF accepts no liability whatsoever in this regard.

Notes

1. This cluster can include intercultural, multicultural, and comparative philosophies assuming some differences.
2. Panikkar (1988) and Weber (2013) have both made similar arguments.

3. See Innocent Asouzu (2013) for an explication of this idea in his theory of complementary logic.
4. Egbai and Chimakonam (2019) raised a similar question in their essay on the appropriate method for intercultural philosophy.
5. Details of the etymology of the technical term conversation translated from the Igbo language-derived concept of arụmarụka have been provided elsewhere, see Chimakonam (2017b and 2018a).
6. For a detailed presentation of the theory of conversational philosophy, see Chimakonam (2015a, 2015b, 2015c, 2015d, 2017a, 2017b, 2018a).
7. For some details, see Chimakonam (2017c, 2018b, 2019, 2020a, 2020b); Ani (2019); Metz (2020); Ofuasia (2019, 2021).
8. This is an Igbo language expression.
9. What we have stated above are propositional logic dimension of the system of Ezumezu logic. For lack of space, we cannot discuss Ezumezu in more detail. The reader is referred to some of the extant literature listed earlier.

References

Angle, Stephen (2010), "The Minimal Definition and Methodology of Comparative Philosophy: A Report from a Conference," *Comparative Philosophy*, 1 (1): 106–10.

Ani, Amara E. (2019), "The Methodological Significance of Chimakonam's Ezumezu Logic," *Filosofia Theoretica: Journal of African Philosophy, Culture and Religions*, 8 (2): 85–95.

Asouzu, Innocent I. (2013), *Ibuanyidanda (Complementary Reflection) and Some Basic Problems in Africa*, Zurich: Lit Verlag.

Burik, Steven (2009), *The End of Comparative Philosophy and the Task of Comparative Thinking: Heidegger, Derrida, and Daoism*, Albany, NY: SUNY Press.

Chimakonam, Jonathan O. (2015a), "Transforming the African Philosophical Place through Conversations: An Inquiry into the Global Expansion of Thought (GET)," *South African Journal of Philosophy*, 34 (4): 462–79.

Chimakonam, Jonathan O. (2015b), "Conversational Philosophy as a New School of Thought in African Philosophy: A Conversation with Bruce Janz on the Concept of Philosophical Space," *Confluence: Online Journal of World Philosophies*, 3: 9–40.

Chimakonam, Jonathan O. (2015c), "Dating and Periodisation Questions in African Philosophy," in Jonathan O. Chimakonam (ed.), *Atuolu Omalu: Some Unanswered Questions in Contemporary African Philosophy*, 9–34, Lanham, MD: University Press of America.

Chimakonam, Jonathan O. (2015d), "Addressing Uduma's Africanness of a Philosophy Question and Shifting the Paradigm from Metaphilosophy to Conversational Philosophy," *Filosofia Theoretica: Journal of African Philosophy, Culture and Religions*, 4 (1): 33–50.

Chimakonam, Jonathan O. (2017a), "Conversationalism as an Emerging Method of Thinking in and beyond African Philosophy," *Acta Academica*, 47 (2): 11–33.

Chimakonam, Jonathan O. (2017b), "What Is Conversational Philosophy? A Prescription of a New Doctrine and Method of Philosophy, in and beyond African Philosophy," *Phronimon*, 18: 114–30.

Chimakonam, Jonathan O. (2017c), "The Question of African Logic: Beyond Apologia and Polemics," in Adeshina Afolayan and Toyin Falola (eds.), *The Palgrave Handbook of African Philosophy*, 106–28, New York: Palgrave Macmillan.

Chimakonam, Jonathan O. (2017d), "African Philosophy and Global Epistemic Injustice," *Journal of Global Ethics*, 13 (2): 120–37, doi: 10.1080/17449626.2017.1364660.

Chimakonam, Jonathan O. (2018a), "The Demise of Philosophical Universalism and the Rise of Conversational Thinking in Contemporary African Philosophy," in Edwin E. Etieyibo (ed.), *Method, Substance and the Future of African Philosophy*, 135–59, New York: Palgrave.

Chimakonam, Jonathan O. (2018b), "The Philosophy of African Logic: A Consideration of Ezumezu Paradigm," in Jeremy Horne (ed.), *Philosophical Perceptions on Logic and Order*, 96–121, Hershey, PA: IGI Global.

Chimakonam, Jonathan O. (2019), *Ezumezu: A System of Logic for African Philosophy and Studies*, Cham: Springer.

Chimakonam Jonathan O. (2020a), "Ezumezu as a Formal System," in Jonathan O. Chimakonam (ed.), *Logic and African Philosophy: Seminal Essays in African Systems of Thought*, 297–320, Delaware: Vernon Press.

Chimakonam Jonathan O. (2020b), "Why Can't There Be (an) African Logic? Clarifying the Squall for a Cultural Logic," in Jonathan O. Chimakonam (ed.), *Logic and African Philosophy: Seminal Essays in African Systems of Thought*, 245–58, Delaware: Vernon Press.

Dottin, Paul (2019), "Sino-African Philosophy: A Re-'Constructive Engagement'", *Comparative Philosophy*, 10 (1): 38–66.

Egbai, Uti. O. (2018), "Why African Philosophers Should Build Systems: An Exercise in Conversational Thinking," *Filosofia Theoretica: Journal of African Philosophy, Culture and Religions*, 7 (1): 34–52.

Egbai, Uti O., and Chimakonam Jonathan O. (2019), "Why Conversational Thinking Could Be an Alternative Method of Intercultural Philosophy," *Journal of Intercultural Studies*, 40 (2): 172–89.

Enyimba, Maduka (2021), "Moderating Conservatism and Radicalism in Post-colonial Sub-Saharan Africa: Some Objections and Clarifications through Conversational Thinking," in Edwin Etieyibo, Obvious Katsaura, and Mucha Musemwa (eds.), *Africa's Radicalisms and Conservatisms: Politics, Poverty, Marginalization and Education*, vol. 1, 31–44, Leiden: Brill.

Enyimba, Maduka (2019), "Sustainable Inclusive Development through Conversational Thinking: The Case for Africa-China Relations," *Filosofia Theoretica: Journal of African Philosophy, Culture and Religion*, 8 (1): 1–20.

Fleming, Jesse (2003), "Comparative Philosophy: Its Aims and Methods," *Journal of Chinese Philosophy*, 30 (2): 259–70.

Krishna, Daya (1986), "Comparative Philosophy: What It Is and What It Ought to Be," *Diogenes*, 34 (136): 58–69.

Littlejohn, Ronnie, "Comparative Philosophy," *Internet Encyclopedia of Philosophy*. Available online: https://iep.utm.edu/comparat (accessed April 30, 2021).

Łukasiewicz, J. (1970), "On Three-Valued Logic," in L. Borkowski (ed.), *Selected works by Jan Łukasiewicz*, 87–8, Amsterdam: North-Holland.

Metz, Thaddeus (2020), "Recent Work in African Philosophy: Its Relevance beyond the Continent," *Mind*, 72: 1–22.

Mou, Bo (2006), "How Constructive Engagement of Davidson's Philosophy and Chinese Philosophy Is Possible: A Theme Introduction," in Bo Mou (ed.), *Davidson's Philosophy and Chinese Philosophy: Constructive Engagement*, 9–19, Leiden: Brill.

Mou, Bo (2010), "On Constructive-Engagement Strategy of Comparative Philosophy: A Journal Theme Introduction," *Comparative Philosophy*, 1 (1): 1–32.

Mou, Bo (2013), "Constructive Engagement of Analytic and Continental Approaches beyond the Western Tradition," in Bo Mou and Richard Tieszen (eds.), *Constructive Engagement of Analytic and Continental Approaches in Philosophy from the Vantage Point of Comparative Philosophy*, 147–62, Leiden: Brill.

Mou, Bo (2018) "Constructive-Engagement Strategy of Doing Philosophy of Language Comparatively in View of Chinese Language and Chinese Philosophy: A Theme Introduction," in Bo Mou (ed.), *Philosophy of Language, Chinese language, Chinese Philosophy: Constructive Engagement*, 1–45, Leiden: Brill.

Nweke, Victor C. A. (2015), "David A. Oyedola and the Imperative to Disambiguate the Term 'African Philosopher': A Conversation from the Standpoint of the Conversational School of Philosophy (CSP)," *Filosofia Theoretica: Journal of African Philosophy, Culture and Religions*, 4 (2): 94–9.

Nweke, Victor C. A. (2016), "Mesembe Edet's Conversation with Innocent Onyewuenyi: An Exposition of the Significance of the Method and Canons of Conversational Philosophy," *Filosofia Theoretica: Journal of African Philosophy, Culture and Religions*, 5 (2): 54–72.

Ofuasia, Emmanuel (2019), "Unveiling Ezumezu Logic as a Framework for Process Ontology and Yorùbá Ontology," *Filosofia Theoretica: Journal of African Philosophy, Culture and Religions*, 8 (2): 63–83.

Ofuasia, Emmanuel (2021), "Review of Ezumezu: A System of Logic for African Philosophy and Studies," *International Journal of African Renaissance Studies*, https://doi.org/10.1080/18186874.2021.1889926 (accessed April 2, 2021).

Panikkar, Raimundo (1988), "What Is Comparative Philosophy Comparing?," in Gerald James Larson and Eliot Deutsch (eds.), *Interpreting across Boundaries: New Essays in Comparative Philosophy*, 116–36, Princeton, NJ: Princeton University Press.

Said, Edward (1978), *Orientalism*, London: Routledge & Kegan Paul.

Said, Edward (1993), *Culture and Imperialism*, New York: Knopf & Random House.

Smid, Robert. W. (2009), *Methodologies of Comparative Philosophy: The Pragmatist and Process Traditions*, Albany, NY: SUNY Press.

Tavernaro-Haidarian, Leyla (2018), "Deliberative Epistemology: Towards an Ubuntu-based Epistemology that Accounts for a Prior Knowledge and Objective Truth," *South African Journal of Philosophy*, 37 (2): 229–42.

Weber, Ralph (2013), "'How to Compare?'—On the Methodological State of Comparative Philosophy," *Philosophy Compass*, 8 (7): 593–603.

Weber, Ralph (2014), "Comparative Philosophy and the Tertium: Comparing What with What, and in What Respect?," *Dao: A Journal of Comparative Philosophy*, 13: 151–71.

Wolff, Christian (1981), "Von den fruchtbaren Begriffen," in Christian Wolff (ed.), *Gesammelte Werke*, 1. Abt. Deutsche Schriften, vol. 21.2, Hildesheim: Georg Olms.

Epilogue

Steven Burik, Robert Smid, and Ralph Weber

One of the primary purposes of this volume has been to capture the present methodological moment in the history of comparative philosophy. This collection of essays from a wide array of contemporary comparativists reflects on the methodological challenges of our day. Although hardly exhaustive, it provides a snapshot of the present moment, a collective record of sorts, representing many of the shared assumptions, live disagreements, and anticipated possibilities for our field of study in the early part of the twenty-first century. Yet in this century, such documentation is hardly enough: the careful record-keeping of modern bureaucracies and a prolific publication industry are now complemented by nearly incomprehensible redundancies in electronic storage, veritably ensuring that even the smallest developments will be permanently recorded for all posterity. What is necessary for our time is, as Rorty (following Hegel) put it, "to capture our time in thought" (Rorty 2006: 85). It requires stepping back from the data of the present moment and attempting to provide it with an overlay of intelligibility, an overlay that not only accounts for the prevailing features of that data but also provides some indication of its directionality. If Hegel's quip about the owl of Minerva is true, then this is surely a fool's errand, but it is one that is nonetheless necessary for the ongoing development of the field.[1]

The State of the Field

Fortunately, it does not take much speculation to observe several key facets for such an overlay across the constituent chapters of this volume. There are several themes that are raised across these chapters, and while not all themes are addressed in all chapters and the themes are not always addressed in the same way or with the same conclusions, they are nonetheless sufficiently prominent as to indicate a significant point of engagement for the present moment in thought. In what follows, we have highlighted just a few of the most prominent, enterprising, and provocative themes, after which we shall try to sketch the direction we envision for comparative philosophy moving forward.

The first and most obvious theme that unites almost all contributors lies in the explicit agreement that one of the major tasks of effective comparison is to leave behind, as much as possible, the lingering presumption of Western priority in the history of comparative philosophy. This presumption can take many forms and is found, for example, in the exclusive, excessive, or inappropriate use of Western philosophical categories, or in the words and phrases chosen for translation efforts, but also and more generally in the things that are considered to be properly philosophical and thus worthy of comparison. As a simple example, Western philosophy has been heavily guided by the Socratic "what is?" question: the question about essence, about how to accurately describe something. This focus has made its way readily into comparative philosophy itself, as demonstrated by the persistent drive to define comparative philosophy (and thus to delineate what "counts" and what does not), as well as by the insistence that non-Western traditions ask similar questions and provide similarly modeled answers. But one can also think of the longstanding focus in Western thought on dualism in its many forms, such as in the pairs sensible/intelligible, mind/matter, public/private, individual/collective, finite/infinite, mortal/immortal, and many other forms. Such dualisms are also usually understood as dichotomies, with a clear preference for one side of the pair over the other. While we do not claim that such divisions are not found elsewhere, or that such distinctions are wrong per se, these focal points of Western thought need not be present in the same intensity in other ways of doing philosophy, or could be present but addressed differently. A tradition of Western thought that overemphasizes such dualistic distinctions and takes a clear hierarchical approach to them, runs a very real risk of not being able to accommodate other ways of thought, since such dualisms are ingrained not only in Western thought but also in its vocabulary.

The realization that Western biases need to be overcome or minimized comes with the call to open (comparative) philosophy to multiple conceptual schemes or approaches, and while this is laudable, care should be taken to avoid some opposite dangers. For example, the principled rejection of Western philosophical categories might bring with it a turn to everyday language, which then risks making non-Western philosophy look mundane and incapable of complex thought, and the comparisons contrived and unclear. So, what language should we use? If we play language down too much, it becomes bland; if we play it up too much, it becomes too particular. And this is not the only problem. The refusal to use Western categories could obscure strong similarities among traditions that such categories are best suited to highlight.

This goes hand in hand with the risks of exoticizing and even romanticizing the non-West, as well as ignoring important challenges to "Western categories" from within "Western philosophy" itself. The continued prominence of structuring comparative discourse in terms of "West" and "non-West" (immense abstractions, like "North" and "South") might help to put the spotlight on the latter, but it might also stand in the way of decentering the former. It could have the effect of essentializing cultural differences, allowing those differences to stand as equivalent to philosophical differences. Our contributors seem generally aware that a careful and site-specific balance must be struck here. Perhaps, if the problem lies with the exclusive, excessive, or inappropriate use of Western philosophical categories, then no principled rejection of those categories might be warranted; rather, what is required is striking a balance between technical language and ordinary language when articulating each position and creating a pluralist scene where some might continue to use Western philosophical categories while others would not—without making the efforts of the latter somehow less philosophical simply by the self-reflective and considered rejection of these categories. This is an explicit theme in the contributions from Neville and Ames, for example, while it is more implicit in the contribution from Ganeri. We find it to be a relevant consideration across both the contributions in this volume and across the field as a whole.

Related to this, a second theme that runs across the chapters in this volume is the matter of translation. This equally important theme is central to comparative philosophy. Although positions on this differ largely amongst our contributors and in the field of comparative philosophy in general, translation is indeed (even if sometimes only implicitly) on everybody's mind. Some of our contributors take a very strong stand for translation, going so far as to call it a necessary endeavor (Freschi calls it a litmus test, Diagne argues that one *must* speak multiple languages in order to do comparative philosophical work), while others take a less strong position (Chakrabarti and Weber argue for the philosophical value of polyglotism). And Soldatenko, for example, argues that the creativity involved in comparative philosophy is more important than translation. In our view, competence in multiple languages, while valuable, is not a necessary condition for doing comparative philosophy, and certainly not a sufficient one.

The fault lines for this difference in emphasis appear to run along contrasting yet complementary accounts of translation: as "coordinating between two (or more) languages" and/or what might be called "finding new ways to communicate ideas." Both accounts are inherently interpretive, even if such interpretation is only readily celebrated in the second account. More importantly, both dimensions are arguably present in any act of translation (at least, if one allows for sufficiently broad definitions of what constitutes a "language" and how much novelty is necessary for something to be considered "a new way"). If this is the case, then—as Ames suggests—a literal translation is not only impossible but perhaps also undesirable.

The questions of what translation constitutes, how central it is to the comparative task, and just how riven it is with interpretation remain live issues within comparative philosophy, and in this respect the essays in this volume appear to reflect the broader diversity of the field. The differences in how these questions are answered may also reflect the particular contexts out of which they arise. One who has spent a career disestablishing misleading linguistic translations may be particularly well attuned to the dangers such translations pose, while one who has spent their career destabilizing longstanding cultural assumptions within a single linguistic tradition may be better attuned to the pervasive role of interpretation in any linguistic act. Similarly, one who has benefited from inhabiting the lingua franca of their time will likely see the question of language quite differently than those who have been persistently obligated to present their ideas in a second or third language. These differences notwithstanding, our contributors seem to agree that a balance must be sought in each case (even if they disagree on what that balance is), and that concepts and terminology used must be carefully explained and justified. It also seems that many of our contributors are in favor of stretching the host language to accommodate the target language's idiosyncrasies as much as possible. This stretching might take the form of neologisms, nonstandard word use, or the introduction of foreign terms and ideas into the host language. These practices are hardly unprecedented in comparative philosophy, but the ongoing concerns with translation suggest that such practices can only be a starting point and must be pressed a great deal further as the practice of comparison continues to develop.

Directly related to the prior two themes, and in part emerging out of them, a third theme that surfaced among several of the essays pertained to the struggle between the need to strive for objectivity and the realization that we are always situated in our comparative endeavors (or, what might be called the struggle between neutrality and interpretation). This theme is present, for example, in van Brakel and Ma's argument for quasi-universals, in Ames's and Jullien's arguments for generalizations while eschewing essentialism, in Diagne's arguments (following Merleau-Ponty) for "lateral universality," and in Smid's challenge to Smith's prioritization of "discovery" over "invention" in comparison. It is also evident in Neville's argument for what he calls "objective comparisons" and, perhaps in its strongest form, in Chimakonam and Chimakonam's argument for a neutral method in conversational thinking. A question relevant to this theme, but not directly addressed in these chapters (although Soldatenko and Burik come close), is whether neutrality is something that should be sought in comparative philosophy, or whether it is only a trapping of the philosophical obsession in some traditions with disinterested explication and description, and therefore not necessarily desirable within comparative philosophy.

The last overarching theme we have identified (again following from and connected to the previous ones) involves the tension between separating approaches and globalizing approaches. Comparative philosophy can seemingly go in two different directions: whereas some contributors favor an approach that sees non-Western traditions as different alternatives that need to disentangle themselves from the dominant center (mostly the West), others are more concerned with seeking hybrid ways of thinking generated specifically by the comparative efforts. For example, whereas Ganeri in his contribution to this volume seeks to provide an Indian alternative to Greek classicism, Soldatenko espouses more of a hybrid form of comparative thought. Most decolonial approaches would fall within the disentangling camp, while most proponents of fusion philosophy would fall into the globalizing camp, although such associations are neither absolute nor invariable. The two different approaches we highlight here should of course be understood as lying on a spectrum, where overlaps can exist, and where scholars can take a different approach in different circumstances. For example, in other works Ganeri has often taken an approach closer to fusion philosophy than the one in this volume might lead readers to believe.

This tension can also be found in issues regarding the definition of comparative philosophy, with its scope, depth, and stated or unstated goals all up for discussion at least partly because of this tension. It remains a challenge to strike a balance between distinguishing philosophical traditions enough to identify them meaningfully as separate traditions and integrating such differences into a wider discourse that would be able to at the same time accommodate and do justice to them, and this challenge has yielded a wide variety of responses. From van Brakel and Ma's ideas of family resemblance to the conversational approach of Chimakonam and Chimakonam; from Ames's, Neville's, and Jullien's concerns with levels and appropriateness of generalizations to Weber and Chakrabarti's ideas about fusion philosophy; from

Soldatenko's implicit question as to how different a philosophical tradition needs to be to warrant "comparative" philosophy, to Chimakonam and Chimakonam's insistence that a tradition needs to be quite different to warrant the comparative approach; and from Burik's argument that methodological claims should be kept minimal to Smid's challenge for comparativists to become proficient in multiple methods, these are issues that make us think that in Freschi's terminology, comparative philosophy is indeed a struggle, not only at the level of the individual philosopher but also when viewed as a collective endeavor. In our view, a vital component of comparative philosophy, especially as it concerns methodology, entails trying to account for and understand that struggle as a whole, including but not limited to—and certainly not defined by—one's own location relative to the broader array.

And it is within that struggle that we must now turn to our defense of pluralism, which will be based on our understanding of these major themes. Above we have noted several times that there is a plurality of positions on the issues or themes we have identified—both among the essays in this volume and in the field more generally. In other words, there is what can be called a *descriptive* pluralism. But this does not tell us anything about the desirability of any such pluralism in the field. We want to ask the question of whether there *should be* a plurality of methodological positions—that is, a *normative* pluralism—or whether this is only a symptom of the lack of sufficient development in the field.

A Case for Pluralism

What initially brought the three of us together to produce this volume was our shared interest not only in methodological issues as such but also with the many diverse ways that comparative philosophy is and has been practiced. Not surprisingly, then, the three of us maintain a commitment to pluralism in comparative philosophy, which is readily apparent in each of our respective chapters in this volume. It should be noted that the pluralism that we endorse is not identical, but our positions overlap enough that it came to inform many of our deliberations about both this volume and the task of comparison more generally. It constitutes what might be called a "meta-pluralism"—a pluralism of pluralisms, if you will—substantive enough to inform our discourse but not so restrictive as to undermine itself. It is our shared conviction that some sort of pluralism is necessary to make sense not only of this volume but also of the diverse array of what comparative philosophy entails today. Given that a commitment to pluralism is by no means universal, much less the commitment to any specific variety of pluralism, we deemed it a worthwhile exercise to attempt, as somewhat discordant methodological pluralists, to provide an argument for why pluralism is our preferred option, followed by a rough sketch of what such a pluralism should entail.

First, we argue that while it is true that we have so far merely provided a description of pluralism currently prevalent within the field of comparative philosophy, this actually suggests that most scholars who really engage with the question of methodology on a deeper level find that the only viable alternative is indeed pluralism. We are of course aware that not all scholars in the field are committed to pluralism, and we are also aware of the fact that some might say that we are mistaking an "is" for an "ought" here. But we would argue that in our specific time, with its issues of decolonization, the struggle with nihilism and relativism, and the abandonment of grand narratives, indeed the only tenable position is one of well-thought-out pluralism. We would also highlight that for any author convinced of the correctness of his/her approach, there is another one equally convinced of an opposite approach, and both of them seem to have a point. If this is thought through on a meta-level, surely this means that, logically, a methodological pluralism is the only way forward for comparative philosophy, at least for anyone who would look beyond their own particular position to account for the broader whole (something that seems intrinsic to the comparative task itself).

Second, we note the disciplinary challenges that have been raised within the practice of comparative philosophy, which call into question the constancy, coherence, and universality of the discipline of philosophy as such. Because disciplinary definitions of philosophy have historically emerged out of Western philosophy, non-Western traditions have often had to adapt, contort, or even redefine themselves to be taken as philosophically significant—struggles that seem to us to run against the grain of comparative engagement. Challenges *to* the discipline as historically formulated should be taken no less seriously than challenges *by* the discipline as historically formulated, and we do not see any better way to remain open to all such challenges than through a pluralistic outlook. Of course, such an openness to disciplinary challenges raises very practical questions about how comparative philosophy can be integrated into traditional philosophy departments. That is, does embracing pluralism relegate comparative philosophy to something more like "area studies"? To answer this question we look back to the history of philosophy itself. Philosophy started out as pluralist, as the early philosophers (not only in the ancient Greek world, but in many other localities as well) were what we would now call interdisciplinary. If we restrict ourselves for a moment to the history of Western philosophy, a clear trend can then be seen in the constant narrowing through the branching off of different segments from the mother discipline, leading to the proliferation of disciplines as we know them now. We will have more to say on this increased narrowing of the disciplines and interdisciplinarity further on, but here we may seriously wonder whether what is now narrowly defined as "real" philosophy (mainly analytic philosophy), has not along the way of this history relinquished too much of its former broadness in scope. While we do not want our position to be understood as a call to return philosophy to some glorious past as an overarching mother discipline, we do advocate "returning" to a vision of philosophy as the more diverse and less exclusive practice that it used to be—and, in at least some quarters, continues to be. If philosophy departments are to retain or regain their relevance to society in a globalized world, then they need to be able to think and communicate across those largely artificial boundaries created by the development of separate disciplines, which would require a commitment to pluralism. For philosophy (and that includes comparative philosophy) this means it needs to make a shift from the history of continuously narrowing itself to "real" philosophy, and thereby relinquishing much of its breadth, to employing the widest range of possible tools at its disposal. This is a point we will return to further anon when offering our version of what pluralism should look like in comparative philosophy.

Third, we have to answer the question of whether taking a pluralist stance is the best approach to meaningfully engage other philosophical traditions, which may or may not be pluralistic themselves. Two things can be said about this. For one, we believe that a pluralist approach takes more seriously the fact that traditions are not static or monolithic, but rather living and moving entities. Insisting methodologically on approaching a given tradition from a single method or standpoint significantly reduces the rich and various ways of thinking within and about that tradition and limits its possible contributions to philosophy in the wider sense. Additionally, our commitment to pluralism is decidedly methodological. Whether the plurality of traditions is in fact irreducible or whether the apparent irreducibility is only a function of the incomplete development of the field is arguably an empirical question; while positions on the issue can be reasonably entertained, we do not find there to be enough evidence to decide either way. To say that our pluralism is methodological is to claim that, under the circumstances, remaining open to all possibilities is the only reasonable response, even if one commits most of one's creative energies to one or another of those possibilities. Thus, while methodological pluralism can fully account for all traditions, including those that are not pluralist, the same cannot be said of approaches that are not pluralist.

Fourth, any attempt at defending pluralism needs to defend against the accusation of relativism. While it may seem that, in pluralism, "anything goes," this is to forget that pluralism assumes a coherence in subject matter to which the plurality of possible positions are related. That is, there is something "relative to" which the plurality is a plurality, and that something has a relative constancy to it that gives its subject matter a reasonable coherence. The difference between our position and relativism is that, in the latter, what anything is "relative to" is always open, and has no broader coherence. The pluralism that we envision does not and should not resort to any unshifting foundations, but acknowledges and relies on the relatively stable yet always malleable grounds of its actual practice at any given time. Two further clarifications are in order here. On the one hand, there must be some organizing principle for this plurality, if any relatively stable coherence is to be claimed. We find van Brakel and Ma's adaptation of Wittgenstein's notion of family resemblance helpful here insofar as it emphasizes the meaningful connections among its members rather than any "essence" to the overarching family itself; to remain meaningful, such connections cannot be infinitely expanded, but must retain some significant connection to many or most of the other existing members. We also find Burik's notion of infrastructure instructive in this regard: an infrastructure only has meaning from different points; there is no center, but it derives its meaning exactly from connecting those different points. Other possibilities include the quasi-universals, provisional generalizations, polycentricity, and conversational thinking described in other contributions in this volume. These are all attempts to hold comparative philosophy together without giving it an essence. On the other hand, there must be some way of accounting for the purported coherence at any given time. Philosophy may be ever-changing, but it has never been without any definition at all. The problem with defining philosophy—whether pluralistically or otherwise—is not that it has had no definition at all but that it has always had multiple competing definitions. How is a pluralist to choose among those possibilities without at the same time undermining itself? If it is family resemblance, for example, what determines the contours of the family? Which connections are meaningful enough to constitute a roughly coherent whole, and which are left outside of the family? As both Burik and Smid argue in their chapters, this question is answered by the history and present of actual practice within the discipline. That is, while the discipline may be a social and cultural construction, it is precisely that construction that—at any given time—lends coherence to its associated practice. Philosophy is whatever a significant proportion of philosophers take to be of interest at any given time, where such interests are understood in connection with the broader history of such interests within the discipline. In their contribution, Chakrabarti and Weber point out the problems around who counts as a philosopher and who is considered an insider to the conversation of philosophy, and how this is itself not mainly a philosophical but a political question. We would add that, while the discipline has, for most of its history, been a Western construction and has construed its family relations accordingly, it is entirely appropriate that comparative philosophy—as a constitutive part of that family—is continuingly challenging those bounds both retrospectively and prospectively.

Finally, pluralism arguably provides the most effective balance between the extremes of objectivity and subjectivity. Unmitigated objectivity, while worth striving toward in many cases, is itself impossible to achieve, and yet a resort to mere subjectivity is unsatisfactory. The only reasonable response is to take responsibility for one's interpretations, acknowledging the mixture of subjectivity and objectivity that they entail and justifying them provisionally on shared epistemological grounds. One need not be a pluralist to do so. Where pluralism gains its advantage is in accounting for the diversity of such approaches as a whole, each one being at least partially a function of its own subjectivity. A non-pluralistic approach can only be reductive, constraining other positions to the contours of one's own subjective perspective—its criteria, its values, its conceptual scheme, and so on—and as such it is implicitly dismissive. While this may be satisfactory for a merely parochial scholar, it is insufficient for the comparative task; indeed, it runs counter to it.

A similar case can be made with respect to the extremes of excessive universalization and excessive particularization, which pluralism can mediate in terms of provisional generalization. One cannot compare without generalizations; one cannot even translate or interpret without generalizations, and claiming to do so only obscures those generalizations. But what is important for us is that the content of these generalizations need not be static or absolute; they can be provisional, historicist, and contextual. While our efforts should avoid as much as possible anything that would distort the ideas of the "other," this must come with the realization that objectivity itself is not something we can expect to reach. We are indeed trying to understand different ways of thinking in and of themselves, but we are also trying to understand what they can say *to us*, here and now. Comparative philosophy needs to be able to do both if it is to maintain its credibility and its relevance, and it must do this in multiple ways simultaneously as its practitioners continue to engage different particularities from different perspectives and aim to present their findings to a coherent community of fellow comparativists. We do not see how it is possible to conceive of this diverse and simultaneous struggle without a methodological commitment to pluralism.

The Shape of Future Pluralist Comparative Philosophy

If we take for granted that methodological pluralism is a necessary characteristic of comparative philosophy, this opens the question of what such pluralism should entail. Perhaps appropriately, not even pluralism is a single thing; there are many varieties of pluralism, such that not even pluralists agree on what it should entail. In what follows, we offer some indications of the methodological pluralism that we take to be most appropriate to the comparative task.

First, we maintain that methodological pluralism should be thoroughly interdisciplinary. In fact, our own commitment to methodological pluralism has been reinforced by the softening of disciplinary boundaries over the last several decades and the associated rise in interdisciplinary studies and their manifold offerings in terms of methodology. We take this development to be not merely a superficial one but a recognition of the social and cultural construction of disciplines and of the inherent connectivity among what can be known. This being the case, the field of comparative philosophy must be informed by other disciplines than philosophy in at least two respects. On the one hand, like philosophy more generally, it must take into account relevant contributions from other disciplines; while in some rarified instances philosophy can be undertaken solely within its own disciplinary boundaries, more often than not it will intersect with the social, political, economic, religious, linguistic, psychological, and other contexts out of which it arises, and to address these in an informed and credible way, it will need to draw on the disciplines who take them as their primary subject matter. These include, but are not limited to, sociology, political science, anthropology, history, religious studies, theology, and philology. Philosophy must—and, increasingly, is—already rising to that challenge; given its tendency to challenge, broaden, and redefine the bounds of what constitutes philosophy and its proper methods, the onus should be all the more on comparative philosophy to take on that challenge. On the other hand, insofar as those disciplines themselves entail an explicitly comparative dimension, comparative philosophy must both contribute to and draw from the broader efforts at comparison among and across the disciplines. This is true above all else for comparative methodology, since while the content of comparisons may differ among disciplines, the task of comparison is largely held in common. This interdisciplinary dimension presents both an opportunity and a challenge for comparative philosophers: it is an opportunity insofar as it opens a vast array of additional resources for comparison, but a challenge insofar as it necessarily extends beyond the possible expertise of a single comparativist. Even extremely gifted and established scholars will not know it all. The real task of comparative philosophy thus lies in making it possible that all these different scholars from different traditions and disciplines, each with their own interests and expertise, are able to meaningfully discuss their issues with each other. Several of the essays in this volume have sought to make such interdisciplinary connections (e.g., Neville, Diagne, Freschi, and Smid), and we take these connections to be more than merely incidental. We believe such connections to be necessary and anticipate that such connections will only become more commonplace and integral as the field progresses.

Of course, this is not to dissolve disciplinary boundaries in their entirety. Philosophy still has its own contents and methods, at least insofar as they are defined by scholars within the discipline itself. However, recalling the status of the disciplines as artifacts and acknowledging its fluidity over the course of its history, we anticipate that the content and methods of philosophy will continue to change over time. Further, we anticipate that this will only intensify as a more global philosophy has an impact on determining what "counts" as philosophy. Comparative philosophy has already challenged the content and methods of what is considered philosophy on multiple occasions over the past century, and those challenges are far from abating. In this connection, it is worth noting that comparative philosophy faces many of the same challenges as interdisciplinary studies, especially as it pertains to its own self-definition among quickly broadening and changing categories. For example, questions pertaining to the differences between "interdisciplinary," "cross-disciplinary," "multidisciplinary," and "transdisciplinary," who lays claim to which monikers, what differences they entail, and what they all have in common are not far removed from debates within our own field about whether it is best understood as "comparative philosophy," "intercultural philosophy," "fusion philosophy," "post-comparative philosophy," "world philosophy," "cosmopolitan philosophy," or some other term, who uses which term (and how), what differences they entail, and what they all have in common. Both contexts entail a certain commitment to pluralism which refuses to allow its subject matter to be defined by a single methodological perspective and which recognizes that there are different ways of looking at a problem and that different perspectives generate different priorities. At the same time, however, both contexts struggle with the challenge of how to navigate that plurality. In the context of comparative philosophy, this challenge finds expression in questions such as the following: what is comparative philosophy? Is it one kind of philosophy, along with other kinds? If so, how does it relate to philosophy more generally? Should it bring greater coherence to philosophy or greater dissonance? What is its relation to related demarcations, such as culture, geography, or rhetoric?

It is our position that, while it is constitutive of comparative philosophy to posit and consider answers to these questions, it would be counterproductive for one to insist on any such answer. While there is ample substance in each of the possibilities to provide for productive discourse about them, there does not seem to be enough to merit sufficient confidence in any one of them to dismiss the others—at least, not if all of the possibilities are considered outside of the specific context out of which they arrived. While some believe that there is enough to merit such confidence, we find their belief to be undermined not only by the lack of such confidence among other pluralists but also by the comparable confidences of those equally assured of their own, opposing positions. This is not to denigrate that value of any of these positions; rather, it is to recognize, as Connolly did, the wisdom in Berlin's quip that "not all good things are compatible, still less all the ideals of mankind."[2] For this reason, as pluralists, while we celebrate the diversity that is to be found within the discipline, we would resist any attempts to essentialize what philosophy is, and we would similarly resist any similar attempts in the field of comparative philosophy and/or its method(s). The task for the present generation of comparativists, as defined by its postcolonial context, should include discussions informed by as wide as possible an array of what "counts" as philosophy—comparative or otherwise—without so stretching the boundaries that the term itself becomes meaningless.

At the same time, as suggested above, the content of philosophy—again, comparative or otherwise—cannot be left without definition. To do so is, as Jullien suggests, to "giv[e] up on philosophy from the start" (p. 73 in this volume). In this respect, the history of interdisciplinarity presents a cautionary tale: if the methods and subject matter of these category-expanding exercises are not given at least some definition, the entire enterprise can lose any sense of coherence or continuity and either collapse into itself or, not without some irony, spin off into simply one more of the subsets that it originally sought to study. The key question, then, is this: how much fleshing out of the relevant subject matter, methods, or associated monikers is appropriate for comparative philosophy, and at what point does this violate pluralist commitments and resort to mere parochialism? We hold that this balance is best achieved by maintaining a minimal set of sufficiently broad terms without requiring them to have narrow or precise definitions, and leaving the rest to the ongoing deliberations of the academy more generally. Thus, for example, we take "comparative philosophy" to be an acceptable moniker for the field as a whole, despite the unnecessarily narrow definitions that have been ascribed to it. We may also take such terms as "intercultural philosophy" or "fusion philosophy" to be more precise descriptions for particular methods of comparative philosophy, but we see little use in proliferating such specialized terms at the expense of the more general ones. We find "comparative philosophy" to be a sufficiently broad and historically rooted moniker for that resemblance and recommend leaving such general terms broadly defined. While we would encourage any attempts to provide greater specification of what it can entail, we would resist any attempts to lay claim to what it must entail. In our experience, comparative philosophy, as a decidedly broad and nontechnical term, is simply too open-ended to support any such claims. This implies of course that the overarching category is not set in stone. Over time social practice might simply see it recede into the background when enough practitioners stop using it and another label comes to take the pride of place. Any label will be problematic and will have reificationary and potentially hegemonic ramifications, all too much focus on labeling the field in this or that way might undercut the pluralism that sustains it. Again, a balance between an ongoing critical discussion of the label (including its eventual rejection) and of doing one's philosophical work without having to be concerned about doing it under the right label should be struck.

Second, this pluralism must be conducive to some general understanding of its overall dimensions if it is to be of any use in informing and driving the ongoing development of the field. Of course, the very notion of pluralism would seem to resist the imposition of any overarching framework as there are multiple possible accounts of such pluralism and there is no reason to believe any such framework would have any enduring stability. This being the case, any such account can only be provisional, with its value determined by its ability to provide a sense of the diverse and irreducible whole. Still, if broken down to the mere mechanics of a comparison, as generally understood in the present context, perhaps some axes of the current pluralism can be indicated.

Few would object to the following presentation of a comparison as implicitly or explicitly at work when engaging in comparative philosophy, even if this presentation is not exhaustive of its full breadth in comparative philosophy: someone is comparing two or more objects of comparison (i.e., the comparanda) along one or more respects (see Weber 2014; Chakrabarti and Weber 2015). Different practitioners of comparative philosophy usually lay different emphases on the importance and role of the comparativist in this endeavor, and they stress the comparanda in different ways (see Weber 2013: 4–6):

1. De-emphasize comparativist, emphasize both comparanda: Some conceptions of comparative philosophy accordingly come to de-emphasize the role of the comparativist, almost trying to take him or her out of the equation as much as possible, and then often emphasize both comparanda. One can imagine a philologically informed comparison of some aspect pertaining to ancient Greek and Indian philosophy on the basis of a well-defined set of texts and with the claim that any other researcher scrutinizing the same texts to do the same comparison in view of the same respects would by and large come to similar-enough conclusions.

Many other conceptions of comparative philosophy emphasize the role of the comparativist. In one or another way, they accommodate and account for the comparativist's specific positionality in view of the comparative task ahead. Instead of reducing the role of the comparativist to a minimum, they make it part of the determination of which comparanda receives more emphasis. Often, there is a direct relation between one comparandum being considered closer to the comparativist than the other.

2. Emphasize comparativist and the one comparandum somehow considered not to be "one's own": Some emphasize the comparandum thought to be exactly not the one of the comparativist, in some important sense therefore constituting "the other" for the comparativist. One might imagine someone at a French university comparing some aspect of European and African philosophy in order to foreground how some account within African philosophy has an attractive version of that aspect. The formulation of the aspect within European philosophy might be quickly summed up, while the main emphasis comes to lie on the aspect within African philosophy.

The inverse is also an active possibility:

3. Emphasize comparativist and the one comparandum somehow considered to be "one's own": An example would be a Chinese philosopher engaged in comparing an aspect of Chinese and European philosophy, making instrumentalist (which does not mean unserious) use of European philosophy in order to foreground the account that Chinese philosophy has to offer. European philosophy would thus come to stand for a detour that is considered necessary for some or another reason, and which could both be positively or negatively connoted.

While these two options seem to make an instrumentalist use of one comparandum, there is also the option of being instrumentalist across the board:

4. Emphasize comparativist, de-emphasize all comparanda: Here, the comparativist is emphasized to the extent of de-emphasizing both comparanda, as no philosophically relevant connection between the context of the comparativist and the contexts within which the comparanda are considered to stand is struck. Fusion philosophers who emphasize the argument that they draw from the comparison and which they come to defend as their argument pursue something along this conception.

The upshot of these different conceptions is that none of them is clearly the only legitimate or effective choice that a comparativist absolutely has to make. These are viable options that are often aligned with specific goals and interests, and that often make choices more or less compelling in terms of which tradition's philosophical categories to employ or whether to rely on translations (and to what extent). Some philosophers pursue the same conception with the same goal in mind over their entire career. Others reserve themselves the right to pursue this conception in one project, that conception in another, and might also pursue different specific goals and interests throughout their career.

There is a pluralism of goals that comparative philosophers pursue with their undertakings. Some are more directly tied to a political agenda, some more concerned with dominantly internal debates that by and large interest and seek to impact the group of comparative philosophers only. In a way that the field still struggles with, the positionality of the individual comparative philosopher or the specific network he or she is engaged in often defines the outlook and evaluation of worthy agendas, philosophical and non-philosophical. Eventually, comparative philosophy is an endeavor that in all of the above options (whether or not the role of the comparativist is emphasized) is largely driven by interest. Although anything can be compared with anything, this does not mean that we should compare just anything. Interests, however, are relative to the people pursuing them. Nothing is intrinsically interesting. We might have discussions over whether something is intrinsically valuable or not, but the concept of interest is clearly relational in that someone has an interest in something. At the level of the field of comparative philosophy, where all these various interests come together in a big jumble of ideas and interests, what counts as an interest within comparative philosophy and what not is perhaps not best determined from a transcendental standpoint, but is a function of discourse within the discipline itself (as Burik argues in his contribution). This take on comparative philosophy thus avoids the relativist dead-end, since it is constitutively grounded in the collective and ongoing life of the discipline.

Against this plurality of emphases and goals, any sort of dogmatist position that would seek to replace this pluralism with one specific set of emphases and one goal would not only seem to estrange a majority of practitioners in contemporary comparative philosophy (thus undercut pluralism, as we see it in the field), but it also would bring the very social practice that sustains the vitality of comparative philosophy to a halt (and thus undercut pluralism, as we should want to see it in the field). There is a fine line running between a dogmatist position as an expression of what one thinks philosophically to be true or right with regard to a specific question in comparative philosophy and one that pronounces the only truth on what the field itself should be about. There is a case to be made (although not everyone will agree) about the former position, but the latter is not so much concerned with a philosophical question but with an anthropological, sociological, political, and even economic question. In other words, philosophy (including comparative philosophy) has a subject matter, but it is also a social practice.

For our meta-level concerns, it is crucial to understand that the many available positions comparative philosophers might adopt with regard to how to place emphasis in a comparison do not in any necessary manner align with a specific goal, but one can follow almost any of the outlined approaches and, at the same time, pursue entirely different goals. The promise of pluralist meta-level engagement with comparative philosophy, as we present it in this volume, is that we encounter and rub against different positionalities, different approaches, and different goals. There is no necessary connection between positionalities, approaches, and goals. Two comparativists with much similar positionality might pursue radically different approaches, and those using the same approach might still seek to achieve very different goals through them. When engaging with comparative philosophy at the pluralist meta-level, we try to figure out and learn how they are legitimate each and if we do not find them legitimate, we would want to make the reasons clear to ourselves why exactly it is that we reject some of them (the point being reasons, not prejudice or gatekeeping or some such thing). Having made our reasons transparent allows us to entertain a self-reflexive stance and understand ourselves against our own positionality (including our own open or hidden, conscious or subconscious agendas).

Finally, we have noted at various points that the pluralism we endorse is a methodological pluralism. This term is multivalent, with several possible meanings; we mean it to be interpreted in two distinct but simultaneous respects. On the one hand, methodological pluralism entails a methodological commitment to pluralism, such that—whether it turns out that reality entails an irreducible plurality or not—the best way to engage the apparent plurality that we encounter is to treat it as such. In fact, that reality does not entail an irreducible plurality is one such position that should continue to be entertained, as long as it is entertained alongside the position that the empirical reality we encounter does entail such a plurality. Methodological pluralism is, in this sense, a provisional philosophical pluralism, operative only so long as the plurality of possibilities continues to resist a unification that would render it no longer a plurality. From the perspective of methodological pluralism, whether such a moment ever arrives is an empirical question, upon which methodological choices in the present moment are in no way contingent.

On the other hand, methodological pluralism also refers to a commitment to a plurality of methods. Just as there is a plurality of traditions, so there is a plurality of methods for comparative philosophy that currently appears intractable. Certainly, one may have good reasons for preferring one method over others, but no set of reasons is currently sufficient to allow for universal assent. This being the case, we maintain that comparative philosophy is best served if comparativists are prepared to employ a wide variety of methods. While sustained attention to a single method may be warranted, insofar as such attention is most conducive to the careful and ongoing refinement of that method, this sustained attention should not be accompanied by an outright dismissal of other methods, let alone ignorance of or indifference toward them. The comparative dimension of comparative philosophy consists of the methods employed, and however comparative philosophers specialize and stake their claims—as, to some extent, they must—it is their responsibility to acknowledge the persisting diversity of those methods and to contribute in their own way to the ongoing deliberation about them. This would entail, for example, an attitude of open-mindedness, acknowledgment of what the alternatives can do, see, or achieve, efforts to keep active conversation going with respect to method, and readiness to give up or alter one's position.

As noted earlier, these two aspects of methodological pluralism do not necessarily implicate one another. It is possible to embrace a methodological commitment to pluralism while employing only a single method to engage that plurality, just as it is possible to champion one tradition, philosophical position, or idiosyncratic standpoint as superior and employ a plurality of comparative methods to demonstrate this. Both of these possibilities would be more engaging than the one-note orchestra of championing a single tradition by means of a single comparative method, but even then they both fall short of the comparative possibilities of an approach that can engage the existing plurality as it appears in both methods and contents. Comparative philosophy exists because there is no uniformity among philosophical traditions, and it is a contested practice because there is no uniformity among its methods. To sidestep either plurality is to sidestep the challenge of comparative philosophy.

This raises the question of what should be expected of any given comparativist. Does being committed to methodological pluralism in the two respects described above require comparativists to be prepared to employ any credible method to any tradition at any given time? Clearly, this is well beyond the realm of possibility for any single comparativist. Not only are philosophers typically required to develop some degree of specialization as part of their professional training, but such specialization is often what allows for the ongoing development of any one tradition or method. As suggested in the introduction, our point is not that there should be no specialization, but rather that such specialization should not be accompanied by a disregard for the broader whole. To be a methodological pluralist is not to forego the possibility of specializing in, endorsing, or consistently engaging one method or tradition, philosophical position, and so on; it is rather to acknowledge that comparative philosophy is most complete when it acknowledges the broader plurality and, collectively, incorporates that acknowledgment into the way comparative philosophy is pursued as a whole.

As for what this means for the future of comparative philosophy, nobody can be certain, but capturing our time in thought includes staking a claim about the directionality of the field as a whole, both as it appears to be heading and as it should be heading. We have argued our case for methodological pluralism, and believe that our moment is one that requires an ongoing and increased commitment to such a pluralism. We would therefore like to end with a vision of comparative philosophy for the future that is self-reflexive to the extent of having created and maintained a more level playing field, that has decentered "Western philosophy," that is polycentric and fused at the same time, and is inclusive without being philosophically conclusive.

Notes

1. Our use of the term "field" is meant to indicate the subject matter and practice of comparative philosophy, as a subset of both philosophy and of comparative studies more generally. It is intended as a contrast to the "discipline" of philosophy, both as it has been defined and as it continues to be redefined. This contrast is meant to highlight at least three points: first, that comparative philosophy is often not recognized as a distinctive or significant part of the discipline of philosophy and must persistently vie for its own legitimacy; second, that it offers a critical global perspective on the discipline, which is both from within and without it; and third, that it ultimately requires looking beyond the boundaries of the discipline, however, it is conceived. Thus, while "field" is meant as a subset of "discipline" as things currently stand, it is also for the time being a critique with the ambition of redefining future philosophy.
2. Quoted from Connolly (2015: 169). The original quote is in Berlin (1998: 238).

References

Berlin, Isaiah (1998), "Two Concepts of Liberty," in Isaiah Berlin (ed.), *The Proper Study of Mankind: An Anthology of Essays*, 191–241, New York: Farrer, Straus and Giroux.

Chakrabarti, Arindam, and Ralph Weber (2015), "Introduction," in Arindam Chakrabarti and Ralph Weber (eds.), *Comparative Philosophy without Borders*, 1–33, New York: Bloomsbury.

Connolly, Tim (2015), *Doing Philosophy Comparatively*, London: Bloomsbury Academic.

Rorty, Richard (2006), *Take Care of Freedom and Truth Will Take Care of Itself: Interviews with Richard Rorty*, ed. with intro. by Eduardo Mendieta, Stanford, CA: Stanford University Press.

Weber, Ralph (2013), "A Stick Which May Be Grabbed on Either Side: Sino-Hellenic Studies in the Mirror of Comparative Philosophy," *International Journal of the Classical Tradition*, 20 (1): 1–14.

Weber, Ralph (2014), "Comparative Philosophy and the *Tertium*: Comparing What with What, and in What Respect?," *Dao: A Journal of Comparative Philosophy*, 13: 151–71.

Contributors

Roger T. Ames is Humanities Chair Professor at Peking University, Academic Director of the Peking University Berggruen Research Center, and Professor Emeritus of Philosophy at the University of Hawai'i. He is the former editor of *Philosophy East & West* and founding editor of *China Review International*. Ames has authored several interpretative studies of Chinese philosophy and culture, almost all of which are now available in Chinese translation, including his philosophical translations of Chinese canonical texts. He has most recently been engaged in compiling the two companion volumes: *A Sourcebook in Classical Confucian Philosophy* and *A Conceptual Lexicon for Classical Confucian Philosophy*.

Steven Burik is Assistant Professor in Philosophy at Singapore Management University. He holds a PhD in comparative philosophy from the National University of Singapore. His research interests are mainly in comparative philosophy, continental philosophy (Heidegger, Derrida), and Chinese philosophy (Daoism). His works include *The End of Comparative Philosophy and the Task of Comparative Thinking* and articles in various journals and books, including *Philosophy East and West*, *Dao*, and *Comparative and Continental Philosophy*.

Arindam Chakrabarti taught at Kolkata, London, Seattle, New Delhi, Stony Brook, New York, and University of Hawaii Manoa, for the past thirty-eight years, after his DPhil at Oxford University under the supervision of Michael Dummett and Peter Strawson. He has edited or authored fourteen books (in English, Sanskrit, and Bengali) and has published more than a hundred papers and reviews in journals or anthologies. Besides *Denying Existence* (1997), his major monograph *Realisms Interlinked: Objects, Subjects and Other Subjects* (2019) has been critically acclaimed. He is currently working on: *The Book of Questions: Indian Philosophical Analysis*, forthcoming from Penguin Random House, India, and a larger book on the moral psychology of emotions.

Amara E. Chimakonam is currently a doctoral student in philosophy at the University of Johannesburg, South Africa. Her research primarily focuses on African philosophy, ethics, world philosophy, bioethics, feminism, philosophy of religion, and political philosophy. As a member of the Conversational Society of Philosophy (CSP), she applies the conversational and interrogational methods in examining these fields from an African perspective. Her thesis is on the idea of transhumanism through an Afro-communitarian lens. She has published and presented research papers in conferences, webinars, colloquia, and workshops on the topics in bioethics, feminism, philosophy of religion, logic, transhumanism, amongst others, from the African point of view.

She recently propounded a personhood-based theory of right action as an African contribution to the field of ethics.

Jonathan O. Chimakonam, PhD, is a senior lecturer at the University of Pretoria, South Africa, and a senior research fellow at the Center for Interdisciplinary and Intercultural Studies (CIIS), Tubingen University, Germany. His teaching and research interests include African philosophy, intercultural/comparative philosophy, logic, environmental ethics, and decolonial thinking. He aims to break new grounds in African philosophy by formulating a system that unveils new concepts and opens new vistas for thought (conversational philosophy); a method that can drive theories in African philosophy and beyond (conversational thinking); and a system of logic that grounds both (Ezumezu). His articles/books have appeared in several refereed and accredited international journals and presses. He is a member of several professional bodies including the Conversational Society of Philosophy (CSP) and has given several invited talks around the world.

Souleymane Bachir Diagne is a professor in the Departments of Philosophy and French and the Director of the Institute of African Studies at Columbia University. His areas of research and publication include history of philosophy, history of logic and mathematics, Islamic philosophy, African philosophy, and literature. His latest publications are: *Open to Reason: Muslim Philosophers in Conversation with Western Tradition* (2018); *Postcolonial Bergson* (2019); and *In Search of Africa(s): Universalism and Decolonial Thought* (in dialogue with Jean-Loup Amselle, 2020). He is an associate member of the Royal Academy of Belgium and a member of the American Academy of Arts and Sciences.

Elisa Freschi studied Sanskrit and philosophy. She works on philosophy in the Sanskrit cosmopolis and more specifically on topics of epistemology of testimony, philosophy of religion, philosophy of language, and deontic logic. She is a convinced upholder of reading Sanskrit philosophical texts within their history and understanding them through a philosophical approach. She is assistant professor at the University of Toronto Department of Philosophy, and is currently busy finishing a book on Veṅkaṭanātha, a fourteenth-century philosopher and theologian. Her publications can be downloaded from her Academia webpage.

Jonardon Ganeri Bimal K. Matilal is Distinguished Professor of Philosophy at the University of Toronto. He is a philosopher whose work draws on a variety of philosophical traditions to construct new positions in the philosophy of mind, metaphysics, and epistemology. His books include *Attention, Not Self* (2017), a study of early Buddhist theories of attention; *The Concealed Art of the Soul* (2012), an analysis of the idea of a search for one's true self; *Virtual Subjects, Fugitive Selves* (2020), an analysis of Fernando Pessoa's philosophy of self; and *Inwardness: An Outsiders' Guide* (2021), a review of the concept of inwardness in literature, film, poetry, and philosophy across cultures. He joined the Fellowship of the British Academy in 2015 and won the Infosys Prize in Humanities the same year, the only philosopher to do so.

Francois Jullien is a philosopher, Hellenist, and Sinologist. He is a professor at the University of Paris and Chairholder of the Altérité Chair at the Maison des Sciences de l'Homme Foundation in Paris. A former pupil of the Ecole normale supérieure (rue d'Ulm), he holds France's professorial agrégation and a French research doctorate (doctorat d'État). He was successively Director of the East Asia Department at the University of Paris-Diderot, President of the International College of Philosophy, and Director of the Institute of Contemporary Thought. Francois Jullien began by deploying his work between the philosophies of China and Europe. He has developed an intercultural reflection as well as a philosophy of existence. He is the author of about thirty books translated into about thirty languages. He has received the Grand Prix de l'Académie française for his body of work as well as the Hannah Arendt Prize for political thought.

Lin Ma currently works as an associate editor of Philosophers at the School of Philosophy of Renmin University of China. She received her PhD (2006) and MA (2001) in philosophy at the Higher Institute of Philosophy, KU Leuven, and BA in English Language and Literature and LLB in Intercultural Communication at Beijing University. She is the author of *Heidegger on East-West Dialogue: Anticipating the Event* (2008), which is a rigorous study of Martin Heidegger's complex and often overly interpreted relations with Eastern thought and his reflection on the question of East–West dialogue. In recent years, she has co-authored *Fundamentals of Intercultural and Comparative Philosophy* and *Beyond the Troubled Water of Shifei: From Disputation to Walking-Two-Roads in the Zhuangzi*, both published by State University of New York Press. In addition, she has published over sixty research papers in international journals such as *Philosophical Forum, Journal of the British Society for Phenomenology*, and *Philosophy East and West*.

Robert Cummings Neville is Professor Emeritus of Philosophy, Religion, and Theology; Dean Emeritus of the School of Theology; and also of Marsh Chapel at Boston University. He is the author of over thirty books and three hundred essays and is past president of the American Academy of Religion, the Institute for American Religious and Philosophical Thought, the International Society for Chinese Philosophy, the Metaphysical Society of America, and the Charles S. Peirce Society.

Robert Smid is an Associate Professor of Philosophy and Religious Studies at Curry College in Milton, Massachusetts. His research interests include classical pragmatist and process philosophy (especially metaphysics and epistemology in Peirce and Whitehead), comparative philosophy (especially as it pertains to methodology), and political philosophy (especially as it pertains to the promises and perils of democracy). His main work on comparative philosophy can be found in *Comparative Methodologies* (2009), although he has since built on that work in a series of conference presentations, peer-reviewed journal articles, and book chapters.

Gabriel Soldatenko is Associate Professor of Philosophy at Kennesaw State University. Professor Soldatenko's areas of specialization are in Latin American, social political, contemporary continental, and comparative philosophies. His most current research projects follow two lines of thought: first, to more clearly trace, define, and plumb the philosophical value of Latin American philosophy and, second, to participate and contribute to the metaphilosophical upshot and consequences of comparative philosophy. Taken together, these two lines of investigation highlight a broad methodological concern for the discipline of philosophy and its future.

Jaap van Brakel is professor emeritus (with special research assignment) in the Higher Institute of Philosophy of the University of Leuven. He published widely on various subjects, including the concept of chance, transport phenomena in porous media, natural kinds, philosophy of chemistry, comparative philosophy, and more.

Ralph Weber is Associate Professor of European Global Studies at the University of Basel. He has been the book review editor (Europe) for *Philosophy East and West* and the President of the European Association for Chinese Philosophy. He has written extensively on comparative philosophy and the philosophy of comparison and pursues research projects in Modern Confucianism, contemporary Chinese Political Thought, and questions surrounding debates on eurocentrism, decolonialism, and the politics of knowledge.

Index

Note: Endnotes are indicated by the page number followed by "n" and the endnote number e.g., 20 n.1 refers to endnote 1 on page 20.

Academic
   comparison 22, 185, 186, 198 n.9
   comparativists 26
   community 187
   interests 198 n.9
   philosophy 125, 145, 149, 154, 155, 161, 173
Adamson, Peter 112 n.5, 113 n.18
Adluri, Vishwa, 169
aesthetics 56, 60, 61, 72, 77, 142, 173
   sympathy 145, 146, 147
Africa 5, 27, 94, 169, 170
Africa, Asia, and the History of Philosophy (Park, Peter) 131
African languages 93, 94
African philosophy 99, 108, 112 n.12, 160, 229, 235, 252, 257
Age of the Sūtra 143, 144
Akan language 93, 94, 169
Alcoff, Linda 136 n.3
Algeria 127
Allende, Salvador 127
Al-Sirafi, Abu Sa'ld 91
alterity 184
American 27–8
   traditions 18, 19
   philosophers 19, 125, 130, 184
Ames, Roger T. 8, 48 n.17, 55, 56, 67, 200 n.29, 243, 244
analogical philosophy 111 n.1
analytic philosophy 18, 165, 203, 246
Andersen, Hanne 48 n.24
Andhra Pradesh 109
Angle, Stephen C. 37, 224
Anglo-American analytical philosophy 100
Ani, Amara E. 237 n.7
Annambhaṭṭa 97, 111 n.2

anthropology 89, 90, 159, 249
Anti-colonial Critique 147–9
Arabic
   language 91, 169, 171
   and Persian 147
   philosophers 91, 102
   philosophy 108
   translation from Greek 139
argumentative pluralism 142, 143
Aristotle 17, 24, 26, 61, 81, 91, 108, 140, 169, 175, 206
   culture 61
   logic 63, 91–2
   metaphysics 19, 59
   onto-logic 93
   substance philosophy 20, 23
   teleology 59
aruṃaruka, concept of 237 n.5
Arvan, Marcus 112 n.6
Asia 5, 169
   culture 67, 120
   philosophies 121, 123, 125, 131
Asouzu, Innocent 237 n.3
Aṣṭādhyāyī (Pāṇini) 144
atheistic cosmology 55, 56, 58
attitude-toward-a-soul principle 35
Augelli, John P. 136 n.5
Augustine 98, 108, 109, 171
Auseinandersetzung (confrontation) 212–13, 218
Axial Age 17, 27

Babylonian philosophy 141, 166
Bactrian Barmakid translation project 139
Bagchee, Joydeep 169
Baghdad 139
Balcerowicz, Piotr 154, 156 n.5
Baldwin, James 133

Bantu
  concept of *Ubuntu* 170
  languages 93
Beardsmore, R. W. 48 n.24
Behuniak, Jim 5, 68 n.2
Beijing 72
beliefs 33, 34, 43, 150–1, 184
Bellah, Robert, N. 27
Bellaimey, James E. 48 n.23, n.24
Benveniste, Emile 92, 93
Berlin, Isaiah 250, 256 n.2
Berman, Antoine 89, 93, 94
Bernstein, Richard J. 163
Bhagavadgita 170, 177 n.4
bhāṣya 144
Bhattacharya, Kamaleswar 156 n.7
Bhattacharyya, Krishnachandra 144–6, 147
Bhaviveka and His Buddhist Opponents (Eckel, Malcolm David) 28 n.1
Bi, Wang 20, 24, 216
Blackburn, Simon 204
blandness 8, 77, 79
Boghossian, Paul 150–1, 153
Bondy, Augusto Salazar 127–130, 134
Book of Changes 60, 68 n.5
Borges, Jorge Luis 58, 68 n.4
Bostrom, Nick 112 n.6
Bṛhatī (Prabhākara) 110
bridge concepts 21, 22
Britain 140
Bronkhorst, Johannes 142, 143
Buber, Martin 97
Buddhist philosophy 17, 24, 139, 144, 150, 152, 164, 167, 171, 173
Burik, Steven 1, 11, 224, 225, 226, 227, 228, 244, 247, 253

Calvino, Italo 97, 105
Canclini, Néstor García 135 n.2
Caribbean Discourse (Glissant, Edouard) 135 n.2
Cassin, Barbara 93
Castro-Gomez, Santiago 135–6 n.3
Césaire, Aimé 126, 133
Cetina, Karin 150, 154
Chakrabarti, Arindam 10, 131, 132, 163, 169, 207, 208, 212, 219, 243, 244, 248, 252
Chakravartty, Anjan 152

Chang, K. C. 55
charity 7, 32, 42, 43–4, 47, 102
Chatterjee, Amita 4
Chile 127
Chimakonam, Amara E. 11–12
Chimakonam, Jonathan O. 11–12, 235, 237 n.4, n.6, 244
China 36, 61, 62, 71, 72, 74, 79, 81, 82, 140, 141, 149, 154, 167, 214, 233
China and the Christian Impact: A Conflict of Cultures (Gernet, Jacques) 68 n.9
Chinese 21, 40, 47 n.1, 84, 109, 169, 171
  cosmology and epistemology 55–6, 61
  culture 56, 62
  language-thought 74, 81
  philosophers 17, 47 n.1, 55, 50 n.47, 60, 102, 109, 160, 203, 252
  philosophy 2, 9, 31, 55, 58, 59, 61, 108, 160, 170, 203
  thought 73–4
  and Western cultures 56
Christian 17, 26, 59, 62, 63, 127, 131, 147, 169, 216
civil philosophy 61, 62
climate crisis 19, 81, 159
Clooney, Francis X., SJ 19, 20, 28 n.3
closure, as concept 56, 61, 210
Colebrooke, Henry 139
Collected Papers (Peirce, Charles Sanders) 199 n.15
colonialism 5, 131–2, 140, 147, 155, 182
Comparative Philosophy Without Borders (Chakrabarti, Arindam and Weber, Ralph) 131
comparative philosophy 17, 101, 111, 113 n.15, 120, 191, 203, 250
  comparison and truth in 24–7
  constructive engagement, method of 231–3
  discursive sphere 227
  fight bias 19–22
  history of philosophy 27–8
  meta-sphere 227
  method and methodology in 212, 213–17
  methodological neutrality 231
  minimal requirements for 217–18
  as philosophy 208–213
  problems in 224–230

purpose of 133–5
reflections on methods of 17
situation for 17–18
tasks of 227
two-faced comparison 22–4
Comparative theology: Deep Learning Across Religious Borders (Clooney, Francis X., SJ) 28 n.3
comparativists 2, 5, 7, 18, 19, 21, 25, 122, 134, 184, 187, 188, 189, 191, 192, 194–5, 241, 245, 252–5
comparisons 111 n.1
  cross-cultural 122
  with historical sources 99
  of languages 98–9
  provisional definition of 183–6
  and truth in comparative philosophy 24–2
  two-faced 22–4
  unavoidability of 98–9
conceptual scheme 31, 33, 37
  Chinese 40
  European 40
conceptualizing 75, 94, 170
Confluence: Journal of World Philosophies 5
Confucian 17
  concepts of *ren* and *li* 170
  moral philosophy 59
  philosophers 60
Confucius 77, 164
Connolly, Tim 1, 207, 211, 250, 256 n.2
constructive engagement 2, 104, 224, 231–3
Context-dependence of Values (CdV) 235
contextualization 73
continental philosophy 18, 19, 203, 213, 217
conversation
  between comparative and Latin American philosophy 119, 131
  partner 198 n.2
  of philosophy 164, 166
conversational thinking 11, 223, 224, 244, 247
  as veritable option for comparative philosophy 233–6
Coquereau-Saouma, Elise 113 n.14, n.16
Cornille, Catherine 20

cosmopolitan
  language 173
  philosophy 250
cosmopolitanism 159
  non-coercive 143
creativity 59, 61, 181, 243
cross-cultural method 122, 224
cross-cultural philosophies 227–8
cross-disciplinary 250
Critica della ragione (Manzini, Antonio) 113–14 n.23
Critiques (Kant, Immanuel) 106
Cuadernos Americanos (Zea, Leopoldo) 136 n.4
Cuban Revolution 127
Cuban Counterpoint (Ortiz, Fernando) 135 n.2
cultural chauvinism 169, 216
cultural essentialism 8, 121
cultural essentialists 55, 56
culturalism 73, 75

Dao: A Journal of Comparative Philosophy 2
Daodejing 20, 48 n.11, 216
Daoism 1, 216
Daoist 17, 24, 209, 216
David, Pascal 79
Davidson, Donald 7, 21, 32, 43
de Bary, William Theodore 18
decolonization 9, 127, 145, 159, 170, 246, 260
deconstruction 84, 205, 216, 218
  of ontology 76–9
Decosimo, David 21
Defoort, Carine 162, 163, 164, 176 n.2
Degérando, Joseph Marie 3
Deleuze, Giles 198 n.5
democracy 19, 82, 99, 140
Dennerline, Jerry 63
Derrida, Jacques 163, 198 n.5, 206–7, 209, 213, 216, 219
de Saussure, Ferdinand 63–4, 68 n.8
descriptive pluralism 245
Despeux, Catherine 49 n.31
Dewey, John 4, 155
Dharmaśāstra 143
Diagne, Souleymane Bachir 8–9, 94n*, 95 n.1, 172, 243, 244, 249

dialogue 17, 26, 99, 101, 104, 108, 112 n.13
  accountable 233
  cross-cultural 135
  global 150
  interpretive 225
  North-South 135
  philosophical 135
  South-South 135
Dictionary of Untranslatables (Cassin, Barbara) 93
Die Religion innerhalb der Grenzen der bloßen Vernunft (Kant, Immanuel) 171
Dignāga (*c.* 480–540 CE) 144
Dilworth, David 193
displacements 80–5
Discourse on the Method (Descartes, René) 90, 93
Dottin, Paul 232, 233, 235
Dreyfus, Hubert 154
Drudgery Divine: On the Comparison of Early Christianities and the Religions of Late Antiquity (Smith, Jonathan Z.) 199 n.19
Durkheim, Emile 4
Dussel, Enrique 133, 134, 135 n.3
Dutch 133

East Asia 5, 17, 60, 259
écart 71, 85 n.1
Eckel, Malcolm David 28 n.1
Egbai, Uti O 235, 237 n.4
Egyptian philosophy 17
Emerson, Ralph Waldo 19
The End of Comparative Philosophy and the Task of Comparative Thinking (Burik, Steven) 226
Engels, Kimberly 112 n.6
English Civil War 111 n.3
English 4, 18, 40, 41, 57, 61, 68 n.6, 94, 133, 169, 173
Enyimba, Maduka 235
epistemic cultures 150, 151, 152, 154
epistemic virtues 7, 32, 44–5, 49 n.44, 206
epistemology 19, 26, 55, 105, 107, 109, 113 n.23, 119, 151, 173, 204
epithetless philosophy 171
essentialism 56, 61, 63, 66, 67, 121, 160, 244

ethical aim 93
ethics 18, 62, 149, 171, 173
ethnocentrism 66, 73, 75, 135, 161
Euro-American
  academia 101
  culture 120
  philosophy 109, 169
Eurocentrism 3, 5, 159
Europe 7, 72, 74, 79, 80
European
  advantage 61–2
  civilization 147
  classicism 145
  concept 40
  conceptual schemes 40
  exceptionalism 139, 140
  language 72, 78, 169
  language-thought 74
  philology 146
  philosophy 109, 163, 166, 252
  thoughts 79–80
  traditions 45
extra-methodological tradition 193
Ezumezu logic 11, 233, 234, 237 n.8

family resemblance principle 32, 35, 37–9, 42, 47, 211, 213
Fear and Trembling (Kierkegaard, Søren) 106
Fear of Knowledge (Boghossian, Paul) 150
fight bias 19
Firstness 184, 198 n.7
Fleming, Jesse 229, 236
Fraser, Chris 45
free spirits 119, 120, 135 n.1
free research 100
Freiberger, Oliver 199 n.15
French 74, 84, 92, 95 n.1, 126, 128, 133, 148, 171, 176, 252
Freschi, Elisa 9, 102, 112 n.9, 113 n.20, 243, 245, 249
Frost, Robert 58
Fulbrook, Mary 111 n.3
fusion philosophy 2, 4, 10, 160, 166–7, 168–9, 170, 171, 212, 219, 244, 250, 251

Gadamer, Hans-Georg 32, 46, 68 n.3, 101, 104, 112 n.10, 163, 207

Galilei, Galileo 99, 111 n.4
Gandhi, Virchand Raghavji 3
Ganeri, Jonardon 10, 243, 244
Gaṅgeśa 107
Garfield, Jay 161, 163, 175
Gasché, Rodolphe 209, 210
Gassmann, Robert H. 163
Genealogy of Morals (Nietzsche, Friedrich) 119
generalizations 11, 26, 5, 56, 62, 63, 66, 211, 213, 244, 247, 248
German 106, 169, 171
  idealism 160
  Romanticism 76
  Sanskritists 177 n.4
Gernet, Jacques 64, 68 n.9
Gibson, James 49 n.33
Gill, Sam 199 n.25
Girardot, Norman J. 28 n.2
Glissant, Edouard 135 n.2
global philosophy 2, 28, 159, 170, 250
  philosophical issues of 161, 164
globalization 9, 159
Glock, Hans-Johann 165, 168, 176 n.3
Goethe 91
Goldin, Paul R. 55, 56, 57
Goodman, Nelson 32, 39, 49 n.39, n.43
Gopnik, Alison 166
Graham, Angus Charles 40, 49 n.35, 55, 56, 63, 64, 65, 210, 214
Granet, Marcel 55, 56
Greece 71, 81, 89, 142, 144, 148, 154
Greek 10, 72, 108, 140, 171
  agorà 108
  Arabic from 139
  civilization 141
  classicism 140, 144, 244
  classics 145
  culture 17
  exceptionalism 142
  grammar 91
  language 93
  philosophy 80, 91, 108, 160, 165, 166, 252
  to Sanskrit 72
  substance ontology 60
  terms 58
ground-level philosophy 173
Gupta, Sujata 3
Gupta, Prabir K. 3

Gupta, Supratim 3

Habermas, Jürgen 213
Halbfass, Wilhelm 3, 4
Hall, David L. 48 n.17, 55, 56, 67, 141, 200 n.29
Hall, Edith 140, 141, 143, 144, 145
Hamlet (Shakespeare, William) 199 n.20
Han dynasty 17, 36, 56
Harbsmeier, Christoph 41, 45
Hawaiian 171
Hegel, Georg Wilhelm Friedrich 27, 105, 129, 171, 174, 213, 241
Hegelianism 3
Heidegger, Martin 27, 32, 36, 47 n.6, 48 n.13, 76, 106, 163, 203, 212, 213, 219, 229
Hellenistic culture 61
henotheist positions 21
hermeneutic relativity 7, 32, 33, 35, 46
Heubel, Volker 164
Heysse, Tim 162, 163, 164, 176 n.2
Hindu 17, 170, 171
  cosmogony 171
  philosophies 23
Hisamatsu, Shin'ichi 164
Histoire Comparee des systèemes de philosophie (Degérando, Joseph Marie) 3
historical contextualism 4, 7, 8, 169
historicism 10, 160, 165-9
History of Indian and Africana philosophy (Adamson, Peter and Jeffers, Chike) 112 n.5
History of Western Philosophy (Russell, Bertrand) 171-2
history 67, 68, 111 n.3, 123, 134, 139, 159
  of comparative philosophy 6
  of Latin American philosophy 127
  of philosophy 3, 27-8, 123, 166, 168, 246
  of Western philosophy 121, 192
holism 31, 34, 42, 55
Hountondji, Paulin 94
Hui Shi 惠施 36
humanist aim 93
humanity 32, 43-4, 134
  philosophy as tool for 120, 135, 148, 149
Hume, David 166, 169
Husserl Archives Leuven 89

Husserl, Edmund 89, 90, 174
hybrid concepts 41, 42, 47, 48 n.29, 49 n.29
Hybrid Cultures (Canclini, Néstor García) 135 n.2
hypergoods 67, 69 n.10

ideal-language paradigm 207
Igbo language expression 237 n.8
India 140, 141–2
  argumentative pluralism 142
  and Greece 142
  non-coercive cosmopolitanism 143
  philosophical systems 142, 146–7, 171, 252
  Sanskrit classicism 146
  specialness of 142
  tradition 10
  transcendental paradigmatism 142
  voluntary vernacularism 143
Indo-European language 65, 72
informed philosophy 26, 27
infrastructural philosophies 226
instrumental historicism 165
intellectual history 2
intercultural philosophy 2, 97, 101, 109, 113 n.15, 206, 209, 235, 237, 250, 251
interdisciplinary 235, 246, 249, 250
interests 2, 3, 6, 33, 132, 183, 184, 186–190, 197, 198 n.9, 199 n.19, n.22, 205, 211, 213, 253
interhuman interpretation, XYZ model for 7, 32–4
interlocutors 42, 104, 174
International Society for Comparative Studies of Chinese and Western Philosophy (*ISCWP*) 223
interpretation 31, 39, 47, 60, 68, 104, 111 n.3, 145, 182, 184, 186, 206, 212, 216, 226, 232, 243
  conditions and constraints of 32
  epistemic virtues 44–5
  family resemblance (FR) principle 37–9
  hermeneutic relativity 45–6
  mutual attunement 42–4
  mutually recognizable human practices 35–7
  quasi-universals, construction of 40–2
  underdetermination of 34–5
  XYZ model for 32–4
interpreters 7, 8, 9, 32, 33, 34, 39, 42, 55, 58, 105, 108, 146, 207, 218
intra-methodological tradition 192, 193
intrinsic historicism 165
invention, value of 142, 181, 190–6, 244
Islam 18, 170
  cultures 64
  theologians 113 n.16
  traditions 26, 27, 121

Jacob 101, 102, 103, 169
Jaeger, Werner 108
Jainism 146
Japanese philosophy 114 n.24, 164, 171, 209
Jaspers, Karl 27
Jeffers, Chike 112 n.5
Jenco, Leigh 214, 220 n.6
Johnston, Elgin H. 156 n.7
Jones, David 207
Journal of World Philosophies 5
Jullien, François 8, 71, 73, 75, 77, 78, 79, 80, 82, 83, 84, 85, 113 n.14, 244, 251
just philosophy 10, 159, 169, 173, 175, 176, 211

Kagame, Alexis 93, 94
Kant, Immanuel 105, 106, 166, 171, 174
Kaufman, Maike 113 n.22
Kearney, Richard 205, 208, 217
Khmer 171
Kierkegaard, Søren 26, 106, 109
Kirloskar-Steinbach, Monika 1, 112 n.8
Kodjo-Grandvaux, Séverine 93
Korean 171
Krishna, Daya 104, 225, 226
Kunst, Arnold 156 n.7
Kwee, Swan Liat 4

La Raza Cosmica (Vasconcelos, José) 135 n.2
Ladmiral, Jean-René 114 n.25
Lange, Elena Louisa 163
languages 41, 42, 43, 98, 100, 106, 132, 144, 173, 242
  Chinese 31
  and conceptual schemes 8

and cultures 1, 3
European 17
explicit comparisons 99
FR-concepts in 39
games 32, 37
ideal 38, 39
implicit comparisons 98
modern 42
natural 38, 39
non-Western 18
ordinary 40, 42
and philosophy 8–9
as proof of power 133
religious 19
sophisticated 40
tacit comparisons 98–9
unnatural 39
Western 18
language-thought 73
Laozi 35, 50 n.47, 164
Larson, A. G. 229
lateral universality 8, 9
Latin America 76, 108, 123, 125, 130, 131, 132, 133, 171
Latin American philosophy 9, 119, 121, 122, 123–4
 sociopolitical character of 127–130
Latini, Micaela 112 n.11
legalist 17
Legge, James 18
Leibniz, Gottfried Wilhelm 61, 62, 63, 64, 107, 125
Levinas, Emmanuel 184, 198 n.5
Levine, Michael 166, 167, 168
Lévy-Bruhl, Lucien 89, 90
Li, Gang 李綱 36
Liberation Theology 127
linguistic philosophy 93
literature 38, 39, 58, 132, 159, 224
Littlejohn, Ronnie 225
Lloyd, Geoffrey Ernest Richard 48 n.17, 154
logic 56, 61, 91, 174, 228, 233, 235
 Aristotelian 92
 bivalent 11
 elements of 75
logocentrism 19
Lord Shiva 171
Lugones, Maria 135–6 n.3
Lukasiewicz, Jan 233

Ma, Lin 7, 41, 47 n.2, n.3, n.4, n.7, n.9, 48 n.11, n.16, n.17, n.18, n.20, n.25, 206, 213, 220 n.2, 244, 247
Maas, Philipp André 112 n.9
Macaulay, Thomas 141
Maffie, James 1, 112 n.8
Mahabharata 171, 177 n.4
mainstream philosophy 109, 110, 159, 163, 175
Maldonado-Torres, Nelson 32, 39, 135 n.3
Malinar, Angelika 163
Manchanda, Nivi 112 n.4
Maṇḍana 107
Manzini, Antonio 113 n.23
Maori philosophy 108
Marchaisse, Thierry 72
Marino, Francesca 112 n.6
Martin, Nicolas 72
Marxist 17, 18, 111 n.3
Masson-Oursel, Paul 4
Matta Ibn Yunus, Abu Bishr 91
Mauss, Marcel 4
Mayaram, Shail 113 n.16
The Meaning and Problem of Hispanic American Thought (Augelli, John P.) 136 n.5
Medin, D. L. 48 n.23
Mencius 26, 83, 164, 206
Mendietta, Eduardo 135 n.3
Merleau-Ponty, Maurice 8, 48 n.25, 89, 90, 91, 174, 244
Mesopotamia 141
metageography 67
meta-language 31, 32, 36, 38, 39, 40, 41
metanarrative 111 n.3, 205, 210
metaphysics 19, 61, 78, 79, 119, 154, 173, 209, 216, 219
meta-pluralism 245
methodological pluralism 6, 11, 195, 197, 246, 249, 254, 255
Methodologies of Comparative Philosophy (Smid, Robert) 193
Methods of Comparative Philosophy (Kwee, Swan Liat) 4
Metz, Thaddeus 237 n.7
Middendorf, Ulrike 49 n.31
Middle East 5

Mignolo, Walter 135 n.3
Mill, John Stuart 173
Mīmāṃsā 104, 109, 113 n.23, 143
Mind and Body in Early China: Beyond Orientalism and the Myth of Holism (Slingerland, Edward) 55
Moghul Muslim philosophies 17
Moist 17
Moiz, Munema 111 n.2
monotheism 21
Moore, Charles A. 4
Moore, G. E. 4, 203, 223
moral philosophy 72
Mote, Fritz 55, 76
Mou, Bo 2, 104, 223, 224, 231–2
Mozi 44, 45, 49 n.44, 164
Msffie, James 1
Mueller, Max 18, 28 n.2
muliplex essential natures 154
multiculturalism 159
multidisciplinary 250
Murphy, G. L. 48 n.23
Muslim philosophers 91
mutual attunement 7, 32, 42–4
mutually recognizable human practices (MRHP) 7, 32, 35–7
myopathy 181

Nāgārjuna 156 n.7, 175
natural language 38, 39, 46–7, 64, 94, 207–8
Needham, Joseph 55
neo-Confucianism 17
neologism 41, 243
neutral monism 171
Neville, Robert Cummings 7, 28 n.4, 198 n.3, 243, 244, 249
new age in philosophy 133, 134
New Confucian 63
New York Times 161
Newman, Saul 210
Ngugi wa Thiong'o 223
Nicomachean Ethics (Aristotle) 140
Nietzsche and Asian Thought (Parkes, Graham) 119
Nietzsche, Friedrich 26, 64, 65, 92, 93, 119, 120, 130, 209, 213
  philosophies of grammar 65, 92, 93
Njikọka 233, 234

Nmekọka 233, 234
nonacademic interests 198 n.9
non-coercive cosmopolitanism 143
non-European cultures 19
non-European philosophy 10, 159, 160, 161, 162, 166, 175
non-Greek classical civilizations 140
nonmainstream philosophy 110
non-Western philosophy 191
  language in study of 132–3
  traditions 121
Normale, École 72
normative pluralism 245
novelty 100, 181, 182, 190, 196
Novissima Sinica (Leibniz, Gottfried Wilhelm) 61
Nweke, Victor C. A. 235
Nyāyakusumanjali (Udayana) 107
Nyāya-sūtra 144
Nylan, Michael 167, 168

Ofuasia, Emmanuel 237 n.7
Olberding, Garret P. S. 44
Olberding, Amy 160
Oldenberg, Hermann 145
Ọnọna-etiti 233, 234
ontology, deconstruction of 59, 60, 75, 76–9
orientalism 56, 74, 161, 182
Origin and Goal of History (Jaspers, Karl) 27
Ortiz, Fernando 135 n.2
otherness 170, 184

Paideia (Jaeger, Werner) 108
Pali 169, 176
Panikkar, Raimundo 224, 225, 226, 228, 236 n.2
Pāṇini 144
Parish, John W. 199 n.16
Park, Peter 131
Parkes, Graham 119
Patton, Kimberley C. 198 n.4
Peirce, Charles Sanders 184, 185, 186, 198 n.6, n.7, n.11, n.13
philologist 110, 146, 169
philosophers 98–9, 113 n.23, 159, 163, 165, 205
  African 9, 94

American 19
analytic 18, 165, 166, 169, 211, 217
Arab 91
Chinese 17, 55, 109
comparative 192, 227, 229, 231, 249
Confucian 60
contemporary 149
continental 217
fusion 168, 253
imperial 148
Jaina 150, 152
Latin American 125, 130, 132, 133
Muslim 91
non-Western 125
pre-Qin 21
Sanskrit 109, 144, 150, 152
South Asian 24
Western 125, 192, 194
philosophia perennis 175
Philosophie comparée (Masson-Oursel, Paul) 4
Philosophy East and West 2, 4, 5, 162
philosophy
  academic 125, 145, 149, 154, 155, 161, 173
  African 108, 112 n.12, 160, 229, 235, 252, 257
  analogical 111 n.1
  analytic 18, 165, 203, 246
  Anglo-American analytical 100
  Arabic 108
  Babylonian 141, 166
  Buddhist 17, 24, 139, 144, 150, 152, 164, 167, 171, 173
  Chinese 2, 9, 31, 55, 58, 59, 61, 108, 160, 170, 203
  civil 61, 62
  Confucian 59
  continental 18, 19, 203, 213, 217
  conversation of 164, 166
  cosmopolitan 250
  Egyptian 17
  epithetless 171
  Euro-American 109, 169
  fusion 2, 4, 10, 160, 166-7, 168-9, 170, 171, 212, 219, 244, 250, 251
  global post-comparative 159, 170
  global 2, 28, 250
  Greek 80, 91, 108, 160, 165, 166, 252
  ground-level 173
  history of 3, 27-8
  humanity, as tool for 120, 135, 148, 149
  Indian philosophical systems 142, 146-7, 171, 252
  informed 26, 27
  intercultural 2, 97, 101, 109, 113 n.15, 206, 209, 235, 237, 250, 251
  Japanese 114 n.24, 164, 171, 209
  just philosophy 10, 159, 169, 173, 175, 176, 211
  Latin American 9, 119, 121, 122, 123-4
  linguistic 93
  mainstream 109, 110, 159, 163, 175
  Maori 108
  moral 72
  new age in 133, 134
  non-European 10, 159, 160, 161, 162, 166, 175
  nonmainstream 110
  non-Western 191
  pluralist comparative 249
  political 72, 105, 173
  Polyglotism to 169
  postclassical Latin 108
  post-comparative fusion 171, 250
  post-fusion 170
  postmodern Continental 19
  precolonial African 99
  Sanskrit 111 n.2, 114 n.23
  sheer 173
  uninformed 27
  videogame-inspired 112 n.6
  Western 120, 121, 129, 203, 209, 242
  world 250
phoenicians 141, 147
Plato 17, 20, 21, 24, 61, 63, 78, 101, 108, 112 n.10, 113 n.17, 211
pluralism 140, 155, 183, 197, 215, 245-8, 249
plurality 181, 205
political philosophy 72, 105, 129, 173
political science 139, 159, 249
Pollock, Sheldon 141, 142, 144
polyglotism 10, 160, 169, 171, 176, 243
polylogue 104
Portuguese 133
positionality 5
postclassical Latin philosophy 108

postcolonialism 159
post-comparative philosophy 2, 250
post-fusion philosophy 170, 171
postmodern Continental philosophy 19
postmodern neo-Orientalists 55
Prabhākara 110
pragmatic virtues 44
pramāṇas 150, 152
prameya 150
precolonial African philosophy 99
pre-Qin philosophers 17, 21
Primitive Mythology (Lévy-Bruhl, Lucien) 89
principle of reasonableness 42–3, 47
Puett, Michael 55, 56, 57
Pūrva Mīmāṃsā 113 n.23
pūrvapakṣa 143
Putnam, Hilary 44, 57
Pythagoras' theorem 141

Qian Mu 錢穆 63
qing 情 41–2, 48–9 n.28
quasi-homonyms 41, 42
quasi-universals (QUs) 7, 35, 37, 40–2, 244, 247
Quine, Willard V. O. 39

racism 19, 126, 131, 135, 161, 182
Radhakrishnan, Sarvepalli 4, 148, 149
Raghuramaraju, A. 104, 113 n.21
Ramana, Geeta 1, 112 n.8
Rāmānuja 107–8
Rāmānujācārya 110
Ram-Prasad, Chakravarthi 112 n.4
rational theology 107
Ray, Benjamin C. 198 n.4
real philosophy 106, 160, 172, 211, 246
Reale, Giovanni 106
reasonableness, principle of 7, 32, 42–43, 47
redescription 66, 68, 189–190
reflective spirits 119, 135 n.1
relativism 8, 10, 38, 56, 75, 93, 151, 215, 246, 247
religious studies 181, 188–9, 190, 199 n.22
Retrieving Realism (Dreyfus, Hubert and Taylor, Charles) 154
revivalism 169
RgVeda 169

Ricci, Matteo 62
Richards, Ivor Armstrong 48–9 n.28
Ricoeur, Paul 93, 112 n.13, 198 n.8
Rocher, Ludo 139
Rocher, Rosane 139
Roetz, Heiner 44
Roman Catholic theologians 20
Rombach, Heinrich 164
Rongmufu 榕木賦 ("Rhapsody on the Banyan Tree") 36, 48 n.13
Rorty, Richard 66, 241
Rudolph, Ulrich 163
Russell, Bertrand 171, 172, 223

Said, Edward W. 64
Śālikanātha 110
Sāṃkhya 145, 146
Saṃvāda project 104, 113 n.16
Śaṅkara 104, 146
Sanskrit 4, 10, 72, 108, 109, 139, 144, 147, 169, 171, 173
  to Arabic 139
  Buddhist philosophy into Tibet 139
  classics 145
  Cosmopolis 141
  epistemic cultures 152
  knowledge systems 150, 151
  philosophers 104, 109
  philosophy 111 n.2, 114 n.23
Sapir–Whorf hypothesis 38, 46
śāstras 150
Schafer, Edward H. 48 n.13
Schwitzgebel, Eric 113 n.18, 161
Seal, Brajendra Nath 3
Secondness 184, 185, 198 n.8, 199 n.17
Seidel, Roman 166
Sein und Zeit (Heidegger, Martin) 106
sense of hearing 81
sense of sight 81
Shakespeare, William 199 n.20
Shantideva 173
sheer philosophy 170, 173, 177
Shepherd, Robert J. 119, 212
Siderits, Mark 166, 167, 176
Sidgewick, Henry 173
silent transformation 8, 80, 81
Sima Guang 49 n.40
Sinhababu, Supriya 198
Sinologists 8

sinology 71–6
Sivin, Nathan 61
Slingerland, Edward 55, 68 n.2
Smid, Robert 10–11, 200 n.29, 203, 213–14, 224, 225, 244, 249
Smith, Jonathan Z. 21, 181, 186, 199 n.17, n.19, n.21, n.22, 198 n.8, n.10, 244
sociology 89, 159, 249
Socrates 91, 108, 109, 142, 149
soft universalism 47
Soldatenko, Gabriel 9–10, 136 n.6, 243, 244, 245
solipsism 175
Sources of the Self: The Making of the Modern Identity (Taylor, Charles) 69 n.10
South Asia 5, 17, 23, 24, 26, 142
South, James 112 n.6
Spanish 121, 133, 171
Spinoza, Baruch 164
Spire, Antoine 72
Stalnaker, Aaron 21, 22
Stambaugh, Joan 47 n.6
Stance Pluralism 10, 149–154
Steineck, Raji C. 166
Strauss, Leo 113 n.23, 114 n.23
Studies in Philosophy (Bhattacharyya, Krishnachandra) 155 n.2, 155 n.3
Studies in Vedantism (Bhattacharya, Krishnachandra) 174
Subject as Freedom (Bhattacharya, Krishnachandra) 174
Sucarita 110
Sufism 104
sūtra-systems 145
Swahili 171
systematic thinkers 105, 225

Taking Back Philosophy: A Multicultural Manifesto (Van Norden, Bryan W.) 161, 200 n.28
Tan, Sor-hoon 2
Tang dynasty 36
Tamil 98
Tarkasaṅgraha 97
Tatia, Nathmal 156 n.5
Tattvacintāmaṇi (Gaṅgeśa) 107
Tavernaro-Haidarian, Leyla 235
Taylor, Charles 27, 67, 69 n.10, 154

Teller, Paul 153
Telugu 98
Testimony 152, 204
theodicy 98, 107
theological approach 98
theology 17, 18, 19, 25, 61, 107, 111 n.1, 249
theory of *rasa* 142, 147
thesis/antithesis 82
Thibaut, George 145
Thirdness 184–5, 186, 199 n.17
tian 天 (Heaven) 57–8
Tibetan 4, 108, 109
Timothy, Williamson 111 n.4
Tractatus (Wittgenstein, Ludwig) 168
Tractatus Theologico Politicus (Spinoza, Baruch) 164
transcendental paradigmatism 142
transcultural philosophy 2
transdisciplinary 250
translation 7, 9, 33, 40, 46, 89, 98, 131, 133, 169, 173, 207, 209, 243
  as method 89, 91, 93, 97, 106, 113 n.19
  projects 17–18, 21
transmission principle 150, 152
Trevi, Mario 105
Truth and Method (Vattimo, Gianni) 106
two-faced comparison 22–4

Udayana 107
Uehara, Mayuko 110, 114 n.24
underdetermination 32, 34–5, 42, 44, 48 n.22
unflaunted polyglotism, to philosophy 169–174
uninformed philosophy 27
universalism 38, 63, 75, 143, 144, 169
unnatural language 39
upanishads 177 n.4
Urban, Hugh 126, 199 n.16, n.25

Vaiśeṣika-sūtra 144, 150
Vākyārthamātṛkā (Śālikanātha) 110
value of invention 190–6
van Bladel, Kevin 139
van Brakel, Jaap 7, 41, 47 n.2, n.3, n.4, n.7, n.9, 48 n.16, n.17, n.18, n.20, n.25, 48–9 n.28, 49 n.32, n.36, 206, 207, 209, 211, 213, 220 n.2, 244

Van de Mieroop, Marc 166
van Fraassen, B. C. 152
Van Norden, Bryan W. 18, 161, 163, 191, 200 n.28
Vasconcelos, José 135 n.2
Vattimo, Gianni 106
Vedānta 102, 104, 107, 145, 146, 174
vedic philosophies 17
Vedic-Puranic-Tantric wisdom 177 n.4
Verhoeven, Martin 167
veritable methodological option 223–4
The Victorian Translation of China: James Legge's Oriental Pilgrimage (Girardot, Norman J.) 28 n.2
videogame-inspired philosophy 112 n.6
Vidhiviveka (Maṇḍana) 107
Vietnam 127
voluntary vernacularism 143
von Stosch, Klaus 113 n.16
Vyāsatīrtha 105

Walsh, Catherine 135 n.3
Wang, Youru 206
Watson, Burton 36, 48 n.12
Watson, Walter 193
weak historicism 10, 160, 165
Weber, Ralph 10, 111 n.1, n.2, n.12, 112 n.7, 131–2, 169, 186, 199 n.18, 203, 207, 208, 212, 219, 224, 225, 228, 236 n.2, 243, 244, 248, 252
Weil, Simone 147, 148, 149
West Asia 17, 23
Western 216, 242
  bias 7, 18, 242
  colonialism 19, 126
  culture 56, 120, 125
  languages 9
  philosophic universality 119, 132

philosophy 17, 120, 121, 129, 203, 209, 242
  thinking 10
Whitehead, Alfred North 56, 59
Williams, Raymond 68 n.6
Wimmer, Franz 113 n.15
Wiredu, Kwasi 93, 94, 223
Wirkungsgeschichte 207
Wittgenstein, Ludwig 7, 32, 37, 38, 39, 47 n.8, 168, 170, 193, 247
Wolff, Christian 224, 226
Wolof 93
world philosophy/philosophies 2, 57, 209, 250
world systems theory 159
wuyong 无用 48 n.13

Xiang, Guo 216
XYZ model for interhuman interpretation 7, 32–4, 45–6

Yāmunācārya 108
yin and *yang* 82
yoga 145, 146, 170
yong 用 48 n.13
youxi 游戏 (games) 38, 40, 48 n.27

Zea, Leopoldo 123–4, 128, 129, 136 n.4
Zen Buddhist 164
zero copula 91, 92
Zhang Longxi 張隆溪 64, 68 n.9
Zhao, Dunhua 224
zhi 知 (know(ing)) 40, 41, 45
Zhuangzi (Zhuangzi 莊子) 35, 36, 42, 48 n.13, n.18, 208, 214, 220
Zhuangzi 莊子 26, 74, 168, 203, 206, 208, 210, 212, 214, 216, 217, 219
Ziporyn, Brook 212, 214, 215, 220 n.4